Public Finance and Economic Growth in Developing Countries

Public finance is crucial to a country's economic growth, yet successful reform of public finances has been rare. Ethiopia is an example of a country that undertook comprehensive reform of its core financial systems, independent of the IMF and the World Bank, and successfully transformed itself into one of the fastest-growing economies in Africa.

With Ethiopia's twelve-year reform as its guiding case study, this book presents new analytical frameworks to help governments develop better financial reforms. It shows in detail how four core financial systems—budgeting, accounting, planning, and financial information systems—can be reformed. One of the principal findings presented is that governments must establish basic public financial administration before moving to more sophisticated public financial management. Other key findings include the identification of four strategies of reform (recognize, improve, change, and sustain), the centrality of ongoing learning to the process of reform, and the importance of government ownership of reform.

This book will be of interest to researchers and policymakers concerned with public finance, developmental economics, and African studies.

Stephen B. Peterson is a specialist in public financial management advising governments, international agencies, and donors in the development field. He initiated the Executive Program in Public Financial Management at Harvard University in 1986 and led it until 2010. He has directed two long-term financial reforms (Kenya 1986–94; Ethiopia 1996–2008), managing the collaboration of national and regional governments and international agencies. Dr. Peterson is Professor of Public Finance at the University of Melbourne, Australia.

Routledge studies in development economics

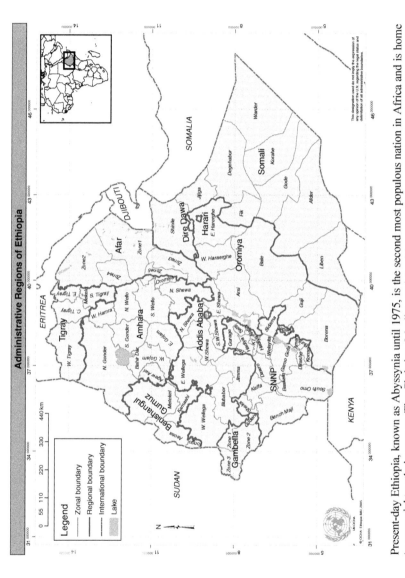

Administrative Regions of Ethiopia

Present-day Ethiopia, known as Abyssynia until 1975, is the second most populous nation in Africa and is home to over eighty ethnic groups. The Christian, Muslim, and Jewish communities of Ethiopia all count among the world's most ancient, and many traditional religions are practiced. The Ethiopian Empire was the only African nation that was never colonized. Map provided courtesy of the UN Office for the Coordination of Humanitarian Affairs. The boundaries and names shown and the designations used on this map do not imply official endorsement or acceptance by the United Nations.

Meles Zenawi (1955–2012), who served Ethiopia as both president (1991–95) and prime minister (1995–2012), at the World Economic Forum Annual meeting in 2012. Meles established the Task Force for Civil Service Reform and took great interest in the reform program's progress, chairing the national steering committee that oversaw implementation of the reform's various programs. He made several key decisions himself—including the decision to exclude the Bretton Woods agencies from the finance reform. Photo copyright by World Economic Forum, swiss-image.ch/Photo by Monika Flueckiger.

The author conferring with Hailemelekot T. Giorgis, vice minister in the Ministry of Finance and Economic Development and chairman of the Expenditure Management and Control Program from 1996 to 2002. Hailemelekot understood that the country faced great challenges and that the reform of its financial management would not be done easily nor quickly. His insights, humor, and relationships with key officials in the federal and regional government promoted trust in the reform. Photo courtesy of Sarah Guebreyes.

Getachew Hamussa (1951–2008), the head of the finance bureau in the Southern Region from 1997 to 2005. His successful direction of that region's financial reform—the first regional implementation of the reform—created a model for other regions to learn from. His fairness and commitment inspired deep loyalty in his staff. He often would show up in the project offices late in the evening after his many other duties to see for himself the progress being made. Photo Corporal Issa Paré, 2006.

Getachew was optimistic about his country's future and communicated it with his boundless enthusiasm. Here he addresses local finance officials of a *wereda* (smaller administrative district). Photo courtesy Kedru Yirga.

Public Finance and Economic Growth in Developing Countries

Lessons from Ethiopia's reforms

Stephen B. Peterson

Routledge
Taylor & Francis Group

LONDON AND NEW YORK

First published 2015
by Routledge

2 Park Square, Milton Park, Abingdon, Oxfordshire OX14 4RN
52 Vanderbilt Avenue, New York, NY 10017

Routledge is an imprint of the Taylor & Francis Group, an informa business

First issued in paperback 2019

British Library Cataloguing in Publication Data
A catalogue record for this book is available from the British Library

Library of Congress Cataloging in Publication Data
Peterson, Stephen B., author.
Public finance and economic growth in developing countries: lessons from
Ethiopia's reforms/Stephen B. Peterson.
    pages cm
Includes bibliographical references and index.
1. Finance, Public–Ethiopia–Management. 2. Fiscal policy–Ethiopia.
3. Ethiopia–Economic policy–21st century. 4. Economic development–
Ethiopia–21st century. I. Title.
HJ1459.P47 2015
336.63–dc23   2014044703

ISBN: 978-1-138-85003-3 (hbk)
ISBN: 978-0-367-87231-1 (pbk)

Typeset in Times New Roman
by Wearset Ltd, Boldon, Tyne and Wear

In memory of my parents, Lillian and Lawrence Peterson
Yes, I did return to Africa

The besetting mistake of expert designers is not designing the thing wrong, but designing the wrong thing.

Frederick P. Brooks, Jr., *The Design of Design: Essays from a Computer Scientist*

Contents

Illustrations

Boxes

Figures

Map

Photographs

Tables

Foreword

Fundamental reform of government and economic institutions is always difficult. Even in high-income countries, where the institutions of a market economy function well and governance is generally effective, reform efforts of institutions ranging from schools to welfare programs to government budgets often fail. The impediments to reform are much greater in developing countries, where the human and financial resources to support reform are weak, where societies are often deeply divided by ethnicity and lack of a common language, or by radical differences between the needs and desires of the urban elite, farmers producing subsistence crops, others producing crops for export, and the many migrants who have left the farm to try to find a better future in low-skill urban jobs. In these terms Ethiopia was one of the poorest countries in the world, and its population was an unusually diverse one, even by developing-country standards. And yet the Ethiopian government of the 1990s and the first decade of the twenty-first century was able to carry out a major reform of its public finance institutions. This book is about those reforms, what it took for them to succeed, and what it will take for that earlier success to be sustained.

International aid agencies played a role in these public sector reforms—some did more harm than good, but others provided critical support. In the latter category was USAID, the agency that provided technical assistance from outside the country, most notably in the person of Stephen Peterson, the public finance and management specialist who led the design and implementation of the Decentralization Support Activity (DSA) project and who is the author of this book.

But this book is not about a failed system and a heroic aid agency and an outside advisor who came in to rescue it. The most indispensable ingredient in the reform was that the Ethiopian government took full ownership of it from the beginning and persevered through thick and thin. This government had come to power after a civil war that was combined with famine and then quickly became embroiled in another war as a region of the country broke away to become an independent country, Eritrea. The DSA project itself was complex in that it involved the decentralization of a core public financial system—budgeting, accounting, expenditure planning, and automation—to the many diverse regions of the country. Implementation required training many thousands of budget staff.

The other critical ingredient in the success of this reform program was that the effort was sustained over a long period, with many of the key people, including Peterson, remaining in place throughout the design and full implementation phases, a process that took twelve years. The essence of institutional reform, particularly but not exclusively in developing countries, is that the changes introduced must fit the reality of the country, and it takes time to figure out and test what works and does not work in the country involved. One cannot take a beautifully designed public finance system, designed with the assumption that all the necessary supporting institutions are in place, set it down in a country where many of those supporting institutions do not exist, and expect it to work. In the case of the program described in this book, the very concept of public finance *management* could not be implemented in the Ethiopian context. A more basic public finance *administration* was required. Even that was a complicated challenge, in that it involved linking the capital and recurrent budgets, adapting a system of performance budgeting, changing from single-entry to double-entry bookkeeping, establishing a needs-based unit-cost fiscal transfer system for intraregional transfer, and then automating this whole system with a state-of-the-art financial management information system—state-of-the-art, that is, for an IT system that could function in a vast country with an antiquated, low-bandwidth electronic infrastructure. Along the way the thousands of personnel needed to run this system also had to be trained.

The obvious success of this effort is not the only lesson to be drawn from the reform. The experience of the Ethiopian DSA project also demonstrates the need for both the government and aid agencies supporting its reform to fully understand what has been accomplished and not to attempt to introduce a variety of further reforms without making sure that the existing system can readily integrate them. In Ethiopia, efforts in recent years have been made to introduce sophisticated public finance management systems without much consideration of what the existing system can absorb, and the result has threatened the sustainability of the earlier effort.

Public Finance and Economic Growth in Developing Countries: lessons from Ethiopia's reforms contains a wealth of information that anyone interested in public finance reform and institutional reform in developing countries in general can learn from. It is particularly relevant to such reform efforts in Africa, but many of the principles are equally applicable to developing countries around the world.

Dwight H. Perkins
Harvard University
Cambridge, Massachusetts
November 2014

Preface

In February 1996 I was scheduled to go to Poland to start a reform of that country's tax administration for the U.S. Treasury. My colleague, John Cohen, asked me to make a detour to Ethiopia for two weeks and help him design a reform project for strengthening the country's decentralization. Cohen's extensive fieldwork and research had made him an authority on Ethiopia, and he was the reason the United States Agency for International Development (USAID) had approached Harvard University for assistance in designing the project—the Decentralization Support Activity project. Stevens Tucker, the governance advisor at USAID, had brought in John after doing the groundwork of this reform through his two-year dialogue with the Ethiopian government in 1995 and 1996.

John's cancer diagnosis prevented him from leading the project, and he asked me if I would do it. His conviction that the Ethiopian government was serious about reform was confirmed by what I saw with my own eyes and the people I met in those two weeks. John was right. It was the most promising opportunity I had yet glimpsed to implement a truly effective reform of government finances in a developing country, and I seized the opportunity before me. I never went to Poland—the two weeks turned into twelve years. John's (and my) faith in the Ethiopian government's seriousness of purpose was vindicated: The World Bank has judged Ethiopia's reform to be one of the best on the continent in recent decades.[1]

Backing up a bit, the context of my decision was that financial reforms on the continent and elsewhere have not fared well. For a period of eight years before I arrived in Ethiopia I had been involved with several financial reforms in Kenya that had had virtually no impact. I learned firsthand about foreign aid fads in the field of public financial management as I managed the World Bank project in the Ministry of Agriculture, which introduced to Africa the bank's latest technique in its portfolio of "international best practice," the public investment program (PIP). PIPs were meant to prioritize projects in the capital budget, but failed, in Kenya and elsewhere, because they were based on the premise that allocating public funds—a fundamentally political process—could be guided by a technique. Eventually the PIP went the way of many such fads in PFM: it was discredited and abandoned.

My experience in Kenya confirmed for me the validity of the teachings of the political scientist Aaron Wildavsky, under whom I studied at the University of California, Berkeley. Wildavsky, renowned for his work on public policy, government budgeting, and risk management, had a great deal to say and to teach on the robust nature of simple financial systems—what the field calls today "the basics"—and the difficulty, danger, and often limited value of moving beyond simple.

In 1996 Ethiopia faced enormous challenges as a country: the need to recover from a long civil war and attendant political challenges, extreme poverty, a youthful new government strongly committed to rapid decentralization yet leery of foreign influence. Basic financial systems were the order of the day. Ethiopia offered an unusual situation and an unusual opportunity that led to a significant success in its reform efforts. This experience was formative for me and gave me the opportunity to make a positive contribution to a dynamic aspect of this fascinating country's development. It also gave me myriad insights into the process of reform that resulted in my creation of a new theoretical model and analytical tools. I integrated these tools into the executive education program I introduced and directed at Harvard University for twenty-four years and was encouraged that these tools resonated with senior officials, from forty-seven countries, who participated in the program.

Especially gratifying was the frequent observation by workshop participants that "what we have [in my own country] is not that bad." This aligned with my own experience, that understanding context, building on existing assets and strengths, and taking an incremental approach to change were keys to the Ethiopian reform's success. Thus was planted the seed of the idea to write this book.

To start to fix the problems in the understanding and practice of PFM, countries and practitioners need examples of success—if only to know that it can be done and how it can be done. With this book I offer a work that describes and dissects a significant achievement of a government in Africa that chose its own path to reform its finances. The book provides tools that support the efforts of practitioners as they guide governments in developing countries—indeed, in developed countries as well. Perhaps most important to success in the field in Ethiopia were training materials. Ethiopia's long political turmoil had decimated the ranks of qualified government personnel, and thousands of competent new staff were needed. Consequently, central to the reform's success was an extensive training program for finance officials at every level of the administration. My goal of advancing understanding of effective PFM reform includes a commitment to making available for study and emulation the training materials the DSA project and the government developed. To this end the procedural manuals and the training materials based on the manuals are available to download on the author's website which complements this book (stevepetersonpfm.com).

The eighteen-year effort to design and execute the reform and, later, to write this book about the experience rested on a network of collaborations, some involving a few individuals and others involving thousands. First and foremost is David Leonard, whose thorough work on rural development in Africa has been an inspiration and a standard to me and many others. David shaped my career in international development starting when I was his student at Berkeley, and has assisted me every step of the way. David introduced me to John Cohen, leading to a friendship that was central to my work in Ethiopia. John's research and fieldwork—and his fluency in Amharic—had given him not only a matchless understanding of the deep structure of Ethiopia's society and economy but also an equally deep love of the country's people and appreciation of its extraordinary history and sophisticated Abyssinian culture. Without him there likely would not have been a reform in Ethiopia.

Reforms in developing countries must be funded, by the country's government, foreign aid, or a combination of the two. Financial reforms take years, so patience and continuity of funding are critical. The DSA project was fortunate in its funders. USAID, the reform's largest donor, stayed the course for all twelve years, effectively managing the funding process yet never micromanaging the project. When additional resources were needed, the governments of Ireland and the Netherlands joined USAID as outside funders. In the final and most extensive phase of the project, the Ethiopian government made the largest financial contribution. The collaboration of all four governments made the reform possible.

The reform was won with leadership and commitment from the top through to the trenches. At the very top, Prime Minister Meles Zenawi provided leadership in the early stages of the reform, taking great interest, making key decisions, and guiding the strategy that allowed those in the trenches to be so effective. From the reform's inception, the prime minister made it absolutely clear that this was to be a government, not a foreign aid, reform.

Hailemelekot T. Giorgis, vice minister for finance, was the senior government official tasked with carrying out the reform. A teacher by training, he appreciated the obstacles confronting the reform and the need for patient learning.

Among many other officials who made enormous contributions, Getachew Hamussa, the head of finance in the Southern Region, stands out. Ethiopia's deep decentralization meant that success hinged on the reform's working in the regions and their smallest budgetary entities, the *weredas*. The Southern Region is one of the largest of Ethiopia's nine regions, and it was the site of the first regional pilot of the reform.[2] Success in this large region would do much to launch the reform nationwide. Getachew's leadership in the Southern Region ensured the success of his country's reform.

Reform is won or lost in the trenches and the trenches delivered. Most deserving of acknowledgment are the more than 72,000 Ethiopian officials who underwent training and delivered the reform to every level of the country's administration.

Within the DSA project it was a privilege to work with our sixty-three staff members. I wish I had space to thank each one individually. Here I wish to thank most especially four people: Sarah Guebreyes, the project manager, made sure that the project's $34.7 million budget was properly accounted for (we passed four USAID audits). She was also a staunch advocate for making the results of the reform known in the form of a book, and helped keep the facts straight. Jim Yardley played a leading role in designing the in-service training program, and gained the trust of government finance specialists not only with his knowledge but also with his down-to-earth demeanor. James Joseph, a project advisor who possessed a quarter century of experience on the continent, worked tirelessly with project staff and government officials to manage and ensure the quality of the in-service training program that was the foundation of the reform. Mebrahtu Araya, a former government official, ensured that the accounting procedures and training were clear and accessible for government staff. Equally important, through his deep network of contacts with government officials he provided the DSA project with invaluable understanding as to how officials viewed the reform.

Other individuals were pillars of support when it came to writing this book. Bill Trautman, a colleague at the Harvard Institute for International Development, in numerous discussions of the DSA project and the book's most controversial issues brought wisdom from his long experience with both developed and transitional governments on how and why they typically don't work well. He helped convince me that something that worked in Abyssinia under such difficult constraints was important to publish. Helen Solomon, for years the DSA project's backstop at the Kennedy School, understood the challenges of its implementation from a granular perspective and provided an endless supply of enthusiasm for both the project and book. Helen also gave generously of her time to read and provide comments on all of the chapters. My editor, Katherine Scott, took on a project that became much larger than she had anticipated. She stuck with it, bringing not only clarity and structure to the manuscript through our many rounds of reorganizing, rewriting, and editing, but also creative input that shaped the work. Without her, there might have been a book—but not this book. Bill Sweetser, my oldest friend, encouraged and supported me in this undertaking and—engaged in an ambitious writing project of his own—swapped writing stories with me. My colleagues David Leonard, Jerome Dendura, Noel Hepworth, Mick Moore, Mike Westlake, and Jim Yardley read selected chapters and provided feedback that sharpened the manuscript. Dwight Perkins, the director of the Harvard Institute of International Development, hired me in 1986 and has supported my work and my professional goals unstintingly since then. He kindly offered to write the foreword to this volume.

Fortune continued to smile on the project when it found a home in Routledge's Development Economics publishing program. My thanks to Helen Bell and Emily Kindleysides for their initial interest, and to Lisa Thomson and the rest of the Routledge production team for their efficiency and professionalism, ensuring a smooth production process.

My work in Ethiopia and on this book could not have been done without the support of my family: Jennefer, Mara, and Claire. I am grateful for their patience and love.

Stephen B. Peterson
Melbourne, Australia
November 2014

Notes

1 For a full discussion of the World Bank's 2010 assessment and recent developments in Ethiopia's financial system, see chapter 8.
2 There are eleven administrative entities below the level of the federal government: nine regional states and two administrative areas. The nine regions are Tigray, Afar, Amhara, Oromia, Somali, Benishangul Gumuz, Harari, Gambella, and the State of Southern Nations, Nationalities, and People's Region, or SNNPR (often called the Southern Region, the usage employed in this book). The two administrative areas are the Addis Ababa City Administration and the Dire Dawa City Administration (www. ethiopia.gov.et/web/pages/regional-states).

Acronyms

BC	budget classification
BDA	budget disbursement accounting
BI	budget institution
BIS	budget information system
BOCB	Bureau of Capacity Building
BOFED	Bureau of Finance and Economic Development
BPR	business process reengineering
BRT	budget reform team
BW	Bretton Woods
CID	Center for International Development
CIDA	Canadian International Development Agency
CIPFA	Chartered Institute of Public Finance and Accountancy
COA	chart of accounts
COFOG	Classification of the Functions of Government (UN)
COPS	context, ownership, purpose, and strategy (drivers of reform)
CPIA	Country Policy and Institutional Assessment
CSRP	Civil Service Reform Program
DFID	Department for International Development (UK)
DoA	Description of Accounts
DSA	Decentralization Support Activity project
ECSC	Ethiopian Civil Service College
EMCP	Expenditure Management and Control Program
EPRDF	Ethiopian People's Revolutionary Democratic Front
FGE	Federal Government of Ethiopia
FIS	financial information system
FMC	financial management and control
HIID	Harvard Institute for International Development
IBEX	Integrated Budget Expenditure (system)
ICT	information communication technology
IFMIS	integrated financial management information system
IFTP	In-Service Financial Training Project
IST	in-service training
IT	information technology

JBAR	Joint Budget and Aid Review
LDSW	locally developed software
MEDAC	Ministry of Economic Development and Cooperation
MEFF	macroeconomic fiscal framework
MOF	Ministry of Finance
MOFED	Ministry of Finance and Economic Development
MTEFs	medium-term expenditure frameworks
NORAD	Norwegian Agency for Development Cooperation
OECD	Organisation for Economic Co-operation and Development
OLF	Oromo Liberation Front
OTS	off the shelf
PEFA	Public Expenditure Financial Accountability (Framework)
PEP	public expenditure program
PFA	public financial administration
PFM	public financial management
PIP	public investment program
PSCAP	Public Sector Capacity Building Project
PSCP	public sector capacity project
PSNP	Productive Safety Nets Program
REPR	regional economic policy review
RMIs	regional management institutes
SIDA	Swedish International Development Agency
SDP	sectoral development program
SNNPR	Southern Nations, Nationalities, and Peoples Regional State
SPVs	special payment vouchers
SSD	second-stage decentralization
TGE	Transitional Government of Ethiopia
TOR	terms of reference
TPLF	Tigrayan People's Liberation Front
USAID	U.S. Agency for International Development
WAN	wide area network
WSU	wereda support unit
ZOFED	Zonal Office of Finance and Economic Development
ZSU	zone support unit
ZTB	zero treasury balance

Part I

Understanding public financial management reform

1 The Ethiopian public finance reform—a case study for *Yichalal!*

> Efficiency is doing things right, and effectiveness is doing the right thing.
>
> Peter Drucker

The financial reform in Ethiopia that took place between 1998 and 2008 is considered one of the best on the continent of Africa since 2000.[1] It succeeded because the right thing was done right. As a success in a field littered with failures, it is worthy of study, for it demonstrates what it means to do the right thing in a developing country. As a success on a continent where failure is all too common, Ethiopia's financial reform demonstrates that African governments can take the lead in designing and implementing financial reforms—a departure from the foreign aid model so prevalent in Africa. The Ethiopian case provides practical frameworks based on a long-term reform which can untangle the morass of current views on public financial management (PFM). It provides an empirical demonstration of how to carry out a financial reform because it provides insight into something that is usually ignored in the PFM literature: learning and how that is achieved through the effective engagement of technical assistance and the alignment of the roles of officials and advisor.

Although the term of choice in the field is PFM, in fact Ethiopia implemented a reform of public financial administration: PFA, not PFM. The failure to make the distinction between the two is a principal source of confusion about PFM and its reform in developing countries. Many financial reforms have failed because they parachuted techniques in that do not fit with how a government is organized: Is it a bureaucracy with weak administration that must strengthen its PFA? Or a strong bureaucracy that has a sound PFA in place, encourages management, and can thus adopt PFM techniques? Regardless of how the bureaucracy is organized, governments must first have financial administration before attempting financial management. Financial administration is compliance, external control, and ensuring the stewardship of public money. Financial management is about establishing internal control, and promoting discretion to achieve policy. Both PFA and PFM are means, not ends. History shows that development does not require PFM—robust PFA is good enough. Developing countries by definition are countries that lack the preconditions for financial management. For such countries, the objective should be to build a robust PFA. The Ethiopian reform provides insights into the principles and nuances of doing this in four key areas: budgeting, accounting, automating (the establishment of financial information systems), and planning. I discuss this issue in greater detail in chapters 9 and 10.

A case study

Public sector financial reforms typically take at least twelve to fifteen years to implement.[2] For twelve years I was the manager of the technical assistance project that supported Ethiopia's public finance reform. Thus I was not only a firsthand observer, but experienced the reform from the inside. This puts me in an excellent—and unusual—position to present a case study of a reform that I observed over a long period of time.

Several years after the departure of the technical assistance to the reform and the end of the project that I headed, I was able to gain an additional perspective as an external observer when I was asked to return and review the reform's performance. The different ways I experienced Ethiopia's reform over a span of sixteen years—as a consultant, implementer, participant, and ultimately, evaluator of its successes and failures—make this case study a first.

In this book I tell the story of what I learned about implementing PFA and, in that process, about the necessary conditions of successful reform.

Ethiopia's PFA reform was crucial in the government's drive to decentralize service delivery to its weredas (the lowest level of government administration responsible for a budget) and confront the country's abject poverty at its roots. Making decentralization work meant that foreign aid could be significantly ramped up by orders of magnitude to support the government's efforts in poverty alleviation. The reform enabled the country, the largest recipient of World Bank concessionary assistance on the continent, to handle these financial inflows. Better financial administration at the wereda grassroots ensured the success of the government's social protection program, the largest in the world, which was scaled up until it provided assistance to up to 9 million people.

The Ethiopian Public Financial Administration reform provides valuable lessons for other developing countries and also strengthens our ability to generalize appropriately from the reform of their public finance systems. The Ethiopian reform is especially striking because it had to overcome the challengingly low level of the country's development. It also illustrates what "local ownership" really means, and what it can accomplish.

Achievements of Ethiopia's reform

The Ethiopian government accomplished significant achievements in four areas that virtually all developing governments grapple with:

1   *Budgeting.* Two reforms were done. First, the capital and recurrent budgets were linked ("crosswalked," in financial management parlance) with a budget

classification and chart of accounts that created cost centers. Second, a system of performance budgeting adapted to context was introduced based on cost drivers and contracts that complemented a toned-up traditional budget.

2 *Accounting.* Single-entry bookkeeping was replaced with double-entry. Cash-basis accounting was replaced with modified cash-basis accounting. Self-accounting that could generate data for a range of annual reports was introduced. Manuals and training materials were created to explain procedures.

3 *Expenditure planning.* A population-based system for intraregional transfer was replaced with a needs-based unit-cost fiscal transfer system. A performance agreement with costing and multiyear planning was installed, establishing accountability by district for the fiscal transfer. Multiyear fiscal planning was established. Multiyear expenditure planning was introduced.

4 *Automation.* A custom-designed integrated financial management information system (IFMIS) was developed that far exceeded international standards yet could run on extremely limited bandwidth. At a cost of less than $1 million, it was far cheaper than the systems said to conform to international standards. It was delivered on time, was beyond scope, and under budget—virtually unheard of for a computer system.

At nearly every turn in this reform there were surprises that defied the predictions of financial specialists. The biggest was the government's successful adoption of an accounting system of international standards, with double-entry bookkeeping and a modified cash basis of accounting, which was done with a mere handful of qualified accountants in the civil service and with finance staff possessing, on average, a twelfth-grade education.

Not one reform but many

Ethiopia comprises nine regions and two administrative areas, vastly different in size, geography, ethnic makeup, political profile, and even history (see the frontispiece). Thus, reform of such a heterogeneous group of states provides examples for other country contexts. Fragile state: Somali. Urban center: Addis Ababa. Extreme remoteness: Gambella. Polyglot: Southern Region. Pastoralist: Afar. State in conflict: Somali. Country within a country: Oromia. (With a population of 18.7 million in 1996, if Oromia state were a separate country, it would be the fifth most populous country in Africa.)

A remarkable feature of Ethiopia's financial reform is that it was delivered in the context of a massive transformation in the organization of government, Ethiopia's second-stage decentralization to its weredas. Thus, it provides a myriad of lessons on how to build financial administration at the grassroots, as well as insights into financial reform in a decentralizing and decentralized government (an issue of great significance to many developing countries, one that is little discussed in the PFM field). PFA reform supported the wave of decentralization and did not delay it.

Scale and location do matter in public sector reform. Quite possibly one reason that New Zealand was in the vanguard of applying the most sophisticated management techniques to the public sector is its demographic context. In 1984, when New Zealand started its financial reform, just 13.4 million humans populated its splendidly isolated 104,000 square miles. Ethiopia, in contrast, is 426,000 square miles (twice the size of Texas), and when the reform started in 1996 it was the second most populous country in Africa, with 59 million people. Furthermore, it is located in one of the most dangerous neighborhoods on earth.

Against the odds

One would be hard put to find a more challenging environment to reform public finance than Ethiopia in 1996. The Four Horsemen of the Apocalypse—war, famine, pestilence, and death—seemed to be permanently stabled in-country. Ethiopia had been devastated by a long civil war, and the revolutionary party that assumed power in May 1991 represented an ethnic minority with tenuous control over a vast country. The bureaucracy was demoralized and many skilled professionals had fled the country. Foreign aid agencies rushed in to support the new regime, producing an inchoate and crowded aid agenda that further burdened a weak administrative system barely coping with daily operations. The government's strategy of ethnic-based decentralization to Ethiopia's eleven regions, implemented shortly after the change of power, further stretched an already strained administration. Less than two years into the start of the reform, the Horsemen rode in with even greater force as a two-year war with Eritrea was followed by the most serious famine in a century. Two years after the cessation of hostilities, Ethiopia embarked on a second stage of decentralization to its weredas, which increased the number of organizations administering finance by a factor of 15. Many of them were in some of the earth's most inaccessible locations. In one of the early training programs in the Southern Region, in the south of the country, some participants required five days to reach the venue, two of them spent on horseback on roads made impassable to vehicular traffic by the weather. The odds of success seemed slim.

Why the reform succeeded

The reform succeeded for three reasons, two of them based in Ethiopia's culture, and one based in the character of the reform itself. Most important was Ethiopia's vigilant protection of its sovereignty. Unique to the continent, the government was absolutely clear that it would own this reform and that it would limit and closely monitor foreign aid. As a newly formed government emerging from seventeen years of civil war, the government was acutely aware of the importance of its need for legitimacy and a free hand to execute its policies and those of the foreigner. Sovereignty was sacred and not to be infringed upon.

Second was discipline, a trait that is deeply ingrained in Ethiopian culture (discussed in more detail in the next section). The foundation of any public finance system is discipline. There is little point in reforming budgeting proced-ures if the budget is a leaky sieve—if you can't track where money comes from and where it goes. There must be a hard budget constraint—governments must live within their means—and there must be good transaction control—the pennies must be counted if the pounds of the hard budget constraint are to be controlled. Ethiopia was able to maintain this requisite fiscal discipline. In fact, it is the only African country that had a single-digit inflation rate for decades before 2000. The United States went off the gold standard in 1971, but Ethiopia continued to use the standard to anchor its currency—further evidence of uncom-mon monetary discipline.

The third reason that Ethiopia's financial reform succeeded was that it was well managed. The government undertook a comprehensive needs assessment of its civil service and then realistically prioritized what most needed doing. It determined the scope of the reform and then budgeted for the funds and time required to make it happen, thus ensuring coherence among scope, budget, and time.

The cultural context

Those familiar with Ethiopia will not find it surprising that the financial reformers overcame incredible odds and adversity to achieve each success. Ethiopia has many ethnic groups, so cultural generalizations are suspect, yet the cultural marker of discipline, mentioned earlier, is discernible across all ethnic groups. Ethiopians' discipline is shown in myriad ways. The virtues were many: seriousness of purpose; prudent, indeed tightfisted use of public money; and the low incidence of corruption. Yet there is a downside to discip-line: a certain rigidity.

Don Levine's *Wax and Gold: Tradition and Innovation in Ethiopian Culture* is one of the most respected sociological studies of the culture of the Amhara ethnic group, which dominated the politics and the bureaucracy for hundreds of years. The expression "wax and gold" (*sam-enna wark*) comes from an ancient form of verse that is very popular with Amharas. The wax is the obvious meaning, the gold the hidden meaning. For Levine, the "wax and gold" ambigu-ity is reflected throughout Ethiopian culture and helps explain its complexities: "The ambiguity symbolized by the formula *sam-enna warq* colors the entire fabric of traditional Amhara life…. Wax and gold is … a way of life [embody-ing] a fundamental indirection in speech by means of the studied use of ambigu-ity." Levine goes on to explain four creative uses of *sam-enna warq* in Ethiopian society as

> the medium for an inexhaustible supply of humor, a means for insulting one's fellows in a socially approved manner, a technique for defending the sphere of privacy against excessive intrusion, and an outlet for criticism of authority figures in a society which strictly controls every kind of overt aggression toward authority, be it parental, religious, or political.[3]

Levine raises the critical question of Ethiopian culture and its nuances and its impact on the modernization process: Do the rigid church, state, village, and family authority structures from top to bottom of the society, which inculcate discipline, impede the innovative impulses of the individual, the essential ingredient to modernization? Following Max Weber, Levine argues that the "cultivation of individuality" by at least a minority of the population is essential for modernization. Yet given the tendencies of Ethiopian society he concludes:

> The weight of Amhara tradition opposes the graceful emergence of such a minority in Ethiopia. The pressures toward conformity and inhibition of self-expression in most areas of life are … characteristic of that tradition. The surly use of authority, the subtle sense of fatalism, the adulation of rank rather than human qualities, the distrust of innovation, the drabness of subsistence, the authority of conventional styles, the narrowness of outlook maintained by mass illiteracy and religious fundamentalism, the interpersonal aspects of wax and gold (deception, insult, and intrigue)—these and related aspects of Amhara culture are formidable obstacles to the development of individuality among Ethiopians.[4]

A contemporary and more positive view for the prospects of modernization and the reforms needed to realize it is expressed by the word *yichalal*, meaning "It's possible!" "*Yichalal!*" is a favorite expression of Haile Gebreselassie, the country's famous marathon runner and a current Ethiopian icon. The concept of *yichalal* seems to promise that the culture, though rigid, would embrace reform if it were done sensibly and on Ethiopian terms and not the terms of the *ferenge*, the foreigner.

Thus, Ethiopia's culture presented reformers with a double-edged sword: the virtues of discipline, the vice of rigidity, inflected by a can-do spirit. The cultural context meant that reform of public finance was likely to succeed with a strategy of recognizing and improving the existing system rather than changing it.

The issues Levine raises about discipline and innovation were at the core of the PFA reform. Finance is one of the most sensitive functions of the state, and so the response to change in that area is inherently conservative. What is striking about Ethiopia's PFA reform is that it melded the tradition of discipline with the modernity of innovation.

Discipline in action

The recent political history reinforced the discipline of the culture. A successful seventeen-year struggle against one of the most ruthless regimes in Africa, one that was armed and supported by the Soviet and Cuban governments, was formative to the new regime's approach to the struggle for *mashashaya*, reform. The revolution stressed the importance of *zemechas*, campaigns, which are all-out efforts to overcome opposition. Steeling the backbone of the combatants in the struggle was the practice of *gemgema*, assessment, which is a thorough, cathartic self-declaration of faults. The struggle honed the collective and individual sources of discipline. A feature of discipline that had far-reaching effects on the financial reform was the belief in not taking shortcuts. Yes, the level of poverty was shocking and needed to be rapidly addressed, but the political order the regime replaced was also shocking and had to be replaced. In the words of the political scientist and noted Africanist Goran Hyden, there are "no shortcuts to progress."[5] You can't cut corners. The new government's decision to clear the four-year backlog of accounts rather than taking the easy path of writing them off speaks volumes for the discipline it brought to the financial reform. Finally, the struggle taught the regime not to take shortcuts and that it takes time—even decades—to achieve one's goals.

The origins of the reform

As one would expect from a government that had recently emerged from a long revolution, Ethiopia brought self-reliance and élan to its reform efforts. In 1996 the government unveiled a five-volume review of the civil service based on an eighteen-month study done without the support or knowledge of foreign aid agencies such as the International Monetary Fund, the World Bank, and others.[6] From its origins, the Civil Service Reform Program of which the financial reform was a component was atypical for Africa and for many developing countries because it was driven by government, not by foreign aid. The government understood it needed financial and technical support from the outside, but it intended to carefully scrutinize who was to be allowed in the reform tent. One of my colleagues observed that the Ethiopians had managed the *ferenge* for five thousand years, and they were not going to stop doing so now.

Ethiopians do respect foreigners who learn their complicated languages and attempt to fathom the wax and gold of their culture. John Cohen was such a foreigner. Cohen served in the Peace Corps in imperial Ethiopia during the 1960s and acquired a deep affection for its people. Fluent in the Amharic language and author of a doctoral thesis on the country's land reform and countless other publications on Ethiopia, he was one of the most respected foreign specialists on Ethiopia. In addition, he led several reform projects in Sudan and Kenya as a senior professional of the Harvard Institute of International Development. The government trusted Cohen immediately, which in turn deepened the Ethiopians' trust of USAID, which was working with Cohen on ways to support the government's administrative reforms. I had worked with Cohen in Kenya's Ministry of Planning, where he directed a four-year reform project, and he brought me with him to the Ethiopia project. Cohen's cancer meant that the design and then the management of what became the Decentralization Support Activity (DSA) project was left to me. It was a twelve-year, $34.4 million project made possible by one patient and continuous patron, USAID; two follow-on patrons, the Irish and the Dutch governments; and, in the final and largest phase, the Government of Ethiopia. This book is written from my vantage point as the project manager of the DSA project.

The purpose of this book

Governments in developing countries need guidance that is clear and informed by reality. In chapter 10 "Recreating the field of PFM for the twenty-first century," I examine the remove from reality that is on display in much of the PFM literature. Failure is ignored, platitudes abound, scholasticism is rampant, and there is a dearth of firsthand knowledge that shows the nuances of reform that are synthesized into frameworks that can guide reformers. This book provides frameworks to guide reformers, and detailed descriptions and discussion of how these frameworks can be translated into practice.

Three frameworks of reform

The book presents three frameworks for understanding public finance reform (explained in greater depth in chapter 9).

1   The Drivers of Reform: context, ownership, purpose, strategy (COPS)
2   The Platforms of Reform: transaction, legal, and policy
3   The Phases of a Reform Project: translation, design, pilot, rollout, and operation

My first framework, the drivers of reform, provides a systematic way of viewing the tapestry upon which a reform takes place. Success in public sector reform depends on alignment of the nondiscretionary driver of reform (context) with the discretionary drivers (ownership, purpose, strategy). Each of these elements of the COPS framework is then elaborated. While context and government ownership are given much lip service, little is said about the purpose of reform and strategy. Purpose is whether the reform is principally about public financial administration or management. A reform strategy can be of one or more types: recognize, improve, change, sustain. Reform is often viewed myopically as being of one type, change. The Ethiopian reform shows that reform can be more complicated, especially when it is done simultaneously with a decentralization reform, and can involve a mix of types, such as recognize-improve-sustain.

My second framework, the *platforms* of PFA/M, provides the menu from which a financial reform is selected. A financial system has to deliver three functions: it must handle transactions, ensure the legality of public expenditure, and promote policy. The various systems (e.g., budgeting in the transaction platform) and what is needed for their execution (institutions, organization, staffing) are located within the transaction, legal, and policy platforms.

The third framework shows how a reform is realized through five *phases*: translation, development, pilot, rollout, and operation. The PFM field has been errant in focusing too strongly on reform as systems and their sequencing and too little on reform as a process of learning. Learning is a natural by-product of the alignment of people, government officials, and technical assistance, and their evolving roles and relationships over the five phases. Learning is where the rubber hits the road because it ensures that a reform is fit for purpose and context and, most important, that it can be sustained once technical assistance departs.

The central argument made in this book is that successful financial reform in a developing country requires coherence—alignment from the macro-level of the drivers of reform to the micro-level of the personnel who deliver the reform.

Using these three frameworks, I examine the four financial reforms at the heart of Ethiopia's public finance, which are at the heart of finance in all governments: budget, accounts, financial information systems, and expenditure planning (chapters 4 through 7). I examine the reform of budgets and accounts in particular detail by walking through the four phases of reform. The fifth phase of these reforms, operation, is presented in chapter 8.

The structure of the book

Chapter 2, "The drivers of public sector reform," uses my COPS framework to show the setting of the financial reform. In chapter 3, "The necessary conditions for a successful financial reform," I examine how the DSA reform project emerged and how the relationship among the government, the funders, and the contractor was established. Chapters 4 to 7 present the four reforms: budget, accounts, automation, and expenditure planning reforms. Chapter 8, "The tests of time: two roads," draws on a year-long assessment of Ethiopia's PFA conducted at the request of the Government of Ethiopia three years after the DSA project ended. It shows how financial systems can deteriorate if they are not adequately sustained. Chapter 9, "How to reform a public financial system," reviews the reform in terms of the three frameworks. Chapter 10, "Recreating the field of PFM for the twenty-first century" examines the state of the PFM field and what the Ethiopia case says about the conventional wisdom.

As a complementary resource to the book I have created a website where the thousand-plus documents produced by the DSA project can be accessed: http://stevepetersonpfm.com. Many of these documents are detailed procedure and training manuals that reformers may well find useful in their own countries and projects. The DSA documents actually cited in this book are listed in the references under "Works cited—DSA project documents," p. 314. I also welcome a discussion on the site not only of the Ethiopian reform but also of other experiences in reform.

The tar pit of public financial reform

One of the best depictions of the trials and tribulations of a PFA-PFM reform in developing countries over the decades of the late twentieth century and early twenty-first is the vivid scenario with which Frederick Brooks begins *The Mythical Man-Month*, his brilliant work on managing complex projects:

> No scene from prehistory is quite so vivid as that of the mortal struggles of great beasts in the tar pits. In the mind's eye one sees dinosaurs, mammoths, and saber-toothed tigers struggling against the grip of the tar. The fiercer the

struggle, the more entangling the tar, and no beast is so strong or so skillful but that he ultimately sinks. Large-system programming [read PFM reform] has over the past decade been such a tar pit, and many great and powerful beasts have thrashed violently in it. Most have emerged with running sys-tems—few have met goals, schedules and budgets. Large and small, massive and wiry, team after team has become entangled in the tar. No one thing seems to cause the difficulty—any particular paw can be pulled away. But the accumulation of simultaneous and interacting factors brings slower and slower motion. Everyone seems to have been surprised by the stickiness of the problem, and it is hard to discern the nature of it. But we must try to understand it if we are to solve it.[7]

This book shows how one very poor country avoided the tar. Others can, too. *Yichalal!*

Notes

1 World Bank (2010a); Hedger and de Renzio (2010).
2 On the time needed for reforms to mature, see Swedish International Development Agency (2007: 93).
3 Levine (1965: 8–9).
4 Levine (1965: 284).
5 Hyden (1983).
6 Office of the Prime Minister, Task Force for Civil Service Reform (1996a).
7 Brooks (1995: 4).

2 The drivers of public sector reform

Ascending to power after a seventeen-year civil war, the new regime faced daunting challenges. The two most important were the need to assert its control throughout the country and to build its legitimacy by delivering development. It seemed as if everything needed fixing at once; on top of that, the government faced a difficult domestic and international environment. In 1994, John Cohen, a fellow with the Harvard Institute of International Development and a leading scholar of Ethiopia, and colleagues conducted an assessment of the challenges confronting the new government, which he enumerated as follows:

- Steady proliferation of demands that threaten to overload the capacity of the government leadership and [to] induce a "crisis management" style of decision-making, marked by institutional drift, confusion, and rising frustration. This is only exacerbated by the institutional gap that exists in government, due to the continued estrangement between the government and inherited ministries.
- Non-democratic cultural inheritance and rising ethnic tensions, in a context in which plans to create interim conditions of stability and introduce competitive electoral politics are poised to begin, organized around regions defined according to ethnic "nationalities."
- A difficult international environment, in which major powers are distracted by events elsewhere and appear unsure of their post–cold war interests in Ethiopia, and in which multilateral agencies such as the World Bank and the IMF press for tight guarantees of [the Government of Ethiopia's] commitment to macroeconomic reform, before answering Ethiopia's immediate emergency needs.
- An institutional void in the countryside, which invites opportunistic banditry among the armed wings of political movements.
- A decimated economy.[1]

These diverse challenges coupled with the new regime's culture of confronting obstacles through self-help *zemechas* (campaigns) and its skepticism of the Bretton Woods agencies meant that reform would be domestically owned to achieve domestic purposes.

Context of the reform

In chapter 1 I presented the COPS framework (context, ownership, purpose, and strategy) as the tapestry upon which a reform unfolds. In this chapter I focus on the nondiscretionary driver, context, especially the economic, political, and bureaucratic contexts. I conclude the chapter by showing how context shaped the discretionary drivers of ownership, purpose, and the strategy of the reform.

Economic context

The economic context when the reform began was an economy that had been decimated, particularly the manufacturing and construction sectors (see table 2.1). Because much of the agricultural sector was subsistence farming, its fortunes were more tied to rainfall and were less affected for the most part by the political transition. Throughout the reform, poverty in Ethiopia was far worse than the average for the continent.

Ethiopia's poverty in 1996 was unspeakable and continues to be so. The country continues to lag behind the development indicators of the group of least-developed countries worldwide and of sub-Saharan African nations (see table 2.2). The country's poverty and isolation in 1996 are illustrated by some stark statistics:

- Seven million to nine million people (8 to 10 percent of the population) did not earn enough to purchase sufficient food.
- Half the population lived on less than 2.5 cents per day spent for food.

Table 2.1 Ethiopia: annual growth rate of sectoral GDP: constant 1980–81 factor cost, 1988–89 to 1993–94 (%)

Fiscal year ending July 7	1988–89	1989–90	1990–91	1991–92
(Ethiopian fiscal year)	(1981)	(1982)	(1983)	(1984)
GDP a constant factor cost	0.2	3.4	−6.7	−3.2
Agriculture sector	−0.1	5.2	2.8	−2.0
Agriculture	−0.5	5.7	3.0	−2.6
Other commodity sectors	−2.5	−4.0	−22.1	−7.6
Manufacturing	0.2	−4.6	−40.8	−9.6
Handicrafts	−10.0	10.4	−13.8	0.3
Building and construction	−7.8	−15.9	−9.2	−14.3
Distribution services	−4.9	1.7	−24.4	−3
Other services				
Public administration and defense	12.9	8.9	−14.1	−14.6
Education	4.2	na	1.3	2.7
Health	4.4	2.5	−4.0	10.1
Nonagricultural GDP	0.5	1.7	−16	−4.7

Source: International Monetary Fund (1994: 78).

Table 2.2 Development indicators for Ethiopia, 1996 and 2011

Indicator	1996 Ethiopia	1996 Least-developed countries	1996 Sub-Saharan Africa	2011 Ethiopia	2011 Least-developed countries	2011 Sub-Saharan Africa
Human Development Index	0.237	0.331	0.379	0.363	0.439	0.463
Life expectancy at birth (years)	47.8	51.0	50.9	59.3	59.1	54.4
Adult literacy rate (percent)	33.6	46.5	55.0	29.8	59.2	61.6
Real GDP per capita (PPP$)	420	898	1,288	934	1,379	2,181
Ranking in the Human Development Index	168 out of 174			174 out of 187		

Source: author's compilation, based on United Nations Development Program (1996: 137); United Nations Development Program (2011: 127–30, table 1; 160, table 9; 164–5, table 9).

- Half the rural population consumed too few calories to contribute at all to agricultural production.
- Eighty-five percent of the population lived in the rural areas.
- Ethiopia was at the bottom of world rankings for the percentage of the population served by roads: half the population lived a two-day walk to an all-weather road.
- Ethiopia was at the very bottom of world rankings for the ratio of cell phones to population.

The principal solution to ameliorating the deep poverty and economic disarray by the regime was political and bureaucratic—to effectively reach the 85 percent of the populace who lived in the rural areas and to do this through a policy of far-reaching decentralization known as regionalization. A comprehensive assessment of regionalization conducted by the Canadian International Development Agency in 1998 concluded that "what becomes essential to the party's success is not so much the EPRDF's [the Ethiopian People's Revolutionary Democratic Front, the ruling party of the new government] capacity to tolerate opposition, as its capacity to reduce rural poverty."[2] The study's conclusion left open the question as to whether the decentralization policy might be a grab for political control disguised as a development policy. Thus, the economic context was closely enmeshed with both the political and the bureaucratic contexts.

Decentralization was central to the government plans for the public sector and thus for the PFA reform. One cannot understand the financial reform or appreciate its achievements without understanding the policy of decentralization. The PFM field is virtually silent on how the structure of government—the extent it is centralized or decentralized—impacts financial reform. It is a far greater challenge to reform a decentralized system than a centralized one, especially one that is in the process of decentralizing. Decentralization to the regions and then, during the rollout of the financial reform, to the weredas (administrative districts within a region), which had limited capacity, meant that this would be a PFA, not a PFM, reform. One reason why some foreign aid interventions never worked in Ethiopia is that these agencies never grasped the implications of the country's decentralization. Some still don't.

Political context

Ethiopia was governed by the Transitional Government of Ethiopia from July 1991 (two months after the victory of the EPRDF over the Derg) under the transitional charter adopted in the national conference in July in Addis Ababa. The Federal Democratic Republic of Ethiopia came into being with the ratification of the constitution in August 1995.[3] It was still in power as of 2014.

There are two interconnected strands of the political context of the Ethiopian reform: first, the triumph of the Ethiopian People's Revolutionary Democratic Front (EPRDF) over the Derg military regime in May 1991 after years of civil war, and second, the pursuit of a policy of ethnic federalism. The EPRDF is an association of regional ethnic parties, in which the dominant player is the Tigrayan People's Liberation Front (TPLF). The Tigrayan ethnic group is the third largest in Ethiopia and holds the key government posts, including, until the death of Meles Zenawi in August 2012, that of prime minister.[4] The new government of Ethiopia, established in July 1991, was dominated by the EPRDF and the Oromo Liberation Front, representing the Oromo ethnic group, the largest in Ethiopia.

Because of the political dominance of the EPRDF and thus the TPLF, it is difficult to separate politics from administration. The party and state distinction is especially blurred at subnational levels, where party officials serve as senior administrators. Beyond the political dominance of the EPRDF, the key political context of the PFA reform was the policy of decentralization based on ethnicity known as regionalization, or ethnic federalism.

Origins of regionalization. The origins of regionalization go back long before the triumph of the EPRDF in 1991. A long-term observer of Ethiopia, Christopher Clapham, noted, "Over a recorded history that stretches back over many centuries, the Ethiopia[n] state has never been restricted to any single nationality or people"; the policy of regionalization was to restore a "system that Ethiopia once possessed, before the centralizing ethos of the twentieth century, backed by firearms, imposed an ultimately unsustainable central autocracy."[5] As to whether it was possible to restore regionalization, Meles Zenawi, the prime minister in 1995, stated, "I don't know; but we have tried everything else, and that didn't work."[6]

The rallying cry of the EPRDF against the military regime was one of ethnic self-determination, and even the possibility of secession. This was enshrined in the Transitional Charter of July 1991, which also immediately recognized Eritrea's autonomy and right to self-determination. In his work on the Tigrayan People's Liberation Front, John Young has argued that the call for ethnic self-determination was a crucial factor in the success of the revolutionary struggle.[7] The Amharas, Ethiopia's second-largest ethnic group, had dominated the state and politics for centuries, until the ascendance of the Tigrayan ethnic group. The Tigrayans, along with the Eritreans, succeeded in overthrowing the military regime in 1991. Yet it is important to distinguish between the dominance of the imperial and military regimes and the dominance through those regimes by the Amhara ethnic group.

The new government had to solve two thorny political issues relating to nation and class.[8] Solving the national question of greater inclusion of ethnic groups was to be done by moving from the unitary state of the imperial and military regimes, which had failed to address problems of centralization, exploitation, and participation, to a federal state defined along national or ethnic lines.[9] The new regime also had to solve the class question of including the peasantry in the polity, which meant reorienting state structures and policies to support the interests of its political constituency: the 80 percent or more of the rural populace engaged in agricultural production. Regionalization was "a forthright, if controversial, response to the legacy of ethnic domination and marginalization in the Ethiopian state."[10] The new government was acutely aware of the need for effective decentralization, which would deliver services more efficiently, and thus build much needed legitimacy for the EPRDF.

Is regionalization for real? Is the push for regionalization genuine, or is it simply a façade for central control by the TPLF-dominated EPRDF? An observer of Leninist regimes, Ken Jowitt, has made the argument that Leninist parties are an organizational weapon designed to penetrate society.[11] What better instrument to penetrate to the lowest levels of a predominantly rural society than decentralization under the guise of ethnic self-determination? One issue that must be clarified and that many observers of Ethiopia have failed to grasp is the distinction between regionalization and fiscal decentralization. Ethiopia does not meet the textbook definition of fiscal decentralization because there is no revenue assignment: subnational governments cannot set tax rates.[12] Regionalization was based on the clear political principle of ethnic self-determination and was not *"primarily aimed at administrative or development efficiencies* [emphasis added]."[13] The challenge of regionalization at the start of the reform (and indeed as of this writing), was summarized by the USAID governance advisor Stevens Tucker, who had several years of in-country experience and became the architect from the donor side of the DSA's PFA reform project:

> The dilemma faced by the EPRDF since it assumed power in 1991 has been how to respond to the political imperative to devolve political and administrative authority to regions whose capacity and accountability are highly uneven, while simultaneously assuring that basic state functions continue, developing regional and sub-regional capacity, and reorienting administrative and political units at all levels to think in terms of partnership rather than command. The approach adopted in practice appears to have been to establish formal, constitutional principles supportive of a devolved system, to focus on rapidly building regional capacity by a variety of means, and to rely during the interim on party structures and informal political linkages to maintain a degree of policy and political coherence.[14]

Tucker makes the further argument that regionalization cannot be simplistically interpreted as central control by the EPRDF for three reasons: policymaking differs significantly from past practices, involving much consultation; policy is implemented locally by locals bringing an ethnic lens and autonomy; and there has been real, not just de jure, transfer of responsibility and capacity to regions, which makes the center dependent upon the regions for monitoring and control. Others have concurred with this analysis, contending that for the foreseeable future there will be the "dynamics of the drive for efficiency through national planning, and the need to develop local capacity for increased effectiveness."[15]

One could add two additional issues to Tucker's description: the limited capacity of central ministries, and unfunded liabilities of the center, which give regions discretion in deciding the depth of implementation they will undertake.

For example, the latter occurred in the Southern Region (complete name: Southern Nations, Nationalities, and Peoples Region) when the DSA project was implementing the first regional reform, which was budgeting. The head of the Bureau of Finance and Economic Development (BOFED) for the Southern Region asked me what he should do, given the recent edict from the central government to establish a farmer training center in every *kebele* (an administrative tier below the wereda, or district, level).[16] To do so would consume the entire budget of the region, as there were several thousand kebeles. I suggested that the region do ten farmer-training centers in the first year.

There were multiple motives behind the policy of decentralization—the sole aim was not necessarily to strengthen the regional level. One example of such nuances was the decision, in 2002, to undertake second-stage decentralization by assigning most regional resources to the wereda level. There are several interpretations as to the origins of this policy, but one that seemed most prevalent was that second-stage decentralization was meant to weaken the influence of the regional parties of the EPRDF, which were becoming less responsive to central direction. This interpretation was based on the initial proposal for second-stage decentralization that block grants be issued from the center and not from the regions. Decentralization can be used to weaken regional political control and not to directly increase the control of the center.

Including foreign aid in a government's financial system is always complicated. It was made even more so with decentralization. Just as the financial reform was getting under way, in 1997, foreign agencies introduced sectoral development programs (SDPs). These programs were intended to increase funding to specific sectors where need was high—the social sector (health, education) and the economic sector (roads)—and were to be financed by means of block grants to the regions funded by the World Bank and other donors. As the federal government and foreign aid agencies shaped the sectoral development programs, there was concern by government that this process actually represented a recentralization of economic and social policymaking, and thus undermined the policy of regionalization. Decentralization is a murky topic at best, although the fiscal federalism literature does try to define its bounds in terms of the horizontal and vertical distribution of resources.[17] In these terms there clearly was from the start and continues to be today significant vertical imbalance, as the regions depend on the center for over 80 percent of their resources. Ethnicity makes Ethiopia's decentralization murkier, from the point of view both of self-determination and the need to reduce the role of Amhara bureaucrats, and of the limited technical capacity of the center and the newness of regional and subregional political and administrative structures. Ethiopia's decentralization was a work in progress in 1996 and remains so to this day—an example of what the legal scholar Cass Sunstein describes as an "incompletely theorized agreement."[18]

Perhaps what is most murky in Ethiopia's regionalization is the need for external control, which is the hallmark of PFA, and the role of political intervention from the center to deliver this control—to ensure the responsiveness of regional and subregional administrations and to curb the potential abuse of discretion, especially corruption. The role of the party as a circuit breaker to ensure responsiveness of local administrations echoes what Jerry Hough found when he studied party-state relations in the Soviet Union.[19] The EPDRF is clearly the glue maintaining coherence in policy and its implementation. Oversight of regions by the party at the center weakened with the advent of the war with Eritrea, which shifted the party's attention to the prosecution of the war. This drastic decrease in political oversight, coupled with the meager capacity of the central finance ministries to support their equivalents in the regions, resulted in de facto decentralization if only because of neglect.

Bureaucratic context

PFA/M can be viewed in terms of systems (e.g., budgeting, accounting) and their execution. In the following sections I examine the execution of systems—institutions, organization, and staffing—that prevailed at the start of the reform and shaped it. (The four financial systems of budgeting, accounting, automation, and planning are discussed in detail in chapters 4 to 7.)

The challenges facing the bureaucracy

A stocktaking of the tough tasks the Ethiopian bureaucracy faced in 1998, two years into the reform, was provided by a Canadian International Development Agency report written by seasoned observers:

> Ethiopia is simultaneously engaged in a least three radical reform processes, any of which would constitute an ambitious undertaking even for a wealthy state. The reforms are as follows: (1) Restructuring the pre-existing state into a federation.... (2) Reform of the civil service into an effective and efficient instrument for the achievement of government policy.... (3) Restructuring of the pre-existing command economy with the introduction of market forces in many sectors.... If one adds to these three areas of fundamental reform, the pressures for change in terms of political culture, transparency and pluralism ("pressures for democratization") the scope of the transition emerges absolutely starkly.[20]

The bureaucracy also had to implement a demanding array of foreign aid development programs, the most significant being the sector development programs.

The most serious task facing the new government was making the decentralization to the regional tier work. This decentralization initiative had been introduced by the new government upon its accession to power, and PFA was an element of this initiative. The regions' limited capacity in financial administration—especially in the four "emerging" regions, Afar, Benishangul Gumuz, Gambella, and Somali—can be seen in their poor performance in spending only a small portion of their budgets.[21]

Already stretched thin by the requirements of the first-stage decentralization, to the regions, the government then extended the decentralization to the weredas virtually overnight, in January of fiscal year 2001–2. With this second-stage decentralization (SSD) the government dramatically moved the goalposts for the PFA reform, increasing fifteen-fold the number of entities that would be managing a budget. Throughout the twelve years of the PFA reform, decentralization continued to be implemented by increasing the number of weredas (by splitting them into smaller entities), as can be seen in the largest region, Oromia: 183 in 2000; 216 in 2003; 287 in 2004; 299 in 2006; 303 in 2008; 308 in 2010.

The leap in the number of budget-managing institutions was a problem not only of quantity but also of quality: limited wereda financial management capacity and a lack of basic infrastructure. One wereda in Amhara region went by the nickname "leave my salary at the road," for access to the wereda was by donkey path, and there were no electricity lines or phone connections.

The policy of SSD to weredas was driven ostensibly by the rationale of improving frontline service delivery, but there was also a strong political rationale: bypassing the regional political parties, which were becoming less responsive to central direction, or were perceived as such. The introduction of SSD could not have occurred at a more challenging time: in January 2002, halfway through the fiscal year, in the year that the DSA project was implementing the first regional reform, the budget reform in the Southern Region. SSD was a huge shock on its own, and for the DSA project, which was in the throes of working through the first regional reform, it was a double shock. Decentralization to the regions with the added plan of SSD to the weredas created a moving target for the PFA reform.

A weak administration

Could the Ethiopian state meet the kinds of challenges that would tax even the most capable state? The Task Force for Civil Service Reform's report, *Task Force Comprehensive Report*, found the administration to be conservative, focused on control, and not responsive to government policy (see box 2.1). The administration had been weakened by the civil war; the quality of the bureaucracy and the bureaucrats was deficient; and while undertaking the reform, this weakened administration was itself undergoing political rectification with the purging of Amhara officials outside of Amhara region.[22] For centuries the bureaucracy had been dominated by members of the Amhara ethnic group; many did not favor the new government and were not trusted by the EPRDF. The ethnic cleansing of the bureaucracy drastically reduced technical capacity, especially at the regional level, but it did eliminate officials who might have blocked reform. It also meant that the highest priority of the PFA reform was to be the rapid in-service training of thousands of new officials.

Box 2.1 Present problems in the civil service—summary of the findings of the Task Force on Civil Service Reform

- Management concentrates on the administration and control of inputs and activities rather than achieving government policy.
- Management systems are outdated and unable to respond to the changing environment in which the civil service operates.
- There has not been a fundamental challenging of the need for government service, regulations, and activities inherited from the past. Public perception is of a bureaucracy that is more of a hindrance than a facilitator, with needless and time-consuming procedures.
- The civil service is under-resourced. Government recurrent expenditure is one of the lowest in the world. The country has, in total, relatively few civil servants.

Country	Civil servants per 10,000 population
France	370
Ghana	182
USA	125
Uganda	83
Ethiopia	50

- The civil service culture gives managers little scope to manage their commands properly. The service is excessively hierarchical and there is little real delegation.
- Staffs are ill paid, generally lack adequate skills, have been isolated from international developments in their field for a number of years, and are demoralized.
- While unethical practices are not institutionalized into the machinery of government, there are significant instances of corruption, embezzlement, and fraud. There is concern that these are on the increase.

Source: Office of the Prime Minister, Task Force for Civil Service Reform
(1996a, vol. 1: 14).

The limitations of the civil service at the start of the reform in 1996 were cataloged in detail in the five-volume *Task Force Comprehensive Report*.[23] Given such deficiencies in the civil service, could Ethiopia's experiment in decentralization prevail despite what forty years of previous research on the topic had found? John Cohen and I reviewed this literature for the United Nations; our central conclusion was that effective decentralization requires "complementary capacity at center and locale, defined as confident states backed by adequate financial and manpower capacity."[24] Ethiopia in 1996 had limited administrative capacity at both the center and locale.

The magnitude of the challenges and the weak administration meant that it would be a PFA, not a PFM, reform. Further, if a PFA reform strategy was to have any hope of succeeding it could not impose excessive burdens on the thin line of senior administrators and newly recruited staff. Under these circumstances, for a PFA strategy of reform to succeed, it would have to limit risk, for there was much risk baked into the system. The fourth driver of reform, strategy, is discretionary—our strategy would have to be a combination of recognize and improve. Change would have to wait.

Institutions

"Institutions" as used here does not refer to the structures of government—the formal organizations. Instead, institutions are the formal and informal *rules* that govern and guide administration. The coming to power of a new government and the transformation of governance with regionalization brought in a flurry of new laws and regulations, which had to be rapidly absorbed by new organizations and, most important, newly minted officials. The magnitude of change and the complexity of decentralization meant that there were bound to be many areas where rules were not clear and, even when legally enacted, still required interpretation in practice. It is axiomatic that decentralization is a process that unfolds over time; although it may be circumscribed by formal rules, the true playing field is defined by practice. In Ethiopia, there was disagreement as to both interpretation and the basic point of whether attention needed to be paid to the formal rules. Some key rules were missing and some were negotiable. Some rules were formal but some were fluid. This was certainly the case with the new financial law, the role of federal audit of regional expenditures, and the disposition of unused transfers by regions.

There is some debate in the PFM literature as to the best timing for putting legal reforms in place, but the debate is often muted or absent because legal reforms must be enacted—unlike procedure reforms, which can be issued by fiat—and this may take years. But in Ethiopia's one-party state the new financial law was passed in weeks, at the urging of the Office of the Prime Minister. Indeed, the first deliverable of the government's Civil Service Reform Program, the new financial law—Financial Proclamation No. 57 (officially: Federal Government of Ethiopia Financial Administration Proclamation No. 57/1996)—was made law on December 16, 1996, a month before the DSA PFA project started. The proclamation provided the legal basis for all aspects of the central government's finances.

Developed with technical assistance from the Government of Canada, the proclamation was a needed overhaul, for the existing legal framework, from 1981, had serious deficiencies: it had never been enacted into law; it was based on a unitary, not a federal, governmental structure; and it was not adequately supported by instructions and manuals to assist line institutions in its implementation.[25] Yet the new law was wreathed in its own ambiguities and its mere existence could not ensure that its requirements would be followed. The Ministry of Finance and the Office of the Auditor General raised concerns about the new law: they felt that it was too restrictive and that implementing it was not feasible, especially a requirement that all donor funds be included in the budget and con-solidated as one lump sum.[26] The discipline of a government hardened by a long revolution led to the financial law differing from that of other countries in speci-fying detailed penalties for violating its provisions. For example, the new finan-cial law specified a ten-year jail sentence for using funds that were not in the budget—which was typically the case of funds from foreign aid.

The considerable attention to penalties in the proclamation underscored the new government's concern, real or perceived, with the need to curb corruption, especially in connection with its policy of decentralization, which gave discre-tion to new entities with limited administrative capacity. Legalism—strict adher-ence to the law—is a strong tenet in the culture, and the proclamation demonstrated the new government's faith that laws can provide an important instrument, along with the party and the administration, to ensure probity. There was a belief in the Office of the Prime Minister that tough laws and a vigilant party could compensate for a weak administration, at least until the administra-tion could be strengthened under the CSRP.

But the reality was not so straightforward. The 1996 financial proclamation raises a number of issues for reformers. The key issue, one with direct relev-ance to the PFA reform managed by the DSA, was the provision for a compre-hensive budget. In budgeting, "the basics" means the line-item, or "traditional," budget (as Aaron Wildavsky called it), a key feature of which is its compre-hensiveness (discussed in more detail in chapter 4, on budget reform). Yet despite the formal legal requirement for a comprehensive presentation of public expenditures, the reform never achieved comprehensiveness because neither the government nor foreign aid entities were interested in full disclo-sure. So much for formal requirements! The mere existence of a formal law doesn't ensure compliance with it.

A second example of the ambiguity of formal rules was the debate about auditing federal subsidies to the regions—how the monies were spent. The federal auditor general claimed this right under the law. The regions disagreed. These federal subsidies were block grants in which federal and foreign aid funds were commingled with regional funds, leading the regions to argue that it was not appropriate for the federal government to audit the expenditures that were funded by commingled monies. What has emerged is a system of either joint audits by regional and federal auditors or simply regional audits.

Another area where formal rules provided little clear guidance was in the con-flict over the disposition, at the end of the fiscal year, of unused funds that had been part of the block transfer to regions. Should the funds be controlled by the region or by the federal Ministry of Finance? And who should decide?

The treatment of the financial transfers from the federal government to regions is important to understand for it goes to the heart of how a decentralized PFA/M system works. There were two types of transfers, those for recurrent expenditures and those for capital expenditures. The recurrent transfer was a monthly physical movement of funds from the central bank in the federal gov-ernment to a bank account of the regional BOFED. This money was used to pay salaries, operating and maintenance expenses, and miscellaneous expenses. Both the transfer and the disbursement of the funds were straightforward.

This could not be said for the transfer for capital expenditures. There was not a physical transfer of cash. Instead, an "advice" setting the limit of what could be spent for capital outlays was sent to the regional bank account. Because capital activities are far more complicated and time-consuming than, say, the payment of an official's monthly salary, virtually none of the regions used up their full capital advice—but they wanted to retain the unspent capital advice balances at the end of the fiscal year. It was the practice of the federal Ministry of Finance to cancel the balance of the capital advice at the end of the fiscal year, and the law was silent on this issue. This type of ambiguity created uncertainty in the fiscal decentralization.

Weak compliance

PFA is about compliance. Once compliance is established, a government can consider moving to PFM and a focus on discretion, and thus professionalism. A challenge this reform faced throughout its life was the weakness of compliance, especially adherence to the directives of the Ministry of Finance.

In most governments, the Ministry of Finance is feared because it has the power of the purse. A virtually unquestioned assumption of PFA/M reform is that even though the Ministry of Finance may have limited technical capacity, it is respected—indeed, feared—and its will shall not be ignored. There is perhaps no more important informal rule in PFA/M than showing respect for the finance organizations. In Ethiopia at the start of the reform these were the Ministry of Finance and the Ministry of Economic Development and Cooperation. In early 1996, USAID convened a meeting with the former minister of finance, Ale-mayehu Dhaba, to hear from him what issues the agency should consider in supporting reform in the government. I kept the former minister's statement in mind throughout the reform and it turned out to be prophetic: "The Ministry of Finance is in danger of becoming a post office." By "post office" he meant that at the federal level the ministry simply sent out budget notices to spending agencies and dished out their monthly cash allotments; they did the same with the transfers to the regions. In short, in the early days of the reform many federal spending agencies simply ignored the Ministry of Finance, using it as an ATM. Two line ministries, the Ministry of Health and the Ethiopian Roads Authority (which had the largest budget in the federal government), were perhaps the worst offenders. They did not submit budget requests or accounts on time. The head of the Accounts Department at the Ministry of Finance simply requested accounting information from the Roads Authority—he did not demand it. The implementation of the budget reform at the federal level was seriously delayed by the failure of the Ministry of Health to respond to Ministry of Finance directives. The country's four-year backlog of accounts was not confined to the far-flung reaches of the country, the regions. Right under the nose of the Ministry of Finance, and indeed within the ministry itself, were several years of backlog.

This failure by the Ministry of Finance to show its teeth may have contributed to the failure to honor the informal rules concerning respect for financial organizations.

In Ethiopia the Ministry of Finance was not sufficiently respected, and in many ways this is still the case with the new federal finance organization, the Ministry of Finance and Economic Development (created from combining the finance and planning ministries in 2003). The formal limitations of the federal finance organization in directing its regional equivalents, coupled with its informal weakness, has meant that the PFA reform in Ethiopia has been largely acephalous.

Both formal and informal institutions establish the behavior of administration. Both types of rules take time to be accepted and shape practice. In 2011, during my assessment of the PFM system, I met with the head of the Oromia BOFED and we discussed the reform at length. He concluded that the procedures were very appropriate but that the system was still "settling," seven years after it had been introduced. By settling he meant the institutions were still being embedded.

Organization

"Organization" refers to the way government is structured. This structure has three principal features: the tiers of government, such as national, region, sub-region; the organization within tiers, such as within one region; and the organization within agencies in a tier (for example, the structure within the Ministry of Finance in the national tier). In Ethiopia, the national tier is referred to as the federal tier. (The term "national" is not used because "nation" refers to the ethnic "nations" in the regions). With decentralization, especially second-stage decentralization, change occurred in all three loci of organization: between tiers, within tiers, and within agencies in a tier. Basically, fragmentation characterized all three types of organization; this had a profound effect on the PFA reform. Fragmentation meant that there was limited coherence or standardization of practices. It meant that there would be significant variations in the actions of regions in both their interpretation of rules, the implementation of procedures, and the design and implementation of the PFA reform.

The decentralization program foresaw principally four tiers: the federal (central) government, region, zone, and wereda.[27] The country's constitution provides for the central and regional tiers of government, but zones and weredas were established under the regional constitutions. The federal, regional, and wereda tiers all have deliberative bodies, but the zone does not; it is an administrative appendage of regional administration and is meant to provide closer support for weredas.[28] Prior to SSD, zones conducted the financial administration of their weredas, though weredas would submit a list of requirements to the zone administration. The SSD to weredas was meant to give this tier the responsibility and resources for frontline service delivery, especially in the fields of health and education. Whether weredas have been accorded genuine discretion to develop and pursue development policies on their own can be debated, but in any case, in practice their discretion is vitiated by unfunded mandates, limited capacity to plan and budget, and a lack of discretionary resources. An argument can be made that weredas are simply agents of the regional government, entities to deliver primary services and collect regional taxes. Weredas are not allowed to make laws, so even though they can issue a budget, the funds for that budget are appropriated under the regional budget law.

Two features of the organization between the tiers had implications for the PFA reform. The first was the inconsistency from region to region as to their own internal tiers, meaning that the regions differed considerably in the number of weredas in them, the population of the weredas, the existence and role of zones, and the ethnic makeup of these entities. The second factor was the absence of an administrative entity responsible for technical coordination. There were no formal mechanisms for technical coordination of the Civil Service Reform Program (CSRP), yet the variations among regions' administrative profiles and characteristics cried out for such coordination and technical support.

The *Task Force Comprehensive Report* summarized the problems between the tiers as follows:

- The policies and directives from the central bodies are insufficiently clear to be useful to the regions. They are not supported by guidelines, manuals, or training which would assist the relevant regional bureaus;
- Central bodies do not respond adequately or quickly enough to requests for assistance from regions;
- Regions fail to supply the central bodies with complete and accurate information on time;
- There is a lack of feedback from central bodies to the regions on the latter's reports;
- The central bodies' inspection departments do not receive the level of cooperation necessary to implement their reports.[29]

The Office of the Prime Minister as the architect of the Civil Service Reform Program took on the role of managing the reform, but this was far beyond its capacity. In fact, as the Civil Service Reform Task Force report pointed out, the OPM itself was in need of reform. (The report found three major problems with the OPM: "lack of clarity in its role [with a weakness in monitoring and review of performance and a tendency to centralize key problem areas onto itself], an absence of action on civil service management and problems of internal organization."[30] Put another way, the OPM did not act strategically and tended to micromanage at both the federal and regional levels. The OPM was not (and still is not) fit for purpose in providing strategic direction and ensuring the establishment of the necessary administrative linkages for policy and its execution, which bring coherence to technical issues. Then, with the advent of war with Eritrea the OPM shifted its attention away from domestic affairs.

The second type of organization of administration was within a tier. The CSR Task Force report found similar weaknesses within the top tier of administration as it had found between tiers—that is, between the federal-tier agencies (such as the Office of the Prime Minister, the Ministry of Finance, the Public Service Commission, the Ministry of Planning and Economic Development, and the Ministry of External Economic Cooperation) and the federal-tier line agencies (such as the Ministries of Health and Education). There was a disconnect both between and within the tiers of administration because the federal agencies were not outward-looking, were not well organized, and focused on minutia.

The third and final type of organization of administration is within an agency of one tier; here we focus on the finance agency at the federal level, within the Ministry of Finance. There were two defining features of this agency. The first was the absence of a permanent secretary or its equivalent—a senior civil servant who is a technocrat, not a political appointee, and is responsible for running the day-to-day affairs of a ministry. The permanent secretary is a civil servant and thus provides continuity and technical direction, regardless of changes in government. In the UK, the official designation of a permanent secretary for finance is "the principal establishment and accounting officer," indicating this individual's two responsibilities: for the personnel and their actions, and for the funds assigned to his or her ministry. Typically, permanent secretaries' superiors are political appointees in ministerial and deputy or vice minister positions who communicate the policies of the government in power and monitor their implementation.

Absent a permanent secretary, department heads in the Ethiopian federal government become the highest-ranking civil servants in a bureaucracy—effectively feudal barons—who can and do act independently of and even at odds with the directives of the politically appointed ministers and vice ministers. This dysfunctional management arrangement characterized the Ethiopian "within-agency" organization. This was illustrated by a meeting in the Ministry of Finance, four years into the reform, where the minister berated the head of the information technology department for turning off Internet access after 5 p.m., which the department head had done because that is when employees typically got online for personal business and entertainment. The minister's tirade made no impact on the department head, and for several weeks, just to show his defiance, he continued to stop Internet access at 5 p.m.

The DSA project was fortunate to have in the first two years of the reform a supportive vice minister for finance, Hailemelekot T. Giorgis, who was also head of the Expenditure Management and Control Component of the CSRP, which was responsible for the PFA reform. The vice minister was a good manager and a forceful individual, but he, too, came up against the feudal fiefdoms of the department heads in the Ministry of Finance. The acephalous organization of the finance function across the tiers of government was thus replicated within the finance agencies themselves.

Compounding the problems stemming from the leaderless nature of the finance function was the second defining feature of the within-agency organization: the separation of the finance function into recurrent budget management (the remit of the finance agencies) and capital budget management (the remit of the planning agencies). This kind of dual budget management was replicated in line agencies as well. For example, in the Ministry of Education there was a department of finance responsible for the recurrent budget and a department of planning responsible for the capital budget. The organizational division of the budget went far beyond separate organizational charts, since the finance and planning ministries had widely divergent philosophies, the Ministry of Finance being conservative and control-oriented and the Ministry of Planning being expansive.

Financial administration was fragmented between tiers, within tiers, and within the agencies of each tier. The fragmentation of the organization of public finance posed a formidable challenge to the PFA reform, for success depended as much on the reform's ability to bridge these organizational crevasses as on the quality of the reformed procedures. Perhaps more so.

Organizational culture

The defining feature of the bureaucratic culture in 1996, and to the present day, is what John Cohen, after many years in governments in East Africa, called "inertia without accountability." This aligns with a common observation of the culture of public officials in Africa that "the nail that stands up gets hammered down." The PFA reform had to work with a cohort of public officials who had survived—literally—for seventeen years under a ruthless dictatorship. That they did survive was testament to their ability, but it reinforced extremely cautious behavior. One former senior member of the Tigray BOFED confided to me during my 2011 assessment, "Senior officials do not make decisions, for making a decision provides grounds for them to be held accountable." Bureaucrats were further intimidated by the extension of the practice of *gemgema*, self-assessment, to all officials, not just party members, throughout the reform; it was vigorously ramped up in the later years of the reform as part of a policy of "business process reengineering reform."

To be proactive was to take a risk. Far better that party officials be the ones to take such risks, as their circumstances are more secure and forgiving. The intimidation of bureaucrats and the virtual absence of reward for initiative have meant that decision-making, and potential innovation, falls to party members. It is no coincidence that Getachew Hamussa, the man who as the head of the region's BOFED largely ensured the success of the first region to be reformed, the Southern Region, was also a highly regarded political cadre in both his region and, especially important, at the highest levels of the central party. The prime minister knew of his exploits and considerable talents. I noted earlier the difficulty of disentangling politics and administration in the context of the far-reaching policy of decentralization. Here I spotlight the underpinnings of the bureaucratic culture that invited decision-making by political cadres and discouraged decision-making by non-party officials. This is still largely the case. Again, what defines PFA is external control and little or no autonomy of the bureaucracy from politics. Such was the case in Ethiopia and still is. PFM is all about discretion, yet in Ethiopia, discretion of bureaucrats, especially those who are not members of the party, is not encouraged—in fact, it is grounds for punishment.

Leadership styles

An important unknown of the PFA reform was whether senior government officials, the managers of the reform, would embrace reform, and not merely accept it: the considerable obstacles needed to be overcome to realize reform required proactive commitment to a continuous and firm effort. Stevens Tucker of USAID, who had been working with the government to design a project (the future DSA project) and had observed the government for several years, contended that "policy makers, elected officials, and civil servants clearly do not have reflexes which condition them to look outward for advice, commentary, or alternative views."[31] And a first reading of Levine's assessment of Amhara culture would make one very pessimistic about the possibility of reform. But things are not necessarily what they seem in Ethiopia (wax and gold again), and cultural conservatism is not absolute. *Yichalal*—It's possible!—is also in play. An absence of certainty leaves the "possibility" of change.

Thus, senior officials' reactions to change, as to decentralization, are complex. Four factors shaped the reflexive responses of government officials to reform:

1   Leadership style of the tier where the official was located
2   Predominant style of leadership
3   Senior officials' openness to external advice
4   The magnitude of change senior officials had to manage

Leadership style by tier. John Young found that the leadership style of the central bureaucracy generally was the same under the new government as it had been under the previous military and imperial regimes: "deeply conservative, resistant to change, extremely hierarchical, preoccupied with concerns about security, and in need of far-reaching reform."[32]

But, as Tip O'Neill, a loquacious U.S. congressman, famously pronounced, all politics is local, and there were dynamics in play in reform under decentralization that often trumped the prevailing conservatism. Decentralization allowed for the emergence of a powerful dynamic of interregional competition. The CSRP was arguably the first tangible, measurable, and high-profile government policy where regions could strut their stuff and demonstrate their ability and autonomy. Immense pride was conferred on the Southern Region when the regional PFA reform was initiated there, and not in the Amhara region, which had dominated the bureaucracies of previous regimes, nor in Tigray, which was home to the reigning political party. This pride tapped Ethiopia's can-do spirit and also meant that regional officials wanted nothing to do with federal officials telling them how to do *their* reform. As the deputy head of the Southern Region's BOFED said, "We don't need the white shoes from Addis" ("white shoes" refers to the ceremonial attire of the Amhara elite). Decentralization throws up many challenges to a reform, such as the difficulty of leveraging a turnkey model from the center or pioneer regions. But it can also unleash a powerful dynamic for rapid change, which no technical assistance project can create. In fact, the dynamic becomes a challenge for a technical assistance project, for the latter must catch and ride the regional reform wave.

Predominant style of leadership. Although the disabling themes found by Young at the federal level held sway to varying degrees in all regions, regions exhibited very different reflexes depending on the style of leadership that predominated there. In 1996, when the PFA reform got under way, there were two very different styles of leadership in the public service: a mobilizing mentality of zemechas (campaigns) born of the long struggle; and its complete opposite, Cohen's inertia without accountability. Clearly, the vigor of the reform would vary by region, depending on which style prevailed. In the home of the struggle, Tigray, the vigor was palpable even to the point of producing failure as a result of trying to do too much. In the second year of the rollout of the reform to regions, Tigray implemented the budget and accounts reform simultaneously, and, said the BOFED head, "It almost broke our backs." The Southern Region was exemplary, for its leadership was a good mix of the vigor of campaigning tempered with the proclivities of the local Gurage ethnic group for pragmatism and a no-nonsense attitude that derived from the group's well-known business acumen.

Senior officials' openness to external advice. In a country that had been isolated for centuries, Ethiopians were suspicious of foreigners. A colleague of mine once commented that Ethiopia had "managed the foreigner for five thousand years." By this he meant that Ethiopia had managed to hold foreigners at bay. For a technical assistance project to succeed, it would have to build trust.

Magnitude of reform. Government managers differed in their tolerance for reform—especially lots of reform. Recipients of aid who are pressed to deal with constant demands to reform often show signs of "reform fatigue." I shall never forget a meeting with Retta Bedada, the seasoned head of the finance bureau of the largest region, Oromia. Within one year his bureau had been subjected to three separate and uncoordinated reforms of its chart of accounts, which is the foundation of a public financial system. In this meeting I was presenting the last of the three changes in his region's chart of accounts, when Badada stated, simply, "I am tired of reform." On another occasion, after I finished presenting the schedule of the budget reform to the head of the capital budget department of the Ministry of Economic Development and Cooperation, he said, "We have been doing this for five thousand years. What is the hurry?" The conservatism bred by the culture affected the process of reform both positively and negatively. It could act as a brake on reform, but on the positive side, it could also serve as a brake on attempts to do things that made no sense, at a speed that was unattainable.

To summarize the influence of the leadership style on the PFA reform, the reform succeeded in large part because it succeeded in the regions. It succeeded in regions because senior officials embraced the reform and were spurred on by interregional competition. The DSA technical assistance project played a role in starting the competition by being left to decide the order of the rollout to regions and by supporting the regional "waves of reform."

Staffing

Unlike the governments in many developing countries, Ethiopia's was under-staffed. Two statistics starkly illustrate Ethiopia's staffing problems at the start of the PFA reform: there was not a single qualified accountant in the government, and four years into the reform only 4.4 percent of regional and 15 percent of total federal personnel had a college-level education and there were few graduates working in financial management.[33] The CSR Task Force report found that staffing of administration, especially at the regional and subregional levels, was inadequate in terms of quantity of staff, their qualifications, and the resources at their disposal—office equipment, vehicles, telephones, and so forth. Table 2.3 presents a picture in early 1997 of the demand for and supply of finance staff in the country available for the public and private sector. For the public sector there was a surplus of bookkeepers (24 percent more than demand) and an adequate number of better-trained accounting technicians (90 percent of demand), but there was not one qualified accountant. In effect, the management of the country's financial trans-actions was principally a bookkeeping operation run by people with a twelfth-grade education or less, and there was very limited actual "accounting"—the

Table 2.3 Demand for and supply of accounting professionals in Ethiopia, 1995 (number of individuals)

	Qualified	Technicians	Bookkeepers	Total
	Professional qualification completed	*Accountancy degree or diploma*	*Vocational certificate: twelfth-grade education or below*	
Total (public and private sectors)				
Demand	774	3,224	11,164	15,162
Supply	21	1,729	8,600	10,350
Surplus/deficit	−753	−1,495	−2,564	−4,812
Public sector				
Demand	354	1,556	5,334	7,244
Supply	0	1,400	6,600	8,000
Surplus/deficit	−354	−156	+1,266	+756
Private sector				
Demand	420	1,688	5,830	7,918
Supply	21	229	2,250	2,500
Surplus/deficit	−399	−1,439	−3,580	−5,418

Source: Coopers & Lybrand (1997).

translation of numbers from the single-entry cashbook to reports. This staffing status at the start of the reform significantly influenced the design of the DSA reform project: planning for the first stage of the budgeting and accounting reform had to be shaped to accommodate both the qualifications of the existing system and staff and the rapid pace of decentralization.

Compounding the problems of understaffing and the limited qualifications of government staff available for managing finances were four other staffing constraints:

1 The policy of cleansing Amhara officials
2 Unattractive conditions in the weredas
3 Delay in making personnel assignments under SSD
4 Inadequate in-service training: lack of infrastructure and low priority.

As noted, the ruling party, the Ethiopian People's Revolutionary Democratic Front (EPRDF), was suspicious of Amhara bureaucrats and consequently rapidly cleansed members of the Amhara ethnic group from regions outside of Amhara and also severely curbed their assignments from the center to the regions. The Amhara made up the major proportion of trained and experienced officials, so removing them from many of the regions severely weakened the capacity needed to manage daily operations, much less implement reform.

A second staff-related factor that hobbled SSD was the unattractive conditions in weredas, especially the absence of adequate schooling for children and access to urban employment opportunities. Though hardship allowances were paid for staff to go to weredas, this compensation did not suffice to recruit and retain skilled finance staff at this tier. It was not uncommon for skilled professionals, especially doctors, to refuse assignments to weredas and only to visit them monthly to pick up their salaries.

The third staff-related factor came as a shock to the DSA project in the midst of the rollout of the first reform in regions, which was the budget reform in the Southern Region: the second-stage decentralization to the weredas far outpaced the ability of the regional tier to make staff assignments. As the bulk of wereda budgets were allocations for salaries, the budget reform at this tier could not progress until staff was assigned. In some weredas in the Southern Region, finance officials dumped budget forms on the desks of wereda council members and refused to start the budget process until the council confirmed staff assignments. The result was that the first budget reform in the regions was not implemented in many weredas until several months into the fiscal year.

The fourth factor affecting staffing was the absence of in-service training. In fact, there was no line-item expenditure code in the budget for training and the budget for what little training was done was buried in the code for "materials." The CSRP Task Force report highlighted the deficiency of training, stating: "Training of civil servants is almost nonexistent."[34]

The discretionary drivers: ownership, purpose, strategy

Having presented the first driver of public sector reform, context, I now briefly consider the other three: ownership, purpose, and strategy.

Ownership

Ownership is a fundamental concept in public sector reform in general and in PFA/M reform specifically. The management of public money goes to the heart of sovereignty. A distinctive feature of this reform is that it was owned by government with little or no influence coming from foreign aid entities or staff. Yes, the government acquired resources for the reform from foreign aid agencies, but it did so under its firm control. Government ownership of the reform was rooted in the political context, the legacy of struggle that had led up to the revolution that overthrew the previous regime. Self-reliance, a distrust of foreigners, and the role of campaigns, zemechas, to achieve political and social goals (in this case, reform, *mashashaya*) meant that government would lead the reform. Reinforcing the self-help approach to reform was a belief shared by many senior officials that foreigners, no matter what their credentials, didn't really understand Ethiopia and so their prescriptions were of limited value.[35] This distrust of the foreign and the respect for what exists—what is Ethiopian—was another reason why a PFM reform involving importing techniques was viewed as suspect.

The political context confirmed the need for sole government ownership and control of this reform. The prime minister personally chaired the Civil Service Reform Program from its inception in 1995 and 1996 until the commencement of hostilities with Eritrea in May of 1998. The CSRP was quietly developed within the Office of the Prime Minister with no input from foreign aid agencies and with the assistance of only one expatriate advisor. The war with Eritrea, which began approximately two years after the CSRP was unveiled, further reinforced government ownership, as most foreign aid agencies dramatically downsized their programs.

Because of the reform's urgency and political roots, the government had to retain full control of the reform. Ownership meant not just domestic ownership of the reform agenda but also ownership by ethnic groups loyal to the regime. Ownership by the latter implied the marginalization of the previously dominant group, the Amhara, and opponents of the dominant political party, the Ethiopian People's Revolutionary Democratic Front.[36] Rapid reform of regional administration was not just about getting budgets right but also about getting the right people doing the budgets.

The government's in-house design of the CSRP and its firm management of foreign aid to resource the reform underscore the fact that from the beginning government was firmly in the driver's seat and owned this reform. In a letter sent to foreign aid agencies in May 1996 when the CSRP was unveiled, the Office of the Prime Minister gave instructions on how foreign aid agencies were to respond to the program and specifically stipulated that "aid agencies refrain from interventions in areas covered by the recommendations until the Government develops its plans and projects."[37] The government applied two principles in resourcing the CSRP: divide and manage bilateral aid agencies, and exclude the Bretton Woods agencies (World Bank, IMF). No bilateral agency was to have too large a portfolio of the reform, and the Bretton Woods agencies were excluded because the government did not want to take out loans and wanted to limit these agencies' influence. It was to be a closely regulated reform.

Clarifying the ownership of reform was critical to the success of Ethiopia's financial reform. But excluding the Bretton Woods and compartmentalizing bilateral donor assistance was not the only ownership to be clarified. The federal government did not have a domestic monopoly over this reform, as regional governments made it very clear when the reform arrived in their jurisdiction that they were responsible for it. So there were two principal tracks of reform, federal and regional, and within the regional track there was considerable diversity. The first track, the federal reform, was where the reform began. In brief, the federal reform developed the crosscutting structures (budget classification, chart of accounts, financial calendar) embedded in an information system that assured consistency of the PFA system among all of the tiers of government.

The second track, the regional and district reform, was focused on building the capacity of weredas (districts) to deliver frontline services, principally primary education, health care, and, eventually, food security. This second-stage decentralization moved the reform's goalposts by increasing by a factor of 15 the number of entities involved in implementing the reform. Second-stage decentralization led to the termination of any significant federal role as well as foreign aid intervention in the PFA reform. The reform was now very granular. It had to be tailored not only to regions but also to hundreds of weredas in a region—over 300 in Oromia—which meant that regions had to take charge of their reforms. It also confirmed a two-track—federal and regional—strategy; within regions, too, there were two tracks, the regional and the wereda levels.

Purpose

The purpose of the reform flowed from the ownership by the government, and was very clear: strengthen PFA to support regionalization, which was arguably the highest political priority of the regime if it was to achieve its goal of solving the political questions of nation and class. Satish Mishra, the economic advisor to the USAID mission prior to the reform, succinctly summarized the rationale of the CSRP's PFA reform: The government of Ethiopia has "attempted to balance the political and economic objectives of regionalization by reliance on *direct control of national revenue* by the center, buttressed by the emphasis on *strengthening the capacity of regional civil servants* to implement development projects [emphasis in original]."[38] The reform was a domestic, not a foreign, agenda. In terms of the specific features of the reform, the purpose was to provide a basic system of financial administration that could work at the regional and subregional levels. The order of the day was not sophistication or "international best practice," however defined, but, rather, improving the effectiveness and timeliness of financial control—specifically, external control.

Strategy

The fourth driver of public sector reform is strategy. There are four types: recognize, improve, change, and sustain. The 1996 context, especially the far-reaching decentralization, meant that change was simply not possible. Reform had to work with what existed, improve it and then sustain it. Some may argue that a strategy of recognizing and improving an existing system is easier than a strategy of change, but in fact, the challenge and effort of reforming a legacy system and bringing it up to date are greater than simply introducing change and keeping one's fingers crossed. It can be argued that the principal problem with public sector reform in general and PFA reform specifically in Africa is defining reform as change, often perpetual, and ignoring the other strategies of reform.

Conclusion

The financial reform that began in 1996 faced a decimated economy, a weak state, and a new regime that had to establish its control and legitimacy. Decentralization was the primary means of supporting the revival of the economy and strengthening the regime. There is little discussion within the PFM field about the dynamics of decentralization in a developing-country environment and its impact on financial reform. Decentralization was itself enormously risky for there were inadequate resources, especially manpower, and the potential for corruption, either real or perceived, was considerable.

Ethiopia's policy of rapid and deep decentralization was already putting considerable strain on the state. A financial reform was needed that could ease, not compound, the strain. Public finance at the start of the reform was fragmented across tiers of government, within tiers, and within organizations. There was a lack of leadership from the federal finance ministries and, more serious, a lack of compliance with their directions. Weak leadership does not augur well for a financial system, and it particularly does not augur well for directing, or guiding, a financial reform. Weak organization coupled with rapidly changing decentralization created a very fluid environment in which the reform project was to operate.

One of the thorniest issues presented by the context in 1996 and throughout the reform was defining an appropriate leadership role of the DSA reform project—to formulate an appropriate response to the acephalous nature of the reform and the entities charged with executing it. The weakness of central authority presented an opportunity for the DSA to assume a leadership role but also posed a real danger of its usurping or being perceived to usurp government ownership. PFA/M requires coherence, and although regional variations are possible, at the end of the day, effective PFA/M requires a coherent system. The "headless" management of the reform by government and the regions' loose coupling with the center as a result of decentralization meant that the project had to serve, at a minimum, as a conduit for communication between and within the tiers.[39] The sources of authority in the Ethiopian reform were elusive. In 2004, the DSA project was deeply involved in assisting the Oromia region's budget reform. As three DSA project advisors and I entered a meeting room in the region's BOFED in Addis Ababa, the head of the accounts department announced quietly, "The third government is here." The following chapters are as much about how the DSA project managed that governance role as they are about the resources the project brought to the reform task.

Notes

1 Cohen, Hammink, and Simmons (1994: 115–16). Hammink later became the director of the USAID mission to Ethiopia.
2 Canadian International Development Agency (1998: viii). The research for this study was conducted from November 1997 to March 1998, so it provides an assessment of regionalization at the start of the PFM reform. See also Ayenew (1998: 15–22).
3 See Federal Democratic Republic of Ethiopia (1995).
4 He was succeeded by Prime Minister Hailemariam Desalegn, who is a member of the Wolayta ethnic group, of southern Ethiopia.
5 Clapham (1995: 3, 11). See also Brietzke (1995).
6 Clapham (1995: 13–14), interview with Prime Minister Meles Zenawi.
7 Young (1996: 534).
8 See Tucker (1998: 8). Stevens Tucker was the governance advisor with USAID and had three years of in-country experience during the transitional period. Tucker was also the key USAID official who managed the design of USAID's decentralization initiative and supervised the development of the DSA project.
9 Tucker (1998: 7–8).
10 Young (1996: 531–2).
11 Jowitt (1978).
12 Purists assert that decentralization involves both expenditure and revenue assignment, and the latter is absent in Ethiopia. Eshetu Chole unpacks the issue of whether regions have revenue assignment by noting that Proclamation 33/1992 stipulates that taxes reserved for joint use by the center and the regions are fixed by the central government. See Transitional Government of Ethiopia (1992). Regarding taxes reserved for regions, Chole (1994a: 22–4) notes that the same proclamation states that "tax systems shall have a unified policy base," which is defined by the central government.
13 Tucker (1998: 18). See also Chole (1994a, 1994b).
14 Tucker (1999: 31).
15 Canadian International Development Agency (1998: 11–92). A more recent assessment of decentralization also confirms that decentralization in Ethiopia is genuine and has introduced significant discretion at regional and subregional levels. See Dom, Lister, and Antoninis (2010: 51–3).
16 Each region has its own Bureau of Finance and Economic Development, or BOFED.
17 One of the most thought-provoking discussions of decentralization was written by one of the most respected organization theorists of his time, Martin Landau, and his colleague Eva Eagle. It was never published, but is available online. See Landau and Eagle (1981).
18 John Kay has said that the post-2008 financial crisis of the European Union has its roots in the evolving nature of the union and has cited Sunstein's comment that the EU is an example of an "incompletely theorized agreement." See John Kay, "What

Europe Can Learn from Kissinger-Style Ambiguity," *Financial Times*, October 5, 2011.
19 Hough (1969).
20 Canadian International Development Agency (1998: vi).
21 The execution of the budget in the smaller regions was low: Afar's low was just 37 percent of the budget in 1994–95; its high was 69 percent, in 1996–97. Benishangul Gumuz's low was 54 percent in 1995–96; its high, 65 percent in 1994–95. Gambella's low was 64 percent, in 1994–95; its high, 82 percent in 1993–94. Somali's low was 56 percent in 1993–94; its high, 84 percent in 1996–97 (see Adem 2001: 22).
22 Clapham (1995: 10).
23 Office of the Prime Minister, Task Force for Civil Service Reform (1996a). See "Works cited–general," p. 309 for a list of the five volumes and their contents.
24 Cohen and Peterson (1999: 130).
25 Office of the Prime Minister, Task Force for Civil Service Reform (1996a, vol. 2: 23).
26 Canadian International Development Agency (1998: 7–62).
27 A holdover from the previous regime was that local (not regional) administration was done by the kebele in the urban areas and by peasant associations in the rural areas. Another administrative jurisdiction below the level of the wereda is the *tabia*. These local administrative entities do not receive formal grants from the region and the wereda is the lowest level of administration where most local public finance is managed.
28 There are variations in the structure of decentralization. Tigray has no zones, and in the Southern Region there are "special weredas" in some areas in lieu of a zone. These special weredas have a deliberative function, and they, not the region, are responsible for providing a fiscal transfer to their weredas.
29 Office of the Prime Minister, Task Force for Civil Service Reform (1996a, vol. 2: 14).
30 Office of the Prime Minister, Task Force for Civil Service Reform (1996a, vol. 2: 6).
31 Tucker (1999: 9).
32 Young (1998: 195), cited in Tucker (1999: 9).
33 On the absence of qualified accountants see Office of the Prime Minister, Task Force for Civil Service Reform (1996a, vol. 1: 8). On the percentages of bachelor's degrees in 1999–2000 see Adem (2001: 21).
34 Office of the Prime Minister, Task Force for Civil Service Reform (1996a, vol. 1: 15).
35 In the first phase of the DSA project there was a macroeconomic component, which was to provide assistance to the Office of the Prime Minister. In one session with an economist of the DSA project from Harvard University, the government minister stated that this economist's "analytic toolbox did not fit the reality found in Ethiopia" (personal communication).
36 See Tucker (1998: 14–24).
37 Office of the Prime Minister, Task Force for Civil Service Reform (1996c: 2–3).
38 Mishra (1995: 2).
39 The DSA project, especially in its first years, made extensive and expensive efforts to bring regions together with the federal government and promote a dialogue on the reform by means of the semi-annual training seminars. They were very well attended, in part because officials had not visited many parts of the country as a result of the years of struggle.

3   The necessary conditions for a successful financial reform

Doing the right thing and doing it right does not assure the success of a public sector reform. There are no guarantees in the reform business, but success is more likely if the necessary conditions are in place. Reflecting on my eight years as a resident advisor working on financial reform in Kenya, I concluded that success had four necessary preconditions: trust, need, help, and urgency.[1] Sadly, most of the financial reforms introduced into Kenya during my eight-year residency amounted to little because the necessary conditions were either weak or absent. A dramatic exception was the automation of the budget, using microcomputers.[2] The technical assistance team from the Harvard Institute for International Development (HIID) was trusted. The need was great because the task of assembling an ever-growing budget book before the start of the fiscal year was becoming unmanageable. The help (solution) was appropriate, given the advent of microcomputers. And the urgency was clear—a failure by the finance ministry to deliver the budget on time was unthinkable.

The first and most important necessary condition of reform is trust. Trust has to be built at many levels: between the government and external funders if the reform is aid-dependent, between the funders and the contractors, and between government officials and technical assistance personnel. Reform involves taking risk, which is rarely supported or rewarded in bureaucracies, which tend to shun risk. If previous reforms have failed or not met expectations, officials will naturally be inclined to discount the virtues of a new reform. Financial reforms in Africa and other developing countries typically involve foreigners, so there is room for distrust, poor understanding, and even outright hostility. Trust is essential because PFA/M reform deals with money, an inherently sensitive issue. Finally, trust is needed because financial reforms change the power structures of bureaucracies. Reformers need to enjoy the confidence of the winners of those power shifts and, if possible, the understanding of the losers.[3]

The second necessary condition is need. It is not always clear to a government that reform is needed. Furthermore, many financial reforms in Africa have been driven by outsiders as a condition of foreign aid. Put simply, is the need real or derived?

The third necessary condition is help. Reform should provide a solution, help that is appropriate and sustainable. Does the help address real need or is it simply what is offered, take it or leave it?

The fourth necessary condition is urgency. Governments face myriad problems, many of which have festered for years. Governments may and often do take a reform approach of ready, aim, aim, aim, aim. One feature of foreign aid–driven reforms is that they usually do demand the government to "fire," but this is little compensation if the reform is not the right thing to do or, if it is, is not done right.

The four necessary conditions for successful reform were in place in 1996 when Ethiopia started its reform. But even having the necessary conditions in place and doing the right thing right did not guarantee success. Necessary does not mean sufficient conditions. I do not believe one can define the sufficient conditions for a public sector reform. Such a "recipe" would be useful, but the complexity of the task makes it impossible to construct. The COPS framework of the drivers of reform gets to the nuances that shape a reform's trajectory, but there are still intangibles at work. One very important intangible is luck. In this chapter I present the four necessary conditions of Ethiopia's PFA reform—and the luck encountered.

The first condition: trust

Public finance goes to the heart of sovereignty. Its reform and who does the reform is sensitive. As a new government, the Transitional Government of Ethiopia was especially vigilant about limiting any encroachments on its sovereignty and also wanted to make very clear that it would be charting its own course. The senior officials of the new government were also very young and had little or no experience with the wily ways of foreign aid agencies and staff. The development of the Civil Service Reform Program (CSRP) in secret and without foreign involvement and making the prime minister the chairman of the reform speaks volumes about the ownership of this reform.

The literature on PFM reform is virtually silent on the role of trust in the process of reform. Some observers say that acceptance of the need for reform is required. This sounds more like resigning oneself to something, rather than embracing it. Trust goes far beyond merely accepting the need for reform. Commentators of PFM reform also argue that commitment is needed, which again is derivative of trust. It is the rare financial reform where senior officials get involved in the trenches, where reform occurs, and ensure its delivery. What is critical is the "tones from the top," and a genuine tone is born of trust. Trust in a reform can be viewed three ways: trust between the government and the funder, trust between the government and the contractor, and trust between the funder and contractor.

The government was going to closely regulate the reform but it also knew it needed external resources for funding and advice. Those it trusted would be invited to the reform.

Distrust of the Bretton Woods organizations

The CSRP financial reform was unique in Africa because the Bretton Woods organizations were virtually excluded. The World Bank was allowed to provide funding for creating a "manager's handbook" and provided some modest funds to the Office of the Prime Minister for logistical support, but was excluded from funding the financial components.[4] When I asked Peter Silkin, the CSRP coordinator, what role the World Bank and the International Monetary Fund would have in the reform, he said none, and for five reasons:

1 Prime Minister Tamirat Layne did not want them in the government.
2 The government did not want to take loans for the reform.
3 The Bretton Woods institutions imposed too many conditionalities for their involvement.
4 The government disagreed with the World Bank's vision of civil service reform, which was principally to reduce the number of civil servants. When World Bank representatives expressed their view to the vice minister of finance, he responded that the civil service was understaffed relative to African and developed countries (he referenced the findings of the Task Force on Civil Service Reform—see box 2.1).
5 The government wanted to retain its independence concerning the direction and implementation of the reform.

Prior to the unveiling of the CSRP, there were lingering mutual suspicions between the government and the Bretton Woods organizations stemming from the initial policy dialogue.[5] In short, the Ethiopian government was not comfortable with the Bretton Woods organizations' involvement; the government knew that these organizations would try to define the reform agenda.

Richard Allen, formerly of the International Monetary Fund's Fiscal Affairs Department, stated on the IMF's *Public Finance Management Blog* that one reason why the IMF is so effective is that they are viewed as a neutral arbiter of reform.[6] Nothing could be further from the truth, so it is ironic that this post was the blog's most-read post of 2010! The Government of Ethiopia was leery of all the Bretton Woods agencies, especially the IMF, which declared Ethiopia "off track" in its program with the IMF two weeks before the start of the war with Eritrea. The Ethiopian government was furious with the IMF's lack of "neutrality."

Trust between the government and the funder

The government did trust USAID and rapidly approved the agency's proposal to support the financial components of the CSRP. In 1996 USAID was the foreign aid agency in Ethiopia best placed to rapidly respond to the government's surprise unveiling of the task force report. For nearly two years before the release of the report, the governance advisor of USAID, Stevens Tucker, had been in discussions with the Ethiopian government over possible USAID assistance to support decentralization. Members of the Ethiopian government trusted USAID because of these discussions and the long support of the U.S. government to the new government during the revolution. It is no exaggeration to state that the Decentralization Support Activity (DSA) project started with enormous goodwill baked in because of the goodwill between the governments of Ethiopia and the United States.

USAID earned the government's trust two ways: through its exceptional staff and by not trying to set the agenda.

Building trust through exceptional staff

The task force report menu offered an embarrassment of riches for the foreign aid agencies shortlisted to participate. As an advisor to USAID and one of the shortlisted, I recommended that the agency support the reform of the budget and accounts components of the PFA transaction platform (presented in chapter 1).[7] USAID sent the government a proposal, which was quickly accepted.

There were several reasons for this rapid approval. First, USAID had done its homework well, observing the evolution of the transition from the very beginnings of the regime in 1991 to a government with a new constitution embarking on massive reforms.[8] Second, the agency had established a respected dialogue with the government and especially with Peter Silkin, the British technical assistance advisor to the Office of the Prime Minister, who unbeknownst to USAID had been coordinating the task force report. This dialogue was principally the professional and personal achievement of Stevens Tucker, who was USAID's governance advisor and who had been in Ethiopia for over two years developing a program for assisting the government's decentralization. Space does not permit a full accounting of Tucker's skills, not just in negotiating a project for a foreign aid agency but also in developing and deepening a dialogue with an array of government officials that helped them think through the translation of challenges they faced to a feasible work plan. Tucker had an uncanny ability to pull together the nuances of Ethiopia—the political, cultural, and regional threads, which were very fluid and very complex.[9] Few foreigners—especially officials of foreign aid agencies, who should have grasped the political-administrative environment— "got" Ethiopia. Few do still. Disentangling the gold from the wax is not easy.

But USAID in Ethiopia in 1996 was not a one-man show—there was a deep bench in the agency. Its director, Marge Bonner, had assembled a very strong team, many of whom had worked together in Indonesia. Again, space does not permit the presentation of all of the mission's dramatis personae, but honorable mention must be given here to Bill Douglass, the program coordinator; Ashton Douglass, who coordinated everything but also brought a very critical eye to what was possible in Ethiopia; and Ron Bonner, who brought an uncommon depth and perspective as to the limits of USAID intervention in a country such as Ethiopia. At a meeting with USAID on the DSA project a few months into the reform, it was clear that Bill Douglass "got" the country, which meant that

USAID "got" it. It was Douglass who, as the meeting started to get sidetracked, cut to the chase and said, "This project is one of the few things we do that the government really wants." The DSA project was fortunate to have from the start the quality and integrity of the professionals at USAID. Most important, they were realists about what could be done.

The professionals assigned to USAID underscored the importance of the U.S. government's support of the Transitional Government of Ethiopia. Long before the regime came to power, the U.S. government supported the revolutionary movement, and key U.S. intermediaries continued their engagement during the transition and the start of the PFA reform. On one of my earliest trips to Ethiopia, in the wee hours of the morn I wandered, jet-lagged, into the lobby of a hotel adjacent to the airport, only to be kept at a distance while a parade of officials, including the head of the CIA and much brass from both governments, arrived and departed for a chinwag. That USAID had "skin in the game" in its association with Ethiopia was further demonstrated in May of 1998, at the commencement of hostilities with Eritrea: although the U.S. government, including USAID, implemented a drawdown of employees in Ethiopia, it took the almost unheard-of step of permitting technical assistance personnel to remain if they assumed personal responsibility for their own safety.

Building trust by not pushing an agenda

An important quality of USAID assistance to Ethiopia that built considerable trust was that it did not push an agenda on the government. USAID staff listened to government officials' needs and for the most part tried to meet those needs on the government's terms. Using our framework of reform, USAID very much *recognized* and respected what the country was trying to achieve. An important benefit of the dialogue established by Stevens Tucker was that once the CSRP report was unveiled, USAID and I as the contractor had access to the government to discuss the translation of the report into a specific reform program. This dialogue was frank and constructive, in good part because USAID was not pressing its own agenda. Part of not pushing an agenda also means that the funder funds just a slice of the reform, not the whole cake. If a funder funds the whole reform, there is considerable potential for the funder to set the agenda, and this weakens government ownership. If a funder only takes a slice, it is buying into the government-driven reform and accepts the overall reform.

Government trust in the contractor

The second dimension of trust in reform is trust between the government and the contractor.

A further reason the government trusted the USAID proposal for the PFA reform was John Cohen, who represented the Harvard Institute for International Development and had worked with Tucker for well over a year in thinking through USAID's intervention in governance.[10] I cannot do justice here to

Cohen's contributions not only to the DSA project but also to the study of Ethiopia and the rest of Africa.[11] One of the world's foremost experts on Ethiopia and fluent in Amharic, he brought a deep cultural understanding and gravitas to the discussions with the government and with USAID. Cohen also brought extensive experience in project management in East Africa, often referring to himself as a "high-altitude rural sociologist." He was a rare combination of academic and practitioner who knew Ethiopia as well as anyone in the world. His considerable presence was perhaps best summed up in a meeting between Tamirat Layne, the former prime minister and briefly the head of the national steering committee of the CSRP, and USAID, where Tucker and Cohen presented USAID's proposal for the PFA reform. Cohen's speaking points reflect a succinct and insightful approach to reform. That meeting "negotiated entrance," as Cohen put it, and Tucker confided to me about the unusual enthusiasm on the part of government. That the meeting started with banter in Amharic between Cohen and Layne did not hurt matters. The tone of that meeting was not surprising to anyone who knew Cohen. Beyond all his credentials and his hard work, he brought a rare enthusiasm to a field populated by pessimists, clock watchers, and seekers of perks of foreign postings. I worked with Cohen in the Government of Kenya for eight years, and he often described the role of the manager of a technical assistance project as akin to being the editor of a high school yearbook—it entailed an ability not only to herd cats but also to bring utter commitment and enthusiasm to a thankless task that few want. Cohen was particularly enthusiastic about working on reform in Ethiopia, and although he had put in over a decade on technical assistance in Kenya, he stressed to me that the project in Ethiopia, unlike that in Kenya, was real development work.

Cohen's reputation and knowledge of Ethiopia brought a sole-source development project to Harvard. One can never know the counterfactual, but given the Ethiopian government's suspicious view of development assistance at the time, it is unlikely, had the selection of the reform project been put out for a competitive bid, that any competitor would have trumped a project to be led by John Cohen.

Another reason HIID got the nod from the government—in addition to Cohen's unassailable knowledge of Ethiopia and reputation for successful fieldwork in Africa—was Peter Silkin's concern with the expense of international commercial consulting firms, which charged extremely high rates. On several occasions, Peter Silkin noted the inappropriateness of high-priced consulting firms delivering services in such a poor country. He felt that these were simply unacceptable, especially given the belief within government that much of the work could be bootstrapped. In fact, Silkin felt, these firms rarely delivered value for their high prices because they often baited and switched: promised top people but sent the third string. Given the unattractive living conditions in Ethiopia at the start of the reform, Silkin was convinced that senior staff of commercial consulting firms would not be posted and, if posted, would not stay long.

Trust between funder and contractor

In 1996 USAID trusted HIID because of its successful implementation of the agency's projects next door, in Kenya, three of which had been directed by John Cohen for ten years. Fortunately, the DSA project implemented by HIID was already three years under way when a scandal emerged in the USAID-funded Russian financial reform project, also implemented by Harvard University. Harvard was sued for $134 million for its mismanagement of U.S. government property.[12] Following this revelation, as the project director of the DSA project I was dressed down several times by USAID mission personnel, but the project had made progress and was establishing its own trust with the government and thus with USAID, which mitigated the distrust of the home office—Harvard.

Limiting foreign influence

The previous regime had rounded up all of the diplomats and housed them in a special compound for the ostensible reason of ensuring their security, but it also made it easier to monitor them. Ethiopia in 1997 continued to closely monitor the flood of foreigners. The regime's concern with restraining foreign influence and its attempts to do so in the early days of the CSRP resulted in some humorous situations. Six months into the start of the DSA project, in mid-1997, the government issued a list of the items a technical assistance advisor posted to Ethiopia could bring into the country duty-free. The short list of about twenty-seven items included a hairdryer, tea service, family photos, a briefcase, and so forth. It also specified that foreign advisors were allowed one duty-free vehicle, whose engine displacement could not exceed two liters—evidence of the government's concern regarding the growing fleet in Addis Ababa of large Toyota Land Cruisers driven by the swelling hordes of foreign advisors. (Fortunately, my own 4.2-liter diesel Land Cruiser had already arrived, along with my forty-foot sea container, whose contents included items that were now considered contraband).

   Foreigners' exit from the country was just as closely monitored. Foreign aid officials and contractors were required to show that they did not have an outstanding balance at the Victory Store and had returned all of the videos rented. The Victory was the only shop in town where imported goods could be purchased in hard currency and where videos could be legally rented. The manifest of goods with which foreign advisors entered the country was carefully scrutinized at the end of their tours to see that all items were leaving the country—had not been illegally sold in the country. The deputy mission director of USAID, who left in 1997, had to explain why he was not repatriating a tea service that had been broken and discarded long ago.

The second condition: need

In June 1996 the Government of Ethiopia unveiled a comprehensive Civil Service Reform Program for overhauling the civil service. They had done their homework. Not unexpectedly for a regime that had been shaped by a successful seventeen-year struggle against a brutal and well-equipped military junta, the government had developed its strategy of the reform in secret, without foreign assistance. In its long struggle, the founding party of the new government, the Tigrayan People's Liberation Front (TPLF), developed a modus operandi called *gemgema* (literally, "assessment"). A *gemgema* was an intensive, no-holds-barred assessment of party members where they first confessed their short-comings and achievements and were judged principally on their frank assessment of their errors. The practice of *gemgema* has continued and extended to bureaucrats, whether or not they are party members. The massive five-volume document, the *Task Force Comprehensive Report*, that presented the Civil Service Reform Program was in many ways a classic example of *gemgema*: it spared no organization, including the Office of the Prime Minister, from a withering assessment. The report demonstrated from the start the seriousness of the regime's commitment to reform and the massive needs of rebuilding the civil service.[13]

The CSRP Task Force report is an impressive document—other governments facing the challenge of designing and implementing such reforms would benefit by reviewing it. Even more impressive was that it was homegrown, produced entirely within the Ethiopian government, with no involvement nor assistance from foreign aid agencies. When the report was released in 1996 it caught foreign aid agencies completely by surprise. Especially important was that it had been funded wholly from government resources. The report provided a comprehensive catalogue of the deficiencies of the civil service and thus the severe constraints that any reform project would face.

The need was articulated from the highest level of government, since the prime minister chaired the national steering committee of the CSRP and key members of his cabinet served on it, resulting in a hands-on approach at the apex of government. The principal architect of the CSRP was Peter Silkin, the lone foreign advisor to the Office of the Prime Minister and the technical coordinator of the Task Force for Civil Service Reform. As an auditor from the National Audit Office of the United Kingdom, Silkin was naturally concerned with mapping out a comprehensive set of reforms in accounts, treasury, and audit (see appendix 3.1).

Rethinking what needs to be done

Despite its scope, there were significant gaps in the CSRP in the area of public finance:[14] Neither the fiscal transfer from the federal to regional governments nor revenue reform were discussed. The name of the financial reform under the CSRP was Expenditure Management and Control Program, rather than Financial Management and Control. The word "financial" implies not only expenditure but also revenue and the fiscal transfer. When I asked why the fiscal transfer was not included in the reform, Silkin said it was too political an issue to be tackled by the reform. When I asked Silkin why revenue reform (tax policy and tax administration) had been excluded, he said the British government had already agreed to support these reforms, and they were outside the CSRP's brief.

Thus, from the beginning the scope of the financial reform proposed by the government was limited, for it did not include revenue nor did it address a fundamental need of financial management in a decentralized government, the management and budgeting of the fiscal transfer. The absence of these two critical processes within the reform meant that the budget reform's goal would perforce be narrow—getting the structure right (reforming the chart of accounts)—and would be only a partial reform of process.

The design of the CSRP had another fundamental weakness: it proposed a reform strategy of change, of leaping from the weak public finance administration that the report so well documented to the sophisticated terrain of public financial management. The report presents pages upon pages of recommendations focusing on performance and its measurement.

When the report was released I was in Ethiopia as part of a team funded by the European Commission conducting a social expenditure review.[15] I had the opportunity to discuss with Silkin the CSRP strategy of leaping to management rather than first strengthening administration.

Viewed in terms of my categories of systems (procedures) and execution (the implementation of systems by institutions, organizations, and staff), the report found that even though there were deficiencies in civil service systems, including those in finance, for the most part the core problem of Ethiopia's civil service was not systems but their execution. My recent findings from the field confirmed these findings of the task force report, and implied weak administration. If existing systems that could be improved were not being adequately executed, then there was little sense in putting in place new systems that, similarly, would not be adequately executed. I argued that the CSRP needed a strategy of transition from a weak bureaucracy to a strong one by first strengthening administration (control over inputs and extensive oversight of spending agencies), and only then moving to the advanced forms of management and planning discussed so eloquently in the task force report. In terms of the four strategies of reform, what was needed initially was a strategy of recognize and improve, not change. I followed up my discussions with Silkin on these issues in a memorandum that I sent to him in June 1996, "The Strategy of Civil Service Reform: Memorandum to the CSRP Advisor in the Office of the Prime Minister":

> Ethiopia's Civil Service Reform is unusual for it is a reform to promote and improve public management. In Africa, civil service reform has usually meant reducing staff. The end state of improved public management is exactly what is needed. Achieving this end state, however, requires a strategy that manages the transition. Does the civil service reform have a strategy [that] adequately takes into account the transition? Can the reform move from weak administration to management? In designing the budget and accounts reforms it is clear that a transition end state is needed. The

weak administrative systems have to be strengthened before they can be reformed into management systems. Ethiopia, like many African and other developing countries, is under-bureaucratized. Roles are not clear, systems are weak, and information is poor or lacking. In both the accounts and budget reforms, it is proposed that the first few years of the reform will involve building strong administration, and only during the later years of the reform will the management reforms be introduced.

Administration and management are very different styles of organization and behavior. Administration is control based on procedure while management is performance based on discretion. To manage is not to control.

The management end state is not, however, a certain linear progression from the administration phase because it is more of a step function. Why? The principal challenge of the management end state is for government staff to exercise discretion, risk resources, and focus on performance. Management is about placing resources at risk to pursue collective goals that also advance individual interests. Without incentives, there is no impetus for discretion or risk taking. The administrative stage does not provide the incentives to exercise discretion.

Another constraint to moving to the management end state is the limited capacity (and confidence) of government staff to combine roles. Effective managers combine several roles, including setting strategy, allocating resources, and accounting for resources. A distinctive feature of administration is the segmentation of roles. Segmenting roles is useful because it promotes accountability as well as task specialization. In very weak bureaucracies task segmentation is especially needed to effectively employ staff with limited capacity.[16]

Ethiopia in 1996 was not in a position to focus on management; it had to strengthen administration first. Indeed, the task force report was somewhat disingenuous in its failure to unpack the "real" organizational backdrop of government in 1996. The report called for a speedy transition to management, but in fact, the political elite in the Ethiopian People's Revolutionary Democratic Front (EPRDF) and especially its core, the Tigrayan People's Liberation Front (TPLF), did not want to build a bureaucracy that exercised discretion and could potentially hold the party accountable. The EPRDF would carry out the mandates of the CSRP to strengthen the state only to the extent that the state could efficiently deliver for the party. Again, the sequencing of PFA/M reforms must be understood within the bureaucratic and political context.

The change in the initial scope of the CSRP was a crystal-clear indication of the EPRDF's intent to limit the strength of the state. Originally, the seven pillars of the initial design of the CSRP were as follows:

Initial Seven Pillars Design of the Civil Service Reform
1   Organization of the central institutions of the civil service
2   Expenditure management and control

3   Human resource management
4   Top management systems
5   Responsibility, authority, and internal accountability of institutional management
6   Service delivery and quality of service
7   Ethics[17]

Pillars 1 and 5 were dropped, which meant that reform of the core state organizations through which the EPRDF exercised control were removed from scrutiny and reform. Most notably, the Office of the Prime Minister was exempt from reform, even though the task force report found several major weaknesses in that body that significantly weakened the civil service.[18] Pillar 5 was dropped because it implied a criticism of the excessive involvement of the political leadership in key ministries, including finance and planning, in the daily operations of administration—the exercise of external control.

> Ministers and vice ministers are heavily involved in the minutiae of day-to-day management rather than concentrating on the strategic direction and oversight of their organizations. In some cases, even the very highest members of the government participate in tasks, which are completely inappropriate to their status and role. For example, Ministers, or their equivalent, participate in payment authorization of even the smallest sums; even where there is an officer with clear delegation of responsibility in an area, there are occasions where top officials still require most decisions in the area to go across their desk ... and delegation over resources is rarely written down except in vague terms.[19]

Regardless of some of the dreams of a management end state contained in the task force report, the political reality was that the regime wanted to strengthen external control. To the political leadership, reform meant improving external control: improving administration, or PFA. They did not want to make the bureaucracy more autonomous by moving it toward internal control, or PFM.

How the reform was to be done

From the start, the task force recognized that how the reform was done was as important as what was done, if not more so. The task force report presented a model of what we call government-led deliverables: an array of consultations and government staff reform committees whose work enabled the government not only to own the reform but also largely to implement it. Peter Silkin, the CSRP reform coordinator, was very concerned to head off the danger that foreign technical assistance staff would weaken government ownership and that it could even be lost. Therefore, the role of foreign technical assistance would be minimal, playing just a background role of transferring experience and skills that implementing government officials lacked. Technical assistance, especially foreign, would not take a lead role. The early planning document of the CSRP presented this "government-led deliverables" model of the reform in considerable detail: "the [CSRP] Steering Committee has *adopted a series of guidelines that are intended to maximize Ethiopian ownership and involvement in all aspects of the development process and minimize dependence on external assistance* [emphasis added]."[20]

Help would be accepted only on the government's terms.

The third condition: help

The government trusted USAID and quickly requested assistance from the agency as soon as the task force report was released. The background work done by Stevens Tucker of USAID and John Cohen of HIID meant that they quickly agreed to assist in the financial reform. Silkin, an auditor, also wanted to fast-track the start of the financial reform. My recent and past experience in working on financial issues in Ethiopia and Kenya also affected the decision to focus the DSA project on financial components.[21] My recent work on the social expenditure review in Ethiopia highlighted the need for reform in budgeting and accounting.[22] The DSA project therefore would work on the budget and accounts components of the CSRP because they were core to PFA/M. From my extensive experience in these areas in Africa, I knew that these components would fit within the limited budget, under $2 million, that USAID could allocate for two years.

The USAID contract

The PFM reform literature is silent about how reforms are contracted, although it is a detail that has significant effects. USAID contributed to the CSRP by contracting with HIID to carry out the Decentralization Support Activity project. I was named chief of party and prepared the Phase 1 proposal with the assistance of Jim Yardley, a professor of accounting who was to be the principal accounts advisor. The proposal was submitted to USAID on November 27, 1996, and in December USAID issued a three-month mobilization contract to the HIID for the project to commence in January 1997.[23]

Given the weakness in PFA and the regime's policy of regional decentralization, the strategy of reform pursued by the DSA project in its Phase 1 contract was one of recognize and improve. Early on in Phase 1 the project conducted a detailed field assessment of the current system and the skills of the staff operating it. This assessment led to the drafting of a strategy for in-service training that showed that the Phase 1 budget was wholly inadequate to meet the training needs necessary to make the existing system function better, much less pave the way for changes to the system.[24] As a result of this memorandum on training, the government requested the DSA project to prepare a proposal for supplementary funding. This proposal, "In-Service Financial Training Project (IFTP)," met the short-term resource requirements for starting training on the existing system but posed a three-fold bureaucratic obstacle for USAID.[25] One problem was that Phase 1 of the DSA project was sole-sourced to Harvard from USAID and had only been operational for a year and a half, and thus had a slim track record. The second obstacle was that Ethiopia was now at war with Eritrea and the U.S. government was hesitant to directly provide funds to the Government of Ethiopia. The third obstacle for the agency was the unfolding scandal of Harvard's project in Russia, which was also funded by USAID. In the end, USAID decided that Harvard was the best option on offer and that the needs in Ethiopia were compelling. USAID expanded its commitment to Harvard to carry out a two-and-a-half-year in-service financial training project (IFTP) to run in tandem with Phase 1 of the DSA project.

The life of the IFTP cooperative agreement extended beyond the Phase 1 contract of the DSA project, so USAID decided to treat all future extensions of the DSA project as extensions of the IFTP, although the project continued to be referred to as the DSA project. This meant that the DSA project was now governed by a cooperative agreement instead of by a contract, and this changed the financial environment in which the DSA project had to sink or swim. The advent of the IFTP meant more than just the crucial funding to start training on the existing system; it was also a change in the modality of USAID's assistance to the reform. Phase 1 of the project was a contract, whereas the IFTP was a cooperative agreement. With a contract, a USAID mission director can intervene and direct the use of funds. With a cooperative agreement (considered "a gift of the American people"), a USAID mission director cannot do this.[26] Thus, a cooperative agreement greatly increases the level of discretion a project director can exercise. In the face of the uncertain and challenging environment of Ethiopia, this financial discretion was an enormous asset that gave the project the ability to respond flexibly to circumstances and was clearly a factor that contributed to the reform's success. USAID never micromanaged the DSA project, and the cooperative agreement status of the project insulated it from this possibility. I would argue that the flexibility of the cooperative agreement meant that the DSA project could expand its brief beyond its technical proposal into crucial areas that, if left unaddressed, would have resulted in a lower-quality reform. The clearest example of this was the project's work on automating financial procedures. The European Commission–funded financial information system (FIS), whose purpose was to automate the procedures developed by the DSA project in budgeting and accounting, was delayed throughout the life of the DSA project. This meant that the DSA project would itself have to provide the FIS—a crucial and expensive undertaking—if the reforms were to be rolled out. The DSA project started work on the automation of the budget and accounts in its second year, but automation was not put into the project contract until Phase 4, which started in June 2004.

The DSA design

The strategy of reform in the DSA design for budget and accounts was a mix of recognize, improve, and sustain. The project was to develop the procedures of budget and accounting while their automation was to be done under a separate project funded by the European Commission. I recognized that there would be considerable risk of being dependent on a separate project for the implementation of the procedures developed by the project under the budget and accounts reform, but that nothing could be done about this. At an estimated $9 million, the FIS project was the most expensive component of the CSRP financial reform and was far beyond the resource level USAID was willing to commit to the first phase of the DSA project. One of the major challenges and changes of the DSA project over the life of the reform was the FIS, and the failure of the EC-funded FIS to arrive meant that the DSA carried out the automation task.

Table 3.1 presents an overview of the DSA design of the PFA reform in terms of the transaction and policy platforms and their discrete systems. (Although the platforms of PFA/M reform include a legal platform, it is omitted from the table because the DSA was not involved in this platform of the Ethiopian reform.)

Table 3.1 The design of the "products" of PFM reform

Platforms and systems	DSA reforms
Transaction platform	
Budgets	
	Chart of accounts
	Budget classification
	Cost centers
	Self-accounting
	In-service training in new procedures
Accounting	
	Documentation of existing procedures
	In-service training in existing system
	Simplification of forms
	Double-entry bookkeeping
	Modified cash basis
	Self-accounting
	In-service training in new procedures
	Management accounting
Financial information system	
	Custom integrated financial management information system (IFMIS)
Treasury	
	Single pool—Treasury Single Account
Policy platform	
Fiscal management	Macroeconomic fiscal framework (MEFF)
Expenditure planning	Public investment program (PIP)
	Public expenditure program (PEP)
Financial decentralization	Transfer formula (region to wereda)
Performance	Wereda performance agreement
Budget policy	Regional economic policy review (REPR)

Source: author.

Having defined what was to be done, the project had to work out how it would be done, given the CSRP policy of a "government-led deliverable" model of reform. The logic of this policy was not a conventional assistance project managed by the contractor. Despite the rhetoric about ownership; the key officials who were to do the reform had their hands full with day-to-day business. The design of the terms of reference for the budget and accounts reform, which were done not by government staff as specified by the CSRP, but by me and the future DSA project accounts advisor, Jim Yardley, demonstrated that government had to be practical about moving forward with design and implementation. This required a "technical assistance deliverable" model of reform. As one of the first projects under the CSRP, the project redefined the government's approach to reform delivery. It never looked back. In the initial and heady days of the reform in spring 1997, a year before the chilling effect of the war with Eritrea in May of 1998, there was much talk and discussion about the reform. The CSRP coordinators in the Office of the Prime Minister did an excellent job of raising awareness and stressing the need for government ownership. But eventually it was time to walk the talk. And for this one needs momentum. The project incorporated many of the recommendations of the task force report on consultative process, as embodied in the budget and accounts reform teams put together using government and project staff, but these never significantly impeded project initiative. Initiative was essential for establishing and sustaining momentum.

The PFA reform in Ethiopia was unusual because the design was a tabula rasa in four respects. First, the task force report had enumerated a huge laundry list of deficiencies, but the government had not translated these into a strategy, much less a detailed program of implementation. Second, there was no technical assistance on the ground already, so that the designers of the budget or accounts reform, which the DSA reform project was to work on, had the flexibility to define a niche. Third, the field of PFM had yet to be fully regimented according to "international best practice" and metrics such as the Public Expenditure Financial Accountability (PEFA) Framework developed by the World Bank, the IMF, and other international bodies. This "metrics vacuum" allowed for an eclectic design appropriate to the fluid context. And fourth, the government's divide-and-manage approach to foreign aid agencies' support of the regime, which excluded the Bretton Woods institutions and siloed technical assistance by function, meant that the technical assistance operating in those silos had a certain latitude, plus insulation from interference. In sum, the reform was a rare case where the government ensured that there would be only one cook in the kitchen, and that cook would be clearly responsible, with government, for the design and implementation of the reform. There would be no debilitating turf struggles.

The fourth condition: urgency

The CSRP was of the highest priority to the government. The government felt an acute sense of urgency and pushed hard to get the ball rolling ASAP. The task force report was released in June 1996, and the government pressed USAID to start implementation of the project as soon as feasible. In late November, USAID requested that HIID submit a proposal to the agency, and by the end of December USAID issued a contract. USAID issued HIID an initial three-month "mobilization," effective January 1, 1997, so that HIID staff could be put in place. As chief of party of the project, I arrived in Ethiopia on February 6, 1997.

The task force report did not specify a time frame for the reform, but Silkin stated that it should be completed "in about four years."[27] Using Silkin's time frame, HIID proposed a three-and-a-half-year time frame. USAID had limited funds and could only commit to a two-year contract for the project, for Phase 1, from January 1, 1997, to December 31, 1998. Thus, from the beginning the project was on a short leash and was starting something that would require much more time and funding to complete than the initial contract permitted.

Plus, luck

As Branch Rickey, the legendary general manager of the Brooklyn Dodgers, once said, "Luck is the residue of design."[28] Perhaps luck is not a necessary condition for a reform project's success, but it certainly helps.

Over its twelve-year life the project faced its share of good luck and bad. Bad luck started in January just as I was preparing to start the project in Ethiopia. Mike Roemer, a brilliant development economist who was to work on the planning reform, died suddenly. Six months into the reform, John Cohen's cancer forced him to retire, depriving him ultimately of his life, and the project of his wise counsel and support at Harvard. Two years into the project, its home office, HIID, was brought down by the scandal surrounding its corrupt project in Russia.

But the project also had its share of good luck. One piece of luck was unlikely: the war between Ethiopia and Eritrea, because it gave the project a critical gestation period for the development of the design. The war also meant that the distraction and detraction by foreign aid agencies was absent, as virtually all of these agencies decamped for safer climes. Unexpectedly, USAID did not pull its contractors out of the country, leaving the DSA project to commence in splendid isolation with one set of cooks in the kitchen, which promoted a coherent design. Thus, the unhappy context of a war had a silver lining for the project. Our early work on the project resulted not only in a reform with confirmed government ownership and deep participation but also in a design fit for purpose and context. In his classic 1967 work on development projects, *Development Projects Observed*, Albert Hirschman argued that a project should not be saddled too early with difficulties, such as fighting turf wars and defending the project design: "A given level of difficulties may be wholly discouraging for the prosecution of the project if it turns up early, while it would be tackled with alacrity and perhaps solved if it arose at a later stage."[29]

A second piece of luck was the EC's delay on and eventual abandonment of a separate FIS project to automate procedures that it had proposed to fund. Coordinating the delivery of a reform with a separate FIS project would have been a prescription for complexity and quite possibly failure, so the EC's abandonment of its FIS project actually promoted coherence. The DSA project was able to step into the breach, and it developed an FIS that exceeded international standards.

Conclusion

This book presents the four reforms that the government implemented with technical assistance from the DSA project: budget, accounts, financial information systems, and expenditure planning. With a hard budget constraint and vigilant party oversight, the PFA reform focused on these four systems and their execution in terms of in-service training. The focus of the PFA reform was on strengthening financial administration—making the core systems of the transaction platform better. The project did work on the policy platform, but the policy elements were marginal and in any case were swept away shortly after the project closed. (The ultimate fate of the reform after the DSA project ended in January 2008 is presented in chapter 8.)

To understand this reform one must understand the people who undertook it and the very unusual context in which they did so. Reform is fundamentally about people—the reform's techniques and sequence flow from the cast of officials and technical assistance providers who cooperate to design and execute the reform. My goal is to convey the tapestry of this reform. As one would expect from the ambiguity of the wax and gold that imbued Abyssinia's culture, the intangible was as important as the tangible—perhaps more so.

Appendix 3.1: CSR task force recommendations (and codes) for the expenditure management and control program[30]

1 Legal framework

1.1. Development of a comprehensive legal framework for the entire financial management regime of the civil service.

2 Budgeting

2.1. Reorientation of budgeting to objectives and strategic plans.
2.2. Introduction of commitment budgeting in line institutions.
2.3. Introduction of a legally binding budget calendar.
2.4. Introduction of an annual review of the effectiveness of the budgeting arrangements.
2.5. Introduction of an in-year review of the implementation of the budget and the need for redeployment of resources.
2.6. Review of the budget classification system to ensure proper separation between capital and recurrent items.
2.7. Provision of a manual, guidance, and training on budgeting.

2.8. All expenditure funded by retained revenues should be used for the receipts side only. The budget should place a legally binding cap on each institution's use of retained revenues; all revenues received over and above the cap should be surrendered to the Ministry of Finance.

3 Cash management

3.1. The restriction on virement should be reviewed with the aim of giving line institutions greater freedom to use funds effectively while leaving central institutions adequate control over key areas.

3.2. Review of the scope for using other forms of payment mechanisms other than cash and checks.

3.3. Introduction of tight controls within line institutions on bank and cash reconciliations.

3.4. There should be a proper up-to-date register of government bank accounts, which should be made available to the Office of the Auditor General for audit purposes.

3.5. All external financing agreements should contain a clause specifying which line institution accounts the donor may deposit money into.

3.6. Review of the causes of the considerable levels of immobilized funds in institutional bank accounts.

3.7. Introduction of cash flow management in the disbursement process. This is for the longer term, once there has been sufficient improvement in institutional accounting.

4 Accounting

4.1. Maintenance of the single-entry accounting system for the foreseeable future.

4.2. The single-entry system to be supplemented by necessary additional financial information on institutions' assets, advances, debtor and creditor positions, etc.

4.3. Improvements in enforcing line institution compliance with the accounting information deadline. All financial returns to be presented to the Ministry of Finance within three months of the end of the financial year.

4.4. Introduction of self-accounting by all government institutions within three to four years. This is to be extended, once embedded in, to each institution producing full annual reports on both financial and physical performance.

4.5. Line institutions to develop their own chart of accounts alongside self-accounting.

4.6. Development of a computer system for the single-entry accounting system, preferably within eighteen months. Computer system to run parallel to the manual system for two years.

4.7. Introduction of instructions on the shelf life of accounting documents.

4.8. Statements on outstanding advances to be produced by all institutions, showing age and nature of advance. Information to be reported, by institution, to the Council of People's Representatives. All institutions to undertake a regular review of advances outstanding with a view to either chasing up or writing off. All write-offs to require prior approval of the Ministry of Finance.

5 Asset management

5.1. Introduction of a comprehensive system, guidance, and training on the management of fixed assets and stock. This to cover both ownership and usage. Ministry of Finance to undertake review of compliance with this system. All write-offs and losses to be reported immediately to the Ministry of Finance for follow-up.

6 Aid management

6.1. Agreements on foreign assistance to contain a clause whereby the donor will provide the Ministry of Finance with full information of all assistance made in the year.
6.2. Review of the financial and performance reporting systems for external assistance with the aim of seeking consistency between donors.

7 Audit

7.1. Responsibility for national development of internal audit to be transferred from the Office of the Auditor General to the Ministry of Finance.
7.2. Arrangements to be set up for all internal audit reports to be sent to the Ministry of Finance.
7.3. Introduction of a comprehensive program of training for internal auditors.
7.4. Review of the legislation covering the external audit of regional funds to ensure complete certification of the national accounts.
7.5. Clarification of the respective roles of the Office of the Auditor General and Ministry of Finance inspection department.
7.6. Proper consideration of how the Council of People's Representatives can best receive and consider the reports of the federal Office of the Auditor General.
7.7. Development of five-year development strategies for the federal and regional Office of the Auditor General.
7.8. Change in arrangements for review of federal Office of the Auditor General's staffing to bring this under the Council of People's Representatives.
7.9. Proper consideration is given to the development of the auditing and accounting profession reports.
7.10. Full human resource and training needs assessments for accounting and auditing staff throughout the civil service.

Notes

1 Peterson (1996e).
2 Pinckney, Cohen, and Leonard (1983); Peterson (1991).
3 In his work with SIGMA (Support for Improvement in Governance and Management, a joint initiative of the EU and the OECD) on the financial reforms that states seeking EC accession must undertake, Noel Hepworth has argued that understanding and managing the changes in the power structures is far more important than the technical issues.
4 Total World Bank assistance to the CSRP was a mere $850,000 (Office of the Prime Minister, Civil Service Reform Management Unit 1997: 22–5). In contrast, USAID funded the Phase 1 of the DSA project at $2.65 million. Over the life of the DSA project, $34.4 million was funded by the governments of the United States, Ireland, the Netherlands, and Ethiopia.
5 The disconnect between government policy and the Bretton Woods agencies began early on in the regime's life: the Transitional Government of Ethiopia's proposal on donor support for regionalization made no reference to the structural adjustment loan negotiated with the Bretton Woods institutions. As Satish Mishra (1993a: 4) noted at the time, since the

> loan and the policy framework paper clearly circumscribe what the regions can and can not do ... short- and long-term priorities should be placed within an economic reform framework and not simply on the perceived administrative and development needs defined in a broad fashion.

See also Mishra (1993b) and the Transitional Government's proposal for donor assistance for regionalization (Transitional Government of Ethiopia, Ministry of Planning and Economic Development 1993). However, in a breakfast meeting of Prime Minister Meles Zenawi with American Ethiopia scholars, held at the Ethiopian embassy in Washington, D.C., on October 20, 1995, when Paul Henze asked Zenawi how he felt about the IMF's and World Bank's views on the government's financial policies, Zenawi responded that the relationships had evolved "from mutually suspicious beginnings, and whereas a policy framework program is usually worked out in Washington, Ethiopia's PFP was designed in Addis"—that is, by the government, though with consultation with the IMF and World Bank. Zenawi added, "Since the two organizations now respect Ethiopia's opinions, there are no serious differences, even if there are divergences about pacing and timing" (see Marcus 1995: 3).
6 Allen (2010).
7 The platform framework for analyzing PFM comprises three platforms: translation (budgeting and accounts), legal (financial law and regulations), and policy (medium-term planning).
8 See Mishra (1993a, 1993b, 1995); Tucker (1998); Cohen, Hammink, and Simmons (1994).
9 See Tucker (1998, 1999).
10 For John Cohen's meticulous assessment of the needs of Ethiopia for a possible USAID intervention in the area of decentralization see Cohen, Peterson, and Smoke (1996) and Cohen and Peterson (1996).
11 John Cohen published prolifically on Ethiopia. His notable works include Cohen (1974, 1987, 1994, 1995), Cohen and Koehn (1977), Cohen and Weintraub (1975) and Cohen and Tucker (1994).
12 See *United States of America v. President and Fellows of Harvard College, Andrei Shleifer, and Jonathan Hay*, U.S. District Court District of Massachusetts, Civil Action No. 00–11977-DPW, "Memorandum and Order," June 28, 2004. For an overview of the issues raised by Harvard's handling of the Russian reforms, see "Harvard's Role in U.S. Aid to Russia," http://janinewedel.info/harvard_boston_globe.pdf.

13 Office of the Prime Minister, Task Force for Civil Service Reform (1996a).
14 Office of the Prime Minister, Task Force for Civil Service Reform (1996a, vol. 1: 1).
15 Peterson (1996d).
16 Peterson (1996f).
17 Author's compilation, based on Office of the Prime Minister, Task Force for Civil Service Reform (1996a, vol. 1: chapter 1).
18 Office of the Prime Minister, Task Force for Civil Service Reform (1996a, vol. 1: 6).
19 Office of the Prime Minister, Task Force for Civil Service Reform (1996a, vol. 4: 3–4).
20 Office of the Prime Minister, Task Force for Civil Service Reform (1996b: 4–5); Office of Prime Minister, Task Force for Civil Service Reform (1996c: 3–6).
21 For my work on the financial reforms in Kenya over eight years see Peterson (1990, 1992a, 1992b, 1992c).
22 Peterson (1996b, 1996d).
23 Peterson (1996a).
24 DSA T-1 and DSA T-2.
25 Peterson (1999).
26 One mission director did want to impose directions on the DSA project but was reminded by the mission's supervising officer that under a cooperative agreement he was not able to impose such directions.
27 The CSRP Task Force issued a memorandum in January 1997 (after the DSA project was contracted) that proposed a four-year time frame of the reform. See Office of the Prime Minister, Civil Service Reform Management Unit (1997: appendix 1).
28 Rickey and Monteleone (1995: 11). I am indebted to Jim Desveaux for pointing out to me the wisdom of Branch Rickey.
29 Hirschman (1967: 18).
30 Based on Office of the Prime Minister, Task Force for Civil Service Reform (1996a, vol. 1: 9, table D-2).

Part II
The Ethiopian reform

4 The budget reform

Toning up tradition

"What about the lions?"

The final task of the federal team responsible for designing the budget reform was to sign off on the design of the new budget forms. We had spent weeks on the design of the forms and I finally asked, "Are we done?" The team unanimously nodded yes.

I asked them what, if anything, should be done about the lions at the top of all of the budget forms. The lions were the symbol of the monarchy that had been abolished by the previous military regime. There was a very long silence.

Eventually I broke the silence with some options: keep the lions, remove the lions, or put in their place the blue and yellow symbol of the new regime, which was now shown on the Ethiopian flag?

Another long silence.

I finally suggested that we remove the lions and replace them with the title "FGE Capital Budget" on the form for capital submissions (FGE for Federal Government of Ethiopia). There was an audible sigh of relief from the team members, who unanimously approved the recommendation. With a click of a computer mouse the lions were gone.[1]

The lions may have been removed from the budget forms, but the actual surviving imperial lions still roar occasionally. They can be seen in the cages where they are kept—ironically enough, across the street from the Ministry of Finance.

In Ethiopia, the lions represent the ancient regime. A budget reform is about change—cultural, organizational, and managerial. In a society with strong traditions and imbued with deep deference to hierarchy, the removal of the lion images from the budget documents was an unmistakable reminder for Ethiopian officials that the times were truly changing. The consternation of Amhara officials—whose ethnic group had dominated Ethiopia politically and bureaucratically for centuries—was palpable. With a click, several thousand years of dynastic rule was erased from the budgeting process in Ethiopia.

The budget is the most important policy document of a government, for it determines how a society allocates its resources. It is a product of history and culture. The background of this reform was one of the oldest cultures on earth. It is a

culture that reveres traditions. Despite the optimism embodied in *Yichalal!*—
"It's possible!"—a slogan recently popularized by Ethiopia's iconic long-
distance runner, Haile Gebreselassie, the reform's success was not a foregone
conclusion. It would certainly take time and would be on Ethiopian terms.
"Budgeting is a fragile tradition," observed Harris Mule, a former distinguished
permanent secretary of the Ministry of Finance of the government of Kenya.[2]
Mule went further and argued that budgets are a language and thus reform
should be done very carefully so as to ensure continued widespread understanding. In Ethiopia the budget tradition was fragile—undocumented and ad hoc.
The culture respected tradition, so the budget reform was likely to be about
improving rather than replacing what existed.

Doing the right thing in a PFA budget reform means toning up what Aaron
Wildavsky called the "traditional budget," the line-item incremental budget, so
that it can reach its potential. "Line-item" refers to the one-line entries for each
revenue and expenditure item such as salaries in a budget document. The task of
toning up is not easy, for it involves the thorniest issues of public finance—
indeed, of governance: setting priorities, routinizing political choice, establishing
responsibility, and ensuring accountability of public money. Governments of
both developing and developed countries struggle with these issues. One reason
why budget reform is always unfinished business is that governments seek,
sometimes in exasperation, to find a technique to solve these conundrums. The
traditional budget addresses the fundamental issues of budgeting, whereas
"advanced" budgeting techniques such as performance budgeting are concerned
with important but not fundamental issues: few governments would be concerned if a performance indicator went missing, whereas most would be concerned if money went missing.

In this chapter I present the budget reform that led the way for the other three
financial reforms—accounting, financial information systems, and expenditure
planning—to which the DSA project provided technical assistance under the
Civil Service Reform Program (CSRP). The chapter provides insights into four
issues:

1   Presenting the features of a traditional budget and the specific tasks and
    challenges needed to optimize it.
2   Strengthening the traditional budget's capacity in promoting performance.
3   Aligning the roles of government officials and technical assistance person-
    nel to do the reform right.
4   Managing the risk to ongoing budget operations posed by reform.

A reform begins with the declaration of a policy—in this case, the CSRP reform.
To realize policy, a reform program is needed, which is often executed by a
reform project. In the case of the reform of the budgeting, accounting, financial
information systems, and expenditure planning components of PFA, the DSA
(Decentralization Support Activity) project was the reform project. A reform
project typically passes through the following phases:

Phase 1: Translation
Phase 2: Development
Phase 3: Pilot
Phase 4: Rollout
Phase 5: Operation.

I shall describe the first four phases of Ethiopia's budget reform in the following sections (phase 5 is discussed in chapter 8).[3]

PHASE 1: TRANSLATION

Phase 1. Translation (role: design).
A reform begins with the declaration of a policy. A design phase follows, which translates the policy into a strategy and specific activities of a program of work. This phase comes to a productive end only with the engagement of the prospect of implementation.

The flawed CSRP recommendations for budget reform

For the budget reform, the Civil Service Reform Task Force report recommended tossing out the traditional budget and installing advanced techniques: zero-based, performance, and program budgeting. These wildly ambitious recommendations for budgeting, which simply were not possible in 1996, were in stark contrast to the prudent, indeed extremely conservative, recommendations for the accounting reform that advocated retention of the most basic of systems: single-entry bookkeeping and a cash basis of accounting. The flawed perspective was due in part to the principal architect of the report, Peter Silkin, who was an auditor from the National Audit Office of the British government, and was not versed in budgeting. The recommendation to install advanced budgeting techniques fit with Silkin's vision of the Civil Service Reform Program as one of leapfrogging basic administration with the aim of installing sophisticated management such as strategic planning and performance systems. In chapter 3 I presented the memo I drafted to Silkin early on in the reform recommending that the CSRP strategy be first one of strengthening administration before attempting management. I followed up my memo with a discussion with Silkin in which I pointed out the incongruence he was promoting between an advanced management focus for budgeting and a ultraconservative administration focus for accounting.

The recommendations of the task force report for reforming budgeting were flawed because the report failed to uncover the fundamental problem of budgeting in Ethiopia: the imbalance in the composition of expenditure. The report mentions many of the symptoms caused by this imbalance but fails to state the cause. The symptoms noted include lack of headroom in the budget for future recurrent costs of current-year capital investments, extensive virement—

the transfers of funds between line items of the budget—and the misuse of retained revenue. These symptoms were the result of the government's policy of favoring capital expenditure over recurrent expenditure, because capital expenditure was viewed as development, whereas recurrent expenditure was viewed as consumption and thus needed to be limited. Underscoring the favored role of capital expenditure, the report notes that capital expenditure is carefully monitored whereas recurrent expenditure is not. (The single most important task in managing public finances to make them sustainable is to manage fixed recurrent costs. Ethiopia did not focus on this in 1996 and continues to fail to do so today, focusing instead on capital expenditures, which are viewed as "development.")

The task force report overlooked the problem of the composition of expenditure, yet it presented the problems of budget execution clearly and in detail.[4] Again one sees the inconsistency in the recommendations for the budget reform: if government is unable to execute a simple traditional budget, it is unlikely that it will be able to execute a sophisticated budget system.

Alignment of roles in the translation phase of the reform

Translating the government's recommendation's for budget reform into a sensible action plan required the project to help the government rethink the assumptions behind the CSRP as outlined in the task force report. The project had to provide a reality check on the dreams expressed in the report. Fortunately, the DSA project had a sympathetic ear in the vice minister of finance, Hailemelekot T. Giorgis, who was a pragmatist and a firm believer that a major weakness of the government was talking big but not delivering. The fact that there was no love lost between him and the CSRP coordinator, Peter Silkin, meant that the DSA project was able to craft a reform strategy focused on getting PFA working well before attempting PFM. The serious problems in budgeting—particularly its execution, coupled with the need to rapidly support decentralization in the regions, which made execution especially challenging—brought the Ministry of Finance to realize the virtue of a strategy of recognize and improve what existed. That meant strengthening PFA.

It cannot be overstressed how important it was to get the requirements revised—dare I say "right"—to convince the government to aim for a different objective than the one laid out in the CSRP report. How many PFA/M reforms founder because they begin with a poor path unaccompanied by effective means of monitoring and self-correction so that they continue on the wrong path until they go over a cliff? The pragmatism of Vice Minister Hailemelekot, responsible for the CSRP expenditure reforms, was a foundation of the reform. Pragmatism also meant that design would fit the context, not unrealistic external models or influence. Pragmatism affirmed a reform strategy of recognize-improve-sustain rather than change.

One of the most gratifying parts of my work over twelve years in Ethiopia was the professional relationship with Vice Minister Hailemelekot. His understanding of the immense challenge of this reform in terms of the limitations but also the opportunities for reform were a key factor in the reform's success. His role in the reform affirms the thesis that reform depends on people, not systems, and it was critical to the reform that he was the right person in the right seat at the right time on the reform bus.

PHASE 2: DEVELOPMENT—cooks, kitchens, and the coherence of reforms

Phase 2. Development (roles: design, implementation).
Enter the implementer. Implementation begins in earnest with the commitment of significant resources to system realization, based typically on the approval of a design and its execution as embodied in a project document (technical and financial proposal). System development is marked by a dialogue between designers and implementers.

Implementation of the DSA project began on February 7, 1997, with my arrival in Ethiopia. The project was housed in a one-room office down the hallway from the cafeteria and its kitchen. The kitchen is a good metaphor for reform. We've all heard the dictum: too many cooks spoil the broth. The same goes for reform. One reason for the success of the reform was that there was only one set of cooks in the kitchen, although many foreign chefs tried to elbow their way in over the years.

As the project expanded it was moved to another wing of the original buildings of the Ministry of Finance—the very same wing that housed the general staff of the Italian military that occupied Ethiopia in the 1930s. Our offices, with the original cracked tiled floor, yellowed and water-stained fiberboard ceiling, and dimly lit hallway, exuded a strong whiff of the past, and sometimes more than a whiff. Work was disrupted one day when gardeners unearthed, near the walkway to our offices, unexploded Italian munitions dating from the Second Italo-Abyssinian War (1935–36), in which Italy attempted to make Ethiopia part of its colonial empire.

In its aging, nondescript one-story offices, the DSA was the back-office operation next to the gleaming new ten-story Ministry of Finance building. The impressive new building with its gilded title over the entryway and large fountain that rarely flowed with water was completely out of step architecturally with its surroundings. It projected an image of modernity and organization that did not exist within, a striking illustration of Ethiopia's "wax and gold"—the collision of the apparent and the real. After construction, the building stood empty for nearly a year awaiting furniture, the Finance Ministry's own headquarters a hard-to-top example of poor expenditure composition.

The two-year war with Eritrea started sixteen months after the start of the DSA project and occurred, fortuitously, during the development phase, giving designers the time they needed to understand the nuances of financial management in Ethiopia and craft an appropriate approach to reform it. What they did can be discussed in terms of doing the right thing right.

Doing the right thing: the design of the budget reform

It was clear to me even before the government released the task force report that doing the right thing in the budget reform was toning up of the traditional budget. In early 1996 I had prepared two assessments of Ethiopia's financial systems, and virtually all of my recommendations concerned improving the line-item budget.[5]

The virtues of the traditional line-item budget

In 1978, Aaron Wildavsky, one of the most respected observers of public budgeting, stated:

> So far, no one has come up with another budgetary procedure that has the virtues of traditional budgeting but lacks its defects.... It is not so much that traditional budgeting succeeds brilliantly on every criterion, but that it does not entirely fail on any one that is responsible for its longevity.[6]

This argument is, unfortunately, unknown by much of the PFM community, or if known, has been largely ignored. The traditional budget meets all the needs of budgeting of a government and does not carry the risk of advanced budget formats such as performance, program, or zero-based. More than any other oversight made by PFM pontificators and advisors, the failure to grasp the virtue of this budget format has led to poor advice to governments and environmental degradation through printing endless tomes on PFM techniques and their sequencing. Table 4.1 presents the six attributes of the traditional budget, the extent these were in place in Ethiopia in 1996, the DSA project's design to rectify the deficiencies, and whether these reforms were adopted. The report card of the budget reform is not encouraging, for four of the six reforms were not adopted by government. The low adoption rate affirms that the traditional budget is concerned with the fundamentals of public resource allocation and reform of fundamentals is very difficult because it is very political. Budgeting and its reform cannot be reduced to technique, as V. O. Key noted many years ago.[7] Like most countries, better budgeting is work in progress and getting a good traditional budget is not a minor achievement.

To understand the features of the traditional budget is to understand the "basics" of budgeting. Current discussions in the PFM field suggest that the basics of budgeting are not understood. Certainly some foreign agencies' PFM initiatives in Ethiopia demonstrate a lack of understanding of various points concerning these basics.

First, the term "basics" is often viewed pejoratively in PFM, as meaning primitive and backward. The basics are anything but backward; they are first principles. If they do not exist or are ineffective, this circumstance will undermine any country's finances.

Second, the basics are about the alignment of function and form. Function is political purpose. Function intersects with form in the design of the budget,

Table 4.1 The traditional budget and Ethiopia's budget reform

Features of a traditional budget	Ethiopia's traditional budget, 1996	DSA project's design for reforming the traditional budget (DSA task number)	Adopted
SYSTEM (Procedures)			
1 Appropriates funds	Very weak Aggregate, not agency-based	Reform appropriation to be agency-based (Task 1)	No
2 Is comprehensive	No There are off-budget expenditures	Expand annual appropriation and present other expenditures in annexes (Task 1)	No
3 Is cash-based	Very weak Aid-in-kind not monetized and budgeted	Monetize aid-in-kind (Task 1)	No
4 Is incremental	Very weak No agency appropriation	Reform appropriation to be agency-based (Task 1)	No
5 Is annual	Very weak No budget calendar	Financial calendar to schedule planning, fiscal transfers, and budgeting (Task 2)	No
6 Line item–based	Very weak No clear budget classification and chart of accounts	New budget classification and chart of accounts (Task 3)	Yes
EXECUTION			
Preparation	Very weak No clear budget forms No budget information system	New budget forms (Task 4) Budget information system (Task 5)	Yes Yes
Training	No in-service training	Introduce extensive in-service training (Task 6)	Yes

Source: author.

which is at the heart of public finance. The traditional line-item budget is the primordial form of budgeting, which endures precisely because it is fit for the political purpose of allocating public money. The operation, principles, and procedures of the line-item budget—the core design of a public finance system—promote a firm alignment of political purpose and form.

The incremental operation of the line-item budget is the reason this budget format lasts: it reflects the political reality of how budgets are made over time. The annual appropriated budget for most governments is largely determined by the previous year's budget—the previous budget is the base of the new budget. The bases of previous years represent the accumulation of political compromises reflected in the government's spending priorities.[8] The budget is a government's most important policy document for it presents the priorities of public policy, priorities that evolve over years of budgeted expenditures.

The second attribute of the line-item budget, its principles, promotes the first principles of managing public money. The principle of annularity imposes discipline on the planning, managing, and control of the mobilization of revenue and its expenditure. The line-item budget is a one-year plan, and if a government cannot implement a one-year plan, its policies have little credibility. Furthermore, of course, the political purpose behind those policies will not be met. From this it also follows—though this is often forgotten—that if you cannot execute a one-year expenditure plan, multiyear expenditure planning is of little use.

The procedures of the traditional budget are also the first principles of public finance. A traditional budget is cash-based and has a line-item format. Public finance is about the stewardship of public money, which is legally appropriated from the citizenry and then legally authorized to be spent. There is no equivalent process in private sector finance, which is about determining marginal cost and thus profitability. The focus of the traditional line-item budget is the control of cash in aggregate (total expenditure balanced against total revenues), by agency (the legal authority of a public body to spend as specified by an article of law—the appropriation), and by item (the specific use of funds). The line-item cash budget therefore meets a first principle of PFA/M: control of cash; the rest of the systems of PFA/M (accounts, disbursement, audit) emanate from a cash basis. Because most governments in the world use a cash-based line-item budget, the other systems of financial administration and management are also often based on cash. Again, Wildavsky notes the virtues of the line-item budget in terms of its simplicity, low risk, and control of cash: "The lesson is that for purposes of accountability, and control, the simpler the budget the better.... For sheer transparency, traditional budgeting is hard to beat."[9] Getting the basics of PFA right means aligning function and form and establishing first principles, the first of which is the control of cash.

Strengthening the traditional budget format

Toning up the traditional budget requires strengthening the six features of this budget format (see also table 4.1):

1 Appropriates funds. The budget format, which presents the organizational base—what an agency and its suborganizations will spend—that easily translates into a legal act of appropriation that authorizes the use of public money.
2 Is comprehensive. The budget presents all expenditures that are authorized through an annual appropriation but does not show expenditures legally authorized by a standing appropriation (e.g., entitlement payments).
3 Is cash-based. The budget is presented in a nominal current cash basis and not in a constant or adjusted basis or an accrual basis.
4 Is incremental. Year on year changes in the budget are largely increases or decreases from the previous year's budget—budget as base.
5 Is annual. The budget and its appropriation is to be used within one fiscal year.
6 Is based on line item. Details of expenditure and revenue are presented granularly using item codes.

The DSA project's design for the budget reform addressed all six of these features and also strengthened execution though the introduction of extensive in-service training, new budget forms, and a financial information system. The project also introduced measures to strengthen the performance capabilities of the traditional budget.

Task 1 of the budget reform: clarify appropriation

The traditional budget delivers the financial trinity—control, management, planning—but is especially strong on delivering control of the budget, which, most specialists would argue, is a first-order requirement of a budget indeed, of a financial system. The preeminent source of control in a government with a legislative body is the budget appropriation—the legal authority to spend. The task force report's failure to discuss the existing deficiencies of appropriation and the need for its reform is further evidence of the report's weakness regarding budget reform.

Britain's late-nineteenth-century prime minister William Gladstone in 1891 underscored the importance of the legislature's power of the purse:

> The finance of the country is ultimately associated with the liberties of the country. It is a powerful leverage by which English liberty has been gradually acquired.... If the House of Commons by any possibility [should] lose the power of the control of the grants of public money, depend upon it, your liberty will be worth very little in comparison.[10]

Most governments appropriate a budget by spending agency, such as, say, the Ministry of Defense, the Ministry of Health, and so forth. Appropriation by agency is how a legislature can hold the executive accountable and is a hallmark of the traditional budget. Appropriation by agency has four purposes. First, the legislature being the voice of the public, it confirms de jure public policy, the priority of this spending. Second, the appropriation gives an agency a degree of certainty that the resources will be forthcoming to fund their budget, even though an appropriation is a ceiling that limits expenditure and not a floor or guarantee that the budget will be fully or promptly funded. Third, an appropriation establishes the "budget as base," which provides stability over successive annual budgets that allows an agency to continue with its current year's initiatives, plan for new ones, and adjust incrementally over time. And fourth, the appropriation sends a crucial signal to agency officials of their role as stewards of public money and trust.

In Ethiopia, however, this agency model of budgeting lacks the needed foundation. There is no viable opposition in the legislature. Without a viable opposition in its legislature, Ethiopia does not have advocates for an agency model of appropriation. The legislature that was voted into office in 2010 is referred to by some as the sports-car parliament—two seats of opposition. Absent opposition in the legislature, appropriation by agency would provide very little de facto accountability of the executive.

Ethiopia's approach to appropriation is unusual: appropriations are made by pools, not agencies.[11] At the federal and regional levels of government two pools of funds, a capital and a recurrent pool, are appropriated. Since zones and weredas cannot make law, the appropriation process does not extend to that level. Agency budgets are in turn "approved" by the respective legislative bodies at the federal and region level and then allocated money by the executive at those levels from the capital and recurrent pools to fund their approved capital and recurrent budgets. Although appropriation is not done by agency, agency budgets are approved by the legislature. This means a legal recognition of intent, but it is not the same as the legal wherewithal to meet that intent: a legal claim to funds through an appropriation. Adding to the ambiguity is the absence of a word meaning "appropriation" in the Amharic language. There is, however, an Amharic word for "approval."

The distinction between appropriation and approval can be clearly seen when one reviews the annual law of appropriation in the federal government's *Federal Negarit Gazeta of the Federal Democratic Republic of Ethiopia*, which publishes all federal laws. The *Negarit Gazeta* clearly presents articles of law that specify the capital and recurrent pools but lacks articles specifying funds to agencies. In addition to the two articles specifying the capital and recurrent pools, the annual budget law at the federal level specifies by article the transfers to be made to the nine regions and two administrative areas. The regional finance laws are similarly constructed and show the transfers to their zones and weredas.

Further illustrating the difference between budget appropriation and approval is the practice at the level of the wereda, or district. Weredas have elected councils that approve the budgets of the spending agencies in their wereda, but weredas do not have the authority to make law—so what is the legal basis of budget "approval" in a wereda? There is none. Since weredas cannot make law they also cannot appropriate budgets. Legal access to public funds for agencies at the wereda level comes from the appropriation at the regional level of a block grant or transfer to each wereda. The wereda in turn allocates this grant to its agencies on the basis of an approval process.

The pool structure of appropriation provides Ethiopia with an executive budget, which the executive—the prime minister at the federal level and presidents at the regional level—can reallocate rapidly, without recourse to the legislature, as long as the overall appropriated ceilings are not breached. Pooled appropriation gives the executive and thus the ruling party enormous discretion in the deployment of resources throughout the fiscal year. Conversely, it emasculates the legislature and marginalizes the role of budget officials in spending agencies.

There is no thornier, more complicated, and more political task in PFA/M than the reform of the appropriation process. The basics are neither simple nor easy. I could have ignored the issue, but did not, for appropriation is the foundation of budgeting. In the early stages of the reform the project made several attempts to reform the process of appropriation. The most specific measure was adding a last chapter to the budget reform manual, "Legislative Approval and Appropriation of the Budget," which clarified the existing practice of appropriation and approval, concepts surrounded with much confusion.[12]

In the early days of the reform I also discussed with the minister of finance the idea of working with the budget committee of parliament, which had requested on-site training in budgeting. He said we would get to it, but we never did. Also in the early days of the budget reform we proposed preparing a more comprehensive budget document with annexes that would include off-budget funding, the World Bank's social rehabilitation funds, and concessionary food imports. None of these suggestions was accepted, although for one fiscal year during a period of large food relief from aid agencies, the project was able to monetize this assistance, worth almost as much as the total budget, and attach it to the annual budget as an annex. As an annex it had no legal standing, but at least it was in the budget book. The foreign aid agencies providing food assistance were ecstatic because there was formal public recognition of these contributions.

Generally, however, foreign aid agencies, especially the Bretton Woods agencies, were not advocates of strengthening the process of appropriation. One reason for this was that a more stringent process would have restricted their maneuvering room and also would have forced them to be much more accountable in terms of the timing and specific amounts of aid they delivered to the country. They preferred flexibility to discipline. In the first year of the budget reform, in 1997, Mike Stevens of the World Bank led the first bank mission to an African government with the explicit goal of studying corruption. I had known Stevens from my work in the early nineties in Kenya and found him to be an exemplary professional. At one stage in our discussions in Addis Ababa he asked me about the status of social rehabilitation funds. I gave him a blank stare—I had never heard of them. He explained that these were funds provided to governments to be used at their discretion—off-budget, off-accounts, and off-statistics. He noted sadly that the existence of "social rehabilitation" funds contradicted the World Bank's public pronouncements on the need for probity and transparency in managing public funds—the much-touted international best practice. Social rehabilitation funds, which were very significant, were never brought onto the budget. Where they went was also extremely sensitive—it was my understanding that most of these funds went to Tigray, the home region of the ruling party.

Foreign aid agencies violate other core principles of financial management, such as that all public money is to be appropriated before being spent. The World Bank's Productive Safety Nets Program (PSNP), the largest such social protection program in sub-Saharan Africa, provides a recent example. The core mission of the PSNP is to provide cash supplements to approximately 9 million of the poorest in Ethiopia so that they can buy food. Starting with the 2010 budget, the Ministry of Finance and Economic Development (MOFED) began disbursing for food relief PSNP funds that had not been appropriated for this purpose, justifying this with the argument that the time-critical nature of food security required flexibility in the financial system.[13] The resident economist of the World Bank mission to Ethiopia agreed with this argument. One can argue that *all* expenditures in a budget are time-critical and need to be executed in a fiscal year. The solution to the requirements of the PSNP and all government activities is a disciplined, efficient system, not a lax system that undermines prudent financial management.

The silence of foreign aid agencies concerning appropriation suggests that they actually prefer "convenient" practice over "best." The silence regarding appropriation on the part of both government and foreign aid also touches on a very sensitive issue: How transparent will government finances be? Indeed, how transparent will foreign aid be? If a budget reform is to be thorough it cannot avoid this issue. Funds that are not presented in the budget are to all intents and purposes not in the public domain—are not public money. "Best practice" in budgeting should begin with accountability and control, but sadly this has not happened in Ethiopia. Some budget reform is good, but more is not necessarily perceived as better if it brings greater transparency—not always desired by either governments or their patrons. Full disclosure makes the management of illusion more difficult. The failure to reform appropriation means that the core basics of budgeting in Ethiopia still remain to be achieved.

Task 2 of the budget reform: introducing a financial calendar

A financial calendar specifies when financial transactions are to occur. In 1996, Ethiopia did not have a financial calendar. A financial calendar promotes good PFA/M for it links the planning cycle to the budget cycle, which follows planning. Ideally, the planning cycle has both a multiyear plan of revenue and expenditure followed by a fiscal forecast, an estimate of revenues and expenditures for the next fiscal year; this shapes the budget cycle, which produces the budget also for the next fiscal year. The objective of the planning cycle is to clarify policy objectives in the medium term and for the upcoming fiscal year with a hard resource constraint. All too often, planning is "blue sky" in terms of resources and is thus irrelevant in defining realistic policy objectives that are to be implemented by the annual budget.

The fiscal plan provides a realistic estimate of resources for the budget. The budget cycle has several sequential activities: (1) a call to spending agencies that gives them a resource ceiling and specifies the schedule of budget bids and discussions; (2) preparation and release of subsidy ceilings to the regions so they can start their own budget process; (3) the review, discussion, and final approval of budgets, ending with the appropriation of funds to execute the budget.

A financial calendar was essential for Ethiopia for two reasons. First, fiscal decentralization required that an additional task be done between the planning and budgeting cycles: the preparation of the formula for determining the financial transfers to regions, and then deciding the size of the regional pool of funds that would be allocated to regions on the basis of the formula. The fiscal transfer needed to be done sufficiently far in advance so that regions could be notified and begin their own budgeting process. With second-stage decentralization, regions themselves had to manage a fiscal transfer process to fund their weredas.

The project's approach to the design of the financial calendar was to keep it simple.[14] The proposed calendar had neither a forward budget nor a scheduled revised budget. This did not preclude a supplementary or a revised budget, should funding have to be increased or decreased within a fiscal year. Eight years of working on budgets in Kenya had shown me how debilitating these multiple budgets were and how they encourage laxity in budgeting. Budget staff in Kenya spend far too much time, indeed most of their time, making and remaking the budget, both before the fiscal year began (drafting a forward budget of the upcoming annual budget) and within the fiscal year (redrafting the annual budget by preparing a revised budget). Budget staff were bogged down in budget preparation and had little time to work on the crucial task of budget execution.[15] Reworking all this paper was a pointless exercise, for the real problem of PFA/M in Kenya was that there was little certainty concerning the resources that would fund these pretty budget books. This "repetitive" budgeting was a scourge in Kenya and I hoped to prevent it in Ethiopia.[16]

The foundation of a financial calendar is cash. All the plans—multiyear, fiscal year, and budgets (the annual budget is a one-year plan of revenue and expenditure)—are for naught if there is no cash. The saving grace to Ethiopia's lack of a financial or budget calendar was the rigid discipline of not spending more than was available—the "hard budget constraint"—and fully funding the budgets of spending agencies, except during the darkest days of the war with Eritrea. Ethiopia had cash, not a calendar.

Like the appropriation proposal, the project's proposals to introduce a financial calendar went nowhere. Government and foreign aid torpedoed this reform. Executive budgeting by the government based on appropriation by pool, not agency, meant that budgeting could be just-in-time, and just before the start of the new fiscal year. Appropriating the capital and recurrent pool was by far the most important budget task, which can be, was, and is to this day done at the last minute. Since the budgets of public bodies were approved and not appropriated, and how the costs of services in their budgets were arrived at were not scrutinized by the legislature—these budgets were not essential. Public bodies were shown to be very lax in responding to the budget call of the Ministries of Finance and Planning, and some very large public bodies, such as the Health Ministry and the Roads Authority, did not complete their detailed budgets before the start of the fiscal year (discussed in a later section of this chapter, on the pilot phase of the reform).

Foreign aid agencies also torpedoed the financial calendar, despite their repeated exhortations that Ethiopia should adopt an authoritative calendar. Simply put: For domestically funded expenditures Ethiopia did not have a calendar but did have cash; for foreign aid–funded expenditures there was no calendar and all too frequently no cash. Ethiopia relied on foreign aid for approximately one third of the funding for total public spending. Since the amount and arrival time of this cash was uncertain, a third of the budget could not be planned and, more important, could not be budgeted and executed. This situation continues today.

A pillar of international PFM "best practice" is multiyear planning systems, called medium-term expenditure frameworks, or MTEFs. The task force report made no mention of the need for MTEFs or for planning the budget. The CSRP architect, Peter Silkin, was an auditor, not an economist nor budget specialist. The DSA project convinced the Ministries of Finance and Planning to add an expenditure planning reform, but the planning reform, like the reform of appropriation and the financial calendar, went nowhere (discussed in detail in chapter 7). It went nowhere because of the refusal in some cases and the inability in most cases of foreign aid agencies to provide the government with firm and timely resource commitments for the upcoming fiscal year, much less the three years of the proposed MTEF. Most damaging was that even when foreign aid agencies did provide information regarding their resource commitments, which were then incorporated into the budget, frequently the funds never arrived, or they arrived too late to be used. The volatility of foreign aid was especially harmful to regional finances because the federal government reduced the domestic funds a region would receive by the amount of foreign funds the region was to receive. The repeated failure of the African Development Bank to deliver on its commitments resulted in repeated shortfalls in regional budgets and eventually forced the government to exclude the bank's funds from the budget.

The failure to implement a financial calendar, like the failure to reform appropriation, means that the basics of budgeting remain to be reformed. A financial calendar holds not just government but also foreign aid accountable. Foreign aid agencies gave lip service to this best practice but were unable to support it with their own policies. Too often, best practice is preached, but convenient practice is actually preferred.

Task 3 of the budget reform: reform of the chart of accounts and budget classification

The principal function of a budget is to allocate resources to the priorities of society. Allocation is a political process virtually impervious to improvement by techniques, but the organization of the budget can be reformed by technique. Budgets are organized by two systems: a chart of accounts (COA) and a budget classification (BC), both of which can be reformed. The chart of accounts is the *what* of the budget (revenue, expenditure, transfer), and the budget classification is the *where* (jurisdiction), *who* (public bodies and their internal four-level hierarchy), and *purpose* (function and subfunction). The COA presents the details of the different entities within a budget such as expenditures, revenues, external resources, transfers. Expenditure in the Ethiopia budget is the 6000 series and revenue is the 1000 series (see table 4.2). The budget classification as developed for Ethiopia locates the entities of the chart of accounts. For example, a salary expenditure is classified as to jurisdiction (say, federal), to budget type (say, capital), to public body (say, the Ministry of Health), to function (say, social), to subfunction (say, health). It is further

Table 4.2 Budget categories and their standardized codes

Classification level	*Code*
Functional classifications	
1 Administration and general	100
2 Economic	200
3 Social	300
4 Other	400
Subfunctional classification—Administration and General	100
Organ of State	110
Justice	120
Defense	130
Public Order	140
General Service	150–170
Subfunctional classification—Economic	200
Agricultural and Natural Resources	210–220
Trade and Industry	230
Mining and Energy	240
Tourism	250
Transport and Communication	260*
Construction	270
Subfunctional classification—Social	300
Education	310
Culture and Sport	320
Health	330
Labor and Social Affairs	340
Prevention and Rehabilitation	350
Subfunctional classification—Other	400
Transfers	410
Debt	420
Contingency	430
Miscellaneous	440

Source: DSA B-16: 24, table 2.5.

Note
* Road construction is listed under "Construction" and not "Transport and Communication."

classified within the public body to a four-level hierarchy—program, subagency, subprogram, and project. Table 4.2, "Budget Categories and Their Standardized Codes," gives a broad overview of the system of standardized codes. Table 4.3, "Budget classification code example: Ministry of Education capital budget," shows an example that drills down vertically into the details of how the system is used to describe and categorize a specific budget item. The COA and BC are standardized and all tiers of government and all public bodies within those tiers have to comply with these two systems.

The COA and BC are the frameworks that organize not only the budget but also the systems that execute the budget: disbursements, accounts, the financial information system, and, ultimately, national statistics. Establishing a good chart of accounts and budget classification system goes a long way toward getting the basics working. Reforming the COA and BC, the organizing frameworks of PFA/M, takes time. Once reformed, they should not be changed unless there are compelling reasons. Changing a COA-BC is not simply introducing a new set of codes—it is about changing how government is organized and how day-to-day finances are done. Returning to Harris Mule's observation that a budget is a language, the COA and the BC provide the grammar of that language, and changing them precipitously or without forethought can reduce comprehension. One reason why PFM reforms that introduce advanced budgeting techniques fail is that they either begin with a poor COA-BC or go overboard in changing them.

DEFICIENCIES IN THE CHART OF ACCOUNTS AND THE BUDGET CLASSIFICATION

In 1996, Ethiopia's COA and BC were seriously deficient. The hierarchy of categories used to organize public bodies—main categories, subcategories, and sub-subcategories—was inconsistently applied by public bodies, so the organization of the budget was neither clear nor consistent. The COA for expenditure items was redundant, featuring a 6000 series for recurrent expenditure, a 7000 series for domestically financed capital expenditure, and an 8000 series for externally financed capital expenditure. The chart also treated domestic revenue and external loan and assistance inconsistently. There were numerous anomalies in the chart, such as item codes that stored funds which could then be transferred to purchase specific goods and services without requiring proper documentation. Items that were significant such as ammunition (which is very material for a country in the Horn of Africa) and training and medical equipment did not have an expenditure code.

REFORMING THE CHART OF ACCOUNTS

Our design focused on rectifying the two most egregious deficiencies in the chart of accounts: simplifying the three series of items of expenditure and introducing material expenditure items such as food. The three redundant series had been created by fiat by the head of the accounts department of the Ministry of Finance

Table 4.3 Budget classification code example: Ministry of Education capital budget, components of complete expenditure code 15/2/311/1/2/ 20/01/114/6322/2641 (for Swedish International Development Agency)

Class of account	Budget	Category	No. digits	Example (code)
	Jurisdiction	2	Federal	(15)
	Budget	1	Capital	(2)
Head	Functional classification	3	Social	(311)[a]
	Subfunctional classification	1	Education	(1)
	Public body (administrative code)	1	Ministry of Education	(1)
Subhead	Program	1	Higher education	(2)
Sub-subhead	Subagency	2	Wondo Genet College of Forestry	(20)
Sub-sub-subhead	Subprogram	2	Forestry Educational Service	(01)
Sub-sub-sub-subhead	Project	3	Strengthening Wondo Genet College of Forestry	(114)
Item	Item of expenditure	4	Construction of buildings—residential	(6322)
Source	Source of finance	4	SIDA assistance	(2641)

Source: DSA B-17, 19.

Note

a The "head" code is a composite of three budget categories: two statistical classifications (functional and subfunctional) and one administrative, naming the agency. Thus, unpacking the 300 code, 3 = the functional classification, social; 1 = the subfunctional classification, education; and 1 = the administering agency, Ministry of Education.

and had no legal standing, so it was possible to quickly reduce the three to one. Much more difficult was adding an additional fourteen items of material expenditure: the Ethiopian officials on the budget reform team stubbornly resisted this. They had their reasons: they understood that day-to-day operations were handled principally by clerical staff with limited education who had committed a handful of codes to memory. However, the team erred in not including some material codes that, in my discussions with spending agencies, I had found to be essential, for example: for medical drugs and medical equipment and for separating salary expenditures of administrative from professional staff. I won some of these battles and lost others. Reform of the COA was done with three strategies of reform—recognize, improve, and change.

REFORMING THE BUDGET CLASSIFICATION

Reforming the budget classification was far more challenging than reforming the chart of accounts because changing a BC is about changing how a government is organized. Reforming the BC meant meeting two challenges. First, the capital and recurrent budgets needed to be "crosswalked"—expenditures in the two budgets relating to the same activity needed to be linked so that the total resources for an activity could be seen.

The second challenge was to create a workable system that met the demands of day-to-day budget administration and the demand for budget analysis based on the United Nations' Classification of the Functions of Government (COFOG), which forms the basis for the UN's statistics.[17]

CROSSWALKING ETHIOPIA'S TWO BUDGETS

Crosswalking was difficult, for the capital and recurrent budgets were like ships that pass in the night: the recurrent budget was driven by subagencies (the locus of salary expenditures), whereas the capital budget was driven by projects (the repository of foreign aid and the locus of expenditures for temporary staff that manned projects). A key innovation in the reform of the budget classification was to bring the recurrent and capital budget categories (subagencies in the recurrent budget and programs and projects in the capital budget) together by function. The four principal functions were "administrative and general," "economic," "social," and "other," which in turn were elaborated into subfunctions. Each principal function had classifications for subfunctions. For example, the "social" function had five subfunctions: "education," "culture and sport," "health," "labor and social affairs," and "prevention and rehabilitation" (see table 4.2).

For each public body we created a composite "head" code category whose first digit indicated the functional classification and whose second digit indicated the subfunctional classification. The final digit, the sub-subfunctional classification, was a unique single digit that identified a public body. For example, the Ministry of Education composite "head" class-of-account code is 311: the first digit, 3, indicates the functional classification "Social"; the second digit, 1, indicates the subfunctional classification "Education"; and the second 1 is a unique number for the Ministry of Education.

Table 4.3 unpacks the complete code that links a specific transaction listed in the COA to the BC, the Ministry of Education public body and its four levels of organization (in this case it is item of expenditure number 2641, "construction of buildings—residential"). The twenty-two-digit string is called a "budget mask" and in this example is 15/2/311/2/20/01/114/6322/2641. The budget mask is the complete expenditure code. This specific expenditure code can be parsed by means of a list:

Expenditure Code 15/2/311/2/20/01/114/6322/2641

15	Jurisdiction: federal
2	Budget: capital
311	Head function: Social/Education/Ministry of Education
2	Subhead, program: Higher education
20	Sub-subhead, sub-agency: Wondo Genet College
01	Sub-sub-subhead, subprogram: Forestry Educational Service
114	Sub-sub-sub-subhead, project: Strengthening Wondo Genet College of Forestry
6322	Item, item of expenditure: Construction of Buildings, residential
2641	Source, source of finance: Swedish International Development Agency Assistance

The system behind this specific example is shown in table 4.3.

Crosswalking the budget was done by introducing the functional and subfunctional classifications and by introducing the program and subprogram budget categories. The innovation of the composite head code at a stroke linked budget management (the agency code) with budget analysis (the function and subfunction code). The budget structure could now be mapped to the top two levels of the UN's Classification of the Functions of Government (COFOG) framework. Our composite approach did not allow mapping to the third and lowest level of COFOG. We intentionally did not envision mapping to the third COFOG level, because we felt that it was too complex to be realistically implemented at that time.

A thorny problem in the dual budget, one that often defeats performance and program budget reforms, is how to assign overhead costs to activities—especially costs related to staff. In Ethiopia as in many developing countries, staffing is the single largest expenditure in the budget, so handling salaries was at the heart of bridging the dual budget. The subprogram budget category, which was one step above the project category and one step below the subagency category, was designed to apportion overheads, especially staffing, which were in the subagency category to projects. The program category, which was above the subagency, subprogram, and project categories, was introduced to aggregate all resources according to a program. When the IMF imposed the requirement that

Ethiopia prepare a consolidated budget that brought together the regional- and federal-tier budgets, the consolidation was done on the basis of programs.

The COA and BC can be very complicated. Some countries have complex coding systems and others have fairly simple ones. The Government of South Africa has more than nine thousand items of expenditure. In our design for Ethiopia we had just ninety-three. I am not persuaded that South Africa has the better system—and neither are some staff of South Africa's National Treasury!

So there is no clear model to follow. Where to begin to design these systems? How complex do they need to be? How many program or functional levels? How many spending categories? As described earlier, we presented a budget classification design with a five-level hierarchy that some government officials thought was too complicated. In the federal government workshop where the draft COA-BC was presented to federal bodies and the senior officials of the Ministry of Finance, the vice minister responsible for the budget reform felt that four levels of organization beneath the public body (program, subagency, sub-program, project) were probably too many and should be reduced to two. He did not provide a rationale for this opinion. Government officials on the budget reform team also wanted to severely restrict the increase in the number of items of expenditure—we increased it from seventy-nine to ninety-three. Fortunately, even with ninety-three items, these could still fit on two sides of one sheet of paper! Ethiopia took a tightfisted approach to all resources, even budget codes and the paper they were written on.

All else being equal, the simpler the design the better. Simple does not mean simplistic. It is a far harder challenge to build a sparse system that meets necessary functionality than a complex system with functionality of little value. A major contribution of the Ethiopian officials on the budget reform team was their continued focus on simplification—not simplicity—in design. Getting the basics working is not just about procedures, toning up the traditional budget; it is also about the degree of complexity in those procedures. Having a COA with 9,000 items of expenditures like South Africa's and a BC scheme with a deep hierarchy would have unduly encumbered the budget. Sleek basics make for clear forms for officials to complete which lessens error, and also makes for clear training materials and user-friendly financial information systems. In many ways, the careful and sparse design of the COA-BC was a key to the success not only of better budgeting but of all the systems that supported the budget—disbursements, accounts, and the financial information system.

An overly complicated COA-BC would not have been fit for purpose for the federal and regional governments when it was designed in 2000, nor would it have been appropriate for the weredas that would soon be given responsibility for financial management. A complicated COA-BC would likely have disrupted and possibly even derailed the reform.

THE INTERNATIONAL MONETARY FUND AND THE COA-BC

The IMF meddled with the government's new COA-BC at the worst possible time, in FY2004, in the middle of the largest one-year phase in the rollout of the budget reform, which included four regions: Oromia, Benishangul Gumuz, Dire Dawa, and Harar. Alone for Oromia, the largest state—with 32 percent of the country's area and 35 percent of its population—8,000-plus officials had to be trained.

Leading the charge in attacking the budget reform was Duncan Last of East AFRITAC (for Africa Regional Technical Assistance Center), a branch office of the IMF located in Tanzania. He along with an IMF team from Washington met with the Donor Assistance Group (DAG), the foreign aid agencies in Ethiopia as well as the minister of finance, and complained vociferously about the poor design of the COA-BC. Last also lashed out at the approach to strengthening the traditional budget and argued that this was not reform and that what was needed was program budgeting.[18] The next evening I received my first ever phone call at my home in Addis Ababa from the minister of finance. My dread quickly disappeared when he said that the IMF team had complained about the COA-BC and he had informed them that it worked for his government and they were deeply involved in its implementation.

This incident illustrates some of the fundamental problems created by the IMF and other foreign aid agencies in PFM reform. The first issue is technical. The COA-BC has two roles, budget administration and analysis. Budget administration is the first-order task and the bottom-line requirement for a government's COA-BC is that it be *mappable* to the various international guidelines such as the COFOG for cross-country analysis of budgets. The IMF has erroneously reversed this, stating that the COA-BC must be *compliant* with the COFOG—hence Last's insistence on going to level 3, even though this was too complex for the Ethiopian setting. The IMF asserts that COFOG is a standard and must be followed, and this logic has been enshrined into the PFM diagnostic of the day, the Public Expenditure Financial Accountability (PEFA) Framework.[19] Simply put, the IMF values formal over substantive rationality.[20] The Ethiopian officials of the budget reform team understood the importance of budget administration and "got" that simple was sensible. The IMF did not.

This incident also provides evidence of the disrespect felt by IMF staff for government systems and reforms. The COA-BC was developed by the budget reform team of the Ministries of Finance and Planning; it was chaired by a vice minister of the Ministry of Finance and was implementing a government policy, civil service reform, that was of the highest priority to the government. Although the DSA project provided technical assistance to the civil service reform program, the reform was a government program and policy. The IMF and East AFRITAC staff exhibited the worst type of behavior that technical assistance could do: dismissing government achievements, being ignorant of policy, and disrupting operations.

The third and most egregious issue raised by this incident was the inappropriateness of the IMF's and East AFRITAC's advice. Program budgeting is the most sophisticated form of budgeting, for it requires governments to relate inputs to outcomes. It made no sense as Ethiopia struggled to get its traditional input budget in regions working well and extend financial management to weredas that had little or no capacity. The vice minister of finance's comment that even a four-level budget classification might be too complicated underscores the importance of budget reforms that are fit for context. Imagine the confusion of wereda budget officials trying to manage a BC based on the three tiers of COFOG pushed by the IMF! Even worse, think of the confusion weredas would have faced if they had had to implement a program budget.

We can let Aaron Wildavsky have the last word on the IMF and East AFRI-TAC's lack of understanding of charts of accounts and budget classification. In "A Budget for All Seasons? Why the Traditional Budget Lasts," he states:

> There is a critical difference between the financial form in which the budget is voted in the legislature and the different ways of thinking about budgeting. It is possible to analyze expenditures in terms of programs, over long periods of time, and in many other ways, without requiring that the form of analysis be the same as the form of appropriation. All this can be summarized: the more neutral the form of presenting appropriations, the easier to translate other changes in program, direction, organizational structure—into the desired amount without increasing the rigidity in categories, and thus erecting barriers to future changes.[21]

In contrast to the IMF and East AFRITAC's response, the World Bank's review of the COA-BC and the entire budget reform volume was very constructive. The World Bank mission in Ethiopia brought in Mike Stevens to review the budget reform. At a meeting I attended at the bank's local office with the director and senior staff, Stevens held up the budget manual, declared, "This is good stuff," and asked, "Has anyone read it?" The bank official responsible for PFM who had sent for Stevens was interested and respectful of the reform throughout his posting. He was replaced by an official who took the bank's acknowledgment of the government reform even further and approached USAID with a request that the DSA project expand its brief to automate financial management throughout the country, especially in the weredas. Although the bank's confidence in our project was gratifying, I informed USAID that such activity would divert the project from finishing the design of the procedural reforms and the rollout of the financial information system that was needed to operate the reforms at just the regional level.

Unfortunately, the budget reform had not seen the last of Duncan Last. A year and a half later, in February 2005, he and Marc Robinson struck again, demanding a meeting with the head of USAID and the IMF resident representative. Last pointed to the deficiencies of the reform, again returning to his hobby horse of the need for advanced techniques of budgeting: performance, and program budgeting.[22] In February 2005 the project was deeply involved in rolling out the accounts reform to the four new regions that were operating the new budgeting system (Oromia, Benishangul Gumuz, Dire Dawa, and Harari), and we were also introducing the budget reform to the last three regions (Afar, Gambella, and Somali), which faced extreme challenges of capacity and remoteness. After Last finished his lecture on international best practice I addressed the IMF and USAID director. I said that these consultants were disrupting a critical phase in the introduction of the reform; the reform is a government reform, not the project's; and these consultants had not done due diligence in understanding Phase 4 of the reform—specifically, the development of a performance framework for the traditional budget.

The absence of professional integrity on the part of Duncan Last is best illustrated by his own words. In a 2002 report to the IMF of which Last is an author, it is acknowledged that the government's policy to devolve financial management to weredas has "massive implications" and is a "shock to the system" and would make financial management and its reform a real challenge.[23] The report authors then praise the work of the DSA project:

> Ongoing reforms to the budget process provide an improved basis for using the budget as an analytic tool. The revised financial calendar, budget classification and chart of accounts that have recently been adopted at the federal level provide a good basis for providing comprehensive information to stakeholders within and outside the executive.... Training in the new financial management procedures is impressive, with thousands of financial management staff trained under the DSA project.... First steps to automating the budget process have been made ... by the USAID DSA project.[24]

Yet Last completely reversed his assessment in 2009. In that year he and Marc Robinson wrote the IMF technical guide for introducing performance budgeting and cited the case of Ethiopia as a failed reform, stating: "In Ethiopia, the civil service reforms went ahead without appropriate improvements in the budgeting process, i.e., ministries were undergoing major changes without corresponding improvements in the way their budgets were being prepared or executed."[25] Last and Robinson's 2009 assessment of the reform is simply untrue. First, the federal ministries were *not* undergoing major changes as a result of the civil service reform because—except for the financial reforms, most of which were being supported by the DSA project—none of the other programs of the CSRP were being implemented (top systems management, human resources, service delivery, and ethics). Second, along with the reforms he duly notes in his 2002 assessment (new chart of accounts and budget classification, financial calendar), the DSA project introduced expenditure planning reforms (Public Investment Program, Public Expenditure Program, Macro Economic Fiscal Framework) that were strongly endorsed by foreign aid agencies, including the IMF.

So why the change of tune? Sour grapes, perhaps. Last wanted in on the game. His 2002 assessment was written while he was discussing with me his and East AFRITAC's involvement in the financial reforms for which the DSA was providing technical assistance. The government had excluded the IMF from this reform, but Last wanted me to collaborate with him and East AFRITAC so he could claim he was involved in Ethiopia's reform. He told me that if I played ball it would ensure future work for me with the IMF. I did not play ball, nor did the government want the IMF anywhere near the reform ball. The 2005 meeting of the IMF, USAID, and the DSA project, where Last and Robinson discredited the project, and the 2009 paper they coauthored that also discredited the project were payback for my not working with Last and the IMF. Last's strategy of gaining admission to financial reforms in Ethiopia was to discredit what he had earlier clearly seen was a good reform, in hopes that the government would ask the IMF for help to sort out the mess.

The IMF and East AFRITAC have never given up their "best practice" agenda for PFM in Ethiopia, and they continued to press the Ministry of Finance to adopt performance-program budgeting for years.[26] In one year they convinced the federal government to create a pilot program for performance-program budgeting in three federal ministries, an experiment that had to be halted because these ministries were unable to prepare their budgets promptly and this was holding up the completion of the federal budget. The inappropriateness of IMF advice on budgeting can best be seen in the context of deteriorating financial reporting in 2010. Instead of MOFED's staff working to get the existing budget and accounting systems functioning, they were diverted to other reforms, including the IMF's performance-program budgeting initiative and business process reengineering.[27]

Reform of the COA-BC was the cornerstone of the budget reform. It is the procedural heart of the budget and has profound effects. The budget reform team achieved a constructive balance in its design in terms of continuity (it did not drastically increase the number of existing expenditure codes), simplicity (there was only one series of expenditure codes), and adherence to international guidelines (it could be mapped to two levels of COFOG).

To put the reform of the COA-BC into practice required the development of new budget forms. These would in turn define the user interface of the financial information system.

Task 4 of the budget reform: reform of the budget forms

After the first year of the budget reform in Amhara region, I debriefed officials from the Bureau of Agriculture in that region on their experience with the new budget system. What struck me most was their enthusiastic praise of the budget forms. They liked the new COA-BC. They liked the new computer system, the budget information system (BIS). Most of all they liked the forms. The greatest improvement to budgeting was the forms that made budgeting clear. Previously, budget forms had been poorly designed and they changed constantly. The devil is in the details, and getting the basics working means getting the details, such as the forms used, right.

THE VALUE OF CLEAR FORMS

Little mention is made in the PFM literature about the importance of forms, but they can make or break a budgeting process. In an environment such as that of

Ethiopia, getting good numbers in the budget was dependent on designing forms well. In 1997, public financial management was done by government officials with an average twelfth-grade education. While there has been improvement in the level of qualification of budget staff, budgeting in weredas is still principally a manual operation, and the high turnover rate and absence of in-service training in budgeting meant that budget forms had to be completed by officials who were learning by doing under the tight time pressure of the inevitable end-of-fiscal-year budget preparation scramble caused in part by the absence of a financial calendar. Clear budget forms also proved their value during the business process reengineering (BPR) reform, started in 2007, which introduced massive reshuffling of government staff and left budgeting in the hands of officials who often had less than one year of experience. The existence of easily completed forms ameliorated the pernicious effects of this reform.[28]

THE McGRATH APPROACH TO DESIGNING FORMS

The importance of getting good budget forms cannot be overstated. The reformed budget system was designed to operate both manually and with a custom computer system developed by the project, the budget information system, or BIS. The budget forms had to be clear because when completed, they became the source documents for the budgets. If the computer system was unavailable or, as in the case of most weredas, had not been extended to that level, the manual forms could be used to prepare the budget. If the BIS was available, the budget forms were the source document for inputting budget data into the system. The BIS had input screens that were identical to the manual forms so that users could easily input data.

The basic suite of forms that we developed for the budget were the following:

- *Form 1, "FGE Capital Budget, Budget Structure for FY ___,"* presented the specific codes for each public body and the four levels of their budget (figure 4.2A).[29]
- *Form 2, "Project Profile for FY ___,"* presented details of projects for the capital budget and sub-agencies for the recurrent budget, which were the principal budget categories for those respective budgets (figure 4.3A shows the form used for a project profile in the Somali Regional State Capital Budget).
- *Form 3, "Project Budget Request for FY ___,"* is where a public body would show, for a specific activity, the various items of expenditure and the sources of their funding—domestic, foreign loan, foreign grant. Thus, this form was the core of budgeting (figure 4.4A).

Shaun McGrath was the DSA project's first advisor on computer technology. One would be hard-pressed to find a better approach to designing budget forms than his. He understood the need to demystify the automation of financial procedures and was committed to making the budget information system very user-friendly. User-friendly software began with the paper budget forms that could serve double duty for preparing a manual budget or as the input forms for the BIS. The McGrath approach to designing these forms was governed by four principles:

1   Integration of the manual with the digital
2   Color coding
3   Flagging key data
4   Instructions provided on all forms

Integration of the manual with the digital. Integration meant replicating the manual forms so that the BIS input screens looked the same as the manual forms that officials were used to using. Those in the PFM field tend to focus too strongly on total integration of PFM systems in a wholly automated Integrated Financial Management Information System (IFMIS). Meanwhile, a major mistake made by PFM reformers is their failure to grasp a truly critical integration task of financial information systems: to link the manual and the digital.[30] No PFM system is ever fully automated—there is always some paper—but the better the link between the pencil and the pixel, the more efficient financial management is, as shown by the budget forms of the Ethiopian budget reform.

Color coding. For those sitting in a well-appointed office on the top floor of the Ministry of Finance preparing budgets for the umpteenth year, the issue of colors had little meaning, but for new recruits at the wereda frontline of budgeting who were learning on the job, with flies and paper flying about and, if they were lucky, a bare bulb providing illumination, any feature that aided clarity was much appreciated. McGrath appreciated the complexity and potential confusion created by the dual budget, and made dramatic use of color to clearly distinguish the two budget types: green forms for the recurrent budget and yellow for the capital budget.

Flagging key data. The design of forms was used to help identify different types of data. Presented earlier are the three types of forms needed for the three key types of data: budget structure, project and sub-agency profile, and the budget submission.

Instructions on all forms. For users, the most revolutionary feature of the forms was the concluding "Instructions" section on all three forms. For the first time, each budget form had line-by-line instructions on how to complete the form. These were printed on the back of each form, which previously had been blank. The BIS operated on the fly in four of the principal languages in Ethiopia—Amharic, Oromiffa, Somali, Tigrigna—as well as English, so the printed forms with their detailed instructions were available in the local language.

Task 5 of the budget reform: introducing a budget information system

McGrath got automation of the reform started on the right foot: forms and the type of information they must present should define the software. The dog (the information requirements of procedures) should wag the tail. In the years that followed, the Ministry of Finance would be visited by purveyors of other financial information systems who argued that the software should determine procedures—the tail wagging the dog.

Developing a budget information system for the PFA reform was not in the DSA project's terms of reference or budget. It was the brief of another project, to be funded by the European Commission.[31] But it had to be done in tandem with the design of forms, and so it was done simultaneously with the design of the budget forms. The project was able to reallocate modest funds from planned work on treasury procedures to develop two financial information systems: the budget information system (BIS) and the budget disbursement (BDA) system for managing disbursement and accounting. If the DSA project had not proceeded with developing a BIS and a BDA system, the budget and accounts reforms would have been delayed for years.

Bringing automation into the project brought coherence to the reform. It also meant that two low-cost, fit-for-purpose, requirements-driven financial information systems (FISs) were developed that were always available to support the reform rather than delay it, as is so often the case with reforms that involve new financial information systems, which are typically late and over budget and, sadly, don't meet the user's requirements. Another danger was avoided, that of assigning the development of procedures to one project and automation to another, which would have led to the near-certain fragmentation of the reform. The potential for the loss of coherence was demonstrated in 2002 when the EC finally restarted its FIS project with the consulting firm of PricewaterhouseCoopers. In an early presentation of its firm's FIS strategy for Ethiopia, Ian Lang, the engagement partner, stated that its system would "mirror" the COA-BC developed by the DSA project. I pointed out to him that a mirror is a reverse image and given that thousands of officials of three of the four largest regions had already been trained with the new COA-BC, the PricewaterhouseCoopers system needed to exactly replicate the COA-BC. I did not get a response from Lang but PricewaterhouseCoopers did get a response from the Ministry of Finance: No, thank you. From 2002 until the DSA project ended in January 2008 there were rumors of restarting the EC's FIS project, but nothing materialized and the EC reprogrammed its funds. In chapter 6 we present the FIS reform in detail.

Task 6 of the budget reform: developing an in-service training program

Once we finished developing and finalizing the new budgeting procedures, we intended to complete a training module as rapidly as possible.[32] The project faced a difficult decision concerning the relative emphasis to be placed on in-service training in the new budget procedures versus training on the existing accounting system in order to clear the accounts. A precondition for rolling out the budget and accounts reforms was that the existing accounting systems had to be up-to-date, so we decided to focus in-service training on accounting. This was a risk, but it paid off, for it meant the backlog of accounts was cleared at the federal level, and then in the Southern Region and the Amhara region, which meant that the implementation of the budget and accounts reform would not be delayed. In the absence of a budget training manual, federal officials were trained in the new budgeting system using the "Budget Reform Design Manual Version 2.1" and the new budget forms. Clear forms with instructions performed double duty as operational training tools. In November 2002 a comprehensive budget training manual was finalized in English and subsequently translated into four national languages: Amharic, Oromiffa, Somali, and Tigrigna.[33]

Going beyond the basics: introduction of cost-center budgeting

The challenge of the budget reform was to realize as much of the potential of the traditional budget as possible. Virtually all PFM reformers overlook the fact that very few governments fully realize the potential of the traditional budget. Arguably the greatest deficiency in budget outcomes in Ethiopia in 1996 and today is poor composition of expenditure. Until one knows all of the inputs, whether capital investment or recurrent costs, that are available to deliver a good or service, one cannot improve the composition of expenditure and thus the quality of that service. Until the dual budget is crosswalked or a unitary budget is installed where capital and recurrent expenditures are brought together in one budget, it is not possible to move to output (performance) budgets or outcome (program) budgets.

The purpose of cost-center budgets—also known as responsibility budgets—is to aggregate inputs and assign responsibilities for funds to specific organizations and individuals. A cost center is a "floating" category that in principle can be at the most macro-level (such as the federal government or a regional government) or the level of a public body (the Ministry of Education) or the four levels within the ministry (programs, sub-agencies, subprograms, projects). Typically, the cost centers were to be based on the four levels of a public body. Table 4.3 shows the cost centers of the sub-agency of the Ministry of Education; the Wondo Genet College of Forestry is a cost center, and under it there is another cost center, a Swedish-funded project, "Strengthening Wondo Genet College of Forestry."

Creating a cost-center budget meant that the budget reform was establishing a foundation for more sophisticated budgeting in the future, should that be needed. Cost centers are to budgeting what double-entry bookkeeping is to accounting. Both provide a more sophisticated treatment of discrete transactions from which to build more sophisticated management and planning of those transactions. For example, double-entry bookkeeping allows an accounting system to include a much wider range of financial entities such as long-term liabilities and assets—not just cash. Cost centers allow a budgeting system to include a much wider range of calculations—cost drivers, better accountability, first inputs, then outputs, and eventually outcomes.

Introducing cost centers into budgeting was a means of aggregating resources across the dual budget but did not take the further step of deepening accountability to the organizational hierarchy within a public body or to officials. The absence of agency appropriation severely weakened the approach to cost centers, as did the absence of formal delegation of authority to an official to incur expenditure.

What the PFM reform merchants to Ethiopia who peddle performance and program budgets fail to grasp is that before officials can be held accountable for outputs (performance) and outcomes (programs), they have to be accountable for inputs, and for that to happen they must know what they are. This is what it means to establish cost centers for the activity they are to manage.

Cost-center budgeting has yet to be widely adopted. Some agencies have done so, many have not, and a few went overboard with this technique. The Ethiopian Agriculture Research Organization introduced over 185 cost centers in the first year of the budget reform, which had to be painstakingly reduced to 48, which significantly delayed the preparation of the entire federal capital budget. I never checked, but perhaps each member of its staff became a cost center. In that agency, clearly a thousand flowers bloomed. There are several reasons why cost centers have not been fully adopted, perhaps the most important of which is the focus of party officials on the capital budget and their neglect of the recurrent budget. The government never embraced the need for a balanced composition of expenditure and continues to pour cement rather than adequately compensate staff. The recurrent budget is an afterthought. A second reason and a broader finding that few PFM reformers take on board is the magnitude, indeed shock, that significant technical changes create in budgeting. Implementing cost centers is not a matter of coding—it is a change of mindset, and this takes time. What is not understood in the PFM literature is the lag time between when a procedural reform is introduced and when it is fully understood and embraced. Put another way, reform has both formal rationality, a new coding system, and substantive rationality, change of mindsets. Beyond the complexity of advance budget techniques pushed by foreign aid, the single most compelling argument for Ethiopia's not adopting them is, again, that the basics are not in place—the inputs are not aggregated.

This concludes part 1 of our discussion of the content of the Phase 2 development of the budget reform. Part 2 presents the process of how the design was collaboratively arrived at with the budget reform team.

The process of designing the budget reform: working with the budget reform team

The initial design work of the budget reform was done by a budget reform team (BRT) consisting of seven officials from the federal finance and planning ministries, MOFED and MEDAC, and me. Neither federal sector ministries nor regional finance officials were included, and although the task force report specified that federal and regional officials should design the reform jointly, it was silent on joint implementation.[34]

Early in the reform, the project convened a meeting of the Ministry of Economic Development and Cooperation (MEDAC) with senior budget staff from the regional equivalent to MEDAC to brief them on the reform. "What are these regional people doing here?" asked Melaku Kifle, head of the capital budget department of MEDAC. The comment is indicative of the compartmentalized character of the Civil Service Reform Program: What's federal is federal, what's regional is regional, and ne'er the twain shall meet.

Collaboration with the regions in the design phase, at the start of the reform, would have had many benefits, including that the federal government would have engaged with regional officials and better understood their constraints. But from the start and throughout the reform, the federal government compartmentalized the reform and never involved the regions with regional design, much less implementation. The consequences of this compartmentalization came home to roost eleven years later, as the DSA project was wrapping up and the time came to turn the reform over to the federal government. The federal government had virtually no understanding of the challenges of regional financial management, which has significantly contributed to the deterioration of performance post-DSA.[35]

The issue of when and how you sweep tiers of government into a PFA/M reform—include them in the process of change—is a crucial question for decentralized countries. The approach of the Ethiopian government was first to design a federal system, implement it, and then hand the federal design to regions to modify as needed. This federal-first approach is simple in terms of logistics—regional staff don't have to trek back and forth—and may seem to save time in the beginning. Nevertheless, I would argue that a more inclusive strategy would have brought greater coherence and certainly sustainability once the DSA project departed.

Fragmentation of the finance function was a fundamental weakness of PFA in Ethiopia, and fragmenting the PFA reform between the federal and regional tiers of government only exacerbated this problem. A major organizational reform that could have been started in the design phase was the establishment of a reform coordinating committee or multiple such committees, made up of federal and regional officials, that could have promoted coherence, not just in reform but also, and far more important, in policy. The DSA project repeatedly sought to establish this coordinating structure and especially pressed that this be a requirement in the 2004 Phase 4 of the project, which was to complete the rollout of the reform countrywide and stand as the conclusion of the project. MOFED refused to establish this organization.

In addition to its lack of connection to the regions, the small federal BRT group had other downsides. It depended on the active participation of government officials who were often called away to operational duties. During budget preparation season, the work of the budget reform team virtually stopped. Working through the BRT easily added a good year to the reform process, which could have been accelerated if more delegation had been made to technical assistance (me). Another downside for me was that it was incredibly frustrating at times, especially when I felt strongly that the team had rejected an important recommendation. But on the whole, most of my recommendations found their way into the design of the reform and the officials curbed complexity.

The value of the budget reform team

Despite the limitations in the composition of the budget reform team, there was much value in the approach. The BRT promoted government "ownership" (meaning participation, buy-in, and commitment) of the reform. The BRT approach to designing the reform was arguably the perfect instrument for a recognize and improve strategy of reform. Ironically, from day one BRT officials made no mention of the findings of the task force report and the need to put in a program budget. The team members understood from the start that the *existing* system of budgeting was the point of departure for instituting reform. From the outset, the budget reform task was obvious. At least initially this reform was not about *change* and especially it was not about change that the foreigner wanted or, worse, demanded. Budget reform in Ethiopia started off down a sensible path.

Much of the BRT's value lay in the fact that the seven Ethiopian officials knew the system better than most; the team was a knowledge bank of the existing system that I could continually tap, giving me a nuanced understanding not only of procedures but, equally important, of how officials interpreted those procedures—the formal and informal system.[36] Throughout our deliberations it was interesting to see how many areas of the budgeting system were not understood by these experienced budget officials. To recognize a financial system is to know a financial system, and the budget reform team gave me a deep understanding of budgeting in Ethiopia.

A second virtue of the BRT was its role as judge and jury about improvements and changes. The Ethiopians on the team passed judgment on what areas needed reform and especially on my recommendations. Unlike what I experienced in Kenya, the Ethiopian team members were not "yes-people" (there was one woman on the team). This is all to the good because ownership means stewardship, being the keeper of the existing system; although the team members differed among themselves on some issues and disagreed with me on a number of others, at the end of the day, it was their system.

The BRT provided a forum for the government and the project to define a working relationship. Decades of civil war meant that Ethiopia had not experienced hordes of technical advisors, although the former government had Russian and Cuban advisors in key ministries, including planning. The new government simply had little or no experience with the proper deployment of technical assistance. The relationship between the government and the project evolved over the life of the DSA project and was characterized at different times by conflict, collaboration, competition, compartmentalization, and cooptation—the five C's.

In the design of the reform, the approach the DSA project adopted to providing technical assistance was to limit "hands on" and be "elbows near," meaning that project staff kept as low a profile as possible and intervened only when asked or when project staff pointed out that an egregious design mistake was being made. During the implementation of the reform, the approach was very much "hands off"—government officials took the lead, except in some critical information system functions. The virtue of a recognize and improve strategy of reform is that the system always remains in the government's hands, so the reforms are more likely to be sustained. A change strategy of reform, in contrast, is more likely to involve more technical assistance in both its design and implementation and thus is likely to be "hands on" on the part of technical assistance, which makes sustaining difficult.

The government-TA relationship varied throughout the reform. The federal reform included all five C's, the most damaging being competition, when the budget reform team on its own initiative started a budget reform in Oromia in 2003 that was a spectacular failure. The Southern Region and Tigray reforms, however, were poster children for collaboration. The Amhara reform proved difficult—the operative dynamic was conflict.

A striking feature of the budget reform team was that it crosswalked the cultures of the finance and planning ministries and not just the techniques that differentiated the recurrent and capital budgets they managed. Public finance management reformers rarely have the interest or take the time to understand the cultural underpinnings of these reforms. The Ministry of Finance, with its conservative outlook and as the keeper of the cash, was often likened to the Orthodox Church, whereas the Ministry of Economic Development and Cooperation, with its visionary and expansive perspective fueled by foreign aid projects whose funding was volatile like rocket fuel, was likened to NASA. Some circles quipped that the merger of the two ministries to form the Ministry of Finance and Economic Development (MOFED) was a hostile takeover by NASA of the Orthodox Church!

Some of the most revealing discussions of the budget reform team occurred when I asked them who had decided to do something a certain way, or where did this come from—not in an accusatory fashion but to establish the source. I could see light bulbs with question marks flash in the faces of the team members at these times. Often the answer was "We don't know—it has always been done this way." This insight was critical, for at a stroke they realized that if procedures were not documented and thus had no authoritative source, it was okay for the team to rethink, document, and indeed become the authoritative source. In effect, team members from a deeply hierarchical and traditional society needed to feel confident and see themselves as agents of change. To move from a system of budgeting that is not documented and that is understood informally to one that is formal and documented is a huge reform. The biggest factor in the reform was not a budgeting technique but rather the value and importance attached by the budget reform team to the need to document and formalize budgeting and their confidence in their ability to do so. In a back office next to the Ministry of Finance kitchen, we were creating budget officials who could throw a rock at tradition.

The team provided a forum for a *gemgema*, the practice of rigorous public self-assessment—it was particularly rare to do this in the presence of a foreigner. The ideal way to do reform is for government officials themselves to point out the deficiencies of their own system and then make recommendations for improvement, for it brings in context. The team took the work very seriously. It was an important process. Being on the budget reform team gave me a means of understanding not only the nuances of the budget procedures, which were not written down, but also of how officials thought about their work and their own role. Getting the basics working is much more than reforming techniques; real reform is about the details of how reform is understood and rethought by the officials who will be using a system.

PFM reformers may be convinced that a traditional budget is backward and must be replaced. They may think that toning up such a budget is not reform because it is not change to something new. PFM reformers rarely, if ever, "sweep users in"—involve them in the reform process. They may offer a perfunctory workshop in which they rely on a PowerPoint presentation to communicate the new system to its future users. Sweeping the user in means making busy government officials part of the process by giving them the time and opportunity to reflect on what they do, why they do it, and whether there is a better way that fits the context. Respecting the views of officials and not preempting them with their own ideas also requires restraint on the part of technical assistance advisors. This process takes time—a lot of time—which is one reason why it rarely happens. Doing reform right takes time.

Moving from an informal system, where little is written down, to a system of formalized procedures requires thinking through and then committing procedures to paper. This process took the budget reform team two years! Foreign donors would have been exasperated by this kind of time line, but fortunately for the Ethiopian budget reform, with the outbreak of war the foreigners had decamped for safer climes. Ironically, the war provided space for the budget reform team to focus on how to make the Ethiopian budget better. To be sure, the BRT was periodically distracted by the day-to-day operations of government, but it was not distracted by alternative designs and foreign aid conditionalities and disbursement schedules. In splendid isolation, sequestered in the dilapidated offices that had housed the general staff of the Italian occupation in the 1930s, the BRT rethought and reformed the budget. As the budget advisor and chief of party of the DSA project, I was very much in attendance and pushed and pulled the team, but in the end, they were the judge and jury and decided thumbs up or thumbs down. It was an Abyssinian reform. The *ferenge* was allowed into the sacred conclave and was listened to, but he did not decide.

The alignment of roles in the development phase

The objective of Phase 2, development, was to promote a dialog between the government official, the user, and the technical assistance advisors, and this is exactly what the BRT accomplished. I have stressed the importance of *recognize* as a strategy of reform, one that has been virtually overlooked in other PFM reforms. Real reform is not about procedures but about understanding the logic or lack of it behind how work is done and what is needed. Recognize means acknowledging and respecting what exists, and also understanding the underlying rationale.

Procedures often exist not for a reason but because some individual just started to do it that way. For example, the head of the accounts department of MOFED created three series of expenditure codes on his own initiative, without consultation or explanation. Yet PFA/M is a transaction system, meaning that it involves a myriad of details that have to work together to manage thousands of actions. Clearly, PFA/M can become unduly complicated very quickly if random decisions are made without rhyme or reason. Getting the basics working means clearing the underbrush of procedures. Achieving coherence requires simplicity that is not simplistic and rationales that are rational. A proverb from Kenya states "It is better to be shown than told." Through the BRT, officials and technical assistance turned a spotlight on the PFA system in Ethiopia and at times put it under a microscope. The officials learned that I was not committed to importing foreign systems, and I learned that the domestic system could be worked with. Above all, the gestation of development built trust.

PHASE 3: PILOT

> Phase 3. Pilot (roles: design, implementation, utilization).
> Implementation enters its second and core stage, the pilot stage, when operation and use of the system begins. The dialogue among designer, implementer, and user is now complete. Adaptation of implementation based on utilization feedback is undertaken, and adaptation of design also continues as before. This phase is the crucial one in the overall realization process. Only here is there mutual learning among all participants.

A budget is visible and time-critical, unlike reforms to accounts and planning. If the budget doesn't arrive on time, it will be noticed. It is almost assumed that government accounts are late and expenditure planning is an esoteric field known by few and certainly not watched by the public. So the budget, no matter how imperfect, has to get a few things right: be completed before the start of the new fiscal year, have numbers that add up, and, hopefully, support policies that also add up.

Learning is the most important aspect of stage 3 of a PFA/M reform, the pilot, for this is when designers, implementers, and users meet. The pilot is the most complex of the five phases precisely because it involves all three actors involved in a reform. It is the defining moment of a reform. The proof of the pudding will be in the eating; the concept of the design comes off the drawing board and is tested in the real world. Budget preparation is a pressured process because of the importance and visibility of the annual budget and its time-critical aspect. It is difficult to learn under stress, and the principal challenge in designing a budget reform pilot is how to limit the level of stress so that government staff can learn. A successful pilot achieves a balance between stress levels and learning. Too much stress inhibits learning, but the crucible of experience promotes learning. Managing the stress of a budget reform pilot is an aspect of risk management.

Risk management involves two questions: Does the pilot replace the existing system or is it run in parallel? How comprehensive is the new pilot system?

Another key issue that budget reformers need to consider is the extent to which technical assistance has to be hands-on during a pilot in order to limit the risk to the ongoing budget process, which must deliver a budget on time. Further, how can technical assistance staff be managed so that the risk created by a pilot is managed by their involvement or joint involvement with government staff? Achieving this balance is not easy and requires getting the mix of people right and focusing on essentials, not bells and whistles. Our approach to achieving this balance was by means of a two-track pilot.

A two-track pilot design

The federal budget reform pilot minimized risk but maximized the management task by running the old budget system, Track 1, in parallel with a comprehensive test of the new system, Track 2, which was the new system set out in Budget Reform Design Manual Version 2.1.[37] The extreme demands on management meant that government staff focused on producing the budget with the old system, which required the staff of the DSA project to step in and exercise extensive hands-on support of the new system. This arrangement limited learning by government staff, which meant that it was not clear whether government staff would be able to fully take over the new budget system the following year. This uncertainty weighed on the project's planning for extending the budget reform to regions the following year: if project staff would have to continue to assist the federal government, then the scope of the rollout to regions would have to be curtailed. Indeed, the partial management of the federal government of the federal pilot was one reason I pressed the government to limit the following year's rollout to regions to only one region (the Southern Region), rather than the four requested by the vice minister of finance.

The learning that took place in the federal budget reform pilot was principally by demonstration, not by doing. Government staff saw firsthand the virtues of the new budget system, even though they only partially managed it.

Track 1: continuing the existing process of budget preparation

Track 1 was the existing budget preparation process. Aggregate appropriation of the two recurrent and capital pools rather than appropriation by agency was the driving force that shaped this pilot. Aggregate appropriation weakens the budget preparation process because public bodies are not required to prepare detailed budgets until the very end of the fiscal year—indeed, some lax bodies fail to do so until well into the fiscal year. Line-item details are not needed until the new fiscal year, for the Treasury Department of the Ministry of Finance would only release funds to public bodies' bank accounts on the basis of line items. To get their cash, the public bodies needed to get their line items sorted out. Sorting out their line items was not essential in the review and approval of an agency's budget for budgeting was about aggregates, not the details of line items. Aggregate appropriation by pool meant that the ceilings of public bodies were very flexible, providing little or no discipline in budget preparation. They could be changed at will.

Under Track 1, budgeting was principally an exchange by the Ministries of Finance and of Economic Development and Cooperation with the Office of the Prime Minister (OPM) over tentative ceilings of the public bodies. The recurrent expenditure requirements of the public bodies were principally salary, thus relatively stable, so the moving target of budgeting was how much the OPM wanted to increase capital expenditure by domestic and foreign resources. Grants from foreign aid were rarely considered in any detail, and most public bodies and even the OPM did not know what to expect from its benefactors. Foreign aid agencies often did not provide credible figures of their support in time to be included in the budget. Foreign aid was not accurately budgeted in the old system, and the budget reform attempted to do this. Budgeting for these gifts from afar was often done by putting a very conservative figure in the capital budget for ongoing projects and a placeholder figure in the capital budget for a new grant.

In summary, Track 1 budgeting focused on recognizing the nondiscretionary recurrent expenditure (statutory payments—interest, pensions; wages), determining the level of the deficit to fit discretionary expenditure (capital), and making it all come in under the resource ceiling by cutting recurrent operating and maintenance expenditures. This approach to budgeting promoted the imbalance in the composition of expenditure. Composition was a casualty of aggregate budgeting, since disciplined costing of activities in the public bodies by the managers of those services was not a focus.

The budget conversation between OPM and the finance and planning ministries was continuous and was done through the preparation of spreadsheets that were continually updated during the budget preparation season. There was no schedule to the preparation of these spreadsheets, and the OPM demanded updates from the Ministry of Finance and the Ministry of Economic Development and Cooperation without notice. These ministries had to drop everything to respond, which meant their not working on Track 2. This ad hoc, chaotic process whipsawed the budget staff of MOF, MEDAC, and the public bodies between Track 1 and Track 2, and since Track 1 was an OPM project and Track 2 was the DSA project, the priority was very clear. Under these conditions continuity in the management and the data processing of Track 2 fell to the staff of the DSA project. Track 1 promoted a lax process of budget preparation, marginalized the public bodies, undermined disciplined budgeting by sector specialists, and relegated MOF and MEDAC budget staff to the status of clerks, preparing and revising spreadsheets for the OPM.

Unfortunately, Track 1 had priority over Track 2, and the latter was not officially sanctioned. The federal budget call, when the MOF and MEDAC notify federal public bodies to present their budgets by a certain date, ignored Track 2 and did not include the new forms and instructions for their completion. This sent a clear message to public bodies that preparation of the FY2001 budget was to be done as in the past, and left the DSA project staff questioning the government's commitment to the reform.

Another bad sign was that once the final spreadsheet of Track 1 was submitted to the OPM, many of the key sector officials in the MOF and the MEDAC took leave—for them, budget preparation was over. Finalizing the budget volumes created under Track 2, which involved the grunt work of correcting spelling errors in both English and Amharic and correcting numerical errors, fell to project staff.

Track 2: the new process of budget preparation

Track 2 was to execute the procedures and processes of Budget Reform Manual Version 2.1 and involved three activities:

1 Procedures: All federal public bodies were to use the new chart of accounts and budget classification and prepare their budgets using the three new budget forms. Completion of the budget forms would be done according to a clear budget calendar.
2 Financial information systems: the DSA project was to complete the development of the budget information system (BIS) which MOF and MEDAC would use to process the new budget forms and prepare the troika of budgets—requested, recommended, and approved—as well as the budget notifications to the public body. The project would also modify the government's budget disbursement accounts information system to manage the new budget formats.
3 Public-body data processing: The BIS would be installed in four federal public bodies (Ethiopian Roads Authority, Ethiopian Agriculture Research Organization, Ministry of Health, and the Ministry of Water Resources) to enter the data from the three budget forms for digital submission to MOF and MEDAC.

Track 2 posed a significant management challenge to MOF and MOFED, for they would be responsible for doing the data processing related to detailed budget submissions of public bodies. Data processing was to be done by the respective sector departments of MOF and MEDAC—a task they had never done before. The management task was a challenge because these offices would have to cope with the old and the new simultaneously: hobbled by the old laissez-faire budget process, where public bodies routinely submitted budgets late and ignored the demands of MOF and MEDAC, which wreaked havoc on the need to systematically process the data of the new system.

The scope of the Track 2 pilot that was implemented was very different from its initial design. The original design was to be partial, and only a test on paper, but what was eventually done was comprehensive and computerized. The initial design was set by the Ministry of Finance in July 1999 and was to be a partial pilot to test the new procedures and the modification of the budget disbursement accounts. The initial design of the pilot was partial because the government was at war and did not want to subject budgeting to undue risk. Track 1 was the preparation and submission of the budget using the old chart of accounts and budget classification and Track 2 would test the new procedures and the modified budget disbursement accounts in five ministries (the Ministries of Finance; Health; Education; Economic Development and Cooperation; and the Ethiopian Roads Authority), whose budgets would, however, be produced using the old procedures. (The initial design of the pilot did not include the budget information system, whose development was begun in July 1999.)

Executing the pilot during a two-front war

As the DSA project was moving from design to implementation in its first reform, the budget reform at the federal level, it was dealing with two conflicts. In addition to Ethiopia's war with Eritrea, the DSA project faced a conflict on another front: its head office at Harvard University, the Harvard Institute for International Development (HIID), was closed as a result of a scandal of its financial reform project in Russia.[38]

There was no way to assess the collateral effects of Harvard's fraudulent management of a USAID contract in Russia on the renewal of a Harvard contract in Ethiopia. The USAID mission director in Ethiopia and the chief technical officer of the mission overseeing the DSA project were extremely displeased with what happened in Russia. There was enormous uncertainty. First, Phase 2 of the DSA contract was to end on December 31, 2000, which meant that halfway through the year leading up to the start of the new budget system and deep into the critical time for its preparation, the contract would expire. Would USAID begin a review of all Harvard contracts and if so, would that delay the extension of the contract and thus scrap the preparations of the budget reform? Second, the Kennedy School at Harvard University would decide which HIID staff would be retained—would it retain me? A third uncertainty was the Kennedy School itself. Even if I was retained and the project continued, what, if any, support would they offer?

The Kennedy School did not exactly put out the welcome mat, but in the end, they retained the DSA project. Through it the school earned $9 million in unrestricted overhead. For several years this cash infusion from one of the poorest countries in the world made the difference in the Kennedy School's running a surplus, not a deficit.

With the cessation of hostilities with Eritrea in June 2000, the Ministry of Finance and the DSA project revisited the design of the federal pilot and it was agreed to change it from selective to comprehensive; it would not be a paper exercise—it would be a full operational test of the new budget system, including the new forms and the new BIS.

Delivering the Track 2 pilot

Executing the federal pilot proved to be very difficult, but in the end it was a success.[39] The three activities of Track 2 listed earlier were completed, and the budget was completed prior to the start of FY2001. The MOF and MEDAC used the budget information system to consolidate the data into two budget books, which were submitted to the Council of Ministers and Parliament well ahead of their review, which had never before happened. When the DSA project started in 1997, the budget was submitted to Parliament the day before it was voted on. The new budget books presented the budget in a far more transparent and detailed manner than previous budgets: volume 1, the summary, was eighty-one pages long and had twenty-two tables; volume 2, the details by public body by line item of expenditure, was 460 pages.[40]

There were two final outputs of Track 2, a two-volume budget book and the detailed notification forms to public bodies by their sub-agencies and projects, which was their official access to cash from the Treasury Department of the Ministry of Finance. But after the last mouse-click of the BIS, the Track 2 output still needed a lot of work. One of the key features of the Track 2 pilot was that the outputs, the budget volumes, would be produced in the Amharic language (later to be expanded to three other Ethiopian languages—Oromiffa, Somali, and Tigrigna). Doing so required intense effort, and vindicated the use of a custom financial information system tailored to Ethiopia's multilingual requirements.

The difficulties faced in assembling the requested budget receded in the eyes of many budget officials as they saw the quality of the output that they could generate from the BIS. The final output of the budget reform, budget notification forms, won over budget officials in the MOF and MEDAC. These forms list the details of a public body's budget by line item and were the means by which the Treasury Department of MOF would transfer funds to the bank accounts of public bodies, so in effect they execute the budget. Preparing the forms traditionally was an onerous task because of the mind-numbing detail, which had to be accurate because they released cash, and also because the task came after the long and arduous budget preparation process—two to three weeks of around-the-clock labor. Now, the BIS churned out 6,000 pages of the capital budget forms in two days and 3,000 pages of the recurrent budget in one week.

Lessons learned from the pilot phase

A pilot program introduces risk into the most high-profile and time-critical task in PFA/M, making the budget. The federal budget reform pilot successfully tested the system and its units. The two-track approach successfully managed the risk. The two tracks made the preparation of the FY2001 budget a management migraine, but risk was virtually eliminated because Track 1 had priority and could have produced a budget if Track 2 had failed.

The pilot provides several lessons for budget reformers.

First, identify and focus on eliminating the key sources of delay; less central issues can be put on the back burner. In this case they were the budget structure and the inflexibility of the financial information system in rolling over the budget stages.

Second, identify what can be dropped for the first year and be picked up in subsequent years. An example in our case was finalizing the commitment codes of foreign aid down to the level of line item and by the sub-agency and project. It was an enormous undertaking that meant, first, knowing the totals by public body and then breaking them down to the item-of-expenditure level. Going from no presentation of the sources of finance in the budget to a granular presentation was a serious leap and should have been done in the following year. Form 2, the basis of expanding the performance and program role of the budget, could have been dealt with in subsequent years. It was effectively dropped by the public bodies themselves, though it was used for half of the capital budget submissions.

A striking achievement of the pilot was that the BIS was flexible enough to be adapted rapidly to meet the challenges that emerged, such as the production of the budget volumes and working with the intricate issues of Amharic fonts.

Conventional wisdom—indeed almost a commandment—in the PFM field is the superiority of commercial off-the-shelf (COTS) software solutions over custom systems for automating finance. The Ethiopian budget pilot provides contrary evidence and demonstrates the value of a flexible financial information system. It can be modified rapidly to meet user needs in a user-friendly way—a crucial asset in limiting the risk of a pilot. Furthermore, one can never plan for all of the contingencies of a reform, and flexibility to adjust the design in real time is essential. Finally, to comprehensively test a system you have to fully test its functionality when it comes to delivering important details such as successful operation in multiple languages. A rigid off-the-shelf system is not flexible enough to do this. There is little doubt in my mind that such a system would have failed in the federal pilot and in all likelihood would have caused the pilot to fail.

The pilot also provides some "soft," human lessons in addition to the "hard" or system issues. A key metric of the success of a reform is whether it promotes the professionalism of staff. Track 2 did this, for the BIS took the donkey work off officials' backs. The pilot succeeded because the efficiency and quality of the recommended and approved budgets and the notification forms more than compensated for the struggle involved in using the new system to assemble a requested budget. The two-track approach ensured that a budget would be done, but this also meant that government staff did not see the need to work hard on Track 2. Some may have reckoned that the output of Track 2 would not be the actual submission. The quality of the output was a big and positive surprise that convinced many officials of the value of the reform—it might even elevate their own status and profile! They now had a tool that the Office of the Prime Minister did not have; they were no longer just cogs in the wheel, just clerks filling in spreadsheets for the OPM. Now they actually were budgeting.

The issue of alignment in a pilot goes to the heart of what a pilot is—how close it is to the real operation, how hands-on are government staff versus technical assistance, and who manages? Pilots are the most complicated phase of a reform, for during the pilot all three roles—architect, builder, user—come together and the purpose of this phase is learning. To what extent did the reform promote the alignment of roles? The most important learning is government's learning to manage the new system. In this pilot, learning by federal staff was limited, for the project managed Track 2. Alignment was never going to be close or perfect in this situation. Risk was successfully managed and a budget, a much better budget, was delivered. And government staff did learn enough to free up project staff to roll out the reform to regions the following year.

PHASE 4: ROLLOUT

> Phase 4. Rollout (roles: implementation, utilization).
> Implementation begins its third and final stage with the near cessation of design activity. This phase includes only adaptation of implementation. Dialogue takes place principally between the implementer and the client.

Officials in one corner of the Amhara region called their wereda "Leave My Salary at the Road." The road in question was many miles away, whence a path over arduous terrain led to Leave My Salary. Their wereda had no power grid, no land-line phone connection (mobile phones lay in the future). In the Southern Region, it took some participants in one of the in-service training programs held for the rollout of the budget reform five days to reach the training venue in Awassa. They traveled for two days on horseback because the rains made the roads impassable for vehicle traffic. Rolling out the reform to regions, zones, and weredas was a very different kettle of fish than the rollout in the federal government, which involved only a few miles of distance on paved roads, with telephone and electricity connections at hand.

Given such basic communications difficulties, how could the budget and wider-ranging PFA reforms best be rolled out to the regions?

Location and scope of the rollout

The decision as to where to roll out the reforms involved issues of both quantity and quality, quantity referring to the size and importance of the region and quality referring to the quality of infrastructure and, indirectly, quality of staff to do the rollout. The decision also involved issues of scope: How much could we expect to accomplish with this first rollout?

Vice Minister of Finance Hailemelekot proposed that the DSA project implement the budget reform for the fiscal year 2002 (July 8, 2002, to July 7, 2003), the year after the federal budget reform, in all of the big four regions—Amhara, Oromia, the Southern Region, and Tigray—to accelerate the reform. I countered with two, the Southern Region and Amhara. We settled on one. Amhara withdrew from the process, saying that it was not ready. So the first pilot to the regions would be in one region, the Southern Region, and would be one task, budgeting.

The eventual reform timetable was the Southern Region (FY2002), Amhara (FY2003), Tigray (FY2003), and Oromia (FY2004).[41] The option of starting the rollout of the reform to one or more of the five smaller regions (Afar, Benishangul Gumuz, Gambella, Harari, Somali) or the administrative areas (Addis Ababa, Dire Dawa) was never considered because they did not have the capacity to absorb such a massive reform. They accounted for less than 5 percent of total public expenditure, so their reform would follow after the other regions were reformed.

Second-stage decentralization and the scope of the rollout

The tsunami of second-stage decentralization hit unexpectedly. In January 2002, six months into the preparations of the regional rollout in the Southern Region for the new budget system, the federal government announced the policy of second-stage decentralization (SSD), which initially was to apply only to the four biggest regions. Suddenly, the scope of the rollout exploded, for now the bulk of regional resources were to be managed at the wereda level. To say that the goalposts of the PFA reform had changed is an understatement. The task of reforming the big four increased seven to seventeen times, depending on the region and the number of weredas in the region, because the number of budget institutions (BIs) multiplied as decentralization progressed. A BI is a government entity that receives and accounts for a budget and the BIs were the locus for carrying out the reform.[42] With SSD the number of BIs to be reformed in the Southern Region increased by 950 percent, going from 288 to 3,024 (see "BIs after SSD" in table 4.4).

Second-stage decentralization and qualitative constraints

In addition to the quantitative change, placing financial management at wereda levels posed a serious qualitative challenge. Isolation and poor physical infrastructure made these unappealing posts for finance staff who had relatively valuable skills and would seek to leave these posts if given a chance. Early assessments of the SSD found that officials posted to weredas complained of the lack of educational facilities for their children and employment opportunities for their spouses and relatives. Hardship allowances were provided for the most remote locations, but they were meager and did not compensate for the harsh conditions.

To our surprise, when we examined the performance of the financial system in 2011, we found that remoteness was not correlated with poor financial performance.[43] Quality of management was what differentiated the performance of financial management of weredas and was a key factor in determining the success of the regional rollouts to the big four between 2002 and 2004.

Reforming PFA in a country as decentralized as Ethiopia is much more difficult than reforming a centralized country. And reforming PFA while decentralizing is

Table 4.4 Conditions in Amhara, Oromia, the Southern Region, and Tigray, by year of budget reform

Driver of PFM (COPS)	Region and year of reform			
	Southern Region, 2002	Tigray, 2003	Amhara, 2003	Oromia, 2004
CONTEXT				
Population	13.53 million	3.95 million	16.18 million	25.21 million
Cultural profile	Diverse	Homogeneous	Homogeneous	Diverse
Administrative				
1 *Institutions*—Financial law in place	Yes	Yes	Yes	Yes
2 *Organization*—Number	Many, complex	Few, stable	Many, stable	Many, changing[a]
Bureaus; BIs	24; 24	23; 23	34; 34	28; 28
Zones; BIs	11; 264	0; 0	17; 578	17; 476
Weredas; BIs	114; 2,736	48; 1,104	123; 4,182	295; 5,900
BIs before SSD	288	69	612	504
BIs after SSD	3,024	1,127	4,794	6,404
Increase in BIs after SSD (%)	950	1,533	683	1,245
3 *Management*—Leadership quality	Exceptional	Good	Very weak	Adequate to good
Style	Inspirational	Discipline	Blaming	Administrative
Continuity	Yes	Yes	Revolving	Revolving, then stable
BOFED staff	Exceptional	Good	Uneven	Uneven but improved
4 *Bureaucratic culture*	Performance	Performance	Inertia	Mixed performance-inertia
5 *Staffing*—Level of establishment	Adequate	Adequate	Mixed	Adequate
Recruitment	Outstanding	Good	Failure	Outstanding
Training	Outstanding	Excellent	Failure	Outstanding
Training materials	Yes	Yes	Inappropriate	Yes
RMIs	Yes	Yes	Poor	Yes
Delivery	Yes	Yes	Poor	Yes
6 *Procedures*—Adaptation (COA-BC, forms, procedure manuals, IT)	Outstanding	Excellent	Poor	Outstanding
Innovation (single pool, transfer formula)	Outstanding	Excellent	None	Excellent
Delivery (logistics, support)	Outstanding	Excellent	Failure	Outstanding (wereda support units)

Source: author.

Notes

a Prior to the budget reform, Oromia significantly reduced the number of BIs at zone and weredas to 20.
BI = Budget Institution; SSD = Second-Stage Decentralization; COA = Chart of Accounts; BC = Budget Classification; BOFED = Bureau of Financial and Economic Development; RMI = regional management institute.

much more difficult than reforming a country where decentralization is well established. The reform of PFA in the big four was done on the fly, as officials and DSA staff scrambled to develop the wereda budget classifications for the Southern Region in the morning and incorporate them in the afternoon into a budget classification by the finance bureau. This high-wire act was exhilarating, but scary, for it posed enormous risk to the reform. Managing the scope of a project is key to its success, and with SSD, the scope exploded.

Limiting the first-year rollout of reform to one region and one task, budgeting, drastically limited the scope and thus the risk to the reform. If the Amhara region had also been done in the first year, along with the Southern Region reform, the planned task would have been to reform 900 BIs—but after SSD it would have ballooned to 7,818, an eight-fold increase in scope. As it was, to do the Southern Region only meant going from 288 to 3,024 BIs. It was a stroke of luck that the first year of the rollout of the reform to regions was confined to one region.

The DSA planning consultant, Perran Penrose, repeatedly stated how Ethiopia was not fiscally decentralized because it did not meet the textbook definition of decentralization, which is revenue assignment to all the tiers. But there clearly was decentralization of financial administration in terms of the autonomy of weredas, which could "burn the money if they wanted," as one official said. There was extensive de jure and de facto decentralization and it happened literally overnight.

PFA reform in Ethiopia meant not the reform of one government but of twelve: one federal, nine regional, and two administrative areas. In many ways, the regions represented a laboratory of contexts: fragile state—Somali; urban center—Addis Ababa; extreme remoteness—Gambella; polyglot—Southern Region; pastoralist—Afar; state in conflict—Somali. Ethiopia is diversity and decentralization.

The Southern Region: a good choice for the first rollout

The Southern Nations, Nationalities and Peoples Region (the Southern Region, for short) is the third largest in Ethiopia. The most diverse region in Ethiopia, it comprises fifty-four ethnic groups in five regional groupings. One of the most important and best decisions I made in the twelve years I managed the DSA project was the decision to make the Southern Region the first site of the rollout of the reform beyond the federal government. The decision was left to me, and I based it on a combination of objective criteria and intuition. Clear decision criteria are important for justifying a reform project's decision to allocate resources to a pilot, and my two objective criteria were that the region had to have cleared the backlog of accounts (four years' worth, on average) and had to have successfully implemented the project's training strategy. These achievements indicated a willingness of a region to work with our project and approach reform systematically.

My decision was also based on a hunch and my sensing a mutual comfort level with senior regional staff, especially Getachew Hamussa, the head of the bureau of finance. The Amhara region's acknowledgment that they were not prepared to do the reform that year meant that the pilot would be done in just one region, which allowed the project to concentrate its resources and better manage the unknown. As it turned out, the two criteria were linked. The Southern Region was able to bring accounts up to date because the project's training had significantly improved the skills and motivation of accounts staff, especially in the region's zones, where the backlog was greatest.[44] A critical unforeseen benefit of this training program was that it included thousands of bookkeepers from zones and weredas the year *before* the government's rapid second-stage decentralization to weredas. The availability of ample numbers of freshly trained finance staff in weredas and zones greatly facilitated the simultaneous reform of decentralization to weredas and the budgeting and accounts reforms. More good luck.

The selection of the Southern Region was politically astute, although I did not take that into consideration, as we offered a pilot to the Amhara region as well. The Southern Region, with its mélange of fifty-four ethnic groups, made political sense because it was the most politically neutral among of the big four states (the political and bureaucratic elites have traditionally come from Amhara; the Tigrayans were currently the dominant political elite; Oromia, with its 40 percent of the Ethiopian population, raised a concern that it would wield too much influence). Reforming the Southern Region first did not have the political undertones of the other large regions. The Southern Region also made sense because it was large, which meant the results there would have impact and would also provide lessons for the other large regions.

The capital of the Southern Region, Awassa, was the reform's "home," where the reform took deepest root and reached its zenith. A failure in Awassa would have had a chilling effect on the reform and most likely would have delayed it for several years or even ended it and possibly the DSA project, too. Fortunately, Awassa was the rock of the reform, maintaining a high standard and becoming a model for all other subnational governments and the central government, not just of how to do it but also of the fact that it could be done and done very well by regions with no help from the federal government. It was definitive proof of concept.

Analysis of the PFA reform rollout across the big four in terms of the COPS drivers

The four large Ethiopian regions—Oromia (the largest), Amhara (second largest), Southern Region (third largest), and Tigray—provided a budget reform laboratory. The Southern Region learned from its success; Amhara learned from its failure and redeemed itself the following year; Tigray and Oromia learned that tenacity can overcome the odds. The pathways of these regional reforms can be analyzed by means of the four COPS drivers of reform: context, ownership, purpose, and strategy (see table 4.4). Space constraints allow me to cover just the highlights of the four regional reforms and only a brief discussion of the rollout to the other five regions and two administrative areas.

Context: administration

The success and failure encountered in the rollout of the budget reform to regions can be understood in terms of four elements of the administrative context: leadership, culture, staffing, and procedures.

Leadership and culture

The regional budget reforms proved that "getting the right people in the right seats on the bus and the wrong people off the bus and the bus will steer itself" is the deciding factor in the success of a reform. Reform is about people, not sequencing techniques. A successful reform requires patience and extremely hard work on the part of a critical mass of government officials. Technical assistance can assist only up to a point. The key unknowns are the critical mass of talent and the overtime required. How much talent and what kind of talent is enough? Assembling a critical mass of government talent is the "tipping point" for a reform.[45]

The Southern Region reform worked well because of exceptional leadership and strong senior staff. Getachew Hamussa, the head of the region's bureau of finance, was a true champion of change and brought to the task a formidable mix of innate intelligence, political savvy, connections at the highest level, a no-nonsense leadership style, and impressive oratory skills. He assembled a very competent and dedicated group at the bureau and in key finance offices throughout the region, providing the project with the necessary depth. His staff revered him and stayed on the job. Reform may start with the top, but the trenches determine its fate. The staff's commitment and continuity at all levels of the bureau ensured that it would work. Hamussa and his lieutenants and their staff worked tirelessly on the reform.[46]

I'd like to introduce a few individuals whose efforts stood out. Tesfaye WoldeMichael, the deputy bureau head and a key lieutenant of Hamussa's, from the beginning understood and strongly supported the reform. He and Hamussa were working on master's degrees in public administration from the University of London, via distance learning. Sahele Haile, a quiet, poker-faced expert in the government accounting system who had gained his expertise in the school of hard knocks, grasped the nuts and bolts of the accounts reform. No nuance escaped him. His depth of understanding saved the project from making numerous errors and ensured that the budget and accounts reforms were tailored to the requirements of the region and thus were relevant and successful. Belaynesh, Negat, and Tadele, who staffed the back office, where budgeting was done in the Southern Region bureau, quickly learned the new budget procedures and information system. The continuity and immense capacity of this Spanish-speaking back office—nicknamed "Fidel's orphans" because they had spent their childhood in Cuba—meant that the budget reform was done efficiently and accurately and that it stuck.[47] Shumye, who worked tirelessly with the project advisors on the budget system and raised more questions than time and patience often allowed, was an admirable detective. He left no stone unturned.

One of the most colorful staff members was Kedru Abza, whose boundless energy and enthusiasm, large frame, wide grin, ready laugh, and charm banned inertia from the bureau. He had fingers in all the key reform pies—accounting, disbursement, information systems—and you could get a thorough briefing quickly from him, for he spoke his mind. With Kedru you had someone at the switch who was very capable and understood the whole of the reform, not just the parts. Kedru performed a critical role of intimidating foreign aid consultants who wandered into the compound, and took special delight in recounting the manifold deficiencies of Ministry of Finance personnel. Kedru was an advocate of the reform and he spread the good word throughout the region.

One finds striking differences in the leadership of the big four as they undertook reform. Tigray's leader of the bureau of finance and economic development was good but lacked confidence, for finance was a new activity for him. Whereas Hamussa's leadership style was inspirational, the Tigrayan's was one of iron discipline. Fortunately for the reform, there was continuity in the leadership in both the Southern Region and Tigray.

Amhara, in stark contrast to the Southern Region and Tigray, suffered from a revolving door of weak leaders and a leadership style of blaming others rather than accepting responsibility. The biggest problem was the failure of the bureau of finance's leadership to take responsibility for the reform. What leadership there was in the first year of the reform in Amhara was locked in a test of wills between the technocrats and the politicians. Unfortunately, the latter won out with disastrous consequences for the first year of reform in the region. An official at the highest political level of the region decided—against the project's advice—to proceed with the budget and accounts reform simultaneously. His reasoning was political—the region could not fall behind the Southern Region and Tigray. I traveled to Amhara several times to warn them of the consequences of undertaking too much. They refused to listen.

In Oromia, the largest region, the leadership initially was unstable, but it stabilized and stood up to similar political demands as those faced by finance officials in Amhara, despite the additional political demand that it catch up to the three other big regions. Memories of the previous year's failed federal-led budget reform and also of Amhara's unsuccessful attempt to do the budget and accounts reforms together were still fresh. In Oromia, dealing with nearly two and half times the number of weredas that Amhara had failed to reform, prudence prevailed. The politicians backed down and the financial technicians were left to make it happen. The effort was weakened by the uneven quality and turnover of the heads of the budget department, but this was more than compensated by the head of the accounts department, Thomas Daga, who was then and is to this day an exemplary professional and provided wise counsel in the preparations of the Oromia reform.

Oromia started its reform two years after the Southern Region. It faced a very tough strategic question: Given its huge scale, how could the task be made manageable? One option was to do a two-step reform with one half of the region reformed in the first year and the second half in the second year. This would dramatically reduce the logistical challenge of the reform, yet it would dramatic-ally increase its complexity, for the region would be running two financial systems simultaneously. The question of whether it would be possible to do such a large reform concerned the project: we were in the process of introducing the budget reform in two other regions, Benishangul Gumuz and Harari, and one administrative area, Dire Dawa, and also assisting Amhara in restarting its reform, so we were already stretched across four governments. This made sim-plifying the logistics of Oromia very appealing to the project. There was no simple answer as to how to reform Oromia—it was a monumental task. Through-out the discussions with officials of Oromia's bureau of finance, I bore in mind the former vice minister of finance's observation, "If you change Oromia you change Ethiopia." The obverse was also on the line: Could you change Ethiopia without changing its largest region? If we failed there, was the whole reform project a failure? Oromia posed enormous risk to the reform.

The sheer challenge we faced forged a very close relationship between senior bureau officials and project staff. When project staff and I arrived for a meeting in the finance bureau's office in Addis Ababa, Thomas Daga announced, "The third government is here"—we were viewed as partners in the effort, not for-eigners imposing something. The project had enjoyed a very collaborative rela-tionship with the Southern Region finance bureau, but it was a different relationship because the risk was far smaller. In Oromia, failure was a real possibility.

Leadership and an organization's legacy define bureaucratic culture. The strong leadership in the Southern Region and Tigray created a culture of per-formance not only in the finance bureau in the regional capital but also in finance offices across the region. Given the much greater depth of experience and exper-tise of officials in Amhara, it was surprising that weak leadership in the region led to inertia without accountability. There were many capable officials of Amhara, but political cadres undercut their contributions. In Oromia, the culture was a combination of inertia and performance; it improved over time and resulted in tangible achievements in the reform.

For the three regions with able if not exceptional leadership and good admin-istration in depth—the Southern Region, Oromia, and Tigray—the two other ingredients of the reform, staffing and procedures, fell into place. In Amhara, which lacked leadership and management, getting the procedures and staff in place was a struggle.

Staffing and training

The Southern Region, Tigray, and Oromia effectively put adequate numbers of adequately trained staff in place (see "Staffing," in table 4.4). In a country with severe unemployment and a strong cultural bias of hiring locals, the Southern Region's Hamussa bucked convention and sought out the best in the land, advertising nationally for personnel to fill finance positions ahead of his region's reform. The Southern Region even accepted Amhara officials with finance experience. Hamussa's catholic approach to recruitment and promotion gave the Southern Region good depth in staff and, when coupled with the Southern Region's well-functioning in-service training, substantially mitigated the risk that staffing posed to the reform.

Oromia was also outstanding in staffing, recruiting, training, and assigning over four hundred new officials in wereda finance offices. Though taking an orthodox approach—hiring only Oromos—it rigorously screened these new staff. As one would expect from the region that was the font of the revolution, Tigray recruited and trained adequate staff—all Tigrayan.

Amhara failed miserably in recruitment. This is particularly ironic because the region had the deepest pool of experienced administrators of any region. Because Amhara was simultaneously implementing the budget and accounts reforms, it had to recruit and train manpower for both tasks. At the last minute and in desperation, the BOFED decided to train several hundred students in accounting who were already enrolled in vocational training. Unfortunately, accounting was not the vocation of most of these students, and they simply could not grasp the materials. The training had to be suspended after a few days.

Training was the rock on which this reform was built and it is the reason that the PFA system continues to function, even after years of neglect and little or no resources devoted to ongoing training. Training materials were central to train- ing. Over 85 percent of the DSA project's resources of $35 million were devoted to the development of training materials and funding the training of nearly 72,000 officials. One commandment of this reform enforced by the project and heartily endorsed by the regions was that training was to be done in the local language. The procedural manuals and the training modules that were derived from the manuals and the financial information system were produced in four of the country's languages (Amharic, Oromiffa, Somali, and Tigrigna) and English.

The efforts of the Oromia BOFED to translate the English version into the Oromiffa language were heroic. There had never been an accounting manual in the Oromiffa language, and many English words, such as "debit," had no equi- valent in Oromiffa. The translation took nearly two years.

In vast Oromia—virtually a country within a country—BOFED leadership and the DSA project erred significantly on the liberal side when it came to determining the number of staff needed, and over eight thousand were trained. Not only finance officials but also guards, drivers, and secretaries were trained in budgeting and accounting. Having a deep bench proved useful, given the remoteness of many of the weredas and also the seemingly inexorable increase in their numbers as decen- tralization progressed. The virtue of such wide coverage was demonstrated a year after the reform in Oromia when one of the DSA advisors providing post-reform support found that a guard was doing the accounting in one wereda.

Procedures

The rollout phase was of course strongly influenced by the experience of the pilot phase. The hard slog of doing a comprehensive pilot at the federal level meant that the technical package had been tested, improved, and, most important, shown to work. The technical package consisted of procedure manuals with the chart of accounts and the budget classification at their core, the budget forms, and the financial information system. Two of the four necessary though not sufficient conditions of project success, *need* and *help*, were secured by the successful federal reform. *Urgency* would come shortly in the form of the demand on regions to implement second-stage decentralization. *Trust* in the DSA project and the reform would be earned through successful rollouts.

The rollout of the budget reform required that regions adapt the procedures to their context (a reform strategy of recognize-improve), and, with second-stage decentralization, innovate by introducing the single finance pool in weredas and zones to simplify financial administration. The single finance pool brought the administration of budgets, accounts, and disbursements under one roof at zones and weredas in their respective finance departments and offices, much as a typing pool concentrates all typing tasks in one area. The pool was needed because of the exponential increase in the number of BIs created by SSD. The value of the pool was felt most in the accounting and disbursement functions, as these were continuous throughout the financial year, whereas budgeting was not a continuous and transaction-intensive process (the single finance pool is discussed in more detail in chapter 5).

Three regions—Oromia, the Southern Region, and Tigray—succeeded in both adapting and innovating, while Amhara failed. The Amhara BOFED "lifted" by stealth the procedure and training manuals developed in the Southern Region and attempted to use them in Amhara. The Amharas failed to adapt the procedural manuals and the training modules to their region but instead claimed that they had properly translated the English versions of these materials into Amharic. The failure of the reform in Amhara was in part due to the use of procedures not fit for context. Context counts, even within one country.

The three successful regions achieved some exemplary results in three parts of the technical package. In the Southern Region, the budget information system and the budget disbursement accounting system, which together formed the financial information system, were rapidly upgraded just prior to the arrival of the budget submissions. The Southern Region faced a crisis with the BIS. Two weeks before the budget forms were to arrive in the BOFED in Awassa, the project's computer consultant threw the computer manual at me—literally—as he stormed out of my office and quit. The strain of the federal reform had burned him out. He was also not proficient in the development of a distributed information system—software that can run on multiple computers using a local area network (LAN). A distributed system was urgently needed in light of the second-stage decentralization and the fact that forms from more than 3,000 BIs were about to arrive and require processing in the Southern Region bureau of finance. In the federal reform the BIS had to manage only 352 budget institutions. Stepping into the breach and turning the situation around was the local firm of Omnitech, which did a yeoman's job of processing the 3,000 forms at short notice. An enormous snafu was averted. (The FIS reform is discussed in more detail in chapter 6.)

Tigray did the near impossible: simultaneous implementation of the budget and accounts reform. Its smaller size—only forty-eight weredas—facilitated innovation. Its exemplary action was rapid introduction of the finance pool, an unexpected bonus in the second year of the reform that led the way for the much larger regions to adopt it for their reforms.

Oromia delivered exemplary results in adapting the budget classification by drastically reducing the number of BIs in its weredas. Where the Southern Region had twenty-nine BIs per wereda and Amhara had thirty-four, Oromia slashed the number to twenty per wereda in its 295 weredas.

The DSA project's footprints were of course all over the adaptation and innovation of the technical package. The project delivered the upgraded FIS, it developed the single finance pool during the first year of the budget reform in the Southern Region, and it worked with the Oromia BOFED in simplifying the finance structure at the wereda level. The project made two other significant contributions to the success of the budget reform: the wereda support unit and superlative logistics. The DSA project introduced the concept of the wereda support unit (WSU)—a team of officials located at the zone and region level who continuously traveled to weredas to provide on-site technical support, mentoring, and training—during the Southern Region budget reform. Although it never took root in that region, Tigray, or Amhara, it did prove crucial to Oromia's success not only in introducing the budget and then accounts reform but also in embedding them. Working with the weaker weredas, the WSUs were particularly important in helping get newcomers on their feet. The Oromia finance bureau never wavered in its wholehearted support for the WSUs, and the project provided continuous resources for this activity. We assigned as lead project advisor one of our very best people, Abaya Terfasa, an Oromo whose experience and the respect he commanded in the region were crucial to the reform's success.

Often overlooked because delivered so seamlessly were the time-critical logistical actions of delivering the funding to remote sites and ensuring that the tons of forms and manuals found their way into the right hands at the right time—in short, "the hard, secretarial grind of running the show."[48] The logistics of this reform were massive, and managing the reform of twelve governments spread across a vast country required a manager of the first order. The DSA project and the country's PFA reform had such a manager in Sarah Guebreyes, who oversaw the logistical work of the project. USAID scrutinized the DSA books frequently; in 2010 (two years after the end of the project), USAID conducted an unprecedented audit of more than two thousand transactions of the DSA project.[49] Throughout its twelve-year history, involving the management of $34.4 million from four governments, the DSA project maintained scrupulous finances.[50]

David Leonard has pointed out, in defining the term "management" in the development field, that even though the top stuff—policymaking, organizational leadership, internal administration—usually gets the most attention, projects succeed or stumble according to their "bureaucratic hygiene," the cleanliness of their finances.[51] Guebreyes's deft management not only kept the PFA reform on track in Ethiopia, it also kept the Harvard Kennedy School's financial position in the black.

Ownership

All four regions retained ownership in their own hands and excluded foreign aid agencies. All four regions did the reform without the federal government. Oromia had learned the importance of leading its own reform the hard way: from the failure the previous year of the federal-led reform. A major difference between the three successful regions and Amhara was the latter's conflict with the DSA project. The other three welcomed close collaboration with the DSA project and viewed us as an indispensable partner.

Purpose

Two purposes drove the PFA reform: the nationwide mandate to implement the civil service reform program and competition. Incentives are crucial in reform, for reforms offer officials a rare chance to be seen, have impact, and be promoted. Decentralization makes possible competition within and between more levels of government and creates incentives. The Southern Region was extremely proud to be the pioneer and show that they could do it, and without federal help. In Tigray they did the budget and accounts reform together so as to catch up with the Southern Region in the second year of the rollout—it "almost broke our backs" said Mekonnen Abraha, head of the Tigray BOFED, but they did it. Competition had a negative effect in Amhara: the region's attempt to catch up with the Southern Region caused it to do too much too soon—the budget and accounts reform together—which backfired. Oromia's politicians also pressed for a catch-up strategy but then backed down. The challenge of reformers under decentralization is how to harness the competitive dynamic to promptly deliver reform while maintaining coherence of PFA along the way and, above all, mitigating unnecessary risk and avoiding failure. The case of Amhara is sobering and instructive.

Strategy

Oromia's, Tigray's, and the Southern Region's budget reform *strategies* were basically a mix of recognize and improve, though they incorporated some change. They recognized the technical package from the federal reform and improved it to their context. They recognized their capacity and responded appropriately in terms of training and post-implementation support. Again, Amhara was the outlier, for it failed to recognize the need to adapt the technical package to its context and failed to recognize the human resources necessary for the reform. Arrogance trumped humility. The three successful big regions adopted change only where needed—the introduction of the single finance pool in weredas and zones—and even then they were cautious.

PFA reform outside the big four

A full account of the PFA reforms in the other regions and administrative areas could easily fill another book. The reform was implemented in the states of Harari, Afar, Gambella, and Somali; in two administrative areas, Addis Ababa and Dire Dawa; and in another remote region, Benishangul Gumuz. Benishangul Gumuz was the first of the regions beyond the big four to clear its accounts backlog, with the able assistance of Elias Ergicho, a DSA project advisor, and this allowed the region to start its budget reform in FY2004 along with Oromia. Addis Ababa and Dire Dawa, desirable urban areas, were able to implement their reforms smoothly for they had access to skilled manpower, although urban employment opportunities also had the downside of causing frequent turnover.

The remoteness of the states of Afar, Gambella, and Somali posed a tough challenge to the reform simply in terms of the logistics of reaching out to them. Nevertheless, Afar and Gambella embraced the reform and effectively implemented it on schedule. Applying the COPS frameworks to these two regions, their performance was similar to that of Tigray (see table 4.4).

Somali did not meet its goal of a complete rollout of the PFA reform. More than half the region's weredas have serious security issues, it suffered from revolving-door leadership, and it was never able accurately to translate the budget and accounting manuals into the Somali language (a key requirement of the reform), so it is understandable that the reform in that region could not be completed. The Somali PFA plateau is still a work in progress.

The fifth phase of reform, operation, is discussed in chapter 8, together with this phase of the accounts reform, the FIS, and the expenditure planning reform.

Lessons learned from the budget reform: doing the right thing right

Toning up the traditional budget was the right thing to do, given Ethiopia's circumstances in 1996 and its commitment to deep decentralization. The government's reform efforts were effective because of close pairing of government officials and technical assistance, which ensured that both sides learned and the outcome was fit for purpose and context.

The uncomfortable truth about politics, foreign aid, and the traditional budget

The budget reform in Ethiopia was incomplete, but this is not unusual for budget reforms. The political nature of the beast is that budget reforms are ongoing and messy affairs. The core of the basics of budgeting—appropriation by agency, a legal financial calendar—were proposed by the DSA project but were not adopted. Government and foreign aid embraced convenient, not best, practice.

Foreign aid was disruptive to good budgeting despite its vociferous complaints and demands for strong controls and international best practice. The Ethiopian case demonstrates the need for governments first to achieve the full potential of the traditional budget—and the difficulty of achieving even a modicum of it (see table 4.1, "Adopted" column). Few governments do. The budget reform illustrates what Wildavsky spoke of at length: budgeting is about politics, not techniques. The PFM reform merchants don't accept that, and the messy nature of budgeting does not fit in their neat boxes of conditionalities. Arguably the best source on budget reform to this day is Wildavsky's pathbreaking work *The Politics of the Budgetary Process*, in which he wrote:

> The budget is inextricably linked to the political system; by far the most significant way of influencing the budget, therefore, would be to introduce basic political change. Further, no significant change can be made in the budgetary process without also affecting the political process. There would be no point in tinkering with the budgetary machinery if, at the end, the pattern of outcomes was precisely the same as before. On the contrary, budget reform has little justification unless it results in different kinds of decisions and, when and if this has been accomplished, the play of political forces have necessarily been altered.[52]

The incompleteness of the reform of Ethiopia's traditional budget confronts us with an uncomfortable truth: PFA is tougher than PFM. The basics are far more difficult than parachuting in advanced financial techniques; indeed, the basics are only marginally about techniques such as improving the budget classification and the chart of accounts. The truth about the traditional budget is uncomfortable for foreign aid agencies that are bent on intervening in public finance because what is important must be done by government and there is, actually, little the aid agencies can contribute. Toning up the traditional budget is quintessentially endogenous, not exogenous. Getting the basics right in budgeting is not a task for foreigners. This explains in part—in large part, I would argue—why foreign aid interventions skirt the traditional budget and press for the imposition of advanced techniques, which have little or no impact on the outcome of expenditure because the basics are not reformed.

Furthermore, foreign aid agencies ignore the core basics of budgeting, for paying attention to them would make the agencies accountable. They prefer "convenient" practice, which is not correct practice. Off-budget, off-accounts, just when we want to do it, is more in keeping with their interests. Foreign aid is about moving money my way.

The DSA project laid the groundwork for a solid budgeting system in Ethiopia, which has the potential to correct one of the key deficiencies of public expenditure in that country, the poor composition of expenditure. The achievements of the budget reform can be viewed in terms of our platform framework of PFA and PFM. A clear chart of accounts and budget classification was a significant improvement on the transaction platform, as were clear budget forms linked to a user-friendly and always available financial information system. The documentation of the new procedures was translated into training materials, and over 72,000 staff were trained. The policy platform was not reformed. On the legal platform, the Canadian International Development Agency reform made progress on the budget law, but the lack of agency appropriation and of a legal calendar left the legal platform reform with far to go.

Three lessons emerge most clearly from the myriad decisions and experiences of Ethiopia's budget reform: the alignment of technical assistance and officials; getting key details right; and managing risk.

Alignment of the personnel designing the reform required a long lead time. In the case of Ethiopia's civil service reform and its PFA component, this time was opened up by the war with Eritrea, which slowed the breakneck pace of foreign aid interventions to Ethiopia in the late 1990s. Though the initial design was a federal conclave that excluded regions, what emerged was a design fit for purpose and context. Government ownership was real, not a slogan. The lions were gone.

Three crucial details stand out: clear forms that served double duty in guiding operations and providing core instructional material; taking time for officials to understand the budget classification, which is not just about codes but, rather, about the organizational side of financial reform; and having a flexible financial information system that could rapidly respond to unforeseen requirements and not delay the time-critical preparation of the budget. How low should you go in the hierarchy of the budget classification is a policy decision that affects details. International guidelines such as COFOG should guide, not dictate, the complexity of the budget system. Reform is contextual, and excessive complexity that has little value creates enormous risk. As Kenya's Harris Mule observed, a budget is a language and needs to be widely and thoroughly comprehended.

The third lesson of the reform is the importance of managing the risks inherent in reform. Budgets are critical and their reform must not disrupt ongoing budgeting. Using common sense is a good place to begin mitigating risk. Oromia's limiting the complexity of financial organization showed common sense. Amhara's attempt at an overly complex reform did not. Oromia and Tigray's recognizing and using as models the achievements and failures of reform pioneers was common sense. Assembling quality materials for daily management procedures, then translating them into training modules and delivering training in depth was common sense. Recognizing that reform is a long game and requires innovative approaches to post-reform support such as the wereda support units was also common sense. Finally, common sense would require recognizing who, at the end of the day, should be responsible for sustaining this critical function. This has not been adequately done. Ethiopia's budget reform remains very much a work in progress.

Notes

1 The revised budget format can be seen in figure 4.2A, which can be found on the book's website, http://stevepetersonpfm.com, in the section "Annexes to Chapters."
2 Harris Mule made this statement during the three-week PFM executive training program, which I started in 1987 in Kenya at Egerton Agricultural College. He and I were co-teaching a session on the reform of capital budgets. This program was expanded and located at Harvard University continuously from 1987 to 2010.
3 This phase structure is based on the work of E. Burton Swanson, as set forth in *Information System Implementation: Bridging the Gap Between Design and Utilization* (Swanson 1988: 38–9). For a detailed description of the activities to be accomplished in each phase of a typical reform project, see chapter 9, box 9.1, "The five phases of reform," p. 261.
4 Office of the Prime Minister, Task Force for Civil Service Reform (1996a, vol. 2: 25–7.
5 Peterson (1996b, 1996d).
6 Wildavsky (1978: 12).
7 Key (1940); Wildavsky (1964).
8 It is important to note that the annual appropriated budget is not coterminous with the total expenditure. Wildavsky (1978: 105–8) uses the term "treasury budget" to denote public expenditures, such as entitlements, that are established by separate legislation.
9 Wildavsky (1978: 509).
10 Gladstone quoted in Dalton (1954: 17).
11 For a discussion on the absence of appropriation by agency and approval see DSA B-16: 202–3.
12 DSA B-16: 202–10. See also DSA B-19 and B-11. The materials produced by the Decentralization Support Activity project can be accessed at http://stevepetersonpfm. com, which is the repository of the DSA project's documents. See "Works cited— DSA project documents," pp. 314–17 at the back of the book for a list of DSA documents referenced in this book.
13 Peterson et al. (2011: 3).
14 The financial calendar proposed by the project can be seen in figure 4.1A, which can be found on the book's website, http://stevepetersonpfm.com, in the section "Annexes to Chapters."
15 Peterson (1992a).
16 On repetitive budgeting see Caiden and Wildavsky (1980: 75–8).
17 COFOG is a statistical tool used for cross-country comparison of budgets to show the services governments provide. There are three levels in the COFOG framework, which present in increasing detail the types of services a government provides. The budget reform started in 1996 and the COFOG then in place was based on the UN statistical paper (United Nations 1980) and was part of the IMF statistical manual (International Monetary Fund 1986: 147–8).
18 Last (2003). See also Last and Robinson (2005).
19 PEFA is a partnership between the World Bank, IMF, European Commission, the UK Department for International Development, Swiss State Secretariat for Economic Affairs, the French Ministry of Foreign Affairs, the Royal Norwegian Ministry of Foreign Affairs, and the Strategic Partnership with Africa. The framework they have developed is foreign aid–driven and uses twenty-eight indicators to assess the performance of a country's PFM at one point in time. For further information see www. pefa.org.
20 The COA-BC was designed between 1997 and 1999 and used the COFOG guidelines of the day (United Nations 1980; International Monetary Fund 1986). The COFOG guidelines were updated in 2001 (International Monetary Fund 2001). The argument of Duncan Last of East AFRITAC that the new COA-BC did not have the third tier of

COFOG reflects his ignorance of the COFOG guideline that states that the "the third level of detail—subgroups—is intended to serve as a *guide* to the exact contents of the group [emphasis added]" (International Monetary Fund 1986: 143).
21 Wildavsky (1978: 508).
22 Last and Robinson (2005).
23 Schiller, Davies, and Last (2002: 7, 23).
24 Schiller, Davies, and Last (2002: 23, 47, 19).
25 Robinson and Last (2009: 11).
26 Chapter 8 contains further discussion of inappropriate advice on PFM that the IMF gave to Ethiopia.
27 Peterson et al. (2011: 57–70).
28 On the staff reshuffling created by the business process reengineering reform, see Peterson et al. (2011: 52–7) and chapter 8 of this volume.
29 Form 1 (figure 4.2A), Form 2 (figure 4.3A), and Form 3 (figure 4.4A) can be viewed at the website, http://stevepetersonpfm.com, in the section "Annexes to Chapters."
30 Peterson (2007a: 325).
31 The CSR Task Force report estimated the cost of the FIS to be $9 million, which was far beyond the $2 million-plus budget that USAID was willing to commit to the initial stages of this reform. This posed a serious risk of undermining the coherence of the budget, accounting, and, in due course, treasury reforms managed by the project. The war with Eritrea started in 1998 and lasted until 2000. The European Commission, which was online to fund the FIS, was unable to procure the system before the war started, and the EC is forbidden to fund countries in conflict. The new budget system was scheduled to go into operation in the federal government on July 8, 2001, which meant that the procedures, training, and FIS would have to be developed and delivered no later than December 2000. With the war still raging in early 2000 (a ceasefire did not come until June 2000), the project made the decision to develop an FIS on its own for budgeting and accounting.
32 The end product of this phase was "Budget Reform Design Manual Version 2.1." The first version of the budget reform manual was completed on February 17, 2000 (see DSA B-16). An updated budget manual for the federal government was finalized in February 2007 (DSA B-213).
33 See DSA T-103 for the English version of the budget training manual. The "T" series of the DSA documents is training materials.
34 Office of the Prime Minister, Civil Service Reform Management Unit (1997: 11).
35 Peterson et al. (2011: 49–56).
36 The budget reform team played a crucial role in correcting some errors in the CSRP report, for example, that budget institutions were allowed to keep retained earnings. Budget institutions were in fact given their budgets gross, and institutions that had activities that generated retained revenue were to remit all funds received to the finance agency.
37 DSA B-16.
38 Wills (2005). The decision of Harvard University to close HIID and distribute select personnel and staff to schools within the university is presented in Thompson et al. (2000).
39 For a detailed assessment of the FY2001 federal pilot see DSA B-31.
40 The Amharic versions of the FY2001 budget are DSA B-37 and B-38, and the English versions are DSA B-39 and B-40.
41 See table 5.2 in chapter 5, on the accounts reform, for the complete schedule of the budget and accounts of the reform.
42 At the federal level, budget institutions are ministries, at the region level they are bureaus, at the zone level they are departments, and at the wereda level they are offices. A federal public body such as a ministry can have one or more BIs within it. At the region, zone, and wereda level, each public body has typically just one BI.

43 Peterson et al. (2011: 31).
44 The Southern Region also has so-called special weredas, which are ethnically defined autonomous governments.
45 Gladwell (2000: 262).
46 For a more detailed discussion on the quality of the leadership in the Southern Region see Peterson (2011c: 6–8).
47 During the war between Mengistu's Ethiopia and Siad Barre's Somalia, Cuba brought thousands of Ethiopian children orphaned by the fighting to live in Cuba. It was a formative experience for them and they received education, health, and nutritional benefits they would never have had in Ethiopia. The three budget officials in the Southern Region bureau of finance who had benefited from this program were very fond of "Uncle Fidel."
48 James (2007: 749).
49 USAID audits of projects typically involve the selection of two hundred or so items—one-tenth the number of transactions selected after the project closed in 2008. Harvard University's mismanagement of the USAID contract in Russia in 2000 perhaps had something to do with the scale of the end-of-project audit of the DSA project.
50 And, it must be said, partially redeemed Harvard's soiled reputation following its mismanagement of the project the USAID funded in Russia.
51 Leonard (1987: 899).
52 Wildavsky (1964: 271).

5 The accounts reform

Against all odds

In Gambella, the cat died.

The hot, muggy Gambella region, in western Ethiopia, on the Sudan border, was always a challenge for the project because of its remoteness. Now, the Gambella Finance Bureau had a problem of rats eating its accounting records, and one of our project advisors recommended getting a cat. The advice was followed, and it achieved the desired results, but the cat's death ended the sustainability of this measure. Asked why the cat had died, officials said that it had starved. And why had it starved? It had been so successful in its assignment that it had finished its rodent supply, and had died during a long holiday. Why hadn't someone taken the cat home during the holiday? Simple: Government property can't be removed.

This little tragedy illustrates a key feature of Ethiopian financial administration as well as a core principle of PFA and PFM. Much is said in the finance literature of the need for the *hard budget constraint* as the sine qua non of prudent finances.[1] The hard budget constraint should be the first-order objective of the policy platform—a government that lives within its means and prudently incurs expenditure that can be sustained. Supporting the hard budget constraint is *transaction discipline*, which should be the first-order objective of the transaction platform. By far the two principal reasons the reform of PFA in Ethiopia succeeded was that the budget constraint and transaction discipline existed before the reform started and continued throughout the reform.

Two government policies illustrate the firm—indeed, near fanatic—commitment to transaction discipline. First, the mammoth task facing the reform of accounts in 1996 was the four-year backlog of reports from both federal agencies and regions. The government had a choice of whether to simply write off the past and start anew or do the painstaking task of clearing up the backlog. This policy decision probably faces most developing countries because most have this type of arrears. Also, if a country intends to introduce double-entry bookkeeping, this system requires a beginning balance—debits must equal credits so that all subsequent transactions will balance. Ethiopia made the right decision: it started cleaning up the accounts even before the release of the *Task Force Comprehensive Report*, which presented the Civil Service Reform Program (CSRP). How one deals with the past says a lot about how one will deal with the future. Clearing the backlog meant that even before the government's CSRP design of the accounts reform was released in February 1996, the government had embarked on a reform strategy of *recognize* what exists before *changing* the accounting system. The DSA project's strategy for the accounts reform, at least initially, was therefore largely defined by the government's *recognize* strategy of reform, which the project complemented by adding *improve* (documenting procedures, designing better forms) and *sustain* (introduction and delivery of an in-service training program) so to support and rapidly execute the clearing of accounts.

The second illustration of government discipline occurred in 2007, the year before the project ended, when the accounts department delayed the completion of the national accounts for three months to chase down a few thousand-dollar errors out of billions expenditure. Few countries are so precise. In fact, one can argue—and I did—that this chase violated the materiality principle of accounting because the error was insignificant and irrelevant. But it does say something about the level of discipline.

Accounting is the wellspring of discipline in a PFA/M system. Budgeting, by comparison, is positively chaotic. In fact, accounting brings discipline to all budget systems through the second and little-remembered system of appropriation accounting, which is distinct from what is typically understood as *the* accounting system, the accounting for discrete transactions.[2] Appropriation accounting is cash-based and records the use of the annual appropriation. It exists for all budget types, not just line-item cash budgets. So accounting has a role in budget control at the macro-level of appropriation. Prior to the PFA reform, the accounting system provided control at the micro-level as the primary accounts ledger card recorded budgeted expenditures (though not commitments). A crucial question in building a robust PFA is establishing budget control and clearly specifying where its responsibility rests—with the budget department, the accounts department, and/or the treasury department. In pre-reform Ethiopia, it rested with accounts. The accounting system was the bedrock upon which the rest of the transaction platform rested.

Yet after seventeen years of civil war it was not surprising that in 1996 the accounting system was in disarray. What was surprising was that it was not in far worse shape. For that, again, one must appreciate the strong transaction discipline. The problems of the state of the nation's accounts as the reform began were truly severe, starting with the deficiencies in execution. The odds truly were stacked against a rapid reform (see table 5.1, "Overview of Ethiopia's accounts reform").

The Ministry of Finance, which should have been the rock of the reform, was actually the biggest obstacle to turning the situation around. It had not been tasked with making policy, nor did it have the capacity to do so. Worse, as noted earlier, the previous minister expressed the opinion that the ministry was in danger of becoming a "post office," meaning not only that it simply doled out cash but also that it lacked the capacity to demand compliance from federal spending agencies and regions to "post" to the ministry timely and accurate

Table 5.1 Overview of Ethiopia's accounts reform

Ethiopia's accounts as of 1996	DSA project's design for reforming accounts—Step 1. Strengthening the basics	Measure adopted?
System		
1 Accounting system based on 1981 law	• Documented the existing system (manuals)	Yes
• Accounting system not defined; no manuals	• Improved the forms	Yes
• No procedures of recording, closing, reporting	COA improved during the budget reform	Yes
2 Chart of accounts based on budget codes	BDA migrated from mainframe to PC	Yes
3 Poor automation	Donor accounting manual created	Yes
4 Foreign aid imposing separate systems		
Execution		
5 Federal agencies and regions not keeping books	Bookkeeping introduced at federal agencies and regions	Yes
6 Federal agencies and regions not reporting		
• Four-year backlog	• Closure done with IST and support	Yes
• Reports not accurate with disbursement	• Reporting improved—IST, forms, procedures	Yes
7 No trained accountants in the civil service	Bookkeepers trained to be apprentice accountants	Yes
8 No training program	IST strategy delivered in regions; training materials based on existing system	Yes

Ethiopia's accounts after 2000	DSA project's design for reforming accounts—Step 2. Beyond the basics	Measure adopted?
System		
9 Self-accounting	Single financial pool instituted	Yes
10 Double-entry bookkeeping and modified cash-basis accounting	Procedures introduced	Yes
11 Financial reporting	Extensive financial reports produced	Yes
12 Automation	BDA upgraded	Yes
Execution		
13 In-service training	Extensive training in bookkeeping and accounting offered	Yes
	Step 3. Building management	
System		
14 Automation	Extensive management reporting with IBEX 1.3	Yes
15 Zero-treasury balance	Manuals prepared	Government discontinued this IMF reform
Execution		
16 In-service training	Management accounting started	No

Source: author's compilation. On the status of Ethiopian accounting in 1996 see Office of the Prime Minister, Task Force for Civil Service Reform (1996a, vol. 2: 37–45). See also DSA A-27.

reports of their expenditures. The Civil Service Reform Task Force report correctly pinpointed the key problem in accounts in line institutions (spending agencies) at the federal and regional levels:

> In our view, the fundamental reason for poor performance in terms of delivery of national accounts is that it is so highly centralized. The Ministry of Finance is responsible for the preparation of accounts, with line institutions only being required to submit base data. This severely weakens the responsibility of line institutions to produce quality financial information on time. There is a lack of understanding and commitment on the part of senior officials in line institutions to the accounting process. The whole system of accounting and accountability fails, therefore, to place a clear responsibility on line institutions to maintain adequate accounting records and to ensure that their accounting systems function properly.[3]

The defining feature of PFA is compliance. In 1996 there was little compliance to the directives of the Ministry of Finance, which contributed in large part to the four-year backlog. Equally serious was the inaccuracy of the reports that were received by the ministry. No sticks were exercised for the carrots distributed. Building a robust PFA requires strong financial organizations at federal and regional levels, and although both levels did impose a hard budget constraint, much work was needed to establish transaction discipline.

Two other daunting challenges the accounts reform faced were the complete absence of trained accountants in the civil service and the lack of an in-service training program in government bookkeeping or accounting (see table 2.3 on the severe manpower constraints in the country for bookkeepers and accountants in the public and private sectors). It is difficult to do an accounting reform without accountants; indeed, a significant aspect of this reform was adding accounting to the role of bookkeepers. Beyond the constraints to *execution*, there were four problems in the accounting *system*: lack of documented procedures and adequate forms; a limited chart of accounts based on a budget chart of accounts; poor automation; and complexity created by foreign aid's imposing separate accounting systems.

Despite some very discouraging odds, over the course of the twelve-year reform Ethiopia transformed an accounting system in disarray into one that exceeds international standards.[4] The government's achievement in reforming accounts is one reason why its PFA system is ranked as one of the best on the continent. From a rudimentary system featuring single-entry bookkeeping, cash basis of accounting, limited reports, poor automation, and a four-year backlog it created a system that boasts double-entry bookkeeping, modified cash basis of accounting, extensive reports, real-time distributed automation nationwide, and current accounts.[5]

The problems of Ethiopia's accounting system in 1996 are found in many developing countries. The Ethiopian case provides insights in six areas that concern governments grappling with turning these systems around:

1   Understanding the basics of bookkeeping and accounting
2   How to move beyond control and build management
3   The pros and cons of clearing rather than writing off a backlog of accounts
4   The importance of getting the execution of an existing system working prior to introducing more advanced systems
5   Standards for modified cash and cash accounting
6   Good practices in designing an in-service training strategy

In the following four sections I describe the first four phases of Ethiopia's accounting reform: translation, development, pilot, rollout (Phase 5, operation, is discussed in chapter 8).

Phase 1 of accounts reform: translation (design)

> Phase 1. Translation (role: design).
> A reform begins with the declaration of a policy. A design phase follows, which translates the policy into a strategy and specific activities of a program of work. This phase comes to a productive end only with the engagement of the prospect of implementation.

Unlike the recommendations for the budget reform, the task force report's recommendation for accounts was sensible. The right thing was advocated—recognizing and improving what existed. In preparing the task force report Peter Silkin gained a deep understanding of the severe limitations of Ethiopia's capacity in public sector accounting. Perhaps the most sobering reality Silkin, a certified accounting professional, saw and appreciated—beyond the backlog, beyond the lack of documented procedures, beyond even the lack of compliance in preparing accounts—was that there was not a single trained accountant in public service (see table 2.3). The reform, at least as initially conceived by the task force report, would be about bootstrapping a bookkeeping system that consisted of simply filling in ledgers to a rudimentary accounting system, a system for preparing and explaining financial reports. In terms of our framework of systems and execution and the four strategies of reform (recognize, improve, change, sustain), the task force report's recommendations for accounts can be summarized as follows:

- Recognize: systems (document the single-entry bookkeeping, cash basis of accounting)
- Improve: systems (additional reports); execution (clear backlog, timely reporting in future)
- Change: execution (introduce self-accounting: agencies prepare their own accounts, as opposed to merely shipping data to a finance organization such as the Ministry of Finance).

The challenge of the CSRP recommendations for a reform project

The task force report proposed the right thing to do for accounts, but the right thing posed considerable uncertainty for crafting a manageable project. Managing a project's scope is the most important of the three variables that define a project, schedule and budget being the other two. Strictly speaking, the accounts reform was about the bookkeeping and accounting systems. Two uncertainties in particular made managing the project's scope problematic: the pressure to extend the project brief from bookkeeping and accounting to reforming the systems that support accounts, and the uncertainty as to when and whether the backlog would be cleared.

PFA/M reforms are multiyear endeavors, and new demands inevitably crop up. This makes it especially important that project managers have a tight and coherent scope at the beginning. The danger to an accounts reform, especially in its early stages, is the tendency to expand the brief from simply recording the transactions of the many financial processes—budget commitments, treasury, physical asset management, cash management, aid management—to becoming directly involved in improving and managing those operations. This was always a tension for the accounts reform managed by the DSA project. Government continually attempted to slip in additional deliverables as part of the accounts reform without making these requests formal by revising the project's terms of reference or increasing the funding of the budget.

The project reluctantly took on the collateral tasks of improving cash management, a function of the treasury, because bookkeepers' handling cash was part of the legacy accounting system. A second enormous collateral task for which the project had no brief was the development of a financial information system (FIS) to support the budget and accounts reform. The DSA project had to step into this activity because of the long delays by the European Commission, which was responsible for the FIS for the CSRP (the FIS is the subject of chapter 6).[6]

Adding to the uncertainty of the initial scope of the accounts reform were two major policy changes that emerged three years into the reform that dramatically changed the scope: second-stage decentralization and the mandate to move to double-entry bookkeeping and modified cash accounting.

Alignment of roles in the translation phase

Unlike the CSRP recommendations for the budget reform, the recommendations for the accounts reform made sense and there was little need for the DSA project to advocate a different approach. Doing the right thing was established, so the challenge for the project was how to do it. The translation of the accounts and budget reforms were done simultaneously, so Jim Yardley, the lead accounts consultant for the DSA project, and I both had an opportunity to discuss the task force report with Peter Silkin and its approach to both reforms. Yardley affirmed Silkin's approach of recognizing and improving what existed. These discussions also confirmed that the two priorities of the accounts reform were clearing the backlog and rapidly implementing an effective in-service training program.

Phase 2 of accounts reform: development

Phase 2. Development (roles: design, implementation).
Enter the implementer. Implementation begins in earnest with the commitment of significant resources to system realization, based typically on the approval of a design and its execution as embodied in a project document (technical and financial proposal). System development is marked by a design-implementation dialogue.

The principal objective of the development phase was to develop a strategy for clearing the backlog of accounts, which would then allow measures to be taken that would lead to the goal of the accounting reform specified by the CSRP, self-accounting. Self-accounting means that spending agencies record and report their own expenditures. From the task force report it was clear that the role of a technical assistance project in assisting the government to clear the backlog was to develop an effective in-service training (IST) program. Thus, the two principal tasks of the project in Phase 2 were first to document the procedures of the existing accounting system and then develop training materials; and second, to develop a strategy for delivering IST as quickly as possible. Ensuring compliance that public bodies executed the accounting system could not be done by a technical assistance project and was the task of the Finance Ministry and finance bureaus at the federal and regional levels. Absence of compliance was the key reason for the backlog.

Clearing the underbrush: clarifying the basics of bookkeeping and accounting

Before we could reform the accounting system, we needed to ensure that all players were on the same page in possessing a clear understanding of what accounting is and what it is not. Achieving this clarity would help define the scope of our work, and only a reform with a clear and limited scope could succeed. The task force report noted that the 1981 financial regulations that were in force in 1996 did not "mention the nature of the accounting system to be employed including procedures for closing and reporting."[7]

To reform a system, one must know what the irreducible features of the system are. An imprecise definition of the system to be reformed sets the stage for scope creep, a key factor—perhaps *the* key factor—that can scupper a reform. It was important to the Ethiopian accounts reform that this financial system be clearly defined (I suspect that accounts reforms in other countries also suffer from a poor definition). A clear definition is especially needed to ensure that the basics are in place before an accounting system is encumbered with additional functionality, which seems to be an inherent tendency. So what are the basics? Following the logical principle of Occam's razor, one can argue that a bookkeeping and accounting system provides a repository of information.[8] Jim Yardley, the DSA accounts advisor who developed all four accounting manuals under the reform, states, "The primary purpose of a government accounting system is not to provide control but to produce information." He elaborates on the uses of this information:

> Information in the form of financial reports is produced for internal purposes to help management within government make decisions. Management decisions that are aided by finance reports include: assessment of fiscal responsibility, assessment of goal achievement, and evaluation of future needs. Information in the form of financial statements is produced for external purposes to hold government accountable for stewardship over public resources and evaluate consequences of government decisions. The major external users of financial statements are legislators, donors, lenders, and the public. Transparency in government begins with full and fair disclosure of financial information.[9]

Defining the "basics of government accounting" was not an academic exercise. A major contributor to the backlog of government accounts when the reform started was that accounts and bookkeeping staff were overburdened with tasks that should properly have been done by others. For example, cashiers performed the treasury function of disbursement, even though they had no training or remit to do so. Control of budgeted expenditures is a budget function, the establishment and management of a commitment system. Control of cash is a treasury function. The simple definition of accounting as a "repository of information" strips away from the accounting function the functions of other systems that support the accounting system. By clearly understanding the irreducible and primary role of an accounting system, one can eliminate activities that impede its reform. But how compartmentalized can this component be as the repository of all financial information? A major challenge of accounts reform in Ethiopia was to keep the focus on fixing the bookkeeping and accounting (the repository of information) without getting entangled in the reform of the other systems.

Clearing away the underbrush of the collateral systems that impacted accounts—at least conceptually—was an important first step of the accounts reform. Some of these systems could not be separated from accounting overnight, but they pointed the way for the need for reforms in other financial components such as budget and treasury. This clear conceptualization of the role of accounting as "a repository," which guided the project, fits with Frederick Brooks's first commandment of system design:

> Conceptual integrity is *the* most important consideration in system design. It is better to have a system omit certain anomalous features and improvements, but to reflect one set of design ideas, than to have one that contains many good but uncoordinated ideas.[10]

Ironically, the definition of the objective of accounting presented earlier brings into question Allen Schick's tripartite sequence of PFM as control-management-planning.[11] With the earlier definition, accounting systems generate the information that internal and external users use for management of public resources and ultimately for control. Accounting as a repository of financial information promotes planning, management, and control, but, most important, does not itself provide control.

Making a large cadre of officials involved in accounting aware of this definition was itself a reform, part of a reform strategy of *recognition.* Building the professionalism of the accounting cadre was as much about defining what they *don't* do as what they do.

Types of bookkeeping and accounting

This chapter presents the reform of the systems of bookkeeping and accounting, so it is essential to provide a brief overview of bookkeeping and accounting, different systems that are commonly lumped together as accounting. The distinctions between bookkeeping and accounting can be understood in terms of *how*, *what*, and *when*.

How—Bookkeeping is about *how* transactions are recorded. Transactions can be recorded by single entry or double entry.

What—Accounting is about *what* the transaction entities are: expenditure, income, assets, liabilities, etc.

When—Accounting is also about *when* the transaction is reported: the financial year in which the transaction is recorded, or "booked."

There are two types of bookkeeping, single-entry and double-entry. The simplest accounting system has single-entry bookkeeping and a cash basis of accounting, meaning that there is just one transaction entity, cash, and all transactions are recorded in the calendar year. Single-entry bookkeeping is a chronological listing of cash transactions. "Single entry" means that each transaction is recorded just once, when it occurs. This is the system that Ethiopia had in 1996. The virtue of this system it its simplicity, and it also fits with appropriation accounting, which records how the budget is spent.[12] Many governments use single-entry bookkeeping and a cash basis of accounting because it is simple, and works basically the same as these governments' budgetary accounting.

Despite the advantages of simplicity, single-entry bookkeeping has a number of weaknesses when compared to double-entry bookkeeping. One is that it is not "self-balancing," which means that it does not provide an arithmetic check on the chronological tally. In single-entry, which is simply a long list of numbers, it is easy for errors to creep in. With double-entry, each transaction must be entered into two separate credit and debit columns. If the two columns do not tally, then an error has occurred and is detected with each transaction.

Another weakness with single-entry bookkeeping is that it only records cash transactions, which in turn means that only a limited range of reports, those based on chronological cash transactions, can be produced. A financial report is a compilation of the transactions that makes it possible to analyze an entity's financial status, in order to better plan and manage. Because it can record all types of transactions, double-entry books can provide a full range of reports.

In addition to the two types of bookkeeping, accounting systems are described in terms of their *bases*. I have defined the cash basis. The other basis is called *accrual*, featuring the matching principle: revenues are matched to expenses and economic events are recognized regardless of when cash transactions occur. Combining the two types of bookkeeping and the two bases gives us four systems of accounting, described in box 5.1.

This discussion of the features of bookkeeping and accounting raises several wider issues that the PFM reform literature is virtually silent on. First, what are the basics of accounting for government in a developing country and what does the slogan "getting the basics right" mean with respect to accounting? Does "the basics" mean single-entry bookkeeping and a cash basis? Or does it mean double-entry bookkeeping? Does one have to have single-entry and a cash basis system working well in order to evolve to more sophisticated double-entry bookkeeping and a more sophisticated basis—modified cash, modified accrual, or full accrual? Much of the discussion in the PFM field is about the need to leapfrog to full accrual accounting, which requires double-entry bookkeeping. Meanwhile, the need first to get the basics, however defined, working well and how to do it have not been addressed.

A second question that has not been discussed—surprisingly, given the PFM field's obsession with "standards"—is the absence of any guidelines for the two intermediate stages of the basis of accounting, modified cash and modified accrual. Accounting standards (IPSAS standards) are set by the International Public Sector Accounting Standards Board (IPSASB), an entity of the International Federation of Accountants.[13] Yet this board has not established any standards for the two intermediate types of accounting systems. The challenge for most governments in developing countries is how to evolve from single- to double-entry bookkeeping and from cash-based to modified cash-based accounting. Without guidelines or standards for the modified cash or accrual basis, how can these governments be advised? Question: Could it possibly be that insecure advisors recommend accrual accounting to governments because there are standards for this basis, and none for the interim basis of modified cash and modified accrual?[14]

Clearing the backlog

Until the backlog of accounts was cleared, it was not possible to change the accounting system to meet the principal CSRP goal for the accounting reform, self-accounting, which means that spending bodies have to record their transactions and summarize them in financial reports. Prior to reform, public bodies at

Box 5.1 The four types (bases) of accounting

Cash-based accounting. Cash accounting measures the flow of cash resources. It recognizes transactions and events only when cash is paid or received. Financial statements produced under the cash basis of accounting cover cash receipts, cash disbursement, and opening and closing cash balances. There are international standards (IPSAS) for cash accounting but so far there is no consensus on a clear definition.*

Modified cash-based accounting. Modified cash accounting records transactions and events that have occurred by year-end and are normally expected to result in a cash receipt or disbursement within a specific period after year-end. Therefore, the accounting period includes a "complementary period or grace period" for payments such as thirty or sixty days after the close of the fiscal year. Payments over the complementary period that are related to transactions of the previous fiscal year incurred during the fiscal year are reported as expenditure of this previous fiscal year. Financial statements produced under the cash basis of accounting cover cash receipts plus receivables within a specified interval from the end of the period (the complementary period) and cash disbursements plus payables within a specified interval from the end of the period (the complementary period). There are no IPSAS standards for modified cash accounting.

Modified accrual-based accounting. Modified accrual-based accounting is sometimes called "expenditure basis" accounting. It records transactions and events when they occur, irrespective of when cash is paid or received. There is no deferral of costs that will be consumed in future periods. Physical assets that will provide services in the future are "written off" (or "expensed") in the period acquired. Financial statements produced under a modified accrual accounting system cover revenues, expenditures, financial assets, liabilities, and net financial resources. There are no IPSAS standards for modified cash accounting.

Full accrual-based accounting. Full accrual-based accounting records transactions and events when they occur, irrespective of when cash is paid or received. Revenues reflect the amounts that came due during the year, whether collected or not. Expenses reflect the amount of goods and services consumed during the year, whether or not they are paid for in that period. The costs of assets are deferred and recognized when the assets are used to provide service. An overriding principle of full accrual accounting is the matching principle, whereby expenses are recorded in the same period as the related revenues are recognized. Financial statements produced in a full accrual accounting system cover revenues; expenses (including depreciation); assets (financial and physical); liabilities; and net assets. There are IPSAS standards for full accrual accounting, but debate is ongoing.

Source: adapted from Schiavo-Campo and Tommasi (1999: 226–7).

*International Public Sector Accounting Standards.

regional and federal levels simply entered their transactions into forms and shipped them to the regional finance bureaus, which in turn shipped these to the Ministry of Finance. Besides inundating the Ministry of Finance with data, this practice severely weakened the accountability of spending bodies. Self-accounting meant that public bodies would administer their transactions (bookkeeping) and would make reports (accounting).

The backlog in accounts was due principally to deficiencies in execution, not in the systems. A DSA report released in September 2001, just five months before the start of preparations for the accounts reform in the federal government, found that six areas of weakness in execution were responsible for the backlog: lack of training, lack of support, lack of information, lack of clarity in roles and responsibilities, lack of a work calendar, and inadequate staff.[15] These problems were formidable—clearing the backlog would not be a matter of simply filling in the ledgers and sending reports up the line. In fact, the backlog was symptomatic of the fundamental weakness in the organization and management of PFA at all tiers, especially in the Ministry of Finance. The most worrisome weakness of the MOF in the effort to clear the backlog was its lack of clout in demanding prompt reporting by regions and also by federal ministries. The MOF assumed, incorrectly, that promulgation of policy was sufficient to elicit prompt action. In assessing this issue, the DSA found that for outstanding reports, no

> deadlines are set, as MOF considers that the outstanding issues are effectively resolved through government policy decisions as several reminders and discussions have taken place between MOF, federal institutions and the regions on the issue related to the reconciliation of loans and advances.

So far, however, the discussions had not "yielded any positive results."[16]

Two tasks needed to be done by the DSA project to support the government in clearing the backlog: develop training materials for the existing system, and develop a strategy for delivering training as quickly as possible.

Developing training materials

The project's accounts advisors worked tirelessly with government staff at federal and regional levels to get a thorough and nuanced view of the needs of the system. Jim Yardley, the first project accounts advisor, took the lead in 1997 to understand what existed in accounts on the ground. He found:

> The Ethiopian accounting system requires accountants to forward information by completing forms. The system is very simple and designed for the skill level of staff in the system.... Anybody with a 12th-grade education [the average level of the staff working on accounts] and some basic training or experience can perform this bookkeeping task satisfactorily. The accounts reform project envisions self-accounting that will require accountants who are more than bookkeepers. A self-accounting unit is a government unit where decisions requiring financial information are made. A bookkeeper only processes information. A self-accounting unit requires an accountant who can perform bookkeeping tasks plus understands the information,

reports the information in an appropriate format, and explains the meaning of the information to decision makers.... [Current bookkeeping] staff are not prepared to perform as accountants in self-accounting units.[17]

Government staff working in accounts were bookkeepers, not accountants; they knew *what to do* in bookkeeping but did not know *why they were doing it* in terms of the broader process of accounting.[18] The accounts reform therefore had to be a two-step process: get the bookkeeping system working effectively, then move to an accounting system that can produce prompt and understandable financial reports. The accounts reform had to broaden bookkeepers' understanding of the recording task they were doing so they would see how it related to downstream accounting tasks such as reporting.

The development of the training materials required first that existing procedures be documented. The project, in close consultation with government staff, prepared a detailed description of the existing system (henceforth referred to as the DoA—description of accounts). This document was in itself a major reform, for it was the first time the country's accounting system had been systematically described and made accessible in one document.[19] The DoA was a key input into Module 1, which was the training document of the existing system. (The project made the distinction between *manuals*, which were comprehensive presentations of procedures, and *modules*, which were the training documents that were based on the manuals). Module 1 was the training document for the existing system and brought together the *how* and the *why*—how to operate the existing system and the technical and legal reasons why procedures were done.

The purpose of Module 1 was not only to inform government staff of the existing system but also to locate that system within the broader principles of accounting. It prepared staff to become accountants and function in self-accounting units. The existing system was presented in specifics and the specifics were used to illustrate the principles of accounting. Further, accounting's relationship to the budget was explained, placing it in the context of overall financial operations.

Module 1 was developed with extensive collaboration between government and project staff and included a complete array of materials needed for training: for trainers, a manual, a guide, a workbook, a book of overheads, and forms; for trainees, a manual and test questions and answers.[20] It was systematically organized to function as a short course in accounting and accounting's role in the government's financial operations—a primer on the basics of accounting. Reformers in other governments might profit by viewing the module's organization and content. Its table of contents provides a good overview of the project's approach to training on the existing system (see box 5.2).

Part 1, "Introduction to Accounting," demonstrated the difference of public and private sector accounting. This was necessary because some of the government staff had been trained in the latter (double-entry and accrual) and needed to understand how those practices relate to government accounting (single-entry and cash). Part 2, "Basic Accounting Concepts," presented the core accounting

Box 5.2 Table of contents of training module 1

PART 1. Introduction to Accounting

1.0 Accounting and Its Role in Governmental Organizations
1.1 The Role of Accounting Within a Government Organization
1.2 The Role of Accounting Outside a Government Organization
1.3 The Difference Between Accounting and Bookkeeping
1.4 Types of Accounting

PART 2. Basic Accounting Concepts

2.1 Learning Objectives
2.2 Introduction to Financial Accounting
2.3 Accounting Principles
2.4 Internal Controls
2.5 Comparison of Government Accounting with Commercial Accounting
2.6 Basis of Accounting
2.7 Double-Entry Bookkeeping
2.8 Financial Statements

PART 3. Basis for Federal Government of Ethiopia (FGE) Accounts

3.1 Introduction
3.2 Comparison of the FGE with Commercial Organizations
3.3 Legal Basis for the FGE Accounts
3.4 Public Body
3.5 Regional Government
3.6 FGE Public Accounts
3.7 Public Money
3.8 Public Property
3.9 Procurement and Contracts
3.10 FGE Chart of Accounts

PART 4. Overview of FGE Financial Operations

4.1 Introduction
4.2 Characteristics of the FGE Government Accounting System
4.3 Legal Basis for FGE Budgets
4.4 The Purpose of Budgeting
4.5 Typical Preparation of the Recurrent Expenditures Budget
4.6 Annual Distribution of Authorized FGE Budget
4.7 Budget Execution
4.8 The Flow of FGE Money
4.9 The Flow of FGE Accounts Reporting
4.10 FGE Annual Financial Reporting

continued

PART 5. Details of the FGE Accounts

5.1 Introduction
5.2 Overview of Cycle 1 (Collection of Money by Budgetary Institutions)
5.3 Overview of Cycle 2 (Receipt of Requested Budgeted Funds from MOF)
5.4 Overview of Cycle 3 (Receipt of Court and Other Deposits)
5.5 Overview of Cycle 4 (Budgetary Adjustments to Revenues)
5.6 Overview of Cycle 5 (Salary Payment and Returns)
5.7 Overview of Cycle 6 (Purchase of Goods)
5.8 Overview of Cycle 7 (Salary Payments)
5.9 Overview of Cycle 8 (Return of Court and Other Deposit)
5.10 Overview of Cycle 9 (Budgetary Adjustments to Expenditures)
5.11 Overview of Cycle 10 (Salary Returns Withheld)
5.12 Overview of Cycle 11 (4020 Transfers)
5.13 Overview of Cycle 12 (4090 Transfers)

Source: DSA T-28.

concepts and illustrated them using specific existing procedures. Part 3, "Basis for Federal Government of Ethiopia (FGE) Accounts," presented the legal framework in which overall financial management—including accounting—operated, with examples of specific existing procedures. Part 4, "Overview of FGE financial operations," located accounting within the broader PFA system and explained budgeting, disbursements, and procurement. Finally, Part 5, "Details of the FGE Accounts," is a logical presentation of what the current accounting system actually does in terms of the twelve cycles of the accounting system.

One does not get a more challenging "capacity building" task in PFA/M than bootstrapping bookkeepers to perform like accountants. Much is said about the need for "capacity building" in PFA/M reforms. Module 1 of the IST in accounts provides a good example in the definition and practice of capacity building. Training materials should teach government staff what they need to do and why; the why should be illustrated in depth with detailed processes and procedures of the existing system. The devil is in the details and there are many moving parts and lots of details in an accounting system. It is not enough to discuss procedures and principles; staffs need heuristics to organize their understanding of the details so they can organize their work. The twelve cycles helped staff to understand the complex organization of accounting.

PFA/M is a practical field, and there is a tendency to focus on "technique," on the procedures. This can lead to a rote "plug-inski" approach—getting the numbers right and getting them in the right boxes. Module 1 went to great lengths to avoid the "plug-inski" approach. First, it proved to be a very effective instrument for bootstrapping bookkeepers into accountants and gave them a crucial capacity that is rarely discussed—confidence and the professionalism that comes with it. Second, by imparting a deep understanding of accounting principles demonstrated in the day-to-day of the existing system, it promoted self-accounting and the significant

leap to much more sophisticated bookkeeping (double-entry) and basis of accounting (modified cash). Module 1 paved the way for Manual 3, the new accounting
system of double-entry bookkeeping and modified cash-based accounting that was
developed in the pilot phase.[21]

Delivering training

The lack of trained staff was, along with lack of compliance in submitting
reports, the central cause of the backlog. With decentralization to regions, thousands needed to be trained as soon as possible, and the project's second task in
the development phase was to devise a strategy for rapidly delivering this training to these people. With Module 1 in hand, the project trained 4,644 officials in
the development and the pilot phases. How was this achieved?

"Let's go. I want to show you something," said Haile Johannes, the head of
the finance bureau in Amhara region, in a meeting in the region's capital, Bahir
Dar. We were speaking about the challenge of in-service training and I had
asked him what he thought the region might do to deliver training. A half hour
later, crossing a large open field on a muddy track in a driving rain, we
approached a primitive compound of corrugated-metal one-story buildings. What
Johannes wanted to show me was barely visible in the mist.

We entered one of the buildings—it was dimly lit and cold and had a dirt
floor. Johannes introduced me to the head of Amhara's Regional Management
Institute (RMI)—we were standing in the institute's administration "building." I
learned that the Amhara RMI was delivering a rudimentary PFM course provided by the United Nations Development Program. It was very broad, was not
based on the government's procedures, and provided little in the way of training
materials. In the last half hour of a two-hour meeting I asked the RMI head what
he needed. His response was succinct: "Everything." They needed a curriculum,
materials, training for trainers, and physical plant. The existence of such a training center was a total surprise—a very positive one that demonstrated initiative
on the part of regional officials.

The DSA in-service training for the budget and accounting reforms emerged
from this July 1997 meeting at the Amhara RMI and from Jim Yardley's August
1997 assessment, eight months into the beginning of the project.[22] Our strategy for
delivery of IST for budgeting and accounting was summarized in a memo (DSA
T-1), "The Training Strategy for Accounts, Budget and Financial Planning Under
Civil Service Reform," presented in September 1997 to the vice minister of finance
supervising the project. Our strategy was to develop a partnership between training
organizations such as the Ethiopian Civil Service College (now the Ethiopian Civil
Service University), which existed at the federal level, and the RMIs.

Soon after we delivered the IST strategy memo my second meeting with
Prime Minister Meles Zenawi and his cabinet took place. Meles (as he is known
throughout Ethiopia), who chaired the CSRP Task Force, began the discussion
by stating the crucial role of IST in the reform and then asked Peter Silkin, the
reform coordinator, to present his strategy for IST. Silkin's strategy was to

import training organizations from the United Kingdom "lock, stock, and barrel." He argued that there was virtually no capacity in Ethiopia to conduct IST at the level needed. He argued that the reform needed to move forward quickly and could not wait until the capacity of Ethiopian training organizations was developed, a circumstance that justified importing trainers from abroad.

Sitting across from me in the meeting was Dr. Alemayehu Areda, the head of the Ethiopian Civil Service College (now the Ethiopian Civil Service University), which at that time was the principal provider of IST for the government. Upon hearing this strategy he remarked, "Over my dead body." It was heard by all. Meles then turned to me and asked me to present the DSA's IST strategy. Before I spoke, most of the members of the meeting, including Meles, placed the project's training strategy memo in front of them. Silkin did not do so for he had not received a copy of it, nor had he and I discussed it. I then presented the strategy, a loose summary of the core statement of the memo, to wit:

> The proposed institutional strategy for delivering training—accounts, budget, financial planning training—will be provided through a partnership of institutions, including, at least initially, the Ethiopian Civil Service College, the Ministry of Finance, the Ministry of Economic Development and Cooperation, and the regional management institutes, with support from the Decentralization Activity Project.[23]

The magic word "partnership" elicited approving nods around the room, especially from the head of the ECSC, which was to take the lead in the partnership.

I then elaborated on the DSA's strategy for delivering IST. First, training would be delivered in the four principal languages in Ethiopia: Amharic, Oromiffa, Tigrigna, and Somali. Second, the ECSC would play a leadership role in the partnership by training resource personnel from the RMIs that would be the focal point for the delivery of the training in their regions. The DSA project would provide technical assistance in curriculum development, course design, and facilitation of the training partnership.

The DSA IST strategy had several advantages:

*   It built upon existing and emerging government training capacity, the ECSC and RMIs.
*   It established a close link between the designers of the CSRP and the training institutes that would disseminate the reforms.
*   It provided a low-cost means of rapidly delivering a wide coverage of training.

The greatest virtue of working with the RMIs was that this strategy developed local capacity. The RMIs provided a broad coverage in their region; participants would have a common background in the nuances of their region's financial systems; and disruption of ongoing administrative activities would be minimal because the RMIs were nearby.

The PM asked Silkin to assess the strategy I had proposed. He made several points against it.

- First, the RMIs were embryonic and completely untested.
- Second, the ECSC was not in a position to deliver.

The second point did not sit well with the head of the ECSC, Dr. Areda, who took the lead in rebutting Silkin's "import" strategy. He criticized the use of British training organizations because they would not deliver training in local languages. Since most of the accounting staff had a twelfth-grade education or less and little or no facility in English, the "import" strategy would not work.

Silkin's strategy was in trouble. The discussion circled back to me on the issue of the capacity of RMIs. I recounted my "discovery" of an RMI in the hinterland of Amhara, where training was being offered in a rudimentary setting—muddy roads, dirt floors, dim lighting. I thought my depiction might put the members of the meeting off regarding the viability of an RMI strategy, but it had the opposite effect—I could see Meles smiling. The RMIs embodied cherished beliefs of his party, the Tigrayan People's Liberation Front: regional initiative (self-help), national and regional ownership, bootstrapping (development grounded in local needs and conditions), and the frugal use of resources. Good things emerge from struggle in the mud—his own revolution had proved that. A recognize-improve-sustain strategy fit with the political culture and convictions of the TPLF.

Meles concluded the meeting with a statement and a question: The local partnership strategy was to be the strategy of IST for the CSRP. And, why doesn't Addis Ababa University deliver training that is of use to government operations?

As a result of this meeting, the strategy for IST in accounting became the blueprint for IST for the whole Civil Service Reform Program.

It is rare for government to issue a definitive and authoritative statement of a policy for reform, one that guides a project's action. The DSA's development of an IST project strategy and its strong endorsement by the PM was arguably the most important event in the history of the twelve-year project. Recall that there are four necessary though not sufficient conditions for a project to succeed: urgency (IST was indispensable if the CSRP was to move forward); need (as set forth in the task force report); help (the substance of the discussion regarding strategy); and trust in those advising and delivering technical assistance. This meeting clarified the urgency, need, help, and trust in the DSA project to deliver the core assistance to the CSRP: technical assistance in the form of in-service training. IST is where the rubber meets the road in financial reforms. It is the core of reform and if it does not succeed, the most brilliant procedure manuals will gather dust on the shelf. The DSA project was now on the road.

With the acceptance of the IST strategy, it became clear that the first DSA contract did not have anywhere near the level of resources required to execute the strategy. Approximately 8,000 staff had to be trained in budgeting account-ing, and planning in order to fill the shortfall of 5,418 accountants alone for both the private and public sectors (see table 2.3). The project prepared a proposal to USAID for a supplemental project, the In-service Financial Training Project (IFTP). USAID approved it, not only because it fit with government priorities but also because the highest level of government wanted it. The project used all of the IFTP funds to train 4,007 accountants, reducing the country's shortfall by 73 percent, to 1,411.

Ultimately Ethiopia's backlog of accounts was cleared, despite some serious blows to our strategy, particularly the failure of the Ethiopian Civil Service College to deliver. Soon after the IST meeting with the prime minister, Dr. Areda accepted a position with an international foundation. The new president, Dr. Haile Michael Aberra, viewed the college as a degree-granting academic institution, and the delivery of short courses needed for the operation of government was not a priority for him. The project and the RMIs were forced to take up the slack in developing the in-depth capacity training that was the heart of the DSA project's IST strategy.

Alignment of roles in the development phase of the reform

It is rare for those running a development project to have the opportunity to discuss at length the cornerstone of their work with the head of a government and his ministers. The two-hour meeting with Meles and his cabinet led to the basic understandings for alignment. This happy outcome would not have occurred but for earlier due diligence and close cooperation with government staff that afforded a nuanced understanding not only of the existing accounting procedures but also of the resources that could be brought forth from the mist and mud.

Phase 3 of the accounts reform: pilot

Phase 3. Pilot (roles: design, implementation, utilization).
Implementation enters its second and core stage, the pilot stage, when operation and use of the system begins. The dialogue among designer, implementer, and user is now complete. Adaptation of implementation based on utilization feedback is undertaken, and adaptation of design also continues as before. This phase is the crucial one in the overall realization process. Only here is there mutual learning among all participants.

The pilot phase is the most complicated phase of a reform, for it is the only phase where all three functions are executed together: design, implementation, and utilization.

Four surprises

The pilot of the accounts reform lived up to this phase's bad reputation for complications: four surprises lay in store for us. The first surprise was a nasty one: the demand by foreign aid for an unplanned separate accounting system for donor accounting, which delayed the reform by several years. The second surprise, though planned and hoped for, was the success of the regional in-service training in Module 1. The third surprise was utterly unexpected: the government abandoned the CSRP recommendation of retaining the existing single-entry, cash-basis accounting system and specified a new double-entry, modified cash-basis system. Fourth was the sobering difficulty of the federal government to pilot the new accounting system, which raised the possibility of potential delay in the rollout of reform to the regions.

The nasty surprise: demand for a separate accounting system for foreign aid

In August 1998, just when the project was set to proceed with the pilot phase and complete the cleanup of the backlog and finally turn to improving the system, foreign aid agencies driven by the World Bank came up with an unexpected demand: that the government rapidly develop and implement an accounting system for their new sector development programs. This system was to be completely separate from the government system and was to be done as soon as possible. The government in turn asked the project to undertake this new task. When I asked the head of the accounts department of the Ministry of Finance, Samson Mekonnen, why it had to be done—it would be very disruptive to the ongoing accounts reform—he answered, "I had no choice, I was told to do it." No mention had been made in the CSRP design of a separate donor accounting system nor was this activity in the project's scope of work or budget.

This initiative is a poster child of international bad practice: ignoring government-led reforms; not building on an existing system and ongoing work; and failing to understand the deleterious effects in delaying all reforms. The separate accounting system foreign aid insisted on is a clear example of duplication, waste, and weakening financial controls resulting from not using a single, good, existing system, which is easiest to staff, manage, and sustain. Multiple systems in a decentralized government are especially disruptive because decentralization is already complex and there is often a shortage of capacity to run even one system, let alone multiple systems.

The impact of this duplicate accounts reform were significant and immediate. The demand on government to develop a donor accounting system unnecessarily complicated the accounts reform and delayed it for at least two years, according to senior officials of the Ministry of Finance. This initiative derailed the schedule for developing and distributing training materials. Instead of finalizing Module 1 from August to December 1998, as planned, the project had to spend this time, and more, developing a brand-new Module 2 for this separate system. We could not complete Module 1.1 until April 2000. This delay meant that the project trained 2,494 staff using the first version of Module 1.0 and only 2,150 with the significantly revised Module 1.1.

The problem of the donor accounts reform was not only one of time, but of staff. The project later learned that over 25 percent of the time of the senior accounts staff of MOF was being devoted to developing this new donor system.[24] In effect, work on the government-mandated CSRP accounts reform ground to a halt.

I reluctantly agreed to assist the government with this unplanned task in my mistaken belief that this initiative could be harmonized with the ongoing reform. The strategy document for the donor accounting system was prepared by a local firm, and the project only learned later that this firm and Ministry of Finance staff had commenced actual development.[25] The project was kept completely in the dark on this situation until the Ministry of Finance requested the project's accounts advisor, Jim Yardley, to return and evaluate the strategy. The subtitle of Yardley's report, "A Need for Harmonization, Coordination and Integration," succinctly states his recommendations. Yardley noted that the report by the local firm restated the documentary work of previous DSA reports and added no additional information. But Yardley's key observation regarding the report by the local firm was that this separate system was not needed, for "it produces no accounting information to donors that the government's accounting system could not produce."[26]

Yardley's report made three principal recommendations to move forward with donor accounting:

1   Agree on a single reporting format and a single chart of accounts.
2   Report in a timely fashion the government accounting system, which required clearing the backlog.
3   Coordinate the donor accounts reform with the CSRP accounts reform.

Unfortunately, the government did not act on these good recommendations. The foreign aid agencies that pushed this initiative did so without any consultation with project staff, who had several years of experience with the country's system, on how their sector development programs could be managed within the government's existing financial system or with some modifications. This duplicate effort slowed down the very activity—clearing the backlog—that would make everyone's financial reporting more efficient. Thus, the saga of the donor accounting system highlights two issues of PFA/M reform that are relevant in aid-dependent countries: foreign aid entities' ignoring government-driven reform, and the importance of a *recognize* reform strategy. To recognize is to respect what exists. This episode provides lessons in internationally driven bad practice:

International Bad Practice: How *Not* to Reform an Accounting System
1   Assume that what exists cannot meet requirements or be modified to meet requirements.
2   Do it in secret—no consultation with officials and staff to learn what exists and what is currently being done in that area.
3   Don't get the requirements right.
4   Sort of use the existing system's procedures and formats.

5   Relax government regulations for the release of funds.
6   Put in a different chart of accounts with a different number of digits.
7   Leap from cash- to an accrual-basis accounting.
8   Don't assess the additional workload of the separate system. Use two new computer systems, both of which differ from what already exists.
9   Implement without a well-developed training program.
10   Roll out without testing.
11   Call the system interim but do not intend to migrate with the existing system and do not make a plan to do so.
12   Require that it be done yesterday.
13   Require that it preempt all other reform activities, including those that would facilitate the new system.[27]

The welcome surprise: the success of regional in-service training

When I presented the IST delivery strategy of building a partnership of federal and regional training organizations, there was a wholehearted agreement that going local rather than importing a UK training organization was the way to go—but were these organizations up to the task? It was another source of uncertainty, along with the primary one of whether the backlog could be cleared and if so, how long it would take. The partnership organizations were in a very early stage of development. Could they deliver enough training fast enough to meet the demanding schedule for implementing the reform (see table 5.2)? IST is critical to any public sector reform, but it takes time to build organizations to deliver IST. Can a reform wait for the creation of an IST infrastructure or can training be delivered simultaneously with building local training organizations?

From this point of view, the partnership strategy was risky. Again, the keys to a successful reform are doing the right thing and doing it right. The RMI strategy was doing IST right. From another point of view, not adopting the partnership strategy would have been risky. The CSRP had been largely a top-down affair with endless workshops where federal officials told regions what was going to happen. The IST partnership brought regional ownership to the reform.

The piloting of Module 1 through the partnership of federal and regional organizations was remarkably successful: 4,007 officials were trained on time—16 percent more than planned. Especially impressive early on was the performance of the RMIs in the Southern Region and Tigray, which consistently delivered their quarterly quotas of trainees. The enthusiasm for the training was infectious and regions that did not have an RMI took action to establish one.[28] Regional officials were getting a demonstration of the value of these institutes.

To promote the coordination of the IST partnership, the DSA project introduced semiannual meetings for officials of the federal government and all of the regions and administrative areas, to review nationwide progress in the delivery of IST. In addition, these meetings provided, for the first time, a forum where senior managers and technical specialists in public finance from all regions could meet one another

Table 5.2 Year reforms adopted by the federal government and in the regions

Jurisdiction	Fiscal year of budget reform (FY in Ethiopian calendar)[a]	Fiscal year of accounts reform (FY in Ethiopian calendar)
Federal	2001 (1994)	2002 (1995)
Southern Region[b]	2002 (1995)	2003 (1996)
Southern Region		2004 (1997)
Tigray	2003 (1996)	2003 (1996)
Amhara[c]	2003 (1996)	2003 (1996)
Amhara		2004 (1997)
Addis Ababa[d]	2003 (1996)	2003 (1996)
Addis Ababa	2004 (1997)	2007 (2000)
Oromia	2003 (1996)	
Oromia	2004 (1997)	2005 (1998)
Benishangul	2004 (1997)	2005 (1998)
Dire Dawa	2004 (1997)	2005 (1998)
Harar	2004 (1997)	2005 (1998)
Afar	2005 (1998)	2007 (2000)
Gambella	2005 (1998)	2007 (2000)
Somali[e]	2005 (1998)	
Somali	2006 (1999)	

Source: author.

Notes
a The Ethiopian Orthodox Church calculates the years differently from the Gregorian calendar and the Ethiopian year number runs about seven years behind the Gregorian calendar. In addition, the two systems label fiscal years differently. In both cases the FY runs from July 8 of the first year to July 7 of the second. But in the Ethiopian calendar the FY designation refers to the second half of the fiscal year, whereas in the European calendar the FY refers to the first half. For example, in the Ethiopian calendar the accounts reform at the federal level was operating from July 8, 1994, to July 7, 1995, or Ethiopian FY1995. In the European calendar, the new system was operating from July 8, 2002, to July 7, 2003, or European FY2002.
b Two years are listed for the Southern Region's accounts reform, for it was significantly redone in the second year.
c Two years are listed for the Amhara region's accounts reform because the first year completely failed.
d Addis Ababa did the first year reform on its own because the DSA, fully occupied in the regions, was not available to assist. Four years later, the project was able to assist and Addis Ababa redid their reform.
e Two years are listed for Somali's accounts reform but they are blank because they failed to do the reform while the DSA project was there.

and discuss financial issues confronting them in their respective jurisdictions, in the presence of federal officials. It was an informal means of coordinating the PFA reform and public financial administration in general throughout the country. The first of these meetings took place in June 1998, at the ECSC; later they rotated through the regions.

Just prior to the February 2000 semiannual meeting in Tigray, the DSA project convened a three-week program where experienced trainers of Module 1 assessed the training. By then, 1,065 staff throughout the country had been trained on Module 1. The assessment found:

1   The objectives of this training are being achieved. This training makes trainees feel proud of their profession. The trainees are highly satisfied because
this training is the first time staff have been offered training that is well
organized and uses a well-prepared manual.
2   Most of the trainees lacked theoretical background in accounting. From the
training they receive in-depth knowledge about accounting principles and
internal controls.
3   Trainees now can explain the government accounting confidently.
4   Trainees are able to interpret government financial statements and understand the goals of accounting.[29]

The IST was working! In regions that had quickly and consistently delivered the
training, the backlog of accounts was being cleared. The Southern Region, which
was executing the training faster than any other region, clearly affirmed that the
training was crucial to clearing its backlog. Still, a more basic training module
was needed for the rapidly expanding cadre of staff the regions were recruiting.
Module 1 assumed that trainees had a working knowledge and experience with
the procedures of the existing accounting system, but also a knowledge of the
responsibilities of different positions (e.g., cashier, head of administration). This
introductory guide, Module A, was completed in December 2000.[30] Module A
explained the budget and accounting and was a source book of detailed procedures that new and even experienced staff could refer to. To ensure that Module
A could be clearly understood by the rank and file, the project hired two senior
accountants, Alemayehu Seifu and Retta Workeneh, who together had more than
fifty years' experience in government. Their assignment was to ensure that forms
to fulfill a particular activity were accurately filled out and that Module A, which
had been drafted in English, was accurately translated into Amharic.

*The total surprise: the move to double-entry bookkeeping and modified
cash-basis accounting*

"If it takes a hundred years, we are going to implement double-entry bookkeeping," pronounced Hailemelekot, the vice minister of finance. Jim Yardley, the
project's accounts advisor, and I had been summoned to the vice minister's
office to hear this game-changing policy. The task force report had been very
clear about retaining single-entry bookkeeping for the foreseeable future. Peter
Silkin, the author of the CSRP recommendations, was convinced that double-
entry could not be done with the current personnel, untrained bookkeepers with
an average education of twelfth grade who had learned their trade on the job, and
some lacking even that preparation. There was not a single qualified accountant
in the civil service. The project's accounts advisors were also skeptical. This
change in strategy posed a huge risk. Could it be done?

The proposed accounting system was to be double-entry bookkeeping with a
modified cash basis of accounting, henceforth referred to as the "new" system.
The new system would promote the principal objective of the accounts reform as

presented in the CSRP: the establishment of self-accounting. The new system promoted this in four ways: better handling of transactions, correcting incorrect practices, expanding the type of transactions that would be recorded, and better reports. The new system would also improve budget control.

Better handling of transactions. Transactions are incurred by budget institutions (BIs), entities that receive a budget. BIs may be congruent with a public body such as a finance bureau in a region, or a public body may comprise multiple BIs, as is the case with large public bodies such as the Ministry of Education. By recording transactions using double-entry bookkeeping, BIs could maintain a set of self-balancing ledgers and a general ledger that summarized all ledgers, including cash, and could provide a wide range of reports on cash flow.

Correcting incorrect practices. Although the existing system purported to be on a strict cash basis of accounting, there were many exceptions. For example, funds to pay gross salary were requested on a monthly basis, but only net salary amount was transferred. But the BI recorded this as if the gross salary amount had been transferred. This was not strictly cash-basis accounting, but the existing system was not able to record gross salary expense in a better manner because it lacked subsidiary ledgers, which in the case of salary would show net and gross. For most entities, salaries were the largest recurrent expenditure, so this was a material weakness. Another example of the weakness of cash control was the treatment of suspense items (items whose value is uncertain, which should be put into a special ledger). Although suspense items could involve large amounts of cash missing from the BI for long periods of time, the accounting system did not record this cash movement. Grace-period payables were another example of the weakness in the existing system of cash control. For thirty days after the end of the budgetary year, BIs were permitted to receive funds and make payments from the previous year's budget. The receipt and payment of funds was recorded as if the cash movement had occurred on the last day of the fiscal year. If the funds received and the payments made for the grace period payables were not exactly equal, the cash balance reported by the BI at the end of the fiscal year would not be the real cash balance existing at year-end.

Comprehensive recording of transactions. With the existing single-entry, cash-basis accounting system, no continuous record of a BI's assets and liabilities could be maintained. Each year's accounts were independent and transactions that occurred over several years left no record. With the new system, each BI would maintain a general ledger that included at least a cash account and some asset and liability accounts, so each unit maintained a balanced and continuous record of its responsibilities and performance. This is self-accounting.

A formalized modified cash basis for accounts meant that all cash movements would be entered into the cash account. Therefore, a running cash balance in the cash ledger would reflect the actual cash available to a BI. As discussed earlier, there are no international standards defining the modified cash basis of accounting, so the procedures of the new system which were presented in Manual 3 used the following guidelines:

- Revenue is recognized when cash is received.
- Expenditure is recognized when cash is paid, except at the end of the year, when expenditure is recognized if payment is made during the grace period.
- Receivables and payables that do not involve cash movements are recognized.
- Other assets and liabilities are recorded in a separate general ledger.

Better reporting. The most tangible outcome of the new system was better reporting. This would promote not only accountability and financial administration but also, eventually, financial management. Self-accounting was achieved by each BI maintaining a general ledger, thus permitting the BI to produce a full set of financial reports: a balance sheet, a statement of cash flows, and a statement of budgeted versus actual expenditures.

With the new system, financial reports would be produced by each BI and accumulated into financial reports at higher levels of the organization. The continuous accounting record of the new system could therefore be used to assess performance over a period longer than one year. The new system included a simplified process for recording all assets and liabilities through a fund balance account. Fund balance is an accounting category used in government accounting to record the difference between assets and liabilities. In commercial accounting, this is the role of equity accounts. Fund balance is the governmental accounting equivalent to equity, representing the government's net investment. A complete general ledger for the BI is maintained when assets and liabilities are recorded in the fund balance.

Problems with budget control. In addition to introducing the new system of accounting, Manual 3 also remedied deficiencies in budget control. The existing system did not record commitments made against the budget on a timely basis, meaning that if too many purchase commitments were approved and not recorded, a BI might exceed its budget. Good commitment control was needed as follows: when a BI approves a purchase order by verifying that budgeted funds are available, the budgetary funds required to complete the purchase should be committed and should not be available for approval of subsequent purchases. In other words, the budgetary funds available to spend on a purchase are the funds budgeted for that item minus previous purchases and minus previous commitments to purchase. The existing system recorded previous purchases, but did not keep a record of commitments to purchase. The new system recorded and controlled commitments and thus strengthened budgetary control.

One of the great and positive surprises of the PFA reform was the successful implementation by government of double-entry bookkeeping and with it, a modified cash basis of accounting. It was truly achieved against great odds, defying the accounting experts' dire predictions. For governments wishing to adopt this approach to reform, the major takeaway from the Ethiopian experience is that significant capacity can be built if you start with a first-rate training program. The reform also puts into question common assumptions as to the basic educational background required to do more sophisticated accounting.

Introducing this new accounting system in the public sector and training some thousands of staff in its use had the significant collateral effect of boosting the quality of accounting in the private sector. Even though the departure of trained staff for the private sector after having been trained by the public sector was and is always an issue and a challenge, the value of these staff to their society is not lost, for they are building the nation in the private sector.

By adopting double-entry bookkeeping and a modified cash basis of accounting, the reform preempted a potential critique by foreign aid agencies. They had already directed withering fire at the budget reform with its focus on toning up the traditional line-item budget. But there was nothing they could say to argue against the new accounting system—indeed, the silence was deafening. Only after the departure of the DSA project and the agencies' long-awaited entrance into the financial reform process did they start promoting the leap to the stars: accrual accounting.[31] I contend that the current system will meet the needs of the government of Ethiopia for decades to come.

People who have a poor or nonexistent grasp of what bookkeepers and accountants do often refer to them pejoratively as bean counters. The uninitiated need to appreciate the aesthetics of double-entry bookkeeping and the broader significance of Ethiopia's achievement in installing this system. Goethe, in *Wilhelm Meister's Apprenticeship*, had a character state that "the system of book keeping by double entry ... is ... among the finest inventions of the human mind."[32] The accounts reform affirms that Ethiopia can modernize, despite severe constraints. *Yichalal!* It's possible!

The sobering surprise: the difficulty of executing the pilot in the federal government

With the development of the first version of Manual 3, the accounting reform could be piloted at the federal level starting in May 2002. Conducting a reform within a few miles of the Ministry of Finance headquarters should have been straightforward, but it was not. In fact, the federal accounts reform highlighted the MOF's two principal deficiencies: its lack of authority and its limited capacity. The former impacted the latter, as shown by the magnitude of the problem of the backlog of accounts:

1   The Ministry of Finance itself had an embarrassing two-year backlog of accounts.[33]
2   There was a two-year backlog of federal accounts, as of October 2001, seven months before the new accounting system was to be implemented at the federal level.
3   There was a four-year backlog of accounts from regions. The regions refused to report their accounts, even after "discussions" with the MOF. This backlog in the regions was the key constraint in moving the accounts reform forward. It meant that the Central Accounts Department of the MOF would be heavily committed to consolidating all of these back accounts.[34]

4   Six months into the fiscal year of the operation of the new accounting system, 29 of 167 federal reporting units had not implemented the new system.[35]

As of April 1, 2003, nine months into the new fiscal year when the new accounting system was to be in operation, twenty federal public bodies, including the Ethiopian Road Authority (ERA), had failed to produce one monthly report using the new accounting system. The failure of the ERA to report was of particular concern, since it accounted for 46 percent of the federal capital budget. (The ERA was a constant problem in the planning, budget, and accounting reform and acted virtually like an independent fiefdom. The principal source of its funding was foreign aid, and so it was more responsive to foreign aid agencies than to government.)

The difficulty and delays of the federal accounting reform were sobering to the project. First, it had been assumed that all project accounts advisors could be redeployed to the regional rollout, which was now not possible. Second, the MOF itself was in such arrears that it clearly would be unable to assist the regions with the accounts or any other reforms—it needed assistance itself! The regions and the project were on their own to make the reform happen.

Alignment of roles in the pilot phase

The pilot phase of a reform is arguably the most critical phase for establishing close coordination between government and technical assistance and for ensuring that the government remains in the driver's seat. This phase is the main opportunity for learning, as all three roles are executed: architect, builder, and user. Although learning and mid-course corrections do occur in the rollout phase, the system is largely established in the pilot phase.

There were examples of both exemplary and appalling role alignment in the pilot phase. First, the exemplary. Of special significance in the reform of a decentralized system is the alignment between tiers of government. The building of the partnership of government IST organizations from different tiers succeeded admirably. Also exemplary was the revision of Module 1 (training on the existing government accounting system). Jim Yardley went to great lengths constantly to work with the IST trainers to obtain feedback from the early training sessions on Module 1, so that Module 1.1, the final version of Module 1, could be significantly improved.[36] The close consultation established between government and project staff carried on into the development of Manual 3, which changed the accounting system and far exceeded the CSRP specifications. Finally, the need to develop a basic introductory training manual for the large influx of new staff was met in this phase by the preparation of Module A.

The alignment was appalling in the development of the donor accounting system, which not only was not mentioned in the CSRP Task Force report and was done outside the CSR program's accounts reform process established by the government and the project, but also was done in secret. Stealth is not a successful reform strategy.

Phase 4 of the accounts reform: rollout

Phase 4. Rollout (roles: implementation, utilization).
Implementation begins its third and final stage with the near cessation of design activity. This phase involves only adaptation of implementation. Dialogue takes place principally between the implementer and the client.

Two formidable challenges confronted the rollout of the accounts reform to the regions. The first concerned the brute magnitude of the task. Accounting was a continuous activity requiring the management of hundreds of thousands of transactions in an ongoing process—unlike budgeting, a once-a year activity that involved few or no changes from the previous year's budget. Our task was to ensure that these accounting transactions were carried out correctly. The second challenge was that the accounting reform had to follow in lockstep with the budget reform. The budget reform, conducted in the first year of the reform, contained a new budget classification and chart of accounts. This budget had to be managed by the new accounting system put in place in the second year of the reform. If the accounts reform did not arrive on time, there would be no way to execute the new budget system. Given the transactional complexity of accounts compared to budgets, it was far less likely for the budget reform to fail or underperform than the accounts reform. Table 5.2 presents the ambitious and tightly linked schedule of the rollout of the budget and accounts reform. Once the budget reform was started in 2001, it eased the way for the rest of the transition. In 2002, the new federal budget system went into operation, the new federal accounting system started working, and the first regional reform started up with budgeting in the Southern Region. After that, progress was swift (table 5.2).

Since the budget and accounts reforms needed to progress in lockstep, anything that caused the two to be out of sync was very disruptive. USAID's surprise $1.5 million reduction of the Phase 3 DSA budget was just such a disruption. This cut effectively eliminated IST from October to December 2002—the worst possible moment, when preparations, especially training, were planned for the first accounts reform, the federal reform. The reduction of the Phase 3 budget forced a last-minute search for funds for the rollout. At the eleventh hour we located a new patron, Irish Aid, but the funding delay held up the rollout, and both the project and regional governments had to scramble to get the reform back on track. Foreign aid is fickle and is often fickle at the worst possible time. The tight coupling of PFA/M reforms highlights the need to avoid relying on the kindness of strangers for resources.

Another shock to the rollout occurred within two months of the funding shock: second-stage decentralization, which created a second formidable challenge—logistics. Sufficient resources—including technical assistance, documents, and computer systems—had to be put in the right place at the right time.

Furthermore, training was still ongoing; throughout the country staff still had to be trained on Manual 3. Oromia alone needed 8,000 accountants trained in Manual 3.

The project hoped that these challenges could be successfully met because several pillars were established in the pilot phase: the regions, especially the four largest regions, which were to be reformed first, had improved their administration with the development of their RMIs. The delivery of the IST had established a strong working relationship between the regional governments and the project. The necessary but not sufficient preconditions for success were in place: trust, need, help, urgency.[37]

Overview of the accounts reforms in the regions

I focus on Amhara, Oromia, Tigray, and the Southern Region, the four largest regions, which with the federal government account for nearly 97 percent of total expenditure in Ethiopia.

The success of a region's reform depended on two issues. First and foremost: Were the COPS drivers—context, ownership, purpose, and strategy—that would promote reform in place? Second, did the region perform well on delivering the tasks needed for the reform?

In chapter 4 I presented a summary of the budget reform of these four regions in terms of their COPS drivers (see table 4.4). The four factors that were found to be especially important in making a region's budget reform a success also were critical to the success of their accounts reform.

1   Good administration of the finance function not only at the top but also in depth in the finance organizations.
2   Enhanced staffing through recruitment and effective IST.
3   Development and adoption of procedures that fit their context, especially the single finance pool.
4   Good working relationship with the DSA project.

Oromia, the Southern Region, and Tigray had successful accounts reforms because these four factors were in place. Amhara's accounts reform failed the first year it was implemented because these factors were not in place.

In addition to having the drivers in place, the success of a region's accounts reform depended on whether it implemented all of the necessary reform tasks, as shown in table 5.3, "Checklist of regional reform tasks and Amhara region's attempted reform in 2003." Oromia, Tigray, and the Southern Region performed all of the thirty-four reform tasks on the checklist, whereas Amhara did not perform them well.

The fifteen-fold increase in the number of budget institutions created by the second-stage decentralization meant that the success of the accounts reform hinged on simplifying the structure of government and financial administration before introducing new procedures. This was a key factor in the success of the

Table 5.3 Checklist of regional reform tasks and Amhara region's attempted reform as of the August 2003 assessment by the DSA

COPS driver and task	Amhara's execution of checklist
Strategy	
1 Regional planners agree to a two-year sequence: first budget reform, then accounts reform.	No. Regional planners insisted on a simultaneous reform.
Resource mobilization	
2 Government and DSA agree on level of support.	No. The DSA project's technical assistance staffs were fully committed to other reforms and no project funds were available to assist Amhara.
3 Identify adequate resources.	The region failed to adequately resource the reform.
Preparation	
4 Implement budget reform.	No. The budget was not yet approved and the new sub-agency budget category was not understood. Reporting was being done by public body and not disaggregated to sub-agency, so expenditures did not match the budget structure.
5 Clear backlog.	No.
6 Prepare and translate appropriate procedure manual.	No.
Simplification	
7 Create organizational structure.	No.
8 Minimize cost centers.	No.
9 Introduce treasury single account.	No.
Staffing	
10 Recruit adequate staff.	No.
12 Train all staff.	No.
13 Assign reform team members.	No.
Forms	New forms needed for disbursement recording and reporting.
14 Make ledger cards for recording available.	No.
15 Translate forms.	No.
16 Print forms.	No.
17 Distribute forms.	No.
Financial information system	
18 Develop regional automation strategy.	Not developed.
19 Procure and install equipment.	Yes.
20 Identify operators.	Yes.
21 Modify application to the region.	No. Failure to understand that the existing BDA (budget disbursement accounts) system needed modification.

continued

Table 5.3 Continued

COPS driver and task	Amhara's execution of checklist
Training	
22 Develop strategy.	No. Training duration not fixed, scheduling inappropriate (done in June during accounts closing—some training suspended, then restarted); classes far too big.
23 Quantify staff needed.	No. No sense of the numbers of trainees required.
24 Prepare materials.	Materials inappropriate because based on an inappropriate procedures manual.
25 Identify sufficient core trainers.	No. Some trainers did not understand bookkeeping.
26 Enforce the selection criteria of trainees:	Inappropriate trainees selected. • Key accounts staff did not participate. • Many trainees selected (storekeepers, guards) who were not directly involved in accounts. • IST participants assigned to positions not related to accounts. • Training had to be suspended because the trainees did not understand the system.
27 Supervise training.	Very little. BOFED was understaffed and was clearing the backlog of accounts.
28 Ensure adequate training facilities.	Insufficient.
29 Information technology training offered.	Limited.
Implementation	
30 Followed directives from BOFED.	No. BOFED's instructions on closing multiple bank accounts not executed by the Commercial Bank of Ethiopia.
31 BIs supervised.	Very little. BOFED busy, zones busy, large number of weredas, many in remote areas.
32 Startup data made available.	Very little. Double-entry accounting can't be started in the zones and weredas because of lack of training and no opening balances for startup entries.
Information technology	
33 Complete data entry.	No. Budget disbursement accounting, the existing financial information system, still being used; data for 2001 backlogged accounts not entered. No budget data entered for 2002. No recording with the new system for FY2003.
34 Quality control of data processing.	Delayed (did not follow BOFED directives).
35 Produce reports.	Delayed (did not follow BOFED directives).
Post-implementation support	
36 Establish wereda support units.	No.

Source: based on DSA A-66.

accounts reform—reformers of PFA/M in decentralized governments take note. Decentralization brings complexity with multiple tiers of government and administration. A thorough simplification that reduces the quantity of trans-actions while improving the quality of financial administration should be of the highest priority. Simplification needed to be both quantitative, reducing the number of budget institutions, and qualitative, improving financial administra-tion. Simplifying wereda and zone financial administration had three elements:

1   Simplify the organizational structure by creating finance pools.
2   Simplify cash management by introducing a treasury single account (TSA).
3   Simplify the budget structure by reducing the number of budget institutions, thus reducing the number of reporting units.

A pool is a shared management of a public service or function. Finance is a function. Because decentralization, especially at weredas, created some twenty-three separate sector offices (health, education, and so forth), the finance func-tion was concentrated in the wereda Office of Finance and Economic Development (OFED) and the zone Department of Finance and Economic Development (DOFED).[38] They called this grouping a pool. Thus, a finance pool carries out financial services for a number of entities, much as a typing pool does all the typing for all of the staff in an office.

The finance pools were established under second-stage decentralization to concentrate and optimize scarce finance staff. The typical pool provided the fol-lowing services: disbursing budgeted expenditures of the sector departments and offices, accounting for those disbursements, and maintaining a single bank account for treasury funds provided by domestic revenue and some foreign aid. Some regions have adopted pools that carry out more functions, including procurement services, public relations, and engineering services.[39]

Many ministers at the federal level did not understand the concept of a pool because the federal government did not use them. But it was important to estab-lish finance pools in the regions because of the staffing constraints. In terms of the PFA reform, with second-stage decentralization the regions faced a range of options for what services were to be shared by public bodies and handled by pools at the wereda and zone tiers (Tigray had no zones). Each region had to make three decisions:

1   What services would the pool provide—just financial, or others?
2   How many pools would each tier have—single or multiple?
3   How many bank accounts would be in the pool? There were four possible options for bank accounts: (a) One pool and all bank accounts at the wereda Office of Finance and Economic Development (OFED); no public body has a bank account, or cash in their office safes. (b) Multiple pools with all bank accounts at the OFED; no public body has a bank account; each pool has a safe and manages the cash for the public bodies in the pool. (c) Multiple pools with each pool managing bank accounts; no public body has a bank

account, each pool has a safe and manages the cash for the public bodies in the pool. (d) Multiple pools where each public body in the pool has at least one bank account, and pools manage the public bodies' bank accounts with a safe in each pool.[40]

The most simple financial pool structure was option a, which concentrated financial administration in a zone's and wereda's finance organizations (the DOFEDs and OFEDs, respectively). Simplifying disbursement was the most important virtue of the single finance pool, which consolidated disbursement by using one bank account, thereby effectively creating a treasury single account for government funds. A treasury single account (TSA) is a single checking account where funds from domestic revenue and some foreign funds (together called treasury funds) are deposited and whence monies are disbursed.

The financial pool concept is a quintessential example of conceptual integrity in implementation. It made a clear division of labor between the finance function and the service delivery functions of sector offices and departments of weredas and zones. Public bodies could better focus on their objectives while financial execution—control of cash, payments, accounting, reporting—would be handled for them by a pool of professionals. Public bodies would still determine their budgets and authorize expenditures against their budgets.

The conceptual integrity of the finance pool was critically needed with second-stage decentralization because the limited finance staff available needed to focus on their principal responsibilities. Conversely, education staff should focus on the delivery of education services and not be worried about accounts. The finance pool brought conceptual integrity to the first-order task of a financial system, the control of cash, for it removed the safes (petty cash) and checkbooks from public bodies. Streamlining the control of cash by having the OFED pools manage cash was a sensible approach, but it never sat well with the sector offices and departments. Removing their checkbooks and the cash in their safes meant they lost discretion over expenditures that might not meet the scrutiny of the OFED such as junkets that got them out of the hinterland.

The success, failure, and timing of the accounts reform in the four largest regions hinged on their decision regarding the pool structure at weredas and to some extent the zones. A key benchmark in starting the reform was whether a region had made a decision on whether to adopt a single finance pool. In the Southern Region, ultimately the accounts reform succeeded, but it struggled more than necessary principally because it did not simplify enough and used a more complicated pool structure (option b). The Southern Region redid its accounts reform the following year by adopting a single pool and reducing the number of BIs at weredas and zones. The Tigray reform was exemplary because it pioneered the single pool. Oromia, too, succeeded because it adopted a single pool. Amhara failed in the first year of its accounts reform because it adopted the Southern Region's multiple pool structure while lacking an understanding of the nuances of the pool concept and the needs of its region. In sum, if a region simplified, it succeeded. If it did not, it either struggled or failed. Further, if it was underhanded and cut corners—Amhara "acquired" the Southern Region's manuals surreptitiously—it failed.

Introducing a single pool and simplifying cash management with a TSA were two of the three techniques for simplifying financial management at zones and weredas, the other being reducing the number of public bodies and thus BIs— reporting entities—at these tiers. Limiting the number of BIs reduced the number of transactions that had to be recorded. Oromia slashed the number of BIs at the zone and wereda tiers from thirty-two to twenty, a 38 percent reduction that greatly simplified financial management. The Southern Region and Tigray limited the number of BIs at these tiers to twenty-four and twenty-three, respectively, whereas Amhara retained an unwieldy thirty-four BIs.

Accounts reform in the Southern Region: success after a struggle

"Don't turn your face from us," Getachew Hamussa, head of the Southern Region's BOFED, said to me as I was leaving his office to return to Addis after two days of consultation and a celebration of his region's successful completion of the budget reform. He knew only too well that technical assistance was often fickle and flighty. He had experienced firsthand the starts and stops of technical assistance in his region. He also knew that even though the budget reform in his region had been successful, the accounts reform would be far more difficult, especially in the context of second-stage decentralization. But after a shaky start the region got on the right track the following year after reviewing the value of a single rather than a multiple pool.

The Southern Region was exemplary in delivering the drivers of reform that were fit for the region's context (see chapter 4). Its leadership was especially strong. And for the most part, they successfully delivered on the reform tasks. One would expect that the implementation of the first regional accounts reform in a large region that had the most complicated structure of government and administration would face problems. Four key problems were found three months into FY2003 by a prompt assessment, which was presented to the head of BOFED.[41] This assessment was conducted in Wolayta zone in two weredas, Boloso-Sore (where the OFED and the Rural Development Pool were assessed) and Damot-Weyde (where the OFED was assessed) that had been identified as weak during the IST.[42]

One of the problems was that the OFEDs were overwhelmed with multiple tasks: managing daily operations, particularly the closure of the previous year's accounts; implementing the budget and accounts reform; and trying to support the wereda in understanding the new accounting system. The same OFED officials were doing all of these tasks. Second, the budget reform was incomplete— indeed, the weredas had no budgets. The absence of wereda budgets was the result of second-stage decentralization, for the wereda council had yet to approve the assignment of staff, the "complement," to wereda sector offices. Complement (the term governments use to refer to staffing) is the principal expense of a wereda, so if this figure is not known, a budget cannot be prepared. Many of the

OFEDs in the Southern Region simply took the budget forms and dumped them in the council offices to make the point that the birr (the Ethiopian currency) and budget started there.

Once the complement was sorted out, another problem emerged with the new budgeting system: the excessive number of sub-agencies. The head of BOFED felt that a large number of sub-agencies was needed to assess the performance of individuals. Although this was a laudable goal, in the first year of a budget reform one should simplify, not introduce an assessment function. Weredas were struggling to know who sat where—assessing staff performance could come later. The region hobbled its reform by not reducing the number of sub-agencies.

Another unforeseen problem was the lack of forms for the new accounting system. Most serious was a nationwide shortage of multilayer paper (for multiple copies) for the vouchers used for manually recording payments, receipts, and transfers. This compromised a critical control. The shortage impacted all the regions, not just those embarking on reform, and highlighted the MOF's inability to ensure the basic viability of the existing system. A further problem with forms was that the ledger cards where transactions were to be entered using the double-entry format were not available.

The fourth and final problem concerned IST. The degree and diploma holders were performing well, but the less-qualified lacked confidence and their performance was substandard. This staff required more assistance.

The prompt assessment by BOFED of the status of the accounts reform and its close monitoring of performance were indicative of the diligence it brought to the reform. From difficulties came solutions, and the project recommended the creation of wereda support units (WSUs) and zone support units (ZSUs) to assist weak weredas and zones.[43] This innovation was embraced by the Southern Region and was adopted and perfected by Oromia, with its hundreds of weredas.

The accounts reform in Tigray: a textbook success

"It almost broke our back," said Mekonnen Abraha, the head of the Tigray BOFED, shortly after Tigray's successful simultaneous implementation of the budget and accounts reform. Tigray was not only a success, it was an innovative success. The region pioneered the single pool advocated by the project to deal with the new realities of second-stage decentralization. Tigray could both innovate and do the budget and accounts reforms simultaneously because, in comparison with the other big regions, it was relatively small (thirty-six rural and twelve urban weredas). Unlike the Southern Region, Tigray did not have the complication of a zone tier, which in the Southern Region has a political as well as an administrative role.

The accounts reform succeeded in Tigray because the drivers of reform were aligned with context and it delivered the tasks of reform. In terms of motivation, perhaps the principal motivation for doing both reforms and for making the ambitious plan a success was that the region was the home of the ruling elite and could not be seen to lag behind in implementing a core government policy. It had to catch up to the pioneer, the Southern Region. In addition, the simultaneous budget and accounts reforms in Tigray exemplified the *zemecha* (campaign) approach to *mashashaya* (reform). A campaign approach to reform fit with the political and bureaucratic culture of the region—a legacy of its leadership of the revolution that had overthrown the Derg regime.

Even the successful Tigray reform demonstrated that it takes time for an accounts reform to fully settle in. An accounting system has a myriad of moving parts that need to work in concert. One month after the first year of the reform's operation the DSA project found a number of weaknesses in Tigray's accounts reform—deficiencies related to the speed of the SSD rollout, not to problems with the reform design.[44] Nevertheless they served as a reminder to the government and the project that reform was not just a one-year rollout; it required continued attention over years to ensure that all of the moving parts performed.

The accounts reform in Amhara: a textbook failure

"I do not agree with you that the budget and accounts reform cannot be done in the same year," pronounced the head of the Amhara Bureau of Capacity Building (BOCB) in early February 2003, and in so saying, he doomed the rollout of the accounts reform in that region. The official was a rigid party member who said that this decision had come from the highest levels of the region and could not be questioned. I had been directed to the BOCB after a testy meeting in the morning with the acting head of BOFED, Haile Johannes. I had traveled to Amhara to review how the region's preparations for the budget reform were proceeding and was caught completely unaware by the region's decision to reform budgets and accounts simultaneously, in the same year. The acting head of BOFED had told me that it was not acceptable to the region to conduct a two-year sequence of reform. I pushed him to explain why. He said the reason was political and directed me to the BOCB.

In my meetings with BOFED and the cadre at BOCB I made four arguments as to why attempting the accounts reform simultaneously with the budget reform in Amhara was very risky and prone to failure. First, the accounts reform in regions had not been tested and the project was concentrating its manpower in the Southern Region to ensure that the new system was implemented and difficulties could be quickly addressed by that region's officials and DSA staff. Second, Amhara was the second-largest region in Ethiopia, larger than the Southern Region, and its size mandated caution in delivering reform. Third, the region was very late in starting, which when coupled with its size, increased the risk of failure. Finally, I made it very clear that the DSA project staff would not be available to provide assistance in Amhara, since they were fully engaged in the Southern Region and Tigray reforms, and the project had no funds for the Amhara accounts reform. I informed both the BOFED and BOCB that the region would be on its own in implementing the accounts reform.

A week after my visit, on February 18, 2003, the DSA project faxed a memorandum to the Amhara BOFED reiterating the project's advice.[45] We suggested a possible way forward for Amhara if they worked closely with the Southern Region so that the DSA advisors could be shared. Such twinning of the two regions made sense from the standpoint of sharing technical assistance resources, the memorandum made it very clear that the Southern Region had a different structure of government so that the Amhara reform could not be a simple turnkey of the other reform. The Amhara BOFED rejected this advice and proceeded on its own. Instead of twinning with SNNPR, Amhara secretly obtained the Southern Region's accounts manual.

Less than a month later, in early March, the project sent accounts advisors to review Amhara's preparations for the reform. The assessment was alarming and clearly showed that this reform was a train wreck waiting to happen. Three poison pills were in place. The most serious was that there was no procedure manual.[46] Amhara had embarked on a stealth turnkey reform, which ignored the significant differences of its structure of government. It was a prescription for failure.

The two other poison pills were that as of March, four months before the new accounting system was to begin operating, the region had not cleared its backlog of accounts and had not developed an IST strategy. Without an appropriate procedure manual and training materials based on such a manual, an IST strategy was irrelevant. The DSA project sent the region our assessment report in the first week of March but the region continued with its reform.

The project continued to monitor events in Amhara, and two months into FY2003, when the new accounting system was to be operating, the project conducted another assessment.[47] The accounts reformed had failed; indeed, six months into that year, no wereda had submitted a financial report with the new system.[48]

Most of the senior finance officials in the Amhara BOFED knew that a simultaneous reform of budget and accounts did not make sense. This was a reform driven by political fiat, and senior officials clearly were not motivated. They did not show due diligence, failing to deliver the checklist of reform tasks (table 5.3), and the actions they did take were incorrect. They failed to align the drivers of reform (see chapter 4). In addition, they were arrogant. They ignored collaboration with the Southern Region and refused to accept the Southern Region's translation from English into Amharic of the Accounts Manual 3. Instead, Amhara wasted valuable time retranslating the Southern Region's Manual 3, which in any case, did not fit Amhara's needs.

I tried to change this course of events by taking the risky and possibly inappropriate step of speaking with the BOFED heads of the Southern Region and Tigray to get them to convince the Amhara BOFED that they were headed for failure. The Tigray BOFED did have this conversation with the acting head of the Amhara BOFED but indicated to me that the decision was a done deal—it was a political decision that could not be overturned by bureaucrats. I briefed the Ministry of Finance and Development (MOFED) minister five months before the start of the new fiscal year in which the new accounting system would have to work in Amhara and thus well in advance of the failure. MOFED undertook nothing to cause Amhara to change course.

Amhara's stealth accounts reform in FY2003 failed and had to be restarted in the following year. The region's attempt to do both the budget and accounts reform also significantly impaired the quality of the region's budget reform. The lack of due diligence seen in the accounts reform seemed to have infected even the budget reform, which had been scheduled for FY2003 and had the full backing of the project. During my visit in February 2004, when I discovered the stealth accounts reform, I also discovered serious implementation problems in the budget reform. Perhaps indicative of the virtual absence of due diligence was the failure of BOFED to distribute the new budget forms that the project had printed and sent to the region. When asked why the forms were still sitting in the container of the BOFED compound seven months into the new fiscal year a senior official informed me that the container did not have a light.

Amhara's failed attempt provided a textbook case of how not to do the reform, but it did have a silver lining: it was a clear demonstration to other regions of the need to follow the checklist and for senior officials to stand up to political demands to accelerate reform. Also, it chastened Amhara to respect the tangibles of reform (the table 5.3 checklist) and review and take on board the lessons provided by pioneering regions in the accounts reform, especially Tigray.

Amhara's failure made ripples in other regions. In a sense, Amhara's failure led in part to Oromia's success the following year. The failed accounts reform in Amhara had a sobering effect and provided a wakeup call just as the project was turning to the massive reform looming in Oromia. As in Amhara, in Oromia there was strong pressure to "catch up" with the Southern Region and especially Tigray. Amhara's failure gave Oromia's financial officials facing the massive task of reform in Oromia the backbone to say no to the politicians, and in the end the politicians accepted that the risk of failure far outbalanced the risks posed by a year's delay.

Doing the right things right—preparing good manuals, designing IST carefully, building relationships with officials, indeed, getting conceptual integrity in both design and implementation—is necessary, but is not sufficient to ensure a reform's success. Reform also requires a certain momentum. In fact, momentum is arguably the most important quality a project of reform has to develop and sustain, and a failure can slow—indeed stop—the momentum. Fortunately, Amhara bounced back the following year by fully implementing the checklist. I will never know the political fallout of the failed accounts reform, but I am sure there was plenty.

The accounts reform in Oromia: meeting a massive challenge

"If you change Oromia, you change Ethiopia." This sage advice, a year before the reform in Oromia started, from the vice minister of finance, Hailemelekot Giorgis, stuck with me—indeed, haunted me at times. A failure in Oromia would at a minimum bring into question the project's role in the entire PFA reform and might well put an end to the project's role in the reform. Oromia is the largest region in Ethiopia, with roughly 40 percent of the country's population—so large that the project and the region briefly entertained the idea of doing the reform in two parts. We discarded this approach, for it would have created two systems in the region and brought needless complexity. Oromia was a serious test of the region's leadership and administration and the project's capabilities in logistics.

Nothing succeeds like failure in getting a government's attention. The accounts reform in Oromia benefited from its own failed budget reform, led by MOFED in 2003, and the failure of the accounts reform in Amhara in the same year. Oromia officials were all too familiar with the former, and the project went to great lengths to explain the latter to the Oromia BOFED.

Senior finance officials and political leaders alike were strongly motivated, and for the most part Oromia got the drivers of reform aligned and adequately delivered the tasks of reform. Oromia's size demanded that the reform be well prepared and systematically executed. Collaboration with the DSA project was intense, for senior finance officials knew that the reform model implemented in the Southern Region and Tigray was sound and that they needed to fully understand it and adapt it, with the assistance of DSA advisors, to the context of their region. The tangibles were now proven and the BOFED had a clear checklist of the tasks and schedule for doing them. Understanding the enormous challenge of reforming Oromia, the project prepared well in advance a detailed assessment of what was needed to implement both the budget and accounts reforms.[49] This assessment provided the region with a work plan to prepare the reform.

Simplification had been shown to be crucial to the success of the accounts reform in the Southern Region and Tigray, but simplification was not so simple in Oromia. Although Oromia reduced the number of transactions by heroically slashing the number of BIs at zones and weredas to twenty each—far fewer than the other large regions—and embraced the single pool, they complicated matters by continuing to expand the number of zones and especially weredas. The expansion continues to this day.

Because of its size, Oromia more than any other region needed to implement an effective post-reform strategy of wereda support units. DSA project staff worked intensively with the region in developing the WSUs and supporting them financially. Sadly, with the departure of the project in January 2008, the region discontinued the WSUs.

The lessons from the four big regions

What does the experience of these big regions tell us about reforming accounting systems specifically and financial reform in general?

The Southern Region illustrates the importance of the intangible factors of motivation, diligence, and collaboration in making a reform work. The Southern Region also got the tangible factors right—the checklist of tasks needed to deliver the reform (see table 5.3, column 1). This region struggled because of its very complicated government structures, which reflected its complex ethnic makeup. Obviously, it is easier to reform simple than complex structures of government.

Tigray was a poster child of a successful reform. It was both systematic and innovative for it not only delivered the tangibles but also far exceeded with the intangibles, pioneering the key innovation that made wereda-level reform possible, the single finance pool.

Amhara's accounts reform failed because it failed to learn from others' experience, align the drivers, and deliver the reform tasks.

Our final case, Oromia, demonstrates that size increases all of the challenges, but they can be managed. The Oromia reform followed the other big three, took on board the lessons and mistakes of the early reforms, and effectively managed a massive reform.

Accounts reform in the rest of the regions

Except for Somali region, the small regions performed far better on the accounts reform than was expected. The smaller regions faced unique challenges. The remoteness of Afar, Gambella, and Somali posed severe infrastructure constraints not found in the large regions. The serious security problems in Somali meant that the reform was not delivered in that region before the project departed in January 2008.

These regions are often referred to as "low capacity." It is politically very sensitive to talk about this, but one reason why the small regions are "low capacity" is that they tend to be neglected. The central government and the party pointed to aggregate funds transferred to these regions and claimed that these regions got a very fair share of the cake, but the problem was not just a matter of resources per se—it was a matter of presence.

The project did make an effort to reach out to the small regions—more than can be said of the MOFED, which didn't even reach out to the four large regions. Senior ministry officials rarely went to the field. In my only visit to Afar, in September 2005, the president of the region convened a morning meeting with his cabinet. I accompanied Melaku Kifle, the head of MOFED's budget department, who had prepared the budget of the federal government for well over two decades. The president opened the meeting with a welcome. He gestured toward me and said, "I know you." Then he gestured toward Kifle and said, "I don't know you." The small regions often received more than their fair share—but never enough face time.

The fact that the smaller regions executed their reforms as well as they did was largely due to the lessons provided by the larger regions' experiences, good and bad. Standouts include Benishangul Gumuz, which cleared its accounts backlog shortly after the Amhara and the Southern Region cleared theirs, and Afar, which rapidly implemented the reform with only modest project assistance. Though small and neglected and labeled "low capacity," for the most part they performed as well as the four large regions.

An eleventh-hour assignment

Phase 4 of the project, which was intended to be its last, was extended for an additional year, from December 1, 2006, to November 30, 2007, to allow time to complete the handover of the reform to government. The Phase 4 extension document was very explicit about the objectives of the extension: "The extension has two objectives: complete the deliverables of Phase 4 and facilitate the handover to Government of the DSA assisted reforms. *This extension is not a new phase of the project and involves no new activities* [emphasis added]."[50]

Nevertheless, during the extension the government decided to introduce the zero treasury balance (ZTB) disbursement system in the federal government and in the four large regions. A zero treasury balance system is a complex system of master accounts and sub-accounts whose purpose is to promote better cash management by having agencies forecast their cash requirements and by eliminating idle cash in the myriad of agency bank accounts. In essence, ZTB means there is one checkbook for all public bodies at a tier of government (say, the federal government). At the end of the day all the outflows and inflows are balanced; if there is a negative balance the government replenishes the account and if there is a positive balance, it is deposited in a government fund, thereby leaving a zero balance of the account, hence the name.[51]

The East Africa Regional Technical Assistance Center, or East AFRITAC, had pressed the government to introduce a ZTB disbursement system. Again, as with the unplanned donor accounting system, the government asked the project to assist with the design and implementation of the ZTB reform.

The government's request posed a tough decision for the project and sparked strong disagreement among the project advisors. Indeed, whether to assist with the ZTB reform was one of the most contentious issues the project experienced. As chief of party I was firmly against it. First, it was not in the contract, which specifically stated that no new activities were to be undertaken. Second, the government had failed to take over the existing reforms and was now embarking on a new reform that would further distract it from taking over the systems developed under the DSA project. Third, with less than twelve months left in this extension to the end of the project, I felt that it was professionally irresponsible to start a reform without adequate time to properly implement and then support it. Doing the ZTB reform would open the project to criticism for undertaking a reform it did not finish. Other project advisors argued that if we did not at least modify the manuals to reflect the ZTB reform before the project closed, they would be obsolete. In the end I accepted these arguments and the project provided assistance. In the final days of the project it came down to the wire as these advisors did yeoman service to modify all of the regional accounts manuals to include the ZTB system.[52]

The ZTB decision was a case of damned if you do and damned if you don't— but the responsibility for this hectic race to the finish lay with the IMF and East AFRITAC, which had told the government to do the ZTB reform without taking into account the overall status of the PFA reform and the delicate circumstances when a twelve-year technical assistance project withdraws. Typical of the IMF's forays into Ethiopia's PFA/M, it directed the government to do something but did not adequately support its development and implementation. The federal government introduced a ZTB system as the DSA project was closing but abandoned ZTB two years later.

Alignment of roles in the rollout phase

The quality of collaboration between regional governments and the project was a defining factor in the success and failure of the regional reforms. The variations among regions meant that the reform could not be a turnkey rollout of the federal reform. In a decentralized government the design task is not over in the rollout phase. Without the second-stage decentralization, it might have been possible to roll out a marginally tweaked version of the federal reform so that little design effort would have been required. But SSD necessitated thorough simplification and the innovations of the single pool, the treasury single account, and a streamlined structure of reporting entities. For simplification—the sine qua non of conceptual integrity—to work required a deep understanding of the nuances of context. This understanding emerged only through intensive collaboration.

Lessons from the accounts reform

The successful move to double-entry and modified cash-basis accounting defied skeptical experts' predictions and for a long time silenced donor agencies' criticism of the PFA reform and the DSA project. The accounts reform was the jewel in the crown of the PFA reform, for accounts is the anchor of PFA/M. An accounts reform also tests the mettle of a technical assistance project because—unlike budget and expenditure planning reforms, where the quality of outcomes is largely political, not technical—accounting is a technical exercise. If a technical assistance project cannot deliver a technical reform, it has no business being in a country.

The lessons for reformers of government accounting can be distilled as follows:

Tone up. Recognize and improve the existing system so that work is current and efficiencies allow the release of staff to work on reform. If the existing system is performing well, failure or delay in implementing a new system does not impact the accounting function.

Simplify. Accounting systems are the most complex component of the transaction platform of public financial management. Bringing conceptual integrity to design and implementation greatly simplifies an inherently complex system.

Train. The principal resource in the reform of an accounting system is the capability of government staff to understand and confidently run a reformed system. In-service training is the core of reform.

Support. Reforms involve a stage of introduction followed by several years of support and, ideally, institutionalization. The need for support is continual, and requirements vary across these three stages. External resources are volatile and those who provide them are not attuned to the longer and deeper stages of support. Institutionalization of finance reforms needs domestic resources to fill the gap.

Sequence. If the accounts reform is undertaken at the same time as a budget reform, sufficient leeway must be provided to manage the inevitable delays of a budget process. Completion of a new budgeting process may well spill deep into the financial year in which the new accounting system is to operate and manage that budget. If the same officials are involved in both reforms as well as being responsible for daily operations, care is needed to ensure a resilient schedule.

Tolosa Degefu, the head of the Oromia BOFED and an accountant, offers advice to other governments in reforming their accounting systems. In a meeting I had with him three years after the DSA project had departed, I asked him about the status of the reform in his region. He said, "It is a good reform, but it still needs to settle." Introducing a reform with manuals and IST is just the first step in a process of reform. Reforms must age, they must settle in, and during this fragile time, additional reform should not be done. Degefu's advice was not heeded in Ethiopia. The failure to let the accounts reform settle and the leap to introduce new systems are two of the key reasons Ethiopia's PFA has deteriorated (discussed further in chapter 8, "The tests of time").[53]

Notes

1 The hard budget constraint is also referred to as aggregate fiscal discipline. See Allen Schick's framework in World Bank (1998: 17–31).
2 On appropriation or budgetary accounting see Schiavo-Campo and Tommasi (1999: 163–6).
3 Office of the Prime Minister, Task Force for Civil Service Reform (1996a, vol. 2: 44).
4 For a summary of the achievements of the accounts reform see DSA M-70.
5 The performance of the accounting system in 2008 was current for domestic funds but was delayed because of late accounting by several foreign aid projects, especially the Productive Safety Nets Program and the Protecting Basic Services II project. See Peterson et al. (2011: 28–35).
6 The DSA project did not have a specific brief to develop a financial information system until the fourth phase of the project, six and a half years in. At this point the project took the initiative to finalize the financial information systems it had developed since the start of the reform. During the twelve years of the reform the EU issued no contract for creation or rollout of the FIS.
7 Office of the Prime Minister, Task Force for Civil Service Reform (1996a, vol. 2: 41).
8 "Occam's Razor: One should not increase, beyond what is necessary, the number of entities required to explain anything.... [It] is a logical principle attributed to the medieval philosopher William of Occam (or Ockham)" (see Principia Cybernetica, "Occam's Razor," http://pespmc1.vub.ac.be/OCCAMRAZ.html).
9 DSA A-27: 61. This view on the role of accounting is from James Yardley, a DSA accounts advisor and professor of accounting systems at Virginia Polytechnic University in the United States.

10 Brooks (1995: 42).
11 In fairness to Schick, his tripartite three-part sequence of control, which comes from Robert Anthony's work in operations research (see Anthony 1965), focused on the sequence of budget reform. But even here, one must question Schick, in light of Wildavsky's formulation of the traditional budget. As Wildavsky noted in his seminal work, "Why the Traditional Budget Lasts," a line-item budget succeeds because, despite not performing best in all three roles of control, management, and planning, it does not fail in any of them. In short, putting in a line-item budget, just like putting in a basic accounting system, does not imply a focus on just the first stage of PFM, control. See Schick (1966); Wildavsky (1978).
12 Most governments use a cash budget, so accounting for the budget appropriation is in cash. Some governments have an accrual budget, which requires that the appropriation be accounted by accrual and cash accounting.
13 For IPSAS standards: www.ifac.org/public-sector.
14 A colleague related a meeting between a foreign aid agency's PFM expert and representatives of an Eastern European government where the issue of accounts reform was discussed. The PFM expert recommended that the government not change from a cash basis to modified cash because there were no standards for the latter.
15 These deficiencies as contributors to the backlog at both the federal and regional level were discussed in a federal workshop held in the Ministry of Finance in Addis Ababa in late September 2001 (see DSA A-33 and DSA A-34).
16 DSA A-33: 10.
17 DSA A-1, A-2, A-3, A-5.
18 In its 1996 survey of government staff working in accounts, the project found that 88 percent of the bookkeepers had one or more years of experience in government bookkeeping. We tested the survey group and found that all were capable of filling in forms, but none could fully explain the purpose of the forms (see DSA A-1: 4–5).
19 DSA A-13 and DSA A-14.
20 Module 1 comprises the "T" series of DSA publications, relating to training test questions and answers. See DSA T-28 to DSA T-34. The DSA changed its nomenclature with the follow-on IST materials. For the existing system, "modules" referred to the training units and "manuals" to the comprehensive documentation of procedures from which the modules were prepared. For the IST in accounting for donor funds (the 2 series) and the final changed system (the 3 series), manuals contained the procedures for which a training module was created. Jim Yardley, the lead project accounts advisor, directed the development of Module 1.
21 DSA A-35.
22 DSA A-2 and DSA A-3.
23 DSA T-1: 3.
24 DSA A-20: 23.
25 The local firm contracted to develop the strategy for the donor accounting system was Excellence Management & Accounting Consultants. See Excellence Management & Accounting Consultants (1998).
26 DSA A-12: 5.
27 Based on DSA reports M-10, A-11, A-12, A-20.
28 The IFTP was designed to support IST training in the four largest regions—Amhara, Oromia, the Southern Region, and Tigray—as well as the Ethiopian Civil Service College.
29 DSA T-6.
30 Module A is part of DSA T-35.
31 International Monetary Fund (2011: 42).
32 Johann Wolfgang von Goethe, *Wilhelm Meister's Apprenticeship*, edited by William Allan Neilson (New York: P. F. Collier & Sons, 1917), 32.
33 DSA A-33: 5.

34 DSA A-33: 10.
35 DSA Q-23: 14.
36 Module 1.1 comprised DSA T-28 to T-34.
37 Peterson (1996e).
38 There is a clear system of nomenclature for government entities at the different tiers of government: at the federal level, *ministries*; at the regional level, *bureaus*; at the zone level, *departments*; and at the wereda level, *offices*. So the finance function is delivered at the federal level by the Ministry of Finance and Economic Development, or MOFED; at regions by the Bureau of Finance and Economic Development, or BOFED; at zones by the Department of Finance and Economic Development, or DOFED; at weredas by the Office of Finance and Economic Development, or OFED.
39 DSA M-18: 2.
40 DSA M-18: 2–8.
41 DSA M-39.
42 DSA M-39.
43 The DSA project recommended the WSU and ZSU innovations to the Southern Region BOFED in May 2004, eleven months into the rollout of the accounts reform (see DSA M-42).
44 On the weaknesses see DSA A-90: 1.
45 See DSA A-61.
46 DSA M-24: 2.
47 DSA A-66.
48 DSA M-34: 2.
49 DSA A-67.
50 Peterson (2006: 1).
51 For a detailed discussion of how a ZTB disbursement system works, see Pattanayak and Fainboim (2010: 14).
52 The project revised the accounts manuals for the federal and the four large regions to accommodate the ZTB system. For the federal manuals see DSA A-166 and DSA A-167.
53 Peterson et al. (2011: 1–3).

6 Financial information systems
Supporting, not driving, reform

"Is it a Lada or a Lamborghini?" mused Kevin Kelly, the head of Irish Aid to Ethiopia.

"It's a Toyota," I replied. We were talking about the financial information systems that the DSA project had developed to support the PFA reform. Tedla Mulugeta, the head of the Ministry of Finance and Economic Development's information technology department, was enamored of state-of-the-art systems and pushed hard at the start of the civil service reform project for a Lamborghini—an advanced Oracle integrated financial management information system. In 2000 he had declared that the budget information system developed by the project for the budget reform was a bicycle, an assessment he charitably upgraded later to a Lada (the Soviet-era vehicles are ubiquitous in Ethiopia, especially the blue-and-white painted taxis).[1]

Like Mulugeta, many in Ethiopia wanted a sophisticated system. As of 1996 the European Commission had committed to funding a $9 million financial information system (FIS) component of the Civil Service Reform Program, but a two-year delay in procurement followed by a two-year suspension of aid to Ethiopia because of its war with Eritrea put the procurement of this expensive system on the back burner for seven years. Throughout the life of the reform, both the government and the foreign aid agencies kept their desire for a Lamborghini alive, even though foreign funding to make this wish come true ebbed and flowed.[2]

The vehicle metaphor is useful for understanding the financial information system reform in Ethiopia and also provides insight into the information technology (IT) decision that virtually all PFA/M reforms face: How sophisticated must their IT system be? Do they need a Lada or a Lamborghini?

IT has proved to be a risky business in the private and public sectors of both developed and developing countries. IT systems fail or underperform far more often than they succeed. In 2001, the Standish Group, a Boston-based company specializing in IT services, surveyed information system project management. It found that success varied, from 59 percent in the retail sector to 32 percent in the financial sector to 27 percent in manufacturing and 18 percent percent in government. The Royal Academy of Engineering and the British Computer Society reported that 84 percent of public sector IT projects resulted in failure of some sort. A 2011 study of the success rate of IT projects in the corporate sector found frequent massive overages.

> Fully one in six of the projects we studied was a black swan, with a cost overrun of 200%, on average, and a schedule overrun of almost 70%. This highlights the true pitfall of IT change initiatives: It's not that they're particularly prone to high cost overruns *on average*, as management consultants and academic studies have previously suggested. It is that an unusually large proportion of them incur massive overages—that is, there are a disproportionate number of black swans.[3]

Turning to the experience of large-scale FIS projects in developing countries, a 2003 study by the World Bank documented an appalling record: less than 19 percent met user needs, only 11 percent were sustainable, and delivery took seven to nine years.[4] In its 2011 review of the eighty-seven integrated financial management information system (IFMIS) projects it has funded since 1984, the World Bank found that four out of twelve projects in Africa failed (the highest failure rate), but it was silent on underperformance—clearly there are IT black swans in Africa.[5] (In fact, on closer inspection, highly publicized success stories of FIS reforms have not been as successful as their proponents claim. For example, the Tanzania FIS reform had serious deficiencies.)[6] None of the IFMIS case studies the bank presents are from Africa, and the report notes that future studies "might usefully explore the significantly higher failure rate for projects in Africa."[7] The obvious question is, if FIS reforms have such a high failure rate in Africa, doesn't this suggest that foreign aid agencies that advise governments on FIS in PFA/M, especially in Africa, are doing something wrong? One would think that their critical priority would be to conduct research aimed toward upgrading the quality of technical assistance. Despite the ubiquitous underperformance, punctuated with spectacular failures, of public sector IT projects in the developed world, governments in developing countries continue to be advised to adopt overly sophisticated FIS systems (unfortunately, foreign aid agencies often provide concessionary loans for these inappropriate "Lamborghini" systems).[8]

Ethiopia's FIS reform was a significant success without a complicated system, and governments in Africa and in other developing countries can learn much from this twelve-year reform.[9] The DSA project delivered a "Toyota" FIS—the Integrated Budget Expenditure, or IBEX—that was fit for purpose, suitable to local conditions, was inexpensive to develop and maintain, and is sustained in Ethiopia by Ethiopian IT specialists. The proof of its success? It never delayed the rollout of the budget and accounting reforms, it has a remarkable near 100 percent uptime availability, and after nine years it is still used to manage Ethiopia's finances, despite being maintained on a shoestring by three former DSA project staff. If the World Bank estimates of the time to delivery of an IFMIS are correct, the IBEX FIS will continue to manage Ethiopia's finances for another decade.

PFA/M is a crucial function of the state and needs to be reliably delivered with limited risk that is well managed. The near certainty of underperformance and the frequent failures of IT systems generally and FIS specifically mean that achieving a rare success in this treacherous field requires effective risk management. Far too often IT is the tail wagging the reform dog. IT is a common cause for the delay and often outright failure of PFA/M reforms. The field's treacherousness is suggested in the title of Gauld and Goldfinch's book on public sector IT: *Dangerous Enthusiasms: E-government, Computer Failure and Information System Development.*[10] Gauld and Goldfinch examine the performance of public sector IT systems in New Zealand, a country that is reputed to have perhaps the most advanced public sector in the world. If the public sector in New Zealand stumbled on IT, it is no wonder that governments in Africa and developing countries should as well.

The principal lesson from Ethiopia's FIS reform is about managing risk in this very risky business. An iterative approach to the FIS reform was the key to managing risk: ever better versions of the FIS were produced that met changing user needs and kept up with a rapid and sequential implementation strategy, which required that multiple versions be operating simultaneously nationwide. In this chapter I present the two stages of the DSA project's FIS reform. The first stage covered the project's initial engagement in automation, to fulfill an immediate and evolving need for IT systems with a focus on rapid and simple development. The second involved consolidating system functionality and meeting additional requirements with a focus on standards, system robustness, and sustainability. Both of these stages involved numerous iterations of development, pilot, and rollout to hone the FIS until it worked as required. There was no translation phase for the FIS reform, because this reform was conceived as a separate project funded by the European Commission and so there was no preexisting design or statement of policy to be "translated." Not until 2001, with Phase 3 of the DSA project, was the FIS made part of the DSA contract—even though the need to support the rollout of the procedural reforms in earlier phases of the project meant that the DSA project had worked on IT since early 1998.

Ethiopia's FIS in 1996

In January 1997, when the project started, the FIS systems of the government were rudimentary. Federal and regional budgets were prepared using Microsoft Excel spreadsheets on microcomputers, and accounts were prepared using an application called the Budget Disbursement and Accounts system (BDA) running on an aging minicomputer. The BDA was limited and delivered three functions: transaction register, budget adjustments, and reports. The earliest version of BDA was a COBOL-based mainframe application featuring single-entry bookkeeping and cash accounting. Perhaps the greatest problem with the BDA was that the IT departments controlled it, and these departments, especially in the Ministry of Finance, marched to their own drummer and ignored the demands of the accounts departments—a significant factor causing the backlog of accounts. The IT people were calling the shots on how accounting and other financial activities should be carried out, and there was a disconnect between the IT systems and the way accounting was being done in the field. The IT departments at both the federal and regional levels were not user-friendly; worse, they were not held accountable for the delay in the preparation of accounts. Thus, the IT staff—a key link in the chain to bring accounts current—did not consider clearing the backlog of accounts a priority.

This conflict within government between users and providers of IT services was arguably a far more serious hurdle than the rudimentary functionality of the budget and accounting systems. As Peter Keen observed many years ago, "The real problem [with information technology-based reforms] is the history of relationships or lack of relationships in most organizations."[11] Given the baseline situation in Ethiopia in 1996, improving the business processes, the relationships within organizations, was critical for an FIS strategy to succeed. And it had to be done at a pace the bureaucracy could absorb. Even if the funds and terms of reference had allowed for a big bang FIS solution, it would have failed. Not only the business processes but also the level of understanding by government staff of automation and the use of computers were rudimentary.

The DSA project's FIS strategy

Two factors shaped the project's FIS strategy: urgent need and lack of funds. There was an urgent need to support the reformed procedures in budgets and accounts that were being rolled out. This proved to be a godsend, for it highlighted the defining feature of a successful IT system: it meets user requirements. The user requirements had been developed through intensive collaboration of government and project staff and were concretized in the budget and accounting manuals. These specified procedures that in turn would be automated.

Funding was lacking because the project's FIS initiative was not part of its contract; it was not specifically funded until 2001. This circumstance, too, proved a blessing in disguise, for it meant that expensive and complicated solutions were ruled out. The lack of time and money demanded an IT solution that was lean and mean with no bells and whistles. Lack of time and money resulted in an FIS strategy that, cross-country research has shown, promotes successful public sector IT systems. Gauld and Goldfinch's study of public sector IT systems found that success in IT came from "smaller projects, often initiated from the bottom up." They also found that success varied dramatically by a project's budget—witness New Zealand's experience: there, IT projects costing less than $750,000 had a 55 percent success rate, whereas all of those costing more than $10 million failed.[12]

In the two IT stages, the project addressed the five sources of risk of IT systems:

1   Acquisition: Frequent delays, legal entanglements, and rents to funders, government officials, and contractors.

2   Functional: Actual users' ability to use the systems.
3   Technical: The potential for technical glitches or failure.
4   Operational: The systems' fit with the administrative structure and capacity.
5   Proprietary: Unclear ownership of the software.

Stage 1 of the FIS strategy: rapid development and introduction of BDA and BIS systems

Stage 1 of the FIS strategy had two objectives: to replicate the procedural reforms in budgets and accounts and to support their rollout to the federal and regional governments. These objectives necessitated a technical solution that allowed for rapid development to minimize the lead time to introduction, and for easy customization in the face of evolving and geographically varied requirements.

To meet these objectives, the project developed the Budget Information System (BIS) and the Budget, Disbursement, and Accounts (BDA) system. These systems managed well the first four risks of an IT system. Although proprietary risk always exists with a custom system, the project judged that this, too, could be managed by having ownership of the source code and developing a system using software tools widely understood in Ethiopia.

We succeeded in sidestepping acquisition-related problems because the budgetary constraints during the first half of the DSA project obliged us to develop the system in-house or via sole-sourcing to a subcontractor, Omnitech. A major source of delay of FIS projects is the long procurement process that results from the scale and complexity of these systems and thus contracting—as well as their high cost. Since the FIS was not in the project's contract or budget, our solution was small and cheap and therefore quick.

We managed functional risk by focusing on user requirements and system usability. Although user requirements were evolving, and most users were new to the computerized tools, the focus on usability rather than on standards and control allowed for the initial acceptance and use of the automated products, especially to reduce the processing backlog. As required by the iterative evolution of the systems and the geographically phased rollout of the reforms (thus, to ensure that automation would not delay the procedural rollout), the project rapidly developed two functional versions of the BIS and three of the BDA systems during this first stage of its information systems efforts. These were in use throughout the country.

BIS 1: New budget classification, cost-center budget, stand-alone application.
BIS 2: BIS 1 with network capability and additional reports.
BDA 2: Single-entry bookkeeping, new chart of accounts, upgraded to run on a personal computer, not a mainframe.[13]
BDA 3-A: New budget classification, single-entry bookkeeping, new chart of accounts.
BDA 3-B: new budget classification, double-entry bookkeeping, new chart of accounts.

Managing the technical risk was critical because the speed of the rollout precluded lengthy testing of the software. We would be testing through operational use—a risky approach. To manage this risk we used simple systems that could be rapidly developed and deployed with low customization costs, in a highly iterative "prototype" approach. This allowed us to integrate evolving requirements and introduce simple information systems to previously noncomputerized environments, where both user and infrastructural capacity for computerization was low. The risk of using an operational prototype for budgeting was limited because if the BIS failed, the new manual formats could be processed using the previous practice of rudimentary spreadsheets. The risk of using an operational prototype for accounts was reduced because there was a legacy BDA available.

We carefully managed technical risk by having redundant systems, by having the new system mirror the new manual formats, and by using development software and database software that are in wide use in Ethiopia. The BIS and BDA systems were developed using the basic development software of the day, which offered ease of change instead of sophistication or robustness. The BDA and BIS systems were initially stand-alone applications developed in the Visual Basic programming language running on a Microsoft Access database (upgraded to the Microsoft SQL Server database for higher-volume installations)—applications that are widely used in Ethiopia. "Stand-alone" meant that although the systems were available to multiple users working on a local area network (say, in a networked office building), they were not usable by users across a wide area network (such as the Internet). Furthermore, the BIS and BDA applications were integrated in the sense that although the BIS system implemented the budget preparation functionality, and the BDA system implemented the budget execution (accounting) functionality, they shared the financial data created by both functions.

We managed operational risk—the timely availability and upgrading of the BIS and BDA systems as well as the administrative tier's capacity to manage these systems—in two ways. First, we subcontracted the development and upgrading of the BDA and the upgrading of the BIS. This allowed for the required short "time-to-market" of these systems without the long process of building IT resource capacity within the project. Second, the project limited the devolution of automation to the zone level and did not venture to weredas—even though the procedural PFA/M reforms were implemented down to the wereda level—because the task of maintaining even simple automated systems at the remote, low-capacity weredas was deemed to be infeasible. This provided a supportable strategy for deployment of the systems. The weredas had fully functioning manual budget and accounting systems, which were mirrored by BIS and BDA systems, so they could produce budgets and accounts manually and have their zones process them with the BIS and BDA.

In this early stage we didn't have to deal with proprietary issues—who owns the software—which cropped up later with the subcontractor and as the project was closing, with select project IT staff. Our relationship with our subcontractor, Omnitech, was interdependent: they needed us and our money as much as we needed them and their expertise.

The BIS and BDA met the reform's requirements, schedule, and budget, and the development of the FIS did not delay the rollout of the reform anywhere in Ethiopia. This outcome can be termed a success.

Stage 2: International standards and sustainability—IBEX

Phase 3 of the DSA contract was set to expire in May 2004, so in mid-2003 the project started to plan for a final Phase 4, in which the rollout of the budget and accounts reforms throughout the country would be completed and the reform would be handed over to the government. In planning for wrapping things up, one of the key issues was FIS. FIS in Stage 1 had been a breakneck run to keep up with the demanding pace of the procedural rollout. There had been no time to revisit the technical platform of the BDA and BIS and improve the software.

Since the project had contracted out the development and support of the BIS and BDA systems, I felt it was essential to have a thorough and independent assessment of the Stage 1 FIS reform and of what should be done in the final phase. To carry out this task the project contracted an independent IT consultant—Adam Abate, an Ethiopian living outside the country who was familiar with current IT practices in the West and was sensitive to the Ethiopian context. Completed in September 2003, the assessment concluded that the information systems met user requirements and, where they had been implemented, greatly improved the efficiency and quality of the budget and accounts processes.[14] The assessment also concluded that there were several deficiencies and recommended that the BIS and BDA be upgraded, and detailed the scale of the upgrade.

The decision to upgrade the FIS

A handful of decisions, both good and bad, define a technical assistance project. Providing the government with a world-class FIS was a defining decision and it became a cornerstone of the final phase of the project. Two reasons compelled this decision. First, I wanted the DSA project to make a professional exit. I knew that the FIS left by the project would run the country for many years. If our FIS was not robust, the country would face serious difficulties. And if we left a poorly performing FIS, our twelve years of work would be discredited. The Bretton Woods agencies had long been attacking the project's budget reform and I did not want them to have ammunition for further attacks. An upgrade was needed not just to correct deficiencies revealed by the September 2003 assessment but also to leave in place an FIS that was above reproach and met international standards. The "bicycle" and "Lada" jibes that had been leveled at the project's FIS had to be put to rest and the final DSA FIS Toyota put proudly on display. What I did not foresee at the time, and what became a major achievement of the project, was that the Integrated Budget Expenditure system, the upgrade to BIS and BDA, would far exceed international standards. We bequeathed to the government a top-of-the-line Toyota.

A second reason for developing a qualitatively better FIS was the government's initiative to construct a wide area network (WAN), named WeredaNet, to reach all tiers of government. WeredaNet is Ethiopia's first step in building an e-government infrastructure. The network connects more than 570 entities throughout the country (weredas and regional and federal government offices). WeredaNet is a terrestrial (cable-based) and satellite-based network designed with the primary objective of providing information and communication technology (ICT) services such as video conferencing, messaging, and phone service through the Internet, as well as Internet connectivity to the federal-, regional-, and wereda-level government entities. WeredaNet is a multiservice IP-based service using terrestrial broadband and VSAT (very small aperture terminal) infrastructure for the delivery of services to government and the citizens and is meant to provide timely information to the lowest levels of government. Video conferencing is used for meetings, trainings, court sessions; audio is being used for telephone connectivity where it does not exist; and the data connection is being used to exchange data, email, and for applications such as an FIS if it has WAN capability. WeredaNet was potentially a game changer for PFA in Ethiopia, for it held the promise of real-time financial administration at all tiers of government, from federal to wereda. With WeredaNet, the FIS software could reside on a server in the regional BOFEDs and its zones and weredas would then access it online and transactions would be instantly recorded. The regional BOFEDs would also be connected to MOFED by WeredaNet, making PFA virtual throughout Ethiopia; the entry of a transaction in a remote wereda in Gambella would be instantly seen in MOFED in Addis Ababa. With an FIS running on WeredaNet, the minister of finance could know, literally on a minute-by-minute basis, the flow of public money throughout the land. Operating an FIS on a WAN, besides delivering real-time PFA, would dramatically improve the efficiency and security of the management of financial data. With the WeredaNet WAN, the FIS software could reside in the MOFED and could be rapidly maintained: bugs uncovered during operations could be quickly corrected, and both the functionality and the technical platform could be rapidly upgraded. Improvements and changes to the software could also be done centrally and then instantly disseminated. Security of vital financial data would be greatly enhanced, as nationwide data would be continually updated to the central server at MOFED, where government and project staff could ensure vigilant backup. Without a WAN, maintaining the FIS would increasingly become a nightmare as IT specialists had to physically visit 208 sites: 152 federal public bodies (20 outside Addis Ababa), 11 regional finance organizations (BOFEDs), and 45 zone finance organizations (DOFEDs).[15] The mammoth task of outreach to maintain the FIS meant that the rollout of the FIS could go no lower than zone level. Extending the FIS to the 584 weredas, whose number was growing by the day, was beyond the means of the project.

The BIS and BDA systems could not run on a WAN and could operate only on local area networks (LAN) or as stand-alone applications on a single computer. The need for an upgrade was clear, but the question remained: Should the upgrade continue the practice of building a custom system (also referred to as bespoke or locally developed software, LDSW) or should an OTS (off-the-shelf) solution be sought? The decision to proceed with a custom solution was based on an assessment of the five sources of risk to an FIS system enumerated earlier: acquisition, functional, technical, operational, and proprietary.

As in Stage 1, we avoided acquisition risk because we continued the Omnitech subcontract, which had been initially sole-sourced. The modest cost of the subcontract coupled with the rationale of the need for continuity in support and development was an acceptable argument to the funders of the project for continuing the sole-source contract with Omnitech.[16]

In managing functional risk, a custom solution was far superior to an OTS solution. First, the functional design would be based on the BIS and BDA FIS, mature systems whose requirements met user needs and were well understood. The same seamless integration of the computer screens with the manual forms would be retained. Unlike with an OTS, the existing proven baseline requirements were stable and could be rapidly and precisely replicated in the upgrade.

Unfortunately, the custom-versus-OTS issue was complicated by the fact that the government, especially foreign aid agencies, started introducing new requirements. In early 2003 while planning for the upgrade was under way, the World Bank, the IMF, and other aid agencies introduced a comprehensive exercise, the Joint Budget and Aid Review (JBAR), to monitor public expenditure, including funds originating with them. The JBAR required government to provide a consolidated picture of nationwide expenditure twice a year with details by sector and programs within a sector. For example, JBAR required MOFED to present total expenditure for the health sector at all tiers (federal, region, zone, wereda) by major program (say, malaria control). The JBAR reporting requirements required a lot of detail and thus took a long time. Furthermore, the requirements were not stable, as foreign aid agencies kept changing their minds about what information was needed. One of the most frustrating tasks in developing the array of reports in the upgraded FIS was the failure of foreign aid agencies to provide the government and thus the project with clear and written reporting requirements for JBAR. Despite repeated attempts, the project never received these requirements and took the initiative to develop report formats.

It is accepted wisdom that an OTS solution requires stable requirements, for it is difficult and expensive to customize OTS software. Thus, it is ironic that throughout the reform the government and foreign aid pressed for a sophisticated OTS IFMIS, yet their own changing demands for financial reporting resulted in unstable requirements, which undermined the very OTS solution they advocated. The unstable reporting requirements of foreign aid were by met by the flexible custom system of the project.

The final deal killer to the option of doing the upgrade with an OTS system was the diversity of procedures operating across the tiers of government, given the sequential rollout of the reform. A critical issue that is rarely raised in the course of FIS acquisition decisions is how to handle legacy systems and their data. Pioneer regions of the reform were operating the new budget classification

(BC) and chart of accounts (COA) and doing double-entry bookkeeping while the regions that had yet to be reformed were still using the old BC and COA and single-entry bookkeeping. At the end of the day, the accounts department of MOFED had to consolidate these disparate systems and prepare national accounts. A migration tool to bring these systems together would be a crucial, indispensable feature of the FIS upgrade. No OTS was adequate for this task.

The FIS upgrade did pose a technical risk for it involved a complete change to the technical platform.[17] A strong argument for an OTS is that its technical platform is well developed and mature, obviating the need to reinvent the wheel, as with a custom system. But we could not avoid the technical risk of building a custom solution because that was what was needed. We had to manage that risk. At the start of the final phase of the project (Phase 4), a well-functioning and mature FIS, the BIS-BDA, was in place, so development of an upgrade did not pose a risk should its schedule be delayed or if the worst case—system failure—should occur.

Even if they get the requirements right, many IT systems founder because the IT specialists are simply not up to the task. Frederick Brooks's seminal recommendation is that a system must have conceptual integrity—best achieved by a small team with a clear leader. In Eric Chijioke, a newly hired project IT specialist, we found such a leader. The Integrated Budget Expenditure system was Chijioke's brainchild.[18] IBEX was a custom upgrade of the FIS that would build on the proven features of the BIS and BDA systems, further reducing risk and ensuring user acceptance. We planned a collaborative project between Chijioke and our subcontractor, Omnitech, which had for four years developed the BIS and BDA systems. Later a problem with our subcontractor developed, and so a confluence of events also ensured that a small in-house team would develop IBEX and the conceptual integrity deemed essential by Brooks would be maintained.

The custom IBEX upgrade beat an OTS system hands down when it came to managing operational risk. Most important, IBEX maintained for users the "feel" of the BIS and BDA systems with which they were familiar. There would be no learning curve to this "front end" of the IBEX. The magic of the "back end" of the system—the technical platform, hidden from the user—was that the unique design of IBEX allowed it to operate on extremely low bandwidth, allowing IBEX to far exceed international standards. Solving the problem of low bandwidth, which bedevils FIS systems running on a WAN not only in Ethiopia but also in many countries, was brilliant. This feature makes IBEX a technical marvel and a model of FIS for other developing countries coping with a limited information communication technology (ICT) infrastructure. The IBEX achieves this feat by loading on to a network only the very minimal part of the software needed to execute a transaction. For example, when entering budget data, the IBEX budget module will only use the specific code of a specific public body rather than the entire list of public bodies. In database-speak: the entire list of public bodies constitutes a "tree," and IBEX only loads a small part of the tree, the needed leaf of a branch. With this feature, IBEX can operate on existing telephone connections with a transmission rate of only 56 kilobits per second (kbits/s) and is even usable with many of the very remote telephone lines found in Ethiopia which have a minuscule transmission rate of 28 kbits/s (slow dial-up).

The significance of IBEX's low-bandwidth capability cannot be overstated, for it minimized the risk that the software would not work in a WAN environment crowded with other users and applications. The IBEX would have to share the "digital road" with other users, and the government's priority was to use WeredaNet for bandwidth-hungry video conferencing, the new style of political mobilization. With WeredaNet, a cable or a terrestrial link with a hefty 1 megabits/s of upstream bandwidth could connect a government site, though most weredas would be connected by satellite through VSAT (very small aperture terminal), which provided a more limited 512 kbits/s upstream bandwidth.[19] The low bandwidth of IBEX meant that it just might be possible for weredas to upload a transaction for the purchase of stationery while the prime minister addressed the party faithful.

A high-end OTS IFMIS such as Oracle cannot operate on low bandwidth. Where IBEX can upload to the network just the leaf of a data tree, Oracle has to upload the entire tree, making it unsuited to a low-bandwidth environment. Even when there is sufficient bandwidth for Oracle to operate, it crowds out all other applications on the network and can quickly become congested if multiple sites are using Oracle. The government of Uganda adopted an Oracle IFMIS and found that during budget preparation by central ministries in the capital city, Kampala, which were well connected by cable, the Oracle system frequently overwhelmed the network and froze up. (Sadly, the Ethiopian government purchased Oracle in 2010.)

The IBEX design also provided a solution to the operational problem of limited modes of operation. Recognizing that, once operational, even WeredaNet could be delayed or not made available to IBEX users, IBEX was designed to operate in three modes: WAN, LAN, and stand-alone. The compact design of the system meant that the existing computers could be used even in the stand-alone mode. IBEX did not require government to incur the significant cost of upgrading all hardware (which the newly acquired Oracle system will require).

A final operational issue raised by the upgrade was time: Would the DSA project have enough remaining time to develop and implement an ambitious upgrade of the FIS? The upgrade was to be done under the twenty-nine-month Phase 4 contract, which ran from July 1, 2004, to the end of November 2006. International experience with the development of financial information systems indicated that twenty-nine months would not be enough, and prudence would have suggested sticking with the BIS and BDA FIS. But the project had achieved a track record over many years of delivering new versions of the FIS on time, on scope, and within budget, and I was convinced that this delivery performance would continue with the IBEX initiative. Within a year of the start of Phase 4, the budget module of IBEX was completed and operating in the federal government and in the Addis Ababa administrative area. Within two years the accounts module and the module for consolidating national accounts were completed. By

July 2006, four months before the end date of the Phase 4 contract, the IBEX was completed.

Frederick Brooks has hypothesized that

> lean, spare, fast programs are almost always the result of *strategic break-through*, rather than tactical cleverness. Often such a breakthrough will be a new *algorithm*. More often, the breakthrough will come from redoing the *representation* of the data or tables. *Representation is the essence of programming* [emphasis in the original].[20]

The tree design of IBEX, which allowed it to limit its bandwidth requirements, and other features of the IBEX development fit this hypothesis. The system met the highest standards of software development and exceeded international standards not only in its conception and technical features but also in its rapid development and rollout.

The fifth risk to an FIS, proprietary, would be greatly reduced in Stage 2 because the technical demands of IBEX required that the project acquire in-house expertise, especially the lead architect. There would be joint development of IBEX by project and Omnitech staff, thereby building redundancy in the knowledge of the system and reducing risk. By partnering with a local Ethiopian firm, the project ensured that there was local capacity to sustain the system once the project ended while it also built local IT capacity.

Innovations of IBEX

The acronym IBEX happily recalled the walia ibex (*Capria walie*), a rare and endangered species of mountain goat unique to the mountains of northern Ethiopia. Like its namesake, the IBEX was indigenous and was suited to the extremes of its environment, and was an endangered species. Along with the BIS and BDA FIS, the IBEX FIS was also viewed by the government as an interim solution to be replaced by an OTS IFMIS.

The technical and functional features of IBEX are described in appendixes 6.1 and 6.2. Here we briefly highlight the key technical and functional innovations of the system. The principal technical innovation, the ability of IBEX to run on low bandwidth, has been discussed. The second technical innovation was its suite of migration tools to support and improve the consolidation of financial information between different levels of financial institutions, both upward, to consolidate low-level data, and downward, to disseminate centralized data. These migration tools are used to consolidate and then notify the regional budgets, consolidate the monthly regional accounting data, consolidate the regional budget adjustment data, consolidate the nationwide accounts, and even to automate the process of bringing a heretofore stand-alone system onto the online system once a previous remote installation gains network access to the WeredaNet. The migration tools simplified an otherwise tedious and tech-heavy process of data consolidation and enabled basic system users to perform the consolidation functions without technical support.

IBEX features two functional innovations. First, IBEX allows for a seamless interaction between manual and automated systems. Thus, although most weredas process their financial transactions manually, these data are processed in automated systems at the zone level and then electronically consolidated further up, at the region level. These systems can all coexist. Seamless transition means that business functions can continue in the absence of computer availability—a fairly frequent occurrence. IBEX, like its predecessors, BIS and BDA, is typically not the first point of data capture, but all the additional features of automated systems (consolidation, aggregation, data mining, reporting, and so forth) come into play after data are captured in manual forms and entered into the software. If a stand-alone IBEX installation at a zone or federal public body is unavailable for a week at a time because of infrastructure problems, officials can simply continue to process transactions using their existing manual collection forms and then enter the data into the automated IBEX system once its availability is restored. Furthermore, wherever possible the user interfaces of the automated systems have been designed to look like the manual forms they supplement.

The second functional innovation of IBEX was its consolidation module, making it possible to consolidate financial data that are coded differently (for example, data from the old and new chart of accounts). The requirement to produce nationwide consolidated accounts, combined with the phased nature of the PFM reforms, created the very unusual and demanding functional requirement of consolidating, at a national level, budgets and accounts stemming from regions with fundamentally different underlying budget and accounting structures. This effort needed to result in the production of consolidated reports, which would merge the disparate regional data into standardized reports. The IBEX accounts consolidation module provided an automated framework for the mapping of data with disparate underlying structures to a standardized structure and automated the production of the reports from these data. No OTS has this capacity.

The strategy for implementing IBEX

The Stage 2 FIS strategy focused on the development and rollout of IBEX along two tracks (see figure 6.1). Track 1 was the phase-out of the BIS-BDA systems, which would be achieved once WeredaNet allowed for IBEX to operate in a WAN mode and once the stand-alone version of IBEX had been rolled out to those sites not connected to WeredaNet. Track 2 was the phasing in of the IBEX on a WAN and stand-alone basis, depending on the availability of the WeredaNet.[21]

The promise of WeredaNet has yet to be realized. The technical feasibility of operating IBEX on WeredaNet at wereda level was demonstrated by the project in a three-month pilot (August to October 2007) in five weredas in Tigray. In this pilot the IBEX software resided on the server in the BOFED of the regional capital, Mekelle, and five wereda finance offices accessed this IBEX by VSAT,

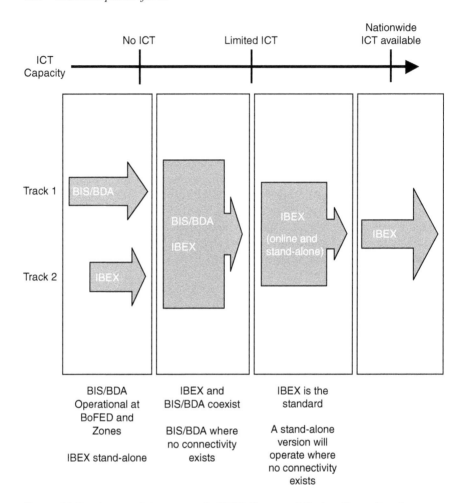

Figure 6.1 Road map of the two-track IBEX (Integrated Budget Expenditure) system rollout.

not cable. The pilot provided proof of concept that weredas could use IBEX online. The congestion experienced from 1 to 6 p.m. seemed related to the use of WeredaNet for Internet purposes—quite possibly personal use, as the congestion cleared an hour after the workday ended. Perhaps the most striking feature of this pilot is that it took the project over a year to get the central government agency responsible for WeredaNet, the Ministry of Communication and Information Technology, to agree to support the pilot. The difficulty of obtaining this cooperation underscored the weakness of the Ministry of Finance, the low priority attached to financial management by other agencies of government, and, most ironic, the failure of MOFED to grasp the importance of a robust ICT to support its desired Oracle OTS. When the project ended in January 2008, virtually all BIS and BDA applications had been replaced with IBEX, but the WeredaNet proved to be too unreliable to operate IBEX online.[22]

The WeredaNet saga illustrates the low capacity of the Ethiopian government to develop and manage complex ICT and IT applications and calls into question the soundness of foreign aid advocacy for a more sophisticated FIS system. WeredaNet was delivered three years late, in 2003, at multiples of its original budget.[23]

The fate of the WeredaNet has four implications for FIS in Ethiopia. First, the country is not in a position to automate FIS at the wereda level. To date, MOFED and BOFED have failed to adequately support IBEX at even regional and zone levels—approximately 250 sites—and have failed to support IBEX at select weredas that have the system.[24] To automate the 800-plus weredas in the country using a stand-alone application, which would require physical support at each site, is beyond the capacity of the government. The DSA project was approached in 2003 by the World Bank through USAID to do precisely that, and was offered commensurate funding, to be provided through the World Bank's Public Sector Capacity Building Project (PSCAP). I firmly declined. Such an initiative would have completely changed the project from one of developing procedures and the training and automation needed to support them to a massive IT project. I firmly believed that we needed to hew to the scope of our project.

Second, the weakness of the ICT validated the DSA strategy of limiting automation to the zone level. Zones are key to supporting the manual processing of financial data at weredas and promptly consolidating this data into an FIS. The obsession with the last mile of automation, weredas, is premature and wrong-headed. It is essential to get the zones properly managing the FIS first. Interestingly, in the assessment I directed at the request of the government and the World Bank of the performance of the financial system in 2010, we found that manual preparation of financial reports did not cause delays—indeed, weredas that had IBEX installed were delayed in reporting in large part because of the absence of support for the system.[25]

Third, the weak ICT infrastructure for FIS means that for the foreseeable future, an FIS must use minimal bandwidth, for there are other applications that are of higher priority to government. Again, the virtue of IBEX is its frugal use of bandwidth.

Fourth, the ICT infrastructure calls into question the wisdom of government's acquisition of an Oracle OTS. It cannot operate on Ethiopia's VSATs and it is yet to be seen that it can operate on even the terrestrial connections. It would appear that both the government and foreign aid have got the cart before the horse here. Until the pathways to regions and zones are adequately paved with silicon, it is premature to embark on implementing an Oracle OTS that in all likelihood will never leave the city limits of Addis Ababa. Far better to first get a robust ICT working and then introduce a more sophisticated system. This argument accords with the World Bank's 2011 review of IFMISs, which stated: "As most contemporary FMIS solutions are Web-based applications, the most important technical precondition before any FMIS implementation is the existence of a reliable countrywide network."[26] It is striking that the FIS recommendations by foreign aid in Ethiopia have completely overlooked the ICT constraints.[27]

What is the future of WeredaNet and thus of an FIS operating on a WAN? As of 2010, WeredaNet had been in operation for eight years and its equipment was reaching the end of its life with many of its routers failing and in need of spare parts. Zone and wereda sites served by WeredaNet suffer from a shortage of staff to manage and operate the network in such remote areas, and the lack of electric power in some weredas poses a constraint to its use. The government has plans to expand VSAT bandwidth to alleviate the problem of congestion and to improve the existing network by linking 460 weredas using ADSL (asymmetric digital subscriber line), a data communications technology that enables faster data transmission over copper telephone lines than a conventional voice band modem can provide, by using frequencies that are not used by a voice telephone call. Since the ADSL will use existing telephone connections, the significance of minimizing bandwidth must be a feature of any FIS solution going forward. But the ministry responsible for the migration from VSAT to ADSL acknowledges that this is a challenging task and will take some time.[28] The deterioration of WeredaNet highlights a failure that hobbles PFA in Ethiopia generally—the failure to sustain existing systems.

Assessing the performance of IBEX

Neither the government nor foreign donors have ever conducted an in-depth assessment of IBEX. Given the significance of IBEX in delivering prompt financial reports on foreign funding, given the millions of dollars committed to replacing IBEX with an OTS IFMIS (which international experience confirms is risky and costly), this is shocking. Basic due diligence would demand an assessment, if only to take on board twelve years of FIS experience when reformers are developing and implementing a follow-on OTS FIS.

In 2006, the DSA funders contracted for a three-week review of all of the activities of the DSA project over ten years. The assessment did focus extensively on the FIS and, after a cursory look at IBEX, concluded:

> IBEX has been designed and developed as a state-of-the-art product and has all the features one would expect in a well designed system—modular design, standard interfaces, uses international standards, uses industry standard relational database interfaces, has a security system appropriate to a central government financial system, comprehensive backup and recovery features. Those modules completed have been proven in practice. None of the users we spoke to voiced any concerns on its performance or reliability and all the evidence is that it forms a sound basis for a government wide FMIS.[29]

The 2010 PEFA (Public Expenditure Financial Accountability Framework) assessment of Ethiopia's PFM found that users were enthusiastic about the IBEX and that it met their needs.[30]

So why spend tens of millions of dollars for an OTS IFMIS at this time, especially since it will not support financial management in weredas, at the front line of service delivery? I raised this very question with the minister of finance in 2005.[31]

Success criteria for an FIS

A government's FIS can be assessed in terms of nine criteria, most of which IBEX's performance in Ethiopia met:

1 *Operational.* IBEX: It works. Upgrades can be seamlessly introduced without disruption of service. IBEX meets this criterion.
2 *Reliable.* IBEX: Is continuously available, with few failures.
3 *Functional.* IBEX: Delivers user requirements in terms of content and operates in four languages.
4 *Capable.* IBEX: Performance meets or exceeds user needs and is especially effective in managing connectivity.
5 *Compatible.* IBEX: Has extensive migration tools for data from legacy systems and fits with and reinforces appropriate manual procedures.
6 *Manageable.* IBEX: Performance is mixed. Government should have an adequate understanding of the capabilities and limitations of the system and should use most if not all of its resources.
7 *Sustainable.* IBEX: Performance mixed. Government should "own" the system, limiting dependence on any single contractor or vendor. The system should be well documented, government should own the source code, and the system should be sustainable within the government.
8 *Expandable.* IBEX: The system can grow with new requirements. The DSA project's FIS has continually evolved and added new functionality.
9 *Affordable.* IBEX: The initial investment and ongoing maintenance meet a "reasonable" social and cost-benefit calculation. Software development costs over the twelve-year life of the project for the different versions of FIS (BIS, BDA, IBEX) were $3.2 million. The IBEX software cost $1.65 million. Using an industry rule of thumb of 15 percent maintenance cost, the current IBEX system can be maintained for approximately $248,000 a year. In terms of social benefit analysis, a cadre of Ethiopian computer specialists have been trained in state-of-the-art systems development who can bring these skills to sustain this system as well as build additional systems for the Ethiopian market.

The IBEX system met seven of these criteria completely. On just two of them the results were mixed. The manageability (number 6) capacity has not been fully developed, in part because of the delay by the government in approving the financial statements for accounting. These are critical reports for accounts and budgets, which meet the basic reporting requirements of government and foreign aid agencies and as discussed earlier, the reporting requirements stipulated by foreign aid were not stable.

Sustainability (number 7), too, is not complete because even though the government owns the source code, it will not be able to fully sustain the system. IBEX is based on open-source frameworks, is extensively documented, and currently has user manuals in English as well as one national language, Amharic. The system was developed in Ethiopia largely by Ethiopians, so although the government will likely not have the capacity to fully sustain this system, it can be sustained within the country.

Managing the development risk of an FIS

As discussed earlier, international experience has shown that IT public and private sector projects in both developed and developing countries have failed or underperformed far more often than they have succeeded. To better understand the causes of this poor performance, developers of IT systems should read the seminal work of Frederick Brooks.[32] Robert Fairly and Mary Wilshire— partially inspired by the fateful loss of the Swedish warship *Vasa* mere hours after she was launched—have also developed a useful framework, "Ten Software Project Problems and Some Antidotes," for understanding why software projects fail (see table 6.1).[33]

I use their framework to assess how the FIS reform overcame these ten problems.

1. *Excessive schedule pressure.* This was the norm for the DSA project's FIS, for we had to keep up and support the very ambitious rollout of the budget and accounts reforms. Three antidotes adopted stand out: better resources, prioritized requirements, and phased release. Since the FIS was not in the initial terms of reference of the project and was only specified five years into the reform, more resources were not available. Better resources were continuously applied with the replacement of the original consultant, Shaun McGrath, with the subcontractor, Omnitech, which in turn was replaced with in-house project staff. Requirements were ruthlessly prioritized—no bells and whistles. But the frequent phased release of the FIS was most likely the principal means of managing schedule pressure. Given the demands of the procedural rollout, the project had to resort to "operational prototypes" because there was little time for testing. These prototypes were vigilantly monitored, and deficiencies encountered in operations were rapidly corrected with a patch or an upgrade.

2. *Changing needs.* User requirements did change over the course of the reform, but these were minimized because the software was driven by user requirements, which were extensively developed in the budget and accounting procedural manuals before they were automated. The commitment to phased release and iterative development managed those changes, which cropped up after the initial development phase.[34]

3. *Lack of technical specifications.* This was never a problem. Both the budget and accounts reforms were designed to operate fully in a manual mode so that the software specifications were detailed in both procedural manuals and physical forms that could be used to process budgets and accounts manually. The software simply had to replicate these documents.

Table 6.1 Ten software project problems and some antidotes

Problem area	Antidote
1 Excessive schedule pressure	• Objective estimates
	• More resources
	• Better resources
	• Prioritized requirements
	• Descoped requirements (reducing the scope of the project)
	• Phased release
2 Changing needs	• Iterative development
	• Change control and baseline management
3 Lack of technical specifications	• Development of initial specifications
	• Event-driven updates of specifications
	• Baseline management of specifications
	• A designated software architect
4 Lack of a documented project plan	• Development of an initial plan
	• Periodic and event-driven updates
	• Baseline management of the project plan
	• A designated project manager
5 Excessive innovation and...	• Baseline control
6 Excessive "secondary innovation"	• Impact analysis
	• Continuous risk management
	• A designated software architect
7 Requirements creep	• Initial requirements baseline
	• Baseline management
	• Risk management
	• A designated software architect
8 Lack of scientific methods	• Prototyping
	• Incremental development
	• Technical performance measurement
9 Ignoring the obvious	• Back-of-envelope calculations
	• Assimilation of lessons learned
10 Unethical behavior	• Ethical work environments and work cultures
	• Personal adherence to code of ethics

Source: based on Fairly and Wilshire (2003: 22).

4. *Lack of a documented project plan.* All three developers of the FIS team prepared extensive planning documents that guided the reform.[35] A project manager was also clearly assigned. Plans are only as good as the staff's discipline to follow them and its professionalism in meeting deadlines. The three developers of the FIS possessed those qualities.

5. *Excessive innovation.* The need to get the IBEX to market quickly to support the reform but also to be completed before the project ended limited innovation.

6. *Secondary innovation.* Frederick Brooks argues that the most dangerous system a developer ever makes is the second system, called "secondary innovation."[36] The temptation to add every bell and whistle possible is nearly irresistible. The temptation comes in part from the desire of developers to be creative, to

devise the new, not just maintain the old, and to have fun. Software development is typically an activity of the young, and although their enthusiasm and creativity needs to be encouraged, it also needs to be well managed and channeled into the delivery of useful and valued systems. The "second system effect" was avoided because of schedule pressures, and the need for frequent releases meant there was no time for bells and whistles. The software architects, especially Eric Chijioke, who designed the IBEX system and led its development, were fully capable of adding interesting features to the system but prudently resisted this temptation.

7. *Requirements creep.* The virtue of having developed procedures to the depth of a fully functioning manual system before automation meant that requirements were very stable. The demand for a rapid rollout of the procedural reforms curbed requirements creep, for the priority was to implement what was proven in the pilot reforms and not add new, untested, features. However, regional variations were accommodated.

8. *Lack of scientific methods.* The most important antidotes were the commitment to prototyping and incremental development. The demand for rapid rollout meant that the project's FIS, especially in the early regional reforms, were operational prototypes, for there was no time to fully test them before deploying them in the field. Incremental development resulted in the three versions each of the BIS and BDA systems.

9. *Ignoring the obvious.* Failing to learn from experience is one way of "ignoring the obvious." The project's approach to FIS development through operational prototyping and incremental development required continuous learning. Learning from the FIS pilots was firmly established from the start by Shaun McGrath, who despite the painful experience of the federal pilot of the BIS prepared an extensive review of it.[37] The rollout of the project's FIS were followed up with assessments of both the adequacy of the software to meet the needs of users and the users' ability to use the software.

10. *Unethical behavior.* The project managed well the first nine problem areas of software development but was blindsided by the tenth, "unethical behavior." Unethical behavior by a subcontractor and three project employees was likely motivated by a conviction that on some level the IBEX program and the information and knowledge that it represented belonged to them, or should belong to them. This is a very basic and central proprietary issue. The work the DSA project did for the government of Ethiopia—including, of course, the very central IBEX system—belonged to the government. It did not belong to the project; it did not belong to the individual DSA staff members who were paid for professional services, including developing the system; it did not belong to outside subcontractors. The USAID contract with Harvard University, which governed the ownership of the DSA deliverables, was very clear: during the life of the project, ownership rested with USAID; after closure all deliverables and the assets, which USAID did not retain, became the property of the government of Ethiopia.

It is essential that proprietary issues be clarified, although doing so may at times be an unpleasant process. Reformers need to be alert to conditions under which proprietary issues can become a source of danger to a project. The first entity to try an end-run around the project to get a monopoly over the software was our sub-contractor, Omnitech, when they refused, in the early stages in the development of IBEX, to collaborate with the project's software designer, Eric Chijioke. This forced the project to bring the whole software design project in-house. The conflict was ultimately resolved via the courts (in the project's favor).

As the termination date of the project approached, the government IT department was in chaos, and the process of handing IBEX off to the government and keeping the FIS functioning smoothly was uncertain. This time it was Eric Chijioke himself, along with Adam Abate and Simon Solomon, the project's three senior IT staff, who attempted to take control of the FIS and the IBEX system. First they delayed the handover, in order, as it later transpired, to secure a lucrative contract for supporting IBEX once the DSA project was closed. Then, two months before the end of the project, they abruptly resigned with great fanfare, writing letters to the minister of finance and Harvard to broadcast their actions. It was clear to all, especially the government, that they were trying to take over IBEX. I met with the minister of finance and his staff to reassure them that the FIS was secure under the leadership of Dula Tessema and Derege Mekonnen, two highly professional and loyal senior project IT specialists.

In addition to managing the ten *Vasa* stumbling blocks, the DSA IT project adhered to good practices in IT management as recently found in successful IT projects in the corporate sector of developed countries:

1 Stuck to the schedule, even after mergers (in this context, organizational changes)
2 Resisted changes to the project's scope
3 Broke the project into discrete modules
4 Assembled the right team
5 Prevented turnover among team members (core team members were retained)
6 Framed the initiative as a business endeavor, not a technical one
7 Focused on a single target, "readiness to go live," measuring every activity against it.[38]

Lessons from the FIS reform

Installing financial information systems is risky and can be nasty. Among the many threats the DSA project faced in its twelve years—the war with Eritrea, the closure of HIID, violent elections, funding cuts, famines, conflicting foreign aid agendas regarding PFA, and massive administrative reorganization in the second-stage decentralization—by far the greatest challenge was the development and support of the FIS. It was the tail that almost wagged the dog of the procedural reform to death.

Why are FISs "such dangerous enthusiasms"? Most obvious, they are complex undertakings that typically take years to develop, during which time the intangible nature of software development makes it hard to monitor progress. "We are almost ready to test it" is a response that unscrupulous developers can use to stave off accountability for years.

The complexity of FIS is illustrated by the five sources of risk that must be managed well if a system is to succeed: acquisition, functional, technical, operational, and proprietary. Acquisition can take years. Changes in function, user requirements, force technical changes that can add years. Turnover of government staff, changes to administrative structures, and the failure or poor performance of support systems (such as ICT infrastructure and training programs) can degrade performance, causing delay and failure.

Finally, FIS systems bring significant de jure and de facto proprietary risk, such that governments can be held hostage to unscrupulous developers tempted by the long-term monopoly rents that can be garnered from FIS systems as governments are locked into these mission-critical systems for years. More than any other component of PFA/M reform, FIS provides foreign aid agencies with a welcome vehicle for moving large sums of money (commodity dumps), which in turn tempt government officials to agree (sometimes with "inducements") to gold-plated systems. Not least, they provide contractors with lucrative long-term cash cows. Lamborghinis are welcome, Toyotas don't fit this tripartite business model. Many observers have noted that foreign aid agencies are not particularly competent in the field of IT and are often willing to go along with the most expensive or best-known product, following the adage "No one ever got fired for hiring IBM." PFM specialists often have stovepiped skills and are not versed in the IT dimensions of their craft. Their short stays in a country also do not fit with the long time scales of FIS development. A good illustration of the poor quality of technical assistance in FIS can be seen in a meeting held in the Ministry of Finance in late 2004 with ministry officials, myself, and the project's three senior IT staff with Ray Walsh, the European Community–funded IFMIS consultant to MOFED. Walsh started the meeting by proudly introducing himself: "I am not an IT specialist, I am not a PFM specialist, I am a project manager." Walsh "advised" the Ministry of Finance for two years on IFMIS; fortunately his efforts came to naught, which put off the OTS IFMIS distraction for the last two years of the project and eased the burden on government, which was scrambling to take over the DSA reform.

Gauld and Goldfinch argue that further IT failures or underperformance can be blamed on four interlocking pathologies that are often at work:

1   *Idolization.* Politicians and public officials believe IT can transform the business of government.
2   *Technophilia.* IT professionals perpetuate the myth that better technology, and more of it, is the remedy for practical problems—the myth of the technological fix.
3   *Lomanism.* The enthusiasm, feigned or genuine, that sales representatives and other employees develop for their company's products (derived from the name of the protagonist, Willy Loman, in Arthur Miller's *Death of a Salesman*).

4 *Managerial faddism.* The tendency for consultants and managers to eagerly embrace the newest management fad, methodology, or utterings of the management guru of the moment and to see problems as largely solvable (or preventable) through improved, or more "rational," management and the appointment of skilled managers.[39]

The debate about custom versus OTS systems

Which is better, a custom system or an off-the-shelf system? I am encouraged that a more catholic view is emerging from the rigid view held in the PFM field throughout most of the past decade that an OTS is a far superior solution—no one ever got fired for procuring Oracle Financials.[40] Perhaps the high failure rate of FIS reforms in developing countries has spurred a rethink of the OTS mantra by the Bretton Woods agencies. The World Bank's 2011 study concludes:

> No single package can provide all the FMIS functionality need for country-specific needs. Hence, most of the new FMIS solutions designed after 2005 integrate [OTS] packages with specific [custom] modules (including open-source software) to cover a broader spectrum of PFM functions.... The current focus on FMIS ICT solution providers and client countries is directed at the development of new open-source software and other innovative solutions to meet core FMIS requirements at a reasonable cost.[41]

Despite this more open view, the finding raises several questions. First, it omits mention of the difficulty and cost of customizing an OTS. Second, the second sentence seems still to recommend that the OTS be the anchor of an FIS and that custom modules support it. Third, the study is silent on OTS upgrades that periodically occur over four- to six-year increments, which promote vendor lock (long dependency on a software provider because of the cost and difficulty of changing software brands), require governments to once again customize the upgrade, and also require rebuilding of the interface with any custom modules.

Another issue, one not mentioned in the quoted passage, is that although the study found that a key technical precondition for an FIS is a robust ICT, the bandwidth found in many developing countries often precludes an OTS, especially the high-end varieties like Oracle.

The study also failed to mention a few other important points, such as the sources of risk of an OTS, custom, mixed OTS-custom or an open-source system. No mention was made of cost containment to reduce risk, nor of the long delays in procurement which in turn delay a PFA/M reform.

There is a serious need in the PFA/M field for a comparative study of the performance of OTS versus custom FIS reforms. There is also a need for a study into the reasons why the FIS failure rate is so high in Africa. The 2011 World Bank's study concludes that this high failure rate is due to "initial attempts to implement ambitious [FIS] solutions without adequate consideration of the limitations in capacity and infrastructure," but provides no detailed case studies.[42]

This conclusion seems quite plausible. In light of it, the bank's recommendation of pursuing a hybrid FIS solution by combining different systems (OTS plus custom plus open source) would seem to result in an overly complicated solution that is likely to fail. A more appropriate solution for African governments would be either a mid-level, not high-end, OTS, if requirements are stable, or a simple custom system if requirements are not stable. If need be, the latter could eventually be migrated to an OTS, once requirements are stable.

Perhaps the most sobering finding of the 2011 World Bank study is that the time to completion of an FIS project has only marginally shrunk, from between seven and nine years (in the 2003 study) to between six and seven years (in the 2011 study).[43] Can any government wait this long to improve PFA/M? I would argue that the key criterion determining the success of an FIS solution is its ability to manage risk, including operational risk—when is an FIS available to support a financial reform. The bank's 2011 study does not deal with the "time to market" issue of an FIS. All else equal, a custom solution is arguably faster to market. A crowning achievement of the project's FIS reform is that it never delayed the rollout of the procedural reform. Systems were built in months—not six to seven years.

Prerequisites of a successful FIS

The 2011 World Bank survey of FMIS found that successful reforms had eight prerequisites: five functional, two technical, and one human resource–related.[44]

Functional
1   Improvement of the budget classification
2   Development of a unified chart of accounts that is integrated with the budget classification
3   Improvement of the operations of the treasury single account
4   Development of commitment controls
5   Establishment of cash management functions

Technical
6   Establishment of a secure countrywide communication network
7   Preparation of system data centers

Human Resources
8   Presence of a core team of ICT specialists within PFM organizations

The World Bank's survey correctly shows the importance of getting good procedures in place before they are automated; this confirms the validity of the DSA strategy whereby procedures drive automation. The Ethiopian procedural reform delivered all five of the functional prerequisites recommended by the bank for an FIS. It did not have the two technical nor the one human resource prerequisite.

The World Bank survey recognized that not enough was known about the failure of FIS reforms in Africa—a point that I, too, have argued.[45] I believe the

Ethiopian FIS reform is very relevant to identifying the reasons for failure, for it demonstrates a different model than the one suggested by the bank, one more suitable to FIS for Africa. For example, the technical and human resource prerequisites recommended by the bank are simply not feasible in many African governments. The Ethiopian model should be seriously considered as a model for Africa.

The Ethiopian FIS reform also refutes the dictum that an OTS is superior to a custom FIS solution or that an OTS should form the anchor of an FIS with supporting custom systems.[46] An OTS FIS would not have not worked in Ethiopia, and if the government had been forced to adopt an OTS solution from the start, the reform would have been delayed for years and quite possibly would never have gotten off the ground. The custom FIS approach adopted by the DSA project was appropriate to the context of Ethiopia, which can be inferred from its performance in managing the five risks of FIS. Acquisition risk was virtually eliminated because of the very rare circumstances under which the project's FIS initiative started—it was not in the terms of reference of the project and was not in the budget. Therefore the initial systems had to be small and cheap and iteratively developed, because user requirements as well as the contract and budget evolved. Functional risk was managed because user requirements were well defined in a detailed manual system, which defined the specifications of the software. Technical and operational risk were managed by using open-source software widely used and available in Ethiopia and by iterative development and phased releases of software that incorporated operational experience. Finally, proprietary risk was managed through frequent delivery of an upgraded FIS so that at all times there was a working system, even if the developers departed.[47] There was sustainability every step of the way.

The DSA FIS strategy affirms the cross-country findings of Gauld and Goldfinch that small-budget IT projects are far more likely to be successful than big-budget projects—big bucks lead to big systems lead to complexity leads to failure—and the budget effects start after only $1 million. The total cost of the IBEX software was $1.65 million. The project strategy also affirmed the finding by the World Bank that a "well-focused, incremental approach is more likely to succeed than [a] comprehensive approach."[48]

The FIS reform provides five key lessons in automating financial reforms in developing countries:[49]

1   Contextual factors are far more important than the technical choice in determining the outcome of automation.
2   Information technology should not be the driver of financial reform. If it had been in Ethiopia, the reform probably would not have been implemented.
3   There is no a priori technical reason to favor either an OTS or a custom solution; the choice depends on the circumstances. However, the opportunities created by a custom solution for learning by doing and creation of ownership provide strong arguments to balance the putative advantages of an OTS solution.

4   Effective project selection and management is a major factor in the success of automation.
5   A financial and social cost-benefit analysis should be undertaken in reviewing a policy of introducing and/or continuing with a custom system or upgrading to an OTS solution.

A word to project managers of PFA/M reform

Perran Penrose, a consultant who worked on the project throughout its life, chided me for spending too much time on IT. He argued that it was a distraction from the more important procedural issues of budgeting, accounting, and planning. I did spend an inordinate amount of time on FIS issues, but I had no choice. PFA/M reform is too important to be left to the techies. IT is an integral aspect of PFA/M reform and must be managed to ensure that it supports, not drives, reform, and that the IT function itself is well managed. IT has a strong propensity to go off track—especially into people's pockets—and can derail a PFA/M reform. The challenge for a manager of a PFA/M project who is not an IT specialist is to learn how to distinguish smoke from substance in a field that is murky. I recommend that managers of PFA/M projects ask themselves, regarding the FIS: In this context what would be a Toyota? And if someone wants a Lamborghini, ask him why it's needed. The capabilities of the IBEX system have yet to be fully realized by the government: the system has generated hundreds of reports that the government has never used. This confirms the virtue of a reform strategy of *recognize*: Do you know what you already have?

This discussion of the FIS reform and of the budget and accounts reforms completes the presentation of the reform of the transaction platform of the Civil Service Reform Program. In chapter 7 I present the expenditure planning reform, the second of three PFA/M platforms, policy. (The DSA project was not involved in the reform of the third platform, legal.)

Appendix 6.1: Technical features of the Integrated Budget Expenditure (IBEX) system, Ethiopia's IFMIS

1   Web-based, browser-based application with no client-side application requirements, except for the browser and Acrobat reader for PDF reports.
2   Ultra-lightweight bandwidth requirement. This is a principle that has been applied throughout application development. Application runs well on a 56 kbits/s (56 kilobits per second) dial-up line and is even usable at 28 kbits/s (slow dial-up). This principle manifests itself in many lightweight application components such as the "on-demand" loading trees, which only load portions of the tree at a time as the tree is expanded by users.
3   Hybrid deployment capability as a WAN-distributed application on the multiserver environment, or as a stand-alone application on a non-networked environment without any additional application development. This is quite unusual for a web-based application. It means that all the code developed

for one deployment mode is completely used for the other deployment mode—a significant time saver in terms of design, development, and testing time. Many IFMISs either do not support a stand-alone mode or require a different client-side application with its own development requirements.

4   Seamless integration between stand-alone non-networked installations and WAN-distributed installations. This serves to functionally integrate the non-connected installations with the central WAN-distributed installations. This is accomplished using the migration tools that are built into the system. This even allows for seamless migration of data from the legacy systems (BIS and BDA) to the centralized IBEX systems as necessary, for example, for budget formulation and accounts consolidation nationwide.

5   The preferential use of robust, enterprise-class open-source frameworks. Everything except the actual database (Microsoft SQL Server) and the web security product (Netegrity Siteminder) uses open-source frameworks. This reduces cost. SQL Server and Siteminder were chosen because the alternatives were not so sustainable in the Ethiopian market. In the case of SQL Server, there was no other high-end database that was supported in Ethiopia—the Oracle database was supported from South Africa. In security matters, it is good to go with a proven, trusted product; Siteminder was the best one available.

6   The application has its own embedded, declarative reporting framework yet is open to integration with third-party reporting tools and systems. "Declarative" means that additional reports can be developed and new reports can be added without changing application code.

7   Highly granular security is embedded in the application but configured declaratively, uses XML and security configurations—again, with no code changes. This means that any application resource (functional module, page, button, link, etc.) and read or write access to any individual piece of application data (such as budget code, account code, etc.) can be secured right down to the individual user level. As is usual, this security can still be applied at the group or role level, such as by region, department, or departmental role.

8   Complete internationalization. The application currently runs in four languages (English, Amharic, Tigrigna, and Oromiffa) and it is very easy to add additional languages. In fact, adding additional languages is just a matter of translating text to the new language and is not a programming task.

Appendix 6.2: The automated financial functions provided by the IBEX system

Budget module. Executes all the budget preparation activities performed by government financial offices prior to the commencement of budget execution processes in a new fiscal year.

Accounts module. Executes all the budget execution activities of government budgetary institutions. More specifically, the accounts module records the financial transactions of the budgetary institutions, records the aggregated monthly accounting reports and provides accounting reports for ledgers, financial statements, transactions, expenditures, and revenues.

Management reports. Over 130 management reports are available to facilitate management accounting and planning.

Financial statements. Two complete sets of financial statements are provided, to fulfill both the Ethiopian government's requirements and international standards for financial reporting.

Budget adjustment module. Provides the functionality to address changes to the approved budget during budget execution. It specifically enables recording of budget transfers and budget supplements and the subsequent production of the adjusted budget.

Budget control module. Enables budgetary control over expenditures by managing the activities of recording budget commitments and disbursement payments.

Nationwide consolidation module. Consolidates the budget and accounting data for the entire country and allows for the generation of regional and national consolidated reports.

Disbursement module. Manages the public treasury functions associated with cash management and disbursing funds between public financial institutions (under development as of fall 2013).

Administration module. Contains the system management functions that are restricted to administrative users such as managing user configuration and access and managing the chart of accounts.

IBEX migration tools. A set of data migration utilities spread across various IBEX modules that, in the absence of a network connection, allows for the seamless electronic export and import of data between IBEX installations, thereby allowing for the consolidation of IBEX data from subsidiary to centralized locations (for example, from a zone to the regional BOFED).

Notes

1 A holdover from Ethiopia's former relationship with the Soviet Union, the decrepit Ladas are miraculously kept running, although their unreliability and rough ride make them suitable only for short trips in cities.
2 In 2009, a year after the DSA project ended, the government realized its wish and embarked on the development of the most sophisticated FIS, an off-the-shelf (OTS) integrated financial management information system (IFMIS) from the Oracle Corporation. As of 2013, much progress has been made—the contractor has renovated the top floor of the Ministry of Finance and installed a cafeteria. Although the government's initiative to acquire an Oracle IFMIS was to be funded without foreign aid, money is fungible, and Ethiopia receives considerable direct budget support. So it is the government taking a loan from the World Bank to buy the system.
3 Flyvbjert and Budzier (2011: 3).
4 Standish Group, "Extreme Chaos," report, 2001 (www.standishgroup.com/sample_research/PDF/pages/extreme_chaos.pdf); Royal Academy of Engineering and British Computer Society (2004: 6); Dorotinsky (2003). Dorotinsky's 2003 study focused on developing countries and presented separate statistics for Africa. A follow-on World

Bank review (Dener, Watkins, and Dorotinsky 2011) of fifty-five completed IFMIS projects funded by the World Bank is more encouraging, but still, 64 percent of these projects were rated as only "moderately satisfactory." However, nearly half of the twenty-five projects surveyed were located in Latin America and the Caribbean region; these areas have much higher success rates than other areas, especially Africa (xiii–xiv). In its review of assistance to PFM reforms in Africa, the IMF also found serious failures with FIS (International Monetary Fund 2006).

5 Dener, Watkins, and Dorotinsky (2011: 30).
6 Diamond and Khemani (2005) argue that the Tanzania FIS reform in early 2000 was the best on the continent. The deficiencies of this reform are presented in World Bank (2001) and Wynne (2005).
7 Dener, Watkins, and Dorotinsky (2011: xix).
8 Parry (2005: 3).
9 At the request of the World Bank, in 2007 I did a comparative review of IFMISs in select countries (see Peterson 2007b).
10 Gauld and Goldfinch (2006).
11 Keen (1991: 214).
12 Gauld and Goldfinch (2006: 10–11).
13 The original BDA, the government's legacy system, ran on a mainframe computer.
14 DSA IT-BIS/BDA.
15 The public bodies at zone level are departments, so the finance organization at this tier is the Department of Finance and Economic Development (DOFED).
16 USAID did due diligence in reviewing the appropriateness of our IT systems and our IT procurement.
17 There were seven components of the technical platform of the FIS upgrade: security and user directory, data warehouse, reporting, auditing, user interface, web distribution, and internationalization (ability to operate in multiple languages). See DSA M-70: 51.
18 Documentation prepared by Chijioke includes DSA IT-IBEX-1, DSA IT-IBEX-2, and DSA IT-IBEX-3.
19 The upstream bandwidth is the volume of data a remote site can send to servers at higher tiers of the system, such as from a zone to an IBEX server in a regional BOFED. The downstream bandwidth is the converse, and this is 32 megabits/s. VSAT (very small aperture terminal) is an earthbound station used in satellite communications of data, voice, and video signals, excluding broadcast television. A VSAT consists of two components, a transceiver that is placed outdoors in direct line of sight to the satellite and a device that is placed indoors to interface the transceiver with the end user's communications device, such as a personal computer.
20 Brooks (1995: 239).
21 Since both the BIS and BDA and IBEX operated in a LAN mode, both tracks of the Stage 2 FIS strategy had LAN capability.
22 As of May 2011, this situation had not changed (see Peterson et al. 2011: 104–6).
23 Unofficial estimates of the cost of WeredaNet are more than $100 million.
24 Peterson et al. (2011: 83).
25 Peterson et al. (2011: 45–6).
26 Dener, Watkins, and Dorotinsky (2011: 71).
27 The centerpiece of the $50.1 million C1 component to support PFA/M under the PBS II foreign aid program is the automation of weredas, yet there is no mention of ICT, much less a budget for improving ICT (Peterson et al. 2011: 60).
28 Information on the WeredaNet from Peterson et al. (2011: 106).
29 Associates for Rural Development (2006: 21).
30 Federal Democratic Republic of Ethiopia, Ministry of Finance and Economic Development (2010b: 25).
31 DSA IT-010.

32   Brooks (1995).
33   Fairly and Wilshire (2003) use the dramatic and tragic failure of the sinking of the Swedish warship *Vasa* in 1628 as a jumping-off point for their concept. The *Vasa* was built top-heavy and had insufficient ballast. The king, conducting a war, was over-eager to see it launched. On its maiden voyage in Stockholm harbor, with the king and nobility watching, the ship had sailed less than two nautical miles when a gust of wind caused it to heel over. Water poured in through the gun portals and the ship foundered, with a loss of fifty-three lives. Key to the country's defense, the *Vasa* could be called a mission-and time-critical system.
34   Iterative software development has for a number of years been viewed as best practice, as compared to the traditional "waterfall" model. According to the latter, one built a complete system end to end with the plan to throw it away and do a second system. Brooks has abandoned the waterfall model in favor of an "incremental-build" model of developing software with progressive refinements (Brooks 1995: 264–8).
35   The key FIS planning documents are DSA B-27, DSA B-31, and DSA IT-002.
36   Brooks (1995: 53–60).
37   DSA B-46.
38   Flyvbjerg and Budzier (2011: 3).
39   Gauld and Goldfinch (2006: 17–18). A classic managerial fad that swept both the private and public sectors in the 1990s was business process reengineering, championed by Hammer and Champy (1993).
40   Diamond and Khemani (2005). At the December 2007 International Consortium of Government Financial Management Conference, "The Use of Financial Management Information Systems (FMIS) to Improve Financial Management and Transparency in the Public Sector," several staff members from USAID (Gail Ostler), the IMF (Bill Dorotinsky), and the World Bank (Peter Murphy) stated that an OTS was far superior to a custom FIS solution. See links at www.icgfm.org/conferenceDocs/2007/Dec/2007WinterConference.htm.
41   Dener, Watkins, and Dorotinsky (2011: xvii, xviii).
42   Dener, Watkins, and Dorotinsky (2011: 30).
43   The 2011 World Bank study reaches no conclusion as to whether the time for implementing an IFMIS in an African government has been reduced, because—as the study notes—most of these systems have failed.
44   Dener, Watkins, and Dorotinsky (2011: 71–2).
45   See Peterson (2007a, 2007b).
46   It should be noted that IFMISs are not common practice in most Organisation for Economic Co-operation and Development countries (see Wynne 2005).
47   Given the significance of the OTS-versus-custom issue, it is striking that there is so little discussion in the PFA/M field of levels of proprietary risk in FIS, particularly in connection with each type of system.
48   World Bank (2002: 12–13). An Organization for Economic Cooperation and Development (2001: 3) study also confirms the virtue of downsizing public sector IT projects:

> Public sector budgeting systems can encourage the funding of large and highly visible IT projects ... that often fail. A radical approach, increasingly adopted in the private sector, is to avoid large projects altogether, opting for small projects instead. One expert has called this change a shift from "whales to dolphins." Adopting dolphins does not mean breaking big projects into small modules. Rather, it involves a shift to a different way of working and thinking, with total project time frames of no more than six months, technical simplicity, modest ambitions for business change, and teamwork driven by business goals.

Heeks (2002) also found that more flexible and improvised approaches are more successful than rigid approaches common with OTS solutions.
49   Peterson (2007a: 347–8).

7 The planning reform

From financial administration to financial management

"Does this mean that the government does not have a policy for economic development that works?" asked Kedru Abza, head of the accounts department of the Southern Region Bureau of Finance and Economic Development (BOFED). His question reflected the uncertainty regarding government planning in light of the headwinds the DSA project had faced in trying to take the reform beyond external control, public finance administration (PFA), to internal control, public finance management (PFM). The answer to Abza's question: The headwinds prevailed and the reform eventually vanished.

Abza's comment came during project staff's debriefing of senior officials of the BOFED on the findings of the recently completed regional economic policy review (REPR), which the project had conducted with BOFED planning staff. It was the capstone of the planning reform, whose purpose was to shape the annual budget by policy that would better promote economic growth to the region.[1] One could hear a pin drop after Abza spoke. Most of the officials realized, perhaps for the first time, why their region was so underdeveloped: because of poor resource endowment and, more disturbingly, the absence of a policy for the region's development. Immediately after Abza's remark, the head of the BOFED, Getachew Hamussa, who was the champion of the reform in that region, stepped into the conversation in his role as a senior party member and declared, "This presentation is about the techniques of planning, not political issues." His interjection quickly ended the presentation, but the point was made: bureaucrats—and these were especially able officials who had embraced and effectively implemented the budget and accounts reform—were not to question political authority. Reform of the transaction platform was fine, but real reform of the policy platform beyond technique was not on the table. The reform could improve the techniques of budgeting, but not the way resources are allocated.

In hindsight, it is no surprise that Ethiopia's planning reform eventually came to naught—virtually all such initiatives have failed in developing countries, especially in Africa.[2] This chapter investigates two issues: What techniques of planning were introduced, and what challenges did they face.

What is a planning reform?

As stated in chapter 1, a good public finance system performs three functions delivered through three platforms: it handles a myriad of *transactions*; it ensures that transactions are *legal*; and it ensures that transactions implement *policy*. A planning reform is about driving the budget by policy: trying to shape the direction of all those line-item expenditures in the traditional budget to achieve better outcomes: economic growth and social well-being.

A useful way to understand the policy platform in which planning reforms are located is in terms of the three objectives of good public finance: aggregate fiscal discipline, allocational efficiency, and operational efficiency.[3] Aggregate fiscal discipline means the hard budget constraint, which is the sine qua non of a public sector reform. If governments are not living within their means, no financial technique can improve outcomes. Once a government has established aggregate fiscal discipline, it can then turn to the relatively easier tasks of planning the distribution of resources among sectors (say, health and agriculture) that best promote growth and social welfare to achieve *allocational efficiency*, and in turn planning how to best deploy resources within a sector to achieve *operational efficiency*. The last stage requires understanding the cost drivers of a service—wages, operating expense, physical plant.

Background on Ethiopia's planning reform

The Civil Service Reform Task Force report made no mention of reforming the policy platform. The principal architect of the Civil Service Reform Program (CSRP), Peter Silkin, was an accountant and auditor by training and profession. He was not versed in macroeconomics nor in the techniques for reforming a policy platform. Silkin did not appreciate the importance of cultivating the planning side of the budget, which would make the existing traditional budget more effective and would introduce performance without fundamentally changing the budget's line-item structure. Changing this structure would have complicated and disrupted budgeting. Although he did advise strengthening external control (PFA) in the areas of accounting and disbursements, he viewed the budget as a vehicle for leaping to management (PFM). He advocated that the traditional budget be rapidly replaced by a performance budget.

On my advice, the government put planning in the CSRP. In Ethiopia I pushed for a planning reform, despite having spent eight years in Kenya working on planning reforms that went nowhere. From 1986 to 1990, I worked in Kenya's Ministry of Planning and National Development. Part of my assignment was to assist the ministry in preparing the development plans of Kenya's forty districts. These plans catalogued the resources of each district in considerable detail, including such items as precise numbers of livestock and data gleaned from censuses based on aerial assessments. Long on data, these plans contained little to no policy: What should be done with the resources?

Even more serious than the lack of policy was the fact that planning was meaningless because the annual budget in Kenya was so uncertain. Kenya, like many developing countries, suffers from repetitive budgeting—constantly remaking the budget.[4] The budget had to be constantly remade in Kenya because the revenue was so unstable—there was insufficient cash to meet the dreams contained in the paper of the budget documents. A budget is a one-year plan of revenue and expenditures, and if a government cannot implement a one-year plan, it is pointless to attempt a multiyear expenditure plan of expenditure. Throughout my eight years in Kenya, the government was never able to fully implement the budget announced at the beginning of the fiscal year because of a shortage of cash. Repetitive budgeting made the eight-year task of reform I was involved in, and much of the work that the Harvard Institute for International Development (HIID) was involved in to improve PFA/M, marginal at best.[5]

From 1990 to 1994 I was the finance advisor to Kenya's Ministry of Agriculture, Livestock Development and Marketing. One of my first assignments was to advise the ministry on a new World Bank financial technique, the Public Investment Program (PIP). This program was designed as a tool to help governments plan their capital expenditures by ranking their projects in order of priority for implementation.[6] The World Bank had chosen Kenya and its agriculture ministry to be the entry point to test and implement the PIP approach in Africa. The ministry had 163 projects in the pipeline that would take up to six years to implement. Most were funded by foreign aid. The PIP approach required department heads to rank the projects from high to low priority so that actions to accelerate their completion and derive their benefits could be undertaken. Not surprisingly, all 163 were ranked as high priority! No department head who had a foreign aid project in his department was willing to assess a project as lower priority. Foreign aid projects were golden geese that not only justified the departments heads' positions but also typically provided the perks of vehicles, travel, per diems, and, if cards were played right, the holy grail of foreign travel. Worse, projects generate rents for corrupt officials. The PIP started with great fanfare but, as is the case with many PFM reforms, was ignored and then quickly disappeared. The Kenya experience taught me firsthand that planning systems could easily degenerate into form, with little substance.

Planning is as inherently political as budgeting—perhaps even more so, because hard decisions do not have to be taken in planning as they do in preparing a budget. Plans also are opportunities for politicians to make promises. The real plan of a government is the annual budget—in effect, a one-year plan—and it is the rare government that shapes the one-year budget within the framework of multiyear planning. Politics can easily infect planning and make it meaningless.[7] Politics also infects budgeting, but a budget, unlike a plan, has the force of law (it is an appropriation) and must be made and delivered and very much has meaning.

Given the discouraging experience of planning reforms over the eight years I was in Kenya, why did I push the Ethiopian government to add planning to the CSRP? In a word, discipline—I was encouraged by the discipline with which the

Ethiopians approached budgeting. Unlike Kenya and many other developing countries, Ethiopia observed the hard budget constraint. They lived within their means, and did not suffer from repetitive budgeting. Their budgets were fully funded. I believed that they would be able to execute a planning reform and stick to it.

Another reason I pressed for at least a modest planning reform was because I strongly felt that it was the right thing to do. For starters, the need for planning is logical. The traditional annual budget falls off a cliff every year and starts more or less from scratch anew. Multiyear planning of a one-year budget is logical and comprehensive, but it is difficult to make it feasible. A further reason I pressed for a planning reform was the belief that it could help rationalize the dual budget—that is, improve the situation whereby separate capital and recurrent budgets were produced by separate organizations at separate times and never looked at together. Even if it did not bring the two budgets together, a new planning system would at least bring the data of the two budgets together in a planning book.

And a third reason why I felt that the planning reform was so important was the government's obsession with capital expenditure (see discussion in chapter 4). It was hard to shake party members' and bureaucrats' conviction that capital expenditure is development, whereas recurrent expenditure is consumption. I felt that the planning function could bring home the error of this assumption. For example it is easily illustrated by the obvious "development" returns of paying good teachers a living wage so they stay in the profession (salaries being part of the recurrent budget).

Finally, from my experience in Kenya I knew that a planning reform could not be done overnight and that if any planning was to materialize from our initiative, it was best to get started sooner rather than later. Eventually, I was sure, the government would see the need for more systematic planning for national development and the needs for budgets to be driven by policy. As Goran Hyden observes, the goal of achieving a policy state in Africa has been elusive, yet must be done if countries are to develop.[8]

> Many governments around the world are not what one would call policy [governments] but, instead, are patronage governments. This is certainly true in many African countries, where rewarding loyal followers becomes so prevalent that it overshadows the effort to achieve public policy goals.... A policy government is committed to providing and implementing public goals that have been duly approved by institutions with legitimate authority to do so. There is a clear separation between official and personal and the distinction between public and private matters. This idea of government is still in the making in African countries.[9]

The Ethiopian government agreed to my recommendation that a planning reform be part of the CSRP, and it came as no surprise that the Ministry of Planning was especially keen on a planning reform.[10] Until this proposal, the Ministry of Planning had been virtually ignored in the preparation of the CSRP and indeed had no representation in the senior government committees that were to coordinate the CSRP. I would like to think that the planning reform was embraced on its technical merits, but clearly, organizational interests were also involved.

Developing the federal and the regional planning reforms

The most important planning reforms are those that help a government maintain a hard budget constraint. The DSA project planning reform proposed assisting the federal government in this crucial area in three ways: policy advising, techniques for integrated revenue and expenditure planning, and budget planning.[11]

In policy advising, a macroeconomic model was to be developed to provide the government with a means to forecast economic growth, which in turn provided a means to forecast what domestic revenues would be generated. A better revenue forecast, coupled with a conservative estimate of what external resources the country could count on from foreign aid, allowed the government to set the hard budget constraint: given the likely level of revenue (domestic and foreign) and a sustainable deficit (how far expenditure could exceed revenue)—how much could be spent? To sustain the macroeconomic model developed by DSA advisors, the government needed to establish an organization staffed by economists who could take over the model once project advisors departed and could gather the data and run the model as needed by policymakers. To pull together all of the data from the forecasting of revenue and expenditure and manage the deficit (or surplus), the project introduced integrated revenue and expenditure planning that would use two techniques, a macroeconomic fiscal framework (MEFF), and a public expenditure program (PEP).

The project's approach to building up the policy platform was to start at the bottom. The mandate of the project was to reform budget and accounting, so our planning reform needed to focus on expenditure planning, which would strengthen the budgeting process. Recall that the annual budget is a one-year plan of expenditure and revenue; the project extended expenditure planning to three years: the upcoming year's budget and the two following years. The planning reform we developed provided a three-year perspective that looked at revenue and expenditure in total, that allocated expenditure by sector, and that was sustainable in terms of the growth of the country's economy and the revenue such growth would generate.

The project proposed a four-step process to build the policy platform in the federal government:

Step 1. A PIP (public investment program), to document the list of projects, many of them multiyear, funded by domestic and foreign resources that have to be placed in the capital budget for the upcoming fiscal year and two following years (a three-year plan of expenditure).

Step 2. An MEFF (macroeconomic fiscal framework), to pull together the forecasts of revenue and expenditure for the upcoming fiscal year's budget, the total amount to be spent at the federal level, the total that would be transferred to the regions, and the deficit target, if any.

Step 3. IPFs (indicative planning figures), to forecast three years ahead the level of
resources public bodies would receive so they can better plan the capital budget.
Step 4. A PEP (public expenditure program), to forecast for the upcoming fiscal year
and two following years the recurrent costs of the projects identified in the PIP.

To summarize the federal planning reform: The PIP would start the process
by presenting the list of each public body's capital projects, which drive the
capital budget. The MEFF would determine the size of the cake, the total funds
available for the federal recurrent and capital budgets and the total amount to be
transferred to regions. The IPFs would cut the cake and assign slices to the
federal public bodies, which would shape their budgets. The PEP would assist
public bodies to divide their slice of cake between the capital budget and the
recurrent budget to support those capital expenditures.

The principal circumstance that determined the context of the regional planning reform was second-stage decentralization, and it made the reform very different from the federal planning reform. The principal task was for us to develop
for regional BOFEDs a suitable process whereby they could allocate funds to
their weredas and monitor how the funds were spent.

The eight planning reforms at the federal and regional tiers

The DSA planning reform initiated eight planning reforms whose purpose was
to help the government meet the three objectives of good public finance:
aggregate fiscal discipline, allocational efficiency, and operational efficiency (see
table 7.1). The eight reforms were as follows:

1   Policy advising
2   Budget planning
3   Integrated revenue and expenditure planning
4   Region-to-wereda fiscal transfer
5   Planning with performance
6   Budget costing
7   Regional budget planning
8   Regional economic planning

Federal planning reform

The first three initiatives were part of federal planning reform. The last five were
part of regional planning reform.

1 Policy advising

The project wanted to plan the planning reform from the bottom up, but Prime
Minister Meles Zenawi requested that we also work at the top. In August 2006,
five months before the DSA project was to begin, I was in Ethiopia working on

Table 7.1 Federal and regional planning reforms, by planning objective

Federal planning reform

Aggregate fiscal discipline	*Allocational efficiency*	*Operational efficiency*
1 Policy advising • Policy studies • Macroeconomic modeling • Building policy capacity		–
	2 Budget planning • Public investment program (PIP)	
3 Integrated revenue and expenditure planning • Macroeconomic fiscal framework (MEFF) • Public expenditure program (PEP)		

Regional planning reform

–	4 Region-to-wereda fiscal transfer • Needs-based unit-cost formula 5 Planning with performance • Wereda performance agreement	
		6 Budget costing Unit costing
	7 Regional budget planning • Public expenditure program (PEP) 8 Regional economic planning • Regional economic policy review (REPR)	

Source: author.

its design with Hailemelekot T. Giorgis, the vice minister of finance. I attended a meeting on the financial reform at the prime minister's office. Prime Minister Zenawi chaired the meeting, which most of his core cabinet attended. It was the first of three meetings I had with him (the third of these meetings, where the in-service training strategy of the CSRP was decided, was described in chapter 5). Prime Minister Zenawi was very interested in the planning reform. At one point in the discussion I asked him where he got advice on macroeconomic policy, and he replied, "from the Bretton Woods." I asked him whether he liked that arrangement and he firmly said no. From the start of his government's tenure in power there had been a very uneasy relationship with the Bretton Woods agencies, especially the International Monetary Fund.[12]

The upshot of this exchange was surprising: Minister Newai Gebre-ab, who served as the prime minister's economic advisor, made a direct request to the DSA project for urgent assistance in economic policy. The request was flattering, to be sure. Advising on economic policy was far beyond the scope of the project, but since the request came from the prime minister himself, it was not possible to duck the issue and say we would be too busy reforming the country's bookkeeping.

I presented this request to the project's home office, HIID, and received an enthusiastic response, especially from Mike Roemer, one of our most seasoned policy economists. Roemer visited Ethiopia in October 1996, shortly after I contacted him, and prepared a three-part program of work in consultation with Minister Gebre-ab: preparation of policy papers on key issues (constraints to economic competitiveness, maize and coffee sector studies), the development of a macroeconomic model, and advice on how to establish an economic policy unit within the Office of the Prime Minister.[13] During Roemer's visit he met with Prime Minister Meles Zenawi. I later learned from Minister Gebre-ab that the prime minister was extremely impressed with Roemer, and likewise from Roemer that he was also very impressed with the prime minister and with the range and depth of his understanding of economic affairs.

Minister Gebre-ab's request certainly got a lot of attention. The IMF's resident representative in Ethiopia, Tom Gibson, came up to me at a U.S. embassy function and thanked me for "doing God's work." The USAID mission director cabled Washington to gush that through the DSA project USAID had "a seat at the policy table of the government of Ethiopia." When I heard about the mission director's cable I said to the USAID official responsible for overseeing the DSA project that not only did we not have a seat at the table, we didn't know where the room was. This initiative was to continue for two years but was crippled from the very start by the sudden passing of Mike Roemer in December 1996, just a month before the project began. He was to lead the policy advising activity and his loss was a huge stroke of misfortune for the project and Ethiopia. One does not find a more accomplished and polished economic policy advisor than Mike Roemer.[14] Then, the start of the Eritrean war, in May 1998, sounded the death knell of the policy-advising component of the project's planning reform. The prime minister's attention turned completely away from reform to the prosecution of war. He met with his economic advisor, Minister Gebre-ab, only a handful of times during the two-year conflict. And the logistics became complicated when USAID imposed a travel ban, which prevented the policy advisors—who were all short-term—from traveling to Ethiopia.

Despite its premature demise, the short-lived policy advising initiative did book some solid achievements. Minister Gebre-ab found the policy studies very useful and said of Mike Westlake's study of the potential direction for Ethiopia's coffee industry that it was one of the best consulting reports he had ever read.[15] Westlake also did a path-breaking study on the need for a commodity exchange, which eventually led to the establishment in 2008 of such an exchange.[16] The macroeconomic model was never used. The advice on establishing a policy organization started the government's thinking about this activity, which came to fruition, if only briefly, many years later, when Minister Gebre-ab brought in Dr. Eleni Gebre-Medhin, a very accomplished economist who had studied in the United States and worked internationally, to spearhead the establishment of the Ethiopian Commodities Exchange.

2 Budget planning

In one of my earliest discussions on the planning reform, I asked Melaku Kifle, the head of the capital budget department of the Ministry of Planning, "Do you know all of the projects that have to be budgeted and what their source of funding is?" His answer, "No," provided a clear rationale for a public investment program—the government needed a list of projects if it was to prepare the annual capital budget. Unlike the PIP in Kenya, where ministries had to prioritize their projects, the PIP I proposed for Ethiopia had a far more modest objective: it was not meant to allocate resources but simply to provide a comprehensive list of projects and key details. For the first time, the government would have in one document a profile of all planned projects. The list would include key data: start and end date, total cost, expenditures to date, balance of expenditures required to complete the project, and recurrent costs (separated into wages and operation and maintenance) needed upon completion.[17]

Although the PIP initially was to be a simple list of projects, the Ministry of Planning and the DSA project quickly decided that projects had to be planned in terms of how much the annual budget could absorb. It was agreed to develop indicative planning figures (IPFs) to be issued to public bodies at the start of the fiscal year when the planning cycle began (July to December), which in turn would lead into the budget preparation cycle (January to June).[18]

Preparing IPFs was a quantum leap in the planning reform; for them to work required three types of information: (1) firm commitments from foreign aid agencies as to their funding of their projects for the next year's budget and preferably for the following two years (a three-year planning horizon); (2) a macroeconomic fiscal framework (MEFF), which is a forecast by government of the total budget available for the federal government; and (3) a planning envelope from the MEFF for each federal public body so that public bodies could plan their budgets. It is important to distinguish between a planning envelope and a budget ceiling. A budget ceiling is a firm statement of resources—although it may be adjusted, it determines the budget. A planning envelope, by contrast, is merely indicative. Thus, preparation of an annual budget would involve two steps: first a planning step, where public bodies are given an indicative envelope so they could set priorities within a rough resource constraint. Second, public bodies are given a budget ceiling that imposes a firm resource constraint for them to finalize their priorities. At this point the planning envelope is affirmed or adjusted up or down.

By establishing IPFs, an MEFF, and a planning envelope, at the federal government tier at least, the planning reform was headed toward achieving the holy grail of international best practice in expenditure planning: a medium-term expenditure framework (MTEF).[19] Unfortunately, although foreign aid agencies, especially the Bretton Woods, extolled the virtue of MTEFs, they torpedoed them in Ethiopia. The Ethiopian budget was dependent on foreign aid for 30 percent or more of its funding, and if this aid could not be dependably forecasted, planning would have little relevance. Nine months into the start of the

DSA project, in October 1997, the Ministry of Planning convened a meeting with the major foreign aid agencies in Ethiopia and presented the planning reform and the information that their agencies needed to provide. The forms requesting the information were distributed and the reform was discussed at length. Two months later only one agency, Ireland Aid, was able to give a very tentative three-year forecast of commitments; the rest begged off, stating that they could not confirm any aid commitments. In fact, the foreign aid agencies were unable to make firm commitments for the upcoming budget year. That meant that not even the annual budget could be forecast. Foreign aid was so unreliable that when public bodies prepared their capital budgets, they simply put a placeholder figure in for a foreign-funded project, for they often did not know until the end of the year what funds would be forthcoming.

The unpredictability of foreign aid was especially damaging in light of Ethiopia's fiscal decentralization. Foreign aid is usually assigned to specific projects, and the value of these projects in the local currency, the birr, is subtracted, or "offset," from the domestic revenue component of the transfer. So if a wereda receives a payment—say, $50,000 for a vehicle—from a foreign donor, the value in birr is deducted from the wereda's regular transfer. If the aid does not arrive, the region's budget is reduced. A further complication was the tendency of foreign aid agencies to favor specific weredas in regions, money that was earmarked for projects, usually capital expenditures. This meant that those weredas could not finance their recurrent expenditures, such as salaries. The weredas needed to pay salaries using birr, but the amount of local currency available to them had been reduced by the amount of foreign aid that was going to projects. Thus, weredas could buy vehicles, but could not pay the salaries of the drivers.

The federal government produced the PIP for several years, but like many planning systems, it became simply a rote exercise and eventually fell into disuse. Ironically, the PIP lasted as long as it did because, as part of this reform, a clause was inserted in the federal financial law stipulating that no project could be implemented that was not in the PIP.

3 Integrated revenue and expenditure planning

The inability of the government to count on foreign aid funds meant that a three-year planning perspective had little meaning. A one-year planning horizon to shape the budget for the upcoming fiscal year would still be useful, however, so the project carried on developing the MEFF and a limited PEP for the federal government's one-year integrated revenue and expenditure plan.

The MEFF and PEP were constrained not only by unreliable foreign aid but also by the federal government's expenditure requirements, which were dominated by defense, the federal capital budget, the regional transfer, and smaller but significant amounts allocated to higher education. Consequently, the federal PEP was meaningful only in terms of those areas. Accordingly, it was decided to incorporate into the macroeconomic tables of the MEFF a broad expenditure element that captured the main federal responsibilities, which meant that the

MEFF became the expenditure forecast of the federal government, but not of all national expenditures. Within that framework the anchor of the budget became a commitment to increase the financial transfers to regions annually. This was a potentially important development because up to that point the policy had been to satisfy federal agency recurrent needs before determining the size of the pool to be allocated to regions. There was, and still is, no formal method of determining the transfer pool to regions, which is therefore discretionary, but in general the total domestic resource transfer has been in line with the MEFF, which has permitted the regions to make some forecasts, notwithstanding the lack of foreign aid forecasts and the lack of MEFF transparency (regions are not formally informed of the MEFF, though there is no formal policy not to inform them). The MEFF has proved useful, for it provides an overview of government policy and, as a preamble to the budget, an adequate budget framework paper.

The MEFF reform proved to be of value, since the MEFF has generally been a sustained and successful activity, but public finance planning at the federal level was not adequate. The reasons for this were many and complex. First, experience elsewhere suggests that responses to dual budget problems that involve the merger of planning and finance ministries take many years to settle down because of staff employment issues. A comprehensive reform of the combined finance and planning ministries to form the Ministry of Finance and Economic Development (MOFED) was long overdue, and until the merger was accomplished it was hard to move planning further along. Second, the relation of the federal government and the regions in respect of financial management has never been adequately defined. MOFED officials had limited awareness of regional issues, and provided little support.

Unlike the MEFF reform, the PEP was of limited use. The "federal government PEP" focused too much attention on forecasting the detailed requirements of over ninety federal public bodies with relatively small budgets and in effect became a budgeting, not a planning, exercise. For the federal PEP to be of value it needed forecasts of foreign aid, which were not forthcoming, so the exercise was abandoned.

In many ways the planning reform at the federal level became trapped in a tar pit: plans should be comprehensive, but they could not be at the federal level because 30 percent or more of total funding came from foreign aid and could not be forecast, so the planning reform could not move forward. The planning reform at the regional level was a very different story, for with second-stage decentralization (SSD), regions had to allocate nearly 65 percent of their funds to weredas, which created the opportunity for the regional BOFEDs not to be merely a post office, à la MOFED, but to allocate resources to achieve regional policy goals in terms of sectors so as best to support growth. As with planning at the federal level, the uncertainty of foreign aid created a serious obstacle, but we felt that it could be outweighed by bringing in a planning perspective.

Regional planning reform: creating a model reform in the Southern Region

Five of the eight planning initiatives were geared to the planning needs of the regions, where the strongest emphasis was on the planning objective of allocational efficiency.

The project had only modest resources available for the regional planning reform and one short-term advisor, and we needed to concentrate the reform. Thus, the project design for the planning reform in regions was to set in place a complete reform in one region rather than to risk incomplete reforms in many regions. The planning reform also needed to pull together and digest a wide range of data—number of schools and teachers, development of unit costs—and gathering this data required focusing in one area. The rollout of the planning reform to the regions would begin with the Southern Region. With a reform up and running in the Southern Region, Southern Region planning officials now had a model to share with other regions, to whom they could offer their experience and support.

4 Region-to-wereda fiscal transfer

The Southern Region was selected for the first planning reform because of its discipline in removing the backlog of accounts and delivering the in-service training program developed in collaboration with the project (described in chapter 5). That the project started its reform work in this region was fortuitous to the planning reform because with the surprise announcement of second-stage decentralization (SSD) in the middle of the fiscal year, the region faced significant and potentially explosive inequalities, and a transfer formula had to deal with these. The region welcomed any assistance we had to offer.

With decentralization, an immediate problem was how to distribute 65 percent of the region's resources to its 114 weredas and special weredas, which are larger, ethnically defined weredas that exist only in the Southern Region. The allocation system had to be politically acceptable. In the Southern Region, with its fifty-four ethnic groups and history of violence between groups—where a conflict in one wereda over which language should be used in its schools had led to more than one death—any system of allocation had to be equitable. Any inequity, or perception of inequity, could literally lead to bloodshed. Yet when the project examined the average expenditures across weredas it found very large variations.

When the federal government issued the edict for rapid SSD, it assumed that regions could simply use the transfer formula the federal government used to allocate resources to regions. This approach would not work for the Southern Region. The federal formula was principally based on population and did not address need. In the Southern Region, some of the least populated weredas had the greatest need and were also the most restive—in fact, the two factors were related. Crisis does spur reform, and a crisis existed in the Southern Region that urgently needed to be dealt with. Even though the project was new on the scene and was still in the process of building trust with regional officials, it rapidly came up with the help the region needed to effect an equitable allocation system.

The transfer formula the project developed was a needs-based, outcome-conditional, general-purpose grant for weredas. The point of its being needs-based was to redress the inequalities of weredas in the short and medium term by giving appropriate weights to weredas' need to adequately finance both their existing and their new activities. For example, existing school students need to be financed, and projected new enrollments also require resources. The formula would be outcome-conditional through the introduction of wereda performance agreements (discussed later), which weredas would commit to in advance of the receipt of their grant. It was a lump-sum transfer, a general-purpose block grant that gave weredas discretion in allocation. The first version of the new formula was approved by the regional council with little debate, which encouraged the Southern Region's Bureau of Finance and Economic Development (BOFED) to continue to develop the system as the staff gained insights into the value of transparency and the power of the formula system to highlight and provide a basis for policy discussions.

The policy basis of the approach can be summarized as follows:[20]

- A transfer formula should be a driver for policy-based allocation and there-fore contain the principal cost drivers that, once highlighted, make people think about efficiency, effectiveness, and equity.
- A comprehensible formula is easy to present to the legislature, and can gain legitimacy by permitting reasoned discussion of assumptions.
- A non-manipulatable formula gives some confidence to lower levels of gov-ernment that it is slightly harder to cheat them than might otherwise be the case.
- The formula should be kept simple, because in the future someone will inev-itably make it more complex.

Essentially, the design principle was derived from output-purchase principles—in this case, the regional government purchases services from wereda govern-ments. Such an approach permits an aggregation of costs that can be integrated into budget output definitions, thereby permitting a combined discussion of budget and performance, where "performance" is the quantifiable improvement that can be demonstrated from an increase in funding. For example, the key cost driver in education is the teacher-to-pupil ratio. Once you determine this ratio—say, one teacher for forty-five students—and estimate an average teacher salary, one can determine what needs to be budgeted and the performance expected by the weredas to achieve the 1:45 ratio.

To summarize, in the Southern Region, with its unique needs for equity, the regional planning reform drove the development of a regional transfer formula that promoted policy (better teacher-to-pupil ratios) and brought rigor into the budget process by introducing costing (identifying the cost drivers of a service, again teacher-to-pupil ratios) combined with unit costs (knowing the average cost of a primary school math textbook). The federal-to-region transfer formula was a blunt instrument that did promote policy or costing of the budget.

Staff from MOFED failed to visit the Southern Region to discuss the planning reform as it proceeded and succeeded—the ministry remained uninterested and uninformed. Worse, the early introduction of the needs-based regional transfer formula was actively opposed by the Ministry of Economic Development and Cooperation (still a separate ministry when the planning reform was started), which insisted that the regions mirror the federal formula, and at times the project experienced the absurd situation of two teams in the Southern Region, one from MEDAC and one from the DSA project, discussing rival proposals, though the preferences of the Southern Region BOFED were in no doubt. The MEDAC people presented a population-based transfer formula that BOFED people compared with the DSA design of a needs-based formula. In a dialogue between government officials—project staff were not present—the project formula was found to be far superior.

5 Planning with performance

A major innovation of the regional planning reform was to introduce performance into wereda-level financial management via the fiscal transfer to weredas. As stated earlier, the region-to-wereda transfer formula was a needs-based, outcome-conditional, general-purpose grant. The wereda performance agreement was the technique to make its outcome conditional, for the wereda had to specify for its key sectors what targets were to be achieved—for example, increasing the school enrollment rates of girls. Since the grant was a block grant and weredas had discretion in its allocation, the agreement also built accountability.

The planning reform introduced a fairly simple but powerful approach by incorporating performance—as measured in terms of quantity, quality, timeliness, and cost—into the outputs. A four-page "wereda performance agreement" was created with three key features. First, the core of the agreement was a listing of the key performance targets, by activity, within the five principal sectors managed by weredas—education, health, agriculture, water, and administration—which was agreed to with the regional BOFED *before* the regional grant was transferred to the wereda (see table 7.2).[21] For example, a key performance target for primary education within the education sector would be the teacher-to-pupil ratio. The second feature of the agreement was that it considered performance capacity—future allocations were conditional on performance. Third, it was signed by both a wereda and a regional representative. If the agreement was not complied with or performance goals were not met, two provisos came into effect: the wereda's allocation for the upcoming fiscal year would—or could—be reduced, and BOFED officials would evaluate the wereda's detailed work plan performance and financial administration and would mandate actions to be taken to improve performance.

Table 7.2 Wereda performance agreement for FY1997, key performance indicators

Sector and program	Key performance indicator
Education	
Primary schools	Number of students to be enrolled
	Primary school teacher-to-pupil ratio
	Number of female students in primary schools
	Budget allocated to schools for operation expenditure
	Number of schools to be constructed
Secondary schools	Number of students to be enrolled
	Teacher-to-pupil ratio
	Number of female students
	Budget allocated for operation expenditure
Health	
	Number of new clinics to be constructed
	Number of health professionals to be hired
Agriculture	
	DA-to-farmer ratio (average DA visits performed to number of farmers)[a]
Water	
	Number of functional water points
	Number of water points to be constructed
Administration	
	Accounts report
	Develop target performance report

Source: author; see also DSA P-63 and P-66.

Note

a DA = Development assistant, a government official who meets with the farmer.

The planning reform actively discouraged a narrow emphasis on performance because wereda budgets were inadequate to achieve very much more than survival, and our initial finding was that weredas were willing to subscribe to the discipline of performance if they received adequate funding for the purpose. For example, in the Southern Region, weredas declined to sign agreements they felt were attached to unfunded mandates such as excessive enrollments. A key lesson for introducing performance into planning or budgeting is that it must develop endogenously at the pace that a subnational government can manage.

A final note on performance. The project introduced what I called a "Type 1" performance budget system at the wereda level: it retained the traditional line-item budget but complemented it with a performance framework, the wereda performance agreement. This approach retained the simplicity and coherence of the budgeting system without unduly complicating it, by, for example, changing the structure of the budget—the budget classification, chart of accounts, and introducing codes for performance. Creating new budget classification, chart of accounts, and codes for performance is a feature of a "Type 2" performance budget, which is often the practice in reforms promoting performance. These changes enormously complicate and confuse budgeting. Indeed, in 2011 the IMF found that its own initiative to introduce performance-program budgeting in 2006 was still in a mess precisely because the design had overcomplicated the budget.[22] Introducing performance is one of the thorniest issues in PFM and is often not done well. The wereda agreement successfully introduced performance at the tier of government with the weakest capacity.

6 Budget costing

The calculation of the wereda transfers, which was done by the regional BOFED, was based on cost drivers (the key physical ratios that determine cost of a service, for example, the ratio of nurses to patients) and the unit costs of the inputs into a service (average salaries of nurses, cost of typically used drugs, and so forth). Setting the amount each wereda received was thus done with objective techniques that were transparent and were shown to the weredas, so weredas knew why they received the total amount they did. Thus, the planning objective of budget costing was operational efficiency. Although the transfer was a block grant and weredas were not required to follow their regional BOFED in their allocations to sectors to calculate their total grant, many weredas started to adopt these costing techniques to determine the allocation among sectors and prepare their budgets. Incremental budgeting was being replaced with calculation of costs. This was a huge leap in budgeting sophistication. Like the performance agreement, it succeeded at the least capable level of government. Once a budget system moves toward a degree of performance orientation, as has been the case in the wereda transfers, input controls (line items) become more difficult, and they need to be replaced by other methods of control, including control by costing. When grant recipients are aware of the costing assumptions used to cal-culate their grants, the conversion of those grants to line-item budgets is in theory influenced by the costing assumptions. Thus, when a specific service, such as a primary school, has a specific unit cost, transfers to weredas and their budgets could be aggregated, for example, one hundred primary schools at X dollars per year. With these planning systems, weredas were moving from exter-nal control (PFA) to internal control (PFM).

When developing multiyear frameworks such as the PEP it is necessary to avoid their degeneration into multiyear incremental budgets, as has occurred in Ghana, Kenya, and Tanzania. The only way to prevent this degeneration was to formulate them using more aggregate costing methods. At the same time, it is desirable that there be a relation between the way annual budgets are costed and the way the PEP is costed. Unit-cost methods serve this dual purpose by provid-ing a standard calculation of, say, how much a primary school costs to run per year. Since the federal government had a limited role in direct service delivery, unit-cost methods were of particular interest at the regional level. A detailed set of guidelines, concepts, and approaches to unit costing was initially developed in the Southern Region in the three main service sectors of education, health, and agriculture. The project also developed a training program for costing for the roads sector.[23]

The DSA strategy was to provide intensive training in costing techniques to support the needs-based formula development and also to give space to the BOFED staff to work through the technical details themselves. The training process involved the gradual identification of competent and committed staff members, who were then brought into the BOFED to form a planning team. As part of the process, the BOFED was restructured (with DSA support) in order better to reflect its moving away from being a purely implementing organization to a more policymaking one.

7 Regional budget planning

The principal focus of the planning reform in the regions was on getting the wereda formula system in place, which meant that the regional public expenditure program (allocating between sectors and determining the recurrent costs of capital expenditure) was slower to develop. For the regional PEP, a fairly simple template was devised into which basic numbers could be inserted. The logic of this approach was that more complex systems require a better policymaking framework, which raises the fundamental question: How independent are regions in terms of setting policy? Autonomy in policy is highly circumscribed because regions are principally partially independent agents of the central government's service delivery policies. If regions have little role in policy, there is little role for a PEP. Restated, if the federal government tells regions what sectors to fund, there is little discretion at the regional level for allocation.

Two other factors weakened the role of PEPs in regions. First was the failure of the central government to develop a satisfactory intergovernmental fiscal transfer system (grants from the federal to regional governments), in terms of both the technical components of a transfer formula and timely revenue forecasting and therefore timely notification to the regions of their likely transfers. While on a visit to the Southern Region in the second year of our work there, I asked Getachew Hamussa, head of that region's BOFED, when he was informed about his region's transfer. He replied that he hears about it "on the television, the week before the new fiscal year is to begin." Regions are dependent on the fiscal transfer from the federal government for upward of 85 percent of their resources—the "vertical balance" of the source of resources between center and local under financial decentralization—so effective regional financial management depends on early notification of their transfer.

The second factor undermining the regional PEP was foreign aid, which not only was unreliable but also distorted the allocation of domestic funds in the transfers to regions because of the offset system.

These factors taken together determined the sequence of actions. Once the wereda transfer system began to take shape, it was easier to set in motion a methodology of medium-term planning, the PEP, in the face of unpredictable revenues. But it was surprisingly difficult to create understanding in the regions of the damaging effects of the offset system and of the obstacles to planning their revenues that this presented. The reason this awareness was so important was that there is a certain degree of back-to-front sequencing in a learning-by-doing approach. Once regions began to understand the revenue issues better, they could think more clearly about both vertical imbalance (the amounts of funds coming from the center versus the region's own revenues) and horizontal imbalance (the differing levels of revenue generation across the weredas within a region). The wereda transfer formula addressed the horizontal imbalance (equity between weredas in revenue generation), while the levels of regional revenue provoked an awareness of the need to increase regional revenues. Given the delays in the federal government's revenue reform for regions, the Southern Region's BOFED asked the DSA project to step in and provide them with a comprehensive revenue reform, which included both policy and administration. This request went far beyond the brief of the project, which was focused on expenditure, not revenue, and I had to firmly say no. Not to be totally unresponsive to the request of the region, I agreed to a modest revenue potential study, which would hopefully jump-start the region's own revenue reform in the absence of a federal reform.[24]

Despite the hurdles, the Southern Region was able to achieve most of the PEP process, and was able to prepare projections of resources to its weredas. This success created awareness of the need to understand the sources of economic growth in the region and ways the budget can better support growth, and to move beyond expenditure planning to wider planning perspectives—to move to regional economic planning.

8 Regional economic planning

In 2005 the DSA embarked on the highest-level stage of the planning reform, which involved a shift of regional policy functions to an increased focus on growth-related policies. The merger of the regional bureaus of planning and finance into one bureau, the Bureau of Finance and Economic Development (BOFED), provided the organizational basis to expand the policy brief. Before the planning reform, the regions had been treated as semiautonomous service delivery agents of the federal government and foreign aid agencies, and had been principally about delivering social services enshrined in the Millennium Development Goals.[25] Now, the regional economic planning reform was to give real meaning to the "economic development" part of the BOFED acronym.

The project launched a regional economic policy review (REPR) in the Southern Region. The review brought in external specialists to take an objective look at growth policies, including competitiveness policies, to ask a fundamental question: What are the competitive advantages of the region?[26] The Southern Region's work on determining the regional GDP and its sources made a significant contribution to the REPR exercise, for it added an element of objectivity to the conclusions of the review. Indeed, the REPR was quite revealing and disturbing. For example, it found that the government imposed rigid input controls on the agriculture sector, from which 85 percent of the region's population derived their livelihood. In the Southern Region, government policy underprovided fertilizer and, worse, brought in the wrong type.[27] The REPR concluded that the region was in a low-level equilibrium trap: savings and investment were inadequate to create growth. The Southern Region had few prospects of escaping the trap, and current growth objectives were unrealistic, reflecting overly optimistic manufacturing-sector growth rates in the presence of physical constraints on agriculture-sector growth. In short, the prospects for regional growth were slim to nil.

When the REPR findings were presented to the Southern Region's council, it was a wake-up call for the regional leadership. Despite Hamussa's warnings concerning factoring in political matters, the region quietly started to incorporate regional economic policy into the budget preparation. It endorsed a greater focus on economic growth, a more rational and focused approach to agriculture extension, and coffee policies more attuned to regional growth needs. The region went on to create a specific-purpose grant for support to "growth driver sectors" in its 1999 budget and the PEP. The REPR also fostered a change in the Southern Region's BOFED, from a focus on implementation, control, and inputs to a more policy-based focus. The Southern Region BOFED combined the budget and planning functions—brought finance and economic development together—which better matched the functions that were needed. The planning reform in the Southern Region started that region on the road from PFA to PFM.

Regional planning reform in the other regions

The strategy for extending the planning reform from the Southern Region to other regions involved a combination of direct technical assistance from the DSA and technical assistance by the BOFED in the Southern Region, the direct costs to be financed by the project. Other regions paid for their staff members to travel to the Southern Region to discuss the reforms.[28] Again, the rationale for this approach was learning by doing: the regional technical experts learned as they interacted. The planning reform was endogenously driven in terms of need, content, and schedule.

Challenges to the planning reform

The planning reform met with four principal challenges: political, organizational, and technical constraints, plus the problems created by foreign aid.

Political constraints on the planning reform

The presence or absence of political commitment determines whether a planning system will exist and if so, whether it will be more than a paper exercise with no meaning. A planning reform raises a crucial question: Does government have coherent policies that are supported by resources? Planning, like budgeting, is a system of allocation—how much to allocate to X versus Y? As such it is inherently political and cannot be reduced to technique. But planning is even more exposed to political pressures than budgeting because it aggregates expenditure and clearly presents the resource choices. As Wildavsky noted many years ago, the virtue of the incremental traditional line-item budget is that it obscures these choices and reduces choice to marginal issues such as whether an incremental increase in funds should be given to education at the expense of defense.

A second political factor weakening planning reforms is the potential for the political leadership to be embarrassed, especially by the scrutiny of bureaucrats—witness the incident described at the beginning of this chapter, when the project presented the results of the REPR to the Southern Region's BOFED. The goal of expenditure planning is to drive budgets by policy. The planning process unveils the weakness or, in the case of the Southern Region, the lack of policy, which embarrasses the political elites.

A third issue that is little discussed in the literature on financial decentralization concerns what tier(s) should bear the shock of instability or a shortfall in funding. This is a sensitive issue that goes deeper than who wins or who loses in the allocation of resources; it gets to who is most vulnerable. It was interesting that the weredas, despite all the lip service paid to their importance to frontline service delivery, were the financial shock absorbers. The most vulnerable tier of government, the one providing the most critical social services, bore the brunt of resource shocks. Federal ministries were the least vulnerable and also bore the mildest financial shocks.

A fourth political factor that weakened the planning reform was the political culture that emerged from the long armed struggle. Our reform received no traction in Tigray, the heartwood of the revolution, because the dominant view of planning in that region was grassroots consultation—in effect, political mobilization—which was not shaped by resource constraints. However, in Tigray this "blue sky" planning was appropriate because there, development was not primarily about budgets; what was important was political loyalty, commitment to the cause, and self-sacrifice for the collectivity.

Organizational constraints

Organizational constraints were operative at the level of the finance organizations—how MOFED and BOFEDs were organized—and at many levels in the structure of decentralization. Even though in theory the planning and finance functions were merged into one organization at all levels of the government, in fact, the issue of the budget predominated. The planning function was virtually all about preparing the capital budget. A key issue in planning is sectoral allocation, which should include both capital and recurrent expenditure. Thus, bringing the two budgets together was a critical step in the right direction. Yet the mentality that focuses on incremental budgeting and inputs is very different from the mindset of viewing policy as a shaper of the budget. Organizational reform does not necessarily lead to change in function, although some success was achieved in changing the mindset of select officials in the Southern Region BOFED. Unfortunately, no change of mindset occurred in the federal government as a result of this reform, so when it came time to decide what activities should be funded in the last year of Phase 5 of the DSA project, the planning reform was left out. In deciding the scope of Phase 5, the minister of finance asked Melaku Kifle, the head of the planning reform in the federal government, "What is planning reform?" Kifle responded, "I don't know." Except for the MEFF, the federal planning reform had little relevance, whereas in the regions it had enormous relevance. The federal government did not appreciate the role of planning for regions.

The way a government organizes decentralization has a significant impact on a planning reform. The key question is how much discretion subnational governments have—how much will the expenditures of autonomous governments be planned in advance. Planning systems have inherently centralizing tendencies: one office or group "plans" for the whole. Comprehensiveness is a key virtue in planning, yet the fragmented nature of financial decentralization runs counter to this vision of comprehensiveness. Early on in the reform, the federal government was pressed by foreign aid agencies to prepare a consolidated budget that included all expenditures in the country, federal and regional, so that these agencies could see the total effect of their aid effort. But a consolidated budget involves advance allocation and thus is about local discretion. Since there was no planning there were no advance allocations and hence no notice of advance allocations—clearly, it was impossible to supply a consolidated budget in advance. An accounting of expenditures was possible after the fact, but not before the fact. This demand of the foreign aid agencies flew in the face of the putative autonomy of regions to determine their resource allocations. Furthermore, the practice of creating a consolidated budget in advance is unheard of in decentralized governments.

A decentralized system raises a critical question about the relevance of techniques used at the central level for planning for subnational governments. The significant differences in the role of central and subnational governments added enormous complexity to a planning reform, for the two levels required different systems. In the case of Ethiopia, the federal MOFED was not interested in understanding the planning needs of regions and thus was unhelpful in assisting regions to craft an appropriate approach to planning. An odd and at times comical situation developed in the Southern Region when the federal MOFED tried to sell its transfer formula to the region—an illustration of the disconnect of planning systems under decentralization.

Decentralization also complicates the financial management of foreign aid. Two years into the reform, at a meeting between government and foreign aid agencies convened in the Oromia city of Nazereth, a frank discussion took place about how government could be accountable for the "budget support" of the aid agencies. "Budget support" referred to the unearmarked transfer of donor funds to the MOFED, where they were commingled with domestic funds before being distributed to federal and regional governments. This commingling posed a serious dilemma for foreign aid agencies, namely: Which tier of government was accountable to them? An official from the World Bank recalled visiting the sector ministries of the federal government (health, education, water) to get signatures on covenants—binding agreements—to ensure that foreign assistance that was sent to the regions would actually be spent in the regional sector where it was intended to be spent. The official got no signatures—the ministries could not take responsibility for regional expenditures, and the covenants idea was abandoned.

Technical constraints on the planning reform

Planning reforms often fail technically because they attempt to implant sophisticated systems. Our planning reform introduced simple but not simplistic systems, powerful instruments for getting government staff thinking about efficiency and policy in allocation. We used a learning-by-doing approach: project advisors would introduce a planning technique such as performance agreements and then leave for a period of time while government staff worked with it and applied it. This was not force-fed planning done by armies of resident expatriate consultants. It was show and tell, leave and see, and more show and tell. Show and tell was two-way, from project advisors to government officials and vice versa. Focusing on one region, the Southern Region, which had demonstrated its strong commitment and capacity in implementing the budget and accounts reform, was appropriate for there was momentum for reform, and, most important, the officials were confident.

Interference by foreign aid

One unplanned-for virtue of the planning reform at the federal level was that for nine years it garnered kudos from the foreign aid community for implementing the "best practice" of introducing the equivalent of an MTEF with the MEFF, IPFs, and PEP. Most foreign aid agencies did not assess the impact of these systems, nor did it seem to matter to these observers. They also did not discuss how the instability of their own and other agencies' commitments had undermined the planning reform.

But not all foreign aid agencies were pleased with our reform. An IMF team, led again by Duncan Last of East AFRITAC (last seen in action in chapter 4), came to Ethiopia to discredit the government planning reform and demand that his reform, which featured a suite of performance indicators, be implemented by the central government. His partner in this mission was Marc Robinson, also of East AFRITAC. Last and Robinson got the IMF head in Addis Ababa and the USAID mission director to agree to a meeting with them and the DSA project— me—to discuss their plan. At the meeting Last laid out his vision for a federal reform to build on the reputed "success" of the performance budgeting reform he had started in the federal government in 2004, by using the performance indicators of his budget reform.[29] He reiterated his critique of the DSA project's budget reform in terms of its chart of accounts and budget classification. Finally he finished, and the USAID mission director asked me to comment. I began by reiterating that the reforms had been collaboratively developed and decided upon with the government, so Last and the IMF were criticizing government policy—the CSRP—not the DSA project. A key principle of responsible foreign aid is not to duplicate scarce development resources, so I next asked Last to explain what he understood to be the ongoing initiatives under the CSRP planning reform. I specifically asked him to explain the planning reforms under way in the regions. He was unaware of these reforms. I then turned to the IMF resident representative and the USAID mission director and explained to them what the government planning reforms were at both the federal and regional levels and that the Last team had failed to do due diligence in understanding what was going on. I also indicated that planning reforms are by nature complicated and can lead to confusion, and introducing a competing reform to governments was likely to produce such an outcome. Duncan Last's work on the planning reform exemplifies foreign aid at its worst—denigrating progress made by others in order to elbow in to implement an inappropriate reform.

Vindication

A month into Phase 5 of the DSA project, and fourteen months before the end of the project, a committee from the House of Federation—a separate body from the parliament or the House of People's Representatives that deals with issues arising from the decentralization policy—visited the DSA project offices and requested assistance in the development of a new federal-to-region transfer system. Parliament had removed the responsibility for developing the federal-to-region transfer system from MOFED because of politicians' widespread view that the ministry had failed in developing an appropriate, equitable transfer system and that there was considerable and growing dissatisfaction with the existing population-based formula. The committee was aware of the transfer formula that had been developed in the Southern Region and wanted to move from a population-based to a needs-based formula, in good part for the same reason the Southern Region had adopted the new format—because it promoted equity and was politically more acceptable.

This request to the DSA project was a huge embarrassment to the minister of finance. Following the slap of removing the responsibility for the transfer formula from his ministry, it showed his lack of understanding of the reform work going on in his own house: the fiscal transfer systems developed for regions by the DSA project. The minister firmly rebuffed the request of the House of People's Representatives, saying the DSA project was fully committed to other activities.

This request by the highest authority in the country, coming in the waning months of the project, vindicated the years of effort on reforming planning. The request held out hope that twelve years after I had raised the question of the need for a transfer formula in the CSRP reform, this need had finally been recognized.

The request also demonstrates the very long time scales required for real planning reforms to take root. Although technique certainly is needed, reforms are not about technique. They are about changing the mindset, and that has to be endogenous and driven by felt need, not by the recommendations of technical assistance.

Conclusion

Planning reforms are difficult. They involve relatively complex techniques and require political support. Indeed, the two principal criteria for assessing the success of planning as introduced into PFM are whether it shapes the budget, and whether it fits with the political agenda and culture. The DSA planning reform succeeded in shaping the budget, especially in the regional pilot in the Southern Region, but it did not fit with the country's political agenda and culture and consequently was not sustained long-term.

Four lessons from this planning reform stand out:

1   Planning reforms must be driven by felt government need, not by derived need such as foreign aid's or technical assistance contractors' need.
2   They must be simple but not simplistic.
3   Government ownership of their development and operation is crucial for keeping them simple and relevant.
4   They take a long time.[30]

These points are relevant to countries that are considering a planning reform or are currently implementing one. The problem with most of the failed planning reforms is that they are hobby horses of foreign aid and there is a strong tendency for the techniques to be complicated and the schedule to be wildly unrealistic. Technical complexity is a major reason why planning reforms in Africa have typically failed or, if they continued, have had little impact. Many technical designs of planning reforms propose complicated schemes, often imported from developed countries. The planning reform in Ethiopia was an innovative response that was appropriate to the context. The technical designs introduced powerful tools that were simple and accessible, yet not simplistic.

Some recent rethinking of planning reforms for developing and especially fragile states has concluded that for these states such reforms are inappropriate because they are difficult.[31] Such thinking can end up throwing the baby out with the bathwater. A planning function is needed by all states. Planning can support the traditional budget; it does not supplant it. If the officials of remote weredas in the Southern Region of Ethiopia, most of them with grade-school education, can operate a Type 1 performance budgeting system, then so can officials of most other developing countries. I am convinced that planning reforms can be done that have impact if they are appropriate in terms of their complexity and the time scales for their introduction. Most important, host governments need to see the need for planning and not do it by rote because foreign aid demands it.

Schiavo-Campo's summary of the experience of introducing the MTEF "international best practice" approach to planning applies equally to the performance of planning reforms writ large in African and other developing countries:

> Costly failures have demonstrated that—as [with] any other institutional reform—successful introduction of a programmatic MTEF takes years of persistent efforts consistent with capacity, resources, awareness, incentives, and institutional realities. The two ingredients of the approach are therefore gradualism and selectivity, and the main conditions of success are simplicity and communication. If prematurely introduced or badly implemented, a formal and detailed programmatic MTEF causes enormous waste, frustration, and illusion—for trivial or non-existent benefits.[32]

From the start of the planning reform, the DSA project pursued, especially in the regions, the practices of gradualism, selectivity, simplicity, and communication. It was a very promising reform, a very innovative technical approach that was fit for context and, most important, was not invasive. Regional governments saw the need for the reform; the Southern Region's government assumed full ownership of it. Sadly, the political system was simply not ready for this reform and for the types of discussions a genuine planning process would inevitably lead to. Foreign aid, specifically the IMF, never took the time to understand this initiative, much less to build on it, and proceeded with conventional approaches that have gone nowhere. The central government's hands-off attitude to the planning reform is a clear indicator that the regime was not interested in moving to financial management, which would promote discretion by bureaucrats, and that the reform would be a PFA reform, with a focus on external control. In the next chapter I discuss the fate of all four reforms: budget, accounts, FIS, and planning.

Notes

1 On the REPR see DSA P-64, DSA P-65, and DSA PA-12.
2 See Wynne (2005); Schiavo-Campo (2008); Beschel and Ahern (2012: 10–11); World Bank (2012d: 60).
3 This framework developed by Allen Schick was published in World Bank (1998: 2).
4 On the consequences of repetitive budgeting see Caiden and Wildavsky (1980: 75–8).
5 Peterson (1992a); Lacey (1989); Lehmann (1986). The principal budget reform in Kenya during the 1980s implemented by HIID was the Budget Rationalization Programme. See Republic of Kenya (1986a).
6 Like Ethiopia, Kenya was heavily dependent on foreign aid at the time, and so the capital budget was and is principally driven by projects funded by foreign aid. For more on that reform, see Peterson (1996c).
7 Wildavsky (1973).
8 I also had a tactical reason for recommending a planning reform. I knew that these reforms are a sacred cow of the Bretton Woods agencies, who view them as "international best practice." If a financial reform did not have a planning reform component—regardless of the actual feasibility of its design—a box would not be ticked and it would become a point of criticism of the whole reform.
9 Hyden (2006: 266).

10 Peterson (1996a: 4).
11 For a more detailed account of the eight technical activities see http://stevepeterson pfm.com, where the seventy-five documents relating to the planning reform are archived.
12 On the disagreements between the government and the Bretton Woods agencies in the early 1990s see chapter 3, n.5.
13 For detailed information on the DSA project's policy-related activities see DSA PA-1 (sector studies on cereal exports), DSA PA-6 (development of the coffee sector), DSA PA-7 (constraints on industrial competitiveness), and DSA PA-11 (creation of a commodity exchange for grain). For some of the activities conducted under the policy initiative with the Office of the Prime Minister see DSA PA-2, DSA PA-4, DSA PA-7, and DSA PA-12. The project's development of a macroeconomic model is presented in DSA PA-3, DSA PA-4, and DSA PA-5. See DSA PA-2 for the project's advice on establishing a policymaking organization.
14 Roemer directed policy advisory teams in many countries, notably Kenya and Indonesia. He was the principal author in 1986 of the blueprint for Kenya's development, which has come to fruition largely along the lines he recommended (see Republic of Kenya 1986b). Roemer also wrote or co-wrote nine books and numerous articles on development, including Roemer and Jones (1991) and Lindauer and Roemer (1994) and was one of four authors of the leading text in the field of development economics (see Perkins et al. 1996).
15 For Westlake's review of the coffee sector see DSA PA-6.
16 See DSA PA-11. For a review of the unique features of this exchange see Tadesse (2010).
17 For the project profile see DSA P-15 and DSA P-16.
18 The financial calendar proposed for Ethiopia is presented in figure 4.1A, which can be found on the book's website, http://stevepetersonpfm.com, in the section "Annexes to Chapters."
19 For a discussion of MTEFs see Schiavo-Campo and Tommasi (1999: 287–306); Oxford Policy Management (2000).
20 The technical details of the wereda transfer formula and its processes are extensively documented in the project's technical reports. See DSA P-49 and DSA P-74.
21 The wereda performance agreement is presented in DSA P-63 and DSA P-66.
22 International Monetary Fund (2011: 14–19).
23 See DSA B-19 and DSA P-54.
24 DSA M-56.
25 Reinert (2006).
26 DSA P-64.
27 DSA PA-12.
28 DSA M-23.
29 The performance budget reform that Duncan Last was so proud of was stillborn: it had to be halted in the four pilot ministries because they could not prepare their budgets, which was holding up the completion of the entire federal budget.
30 See also the extensive documentation of this reform at http://stevepetersonpfm.com.
31 The classic discussion of the difficulty and, often, irrelevance of planning in developing countries is Caiden and Wildavsky (1980: 264–7). More recent reviews have questioned the value of planning reforms on the continent in Africa, especially the medium-term expenditure frameworks. In his review of MTEFs Jim Brumby (2008: 3) found that this technique made little or no improvement in PFM: there was "virtually no evidence of improved macroeconomic balance; some limited evidence of reallocation to priority subsectors; no evidence of a link to greater budgetary predictability; and no evidence of efficiency gains in spending." According to Brumby these findings from Africa also applied in South and Southeast Asia, parts of East Asia, and in some countries of Latin America and the Pacific.
32 Schiavo-Campo (2008: 26).

Part III

Lessons for the developing and the already developed

8 The tests of time
Two roads

With the departure of the DSA project in January 2008, the government of Ethiopia had to decide which road to take—sustain the twelve-year reform or embark on new reforms. It chose the road of perpetual reform and that made all the difference—financial performance deteriorated so quickly that some foreign aid agencies suspended funding.[1] This wrong turn also brought in a new driver, foreign aid—the IMF and the World Bank—as the central government relinquished ownership of the reform. Most damaging was the loss of ownership by regional governments, which was a key factor in the reform's success. Three oft-touted principles in PFM are government ownership of reform, contextualization of reforms, and getting the basics right. The new road violated all three of these principles, which is why finances have precipitously deteriorated since 2008.

In this chapter I examine why the road of perpetual reform, with a goal to leap to sophisticated PFM, was taken and the road of sustaining the reformed PFA system was not. Both roads provide lessons for would-be reformers. The post-2008 experience in Ethiopia also affirms the need to distinguish financial reforms in terms of PFA, public financial administration, versus PFM, public financial management.

The recent deterioration of public finances

It is rare to have a comprehensive operational assessment of a financial system's support of service delivery several years after its reform. Nearly three years to the day after the DSA project ended in January 2008, I returned to Ethiopia to lead a team of five Ethiopian financial specialists to assess why the reformed system was not producing prompt and quality financial reports for the country's two largest foreign aid projects: the Protection of Basic Services Program, Phase II (PBS II), and the Productive Safety Nets Program (PSNP).[2] The purpose of the PBS II program is to provide funds for recurrent expenditures, especially salary, and to expand social services, principally healthcare and primary education. The PSNP provides monthly payments to families to purchase food. There are seven channels by which funds from the government and foreign aid are distributed in Ethiopia. Our review was called the Channel 1 assessment because Channel 1 is the treasury system and we were reviewing only this system.[3]

The Channel 1 assessment was conducted from February to August 2011, including five months of fieldwork covering five regions, eight zones, and thirty-two weredas.[4] A key feature of the assessment was the attachment of finance specialists from the region being visited, giving the assessors contacts and invaluable insights and lending credibility to the findings in our closeout meetings with the five regional BOFEDs. I had requested that the Ministry of Finance also attach finance specialists to our teams, but none were assigned. Even though the number of zones and weredas assessed constituted only a fraction of the total number in the country, in our closeout meetings, administrators in zones and regions found the findings applicable throughout their jurisdictions. Indeed at the end of a two-hour debriefing of our findings to a zone finance department in Oromia, the head of the department thanked me for the efforts of the team and suggested that we "stick around—the situation is even worse than you have said."

Briefly, the Channel 1 assessment found that the principal problem causing delayed and poor-quality reporting for the PSNP and PBS II programs was poor execution. It was not the systems—that is, the procedures. The reform had developed robust systems. This conclusion was confirmed by the finding of the coexistence of good and poor performance in many locales. Underscoring the mixed picture were several anomalous findings: that remoteness was not correlated with delay in submission, and lack of access to a functioning (meaning supported) IBEX computer installation at the zone level did not delay the preparation of reports. The good news was that since the deterioration was caused by problems in execution and not poor procedures, in principle the situation could be rapidly improved if the systems were better sustained, especially by in-service training (IST).

The deficiencies that were found in some of the locales assessed were very worrisome. There were two principal types: lack of budgetary discipline and weaknesses or loss of financial control. In 38 percent of the weredas and zone offices visited by the assessment teams, expenditure was incurred without being budgeted for.[5] Cabinet members who were party cadres pressured financial staffs to violate financial procedures set down in the financial law, regulations, and directives. They faced the choice of following cadres' orders or losing their jobs. Unbudgeted expenditures were recorded on so-called special payment vouchers (SPVs) and were not recorded in the accounting system. Many were found to be unresolved for more than a year and there was considerable risk that repayment would never be made. In some region, zone, and wereda finance offices, SPVs had gone missing and thus repayment had not been made. Cash had gone missing.

Serious weaknesses in financial controls were also found in 71 percent of the finance offices visited. Bank reconciliation—reconciling the cash balance at the bank as stated on bank statements with the cash balance shown on the ledger card on the same calendar date—is a key control. It was not done by 58 percent of the finance offices assessed. Either the finance offices did no cash count, or the count did not reconcile, or they had discontinued the practice.[6] Internal audit, another key safeguard to ensure that adequate control is exercised, was undercut by heads of finance in select weredas and zones, who instructed internal auditors to look at marginal activities outside the pool, such as health centers, but not examine the financial pool. External audits by the regional and federal auditor general have had little impact, because their audit findings have generally been ignored.

Adding to these serious deficiencies was the decline in the performance of funds flows from regions to the zones and weredas, which has significantly impacted the quality of budget execution. Over a quarter of the wereda and zone finance offices and departments reported that their subsidy transfers were delayed for several months. For example, North Gondar zone reported it received its transfer in November, five months late.[7] Delays in funding have had serious consequences, including delays in payments to beneficiaries for purchasing food.[8]

Budgetary indiscipline and poor financial control have combined to create an environment conducive to corruption. The Channel 1 assessment found corruption in select locales; a head of a zone finance department in Oromia told us that it is probably worse than what we turned up.

The World Bank's own metrics for monitoring the performance of the PBS II are evidence of the serious decline in financial controls between May 2009 and May 2011. The bank used what it calls its SAFE principles—sustainability, accountability, fiduciary standards, and effectiveness—to monitor the PBS II program and assess it in terms of these principles on a semi-annual basis. The SAFE principles are a useful composite proxy not only for how a host government's financial system is performing (the fiduciary principle) but also for how the program as a whole is performing. The overall SAFE rating declined two levels between April 2010 and May 2011 from highly satisfactory to marginally satisfactory, and the fiduciary component declined in two years from satisfactory in May 2009 to somewhat satisfactory in November 2009 to marginally satisfactory in April 2010 and May 2011 (table 8.1).[9]

Why have public finances deteriorated so significantly in Ethiopia? Perhaps the most striking finding of both assessments is that much of the "conventional wisdom" about why financial management is eroding was discredited by their findings. The most oft-cited cause of the deterioration of public finances is "staff turnover."[10] Yet the Channel 1 assessment found that the staff in the regional and local finance offices is more than adequate in virtually all locales. Furthermore, although vacancies do occur, they are rapidly filled, often with staff who have better qualifications than the individual being replaced. It is important to differentiate between "turnover" as shuffling within the service and turnover as departure from service. The business process reengineering reform has had a very disruptive impact on financial administration because it continually rotates staff so that officials don't stay on the job long enough to learn it.

A second tenet of conventional wisdom is that remoteness leads to delay of their subsidy transfers. This notion, too, did not hold up under the scrutiny of the Channel 1 and World Bank assessments.

Table 8.1 Scoring of the PBS II SAFE (stability, accountabilility, fiduciary standards, effectiveness) principles

	2009 May	2009 Nov	2010 April	2010 Nov	2011 May	2011 Nov	2012 May	2012 Nov	2013 May	2013 Nov
Stability in additionality	S	S	MS	S	MS	MS	P	P	NS	P
Accountability and fairness	S	S	HS	HS	HS	HS	NS	P	NS	P
Fiduciary standards	S	SS	MS	MS	MS	S	NS	NS	NS	NS
Effectiveness	S	S	S	MS	S	S	NS	NS	NS	NS
Overall	**S**	**HS**	**HS**	**S**	**MS**	**S**	**S**	**S**	**S**	**S**

Sources: author's compilation, based on World Bank (2009b, 2009c, 2010a, 2010b, 2010c, 2011a, 2011b, 2012a, 2012b, 2013d, 2013e).

Notes
Key: HS = highly satisfactory; S = satisfactory; SS = somewhat satisfactory; MS = marginally satisfactory; NS = not scored; P = passed.

A third discredited notion is that the time frame for submitting monthly financial reports of expenditures is too short. In summary, the conventional view is that the procedures for preparing and processing financial reports were at fault, but in fact the assessments showed that the procedures were not at fault.

The real reason for the deterioration in public finances is that the Ethiopian government has made a wrong turn—onto the road of perpetual reform.

The road taken: the wrong turn to perpetual reform and the leap to PFM

The hallmarks of the Civil Service Reform Program was government ownership of the financial reform and a clear purpose of building financial systems that would support decentralization. This implied a reform strategy of *recognize-improve*. Instead of completing this reform with a strategy of *sustain*, a new road has been taken, one that is all about *change*. In taking the change road, the government has relinquished its ownership over public finance—the gravest mistake, I feel—and done so in two senses. Domestically, the Ministry of Finance has relinquished ownership of the financial system by failing to exert leadership in how the government-wide management reform of business process reengineering (BPR) is done in finance. As we shall see, BPR has had disastrous consequences and has significantly and directly contributed to the budgetary indiscipline and poor financial control presented earlier.

Internationally, the Ministry of Finance has also relinquished ownership of the financial system to the Bretton Woods agencies, which are pursuing a reform agenda of installing advanced PFM (public financial *management*, as opposed to *administration*) techniques: a high-end Oracle IFMIS (integrated financial management information system), program budgeting, and accrual accounting. The combined effects of the domestic-led BPR reform and the foreign aid–led PFM reforms is that PFA (public financial administration) continues to deteriorate and deteriorate at the most vulnerable level—in the zones and weredas, the locus of frontline service delivery. The Ministry of Finance has not only relinquished ownership, it has relinquished purpose—it has withdrawn support of a financial system that supported decentralization. The zones and weredas are still weak administrative systems. They are not ready to make the leap to management—BPR and PFM.

The domestic-led management reform: business process reengineering

Business process reengineering (BPR) is a management reform, originally pioneered in the early 1990s in the United States, whose focus is the analysis and design of workflows and processes within an organization with the aim of improving efficiency.[11] The government introduced BPR in 2007 and accorded it the highest priority in the belief that it would significantly improve public sector service delivery. Unfortunately the government executed the BPR with its campaign (*zemecha*) approach to reform (*mashashaya*) and did not prudently adopt a "learning" approach to see how a foreign management reform would fit the Ethiopian context. The problem with BPR in the context of the finance function is that it sought streamlining at the expense of control (public finance administration).

BPR has arguably been the most serious challenge to the reformed financial systems. It has had a serious negative impact on the organization, staffing, and procedures of government financial administration. It also dramatically shows the error of leaping from administration (external control) to management (internal control).

The introduction of BPR in early 2007 could not have come at a worse time. Under BPR the government sought to reorganize the finance function while the procedural reforms were still being absorbed and finance officials were still coping with the merger of the finance and planning function in one agency: the Ministry of Finance and Economic Development (MOFED) and its equivalents at the region, zone, and wereda tiers. Just as the DSA project was winding down and attempting to hand over the reform to the government and ensure that it would be sustained, BPR was being introduced. And the push for BPR was drawing finance officials into the tsunami of this needless and inappropriate management reform; they could not focus on taking over the support for the new financial systems put in place by the DSA project.

The profound impact of the BPR reform on the organization of the finance function is best illustrated by the experience of Amhara region, which significantly changed the organization of its finance function three times in three consecutive years. This reorganizing diverted senior staff from day-to-day operations, which in turn directly diminished the quality and timeliness of financial administration—the deterioration in financial reporting that occasioned the Channel 1 assessment.

The impact of BPR on finance staff has been devastating. First, under BPR, finance has been relegated to a secondary function. The finance function is defined as "support," not a "first priority" of public service. To be sure, finance is not at the "frontline" of service delivery; nevertheless it is one of the most important inputs to good service delivery. The message conveyed by BPR and certainly taken on board by finance staff was that finance, and thus they, were second-class. The effects have been immediate and significant: senior finance personnel who desire to remain in public service have sought positions outside of finance in the "priority" services, education and health. This career-sustaining decision has also been encouraged by the policies of BPR, where in some locales top finance staffs have been "cherry-picked" to serve in other sectors.

Second, BPR has resulted in a "deprofessionalizing" and "despecializing" of the financial function. Under BPR, regions have discretion in defining what BPR is. There is no central guidance—indeed, the senior staff of the Southern Region BOFED confided to the Channel 1 team that "they were very confused." So a further erosion of professionalism comes from the interpretation of BPR that has emerged in the Southern Region: that "generalists," not "specialists," are what is needed. (So far no other region has adopted this interpretation of BPR staffing notions.) This approach to staffing has led directly to rapid deterioration of PFA in the Southern Region, heretofore the pioneer and regional star of the financial reform. PFA/M is a technical field requiring specialists trained in relatively arcane procedures such as bookkeeping and financial audit. Assigning personnel to be ledger accountants who have never been trained in the government book-keeping system, have no bookkeeping experience, and are freshly appointed on the basis of credentials alone is a prescription for poor PFA/M.

The Channel 1 assessment found that from 2008 on Ethiopia's colleges had produced an ample supply of staff to the public service so that vacancies could be rapidly filled with staff with better official credentials than were previously recruited. But one of the dictates of the BPR is that personnel should be moved around frequently so that they learn about the whole organization (related to the "generalist is better than specialist" trope). Thus, inexperienced staff with bright new credentials are elbowing out more experienced personnel with fewer credentials. The Channel 1 assessment confirmed that most vacancies were filled, but the recruits often did not have experience. The performance of PFA crucially rests on the quality, not the quantity, of staff. Freshly earned credentials do not translate into quality, for quality is a function of experience and commitment—neither of which the new recruits have. To make matters worse, the new recruits are denied the opportunity to obtain the experience they need if they are to turn in a professional performance because they are constantly moved to accommodate the change of organizational structure—in some cases three times in as many years. It is ironic that staff capacity should be a constraint to the financial system years after the reform was introduced, yet BPR has indeed whipsawed the staffing of the finance function.

Third, BPR has brought disincentives in compensation. Some regions have adopted a flat compensation scheme, which gives no incentive for qualifications and experience. A fresh recruit receives the same compensation as a member of staff with a decade of experience. The impact of these schemes is that experienced personnel have to find other positions either inside or outside the civil service if they want compensation commensurate with their years of service.

In addition to disrupting the organization and staffing of the finance function, BPR has led to confusion in procedures. BPR has given the country a third basis of accounting, for Amhara region now has adopted modified accrual. Obviously, this cannot fit with the federal financial law, which states that reports from regions will be presented to MOFED in the form specified by the minister of finance—cash basis for recurrent expenditure and modified cash basis for capital expenditure.[12]

BPR has not only introduced unnecessary complexity into financial procedures, it has significantly weakened control by violating generally accepted principles of financial administration. Specifically, the BPR allows for only a single signoff by a wereda staff member of expenditures up to 20,000 Ethiopian birr (approximately $1,200), which violates the principle of segregation of duties. Finally, BPR violates the principle of segregation of responsibilities, for accountants who record and report are also assigned the task of payment.

The BPR reform demonstrates that external control (PFA) must be well established before one can leap to financial management—internal control (PFM). Internal and external audit were orphans of the Civil Service Reform Program's financial reform and were never done. Before one introduces far-reaching efficiency measures such as giving discretion for an individual to sign off on 20,000 birr and remove segregation of duties, strong controls must first be in place whereby these streamlined procedures can be monitored. BPR has significantly weakened control, and international experience has shown that once control is weakened, it is difficult to restore.

BPR of the finance function was done rapidly, was not adequately resourced, was not systematically executed, and, most serious, lacked central guidance and proactive critique from the Ministry of Finance. The ministry simply stood by and watched as prudent financial principles were swept away. Changes to the enabling legal framework were ignored and procedural manuals and training materials were not developed and properly vetted. No provision was made for the massive task of retraining finance staff in the legal and procedural basis of the new system.

The Channel 1 assessment also found another and quite worrisome reason that finance staff were not performing—the use of senior staff for nonfinance tasks. Nearly 80 percent of the heads of the wereda finance offices spent 85 percent of their time off-task.[13] To understand the capacity of the finance function one must go beyond the aggregate figures of in-post establishment and look at the quality of leadership of the function. In Ethiopia, the leadership of wereda and zone finance offices and departments was unavailable.

An internationally led management reform: the leap to PFM

The World Bank failed to provide adequate support to Ethiopia's reformed PFA. The World Bank and the IMF have pushed a reform agenda of PFM.

The World Bank's program for public finance: IT is the magic bullet

As part of its PBS II project, the World Bank included a finance component, which is referred to in the project document as Part C1 (C stands for *component*).[14] The C1 reform was put in place to initiate a new round of PFM reform. One of the C1 reform's many problems was that it had a very large annual budget—$86.6 million in November 2010, which was pared to $67.8 million in 2011.[15] By comparison, the budget for the DSA project over twelve years was $34.4 million. The C1 project has failed to support the PFA system and is one reason why the World Bank's SAFE metrics for the PBS II program (discussed earlier) have deteriorated, especially the fiduciary standards. The C1 reform failed for three reasons: too much emphasis on a new financial information system (FIS), significant underfunding of external audit, and failure to develop an in-service training program.

Table 8.2 starkly presents the priorities of the C1 reform in supporting PFA. Approximately 50 percent of the revised budget (column 4) was allocated two new FIS systems (item 1), while the crucial support needed to sustain the reform, procedural training (item 5), was allocated a paltry 4.6 percent. The most egregious mistake in the bank's strategy was to weaken external control: external audit (item 4) was slashed 74 percent, from $26.5 million to $7 million. As noted in the earlier discussion of the BPR reform, external and internal audit were orphans of the CSRP and were not funded. The continued underfunding of these crucial PFA techniques of external control during the leap to PFM underscored the inappropriateness of World Bank support of public finance.

The aggregate figures and percentage of the budget do not fully convey how poorly designed and implemented the C1 reform was. In terms of design, there was no needs assessment nor a formal design for this $86.6 million component—it was basically a shopping list. Particularly worrisome was the absence of an assessment of the ongoing FIS upgrade (known as the IBEX 2) by the World Bank, which was committing $18.2 million for the completion and rollout of this system under the C1 reform, which was to be the cornerstone of sustaining PFM. The IBEX 2 was "vaporware"—it failed to materialize after three years and $3 million.[16] Furthermore, the World Bank failed to assess the status of the Ethiopian Information and Communication Technology (ICT) Wide Area Network infrastructure that would be needed for the IBEX 2 and the Oracle systems to reach regional and subregional governments (see the discussion of WeredaNet in chapter 6). In short, the bank did not do due diligence in assessing the vehicle, IBEX 2, or the road, WeredaNet, that the vehicle would travel on.

In terms of implementation, fortunately, after two years (2011 to 2012), less than 3 percent of the C1 funds had been disbursed, principally because of delays

Table 8.2 MOFED's initial and current budget for the C1 component of the PBS II program[a] (unit as indicated)

1 Description	2 Initial budget November 25, 2010 (US$)	3 Initial budget: function as percentage of total budget	4 Revised budget March 14, 2011 (US$)	5 Revised budget: function as percentage of total budget
1 Financial information systems	$36,286,623	42.0	$33,799,326	49.8
2 Financial transparency and accountability	7,224,292	8.4	9,454,697	13.9
3 PPFM support	5,200,452	6.0	8,159,642	12.0
4 External audit	26,500,000	30.6	7,025,977	10.4
5 Procedural training	5,081,970	5.9	3,095,249	4.6
6 Procurement reform	4,256,500	4.9	3,621,711	5.4
7 Contingency	0	0	2,559,875	3.8
8 Coordination of the reform	0	0	1,088,664	1.6
9 Development of the accounting profession	2,000,000	2.3	120,874	0.2
Total	$86,549,837		$67,837,351	

Source: author's calculation, based on Federal Democratic Republic of Ethiopia, Ministry of Finance and Economic Development (2010a, 2011).

Note

a Includes $18 million for the Oracle IFMIS and the budget of $49,837,351 requested under the C1 component of PBS II (Ministry of Finance and Economic Development 2011). There is an error in the MOFED budget: the total submitted is $50,170,770 but the total for the items listed is $49,837,351. The $1,088,664 budget for the Channel One Program Coordinating Unit (COPCU) has here been put under the category of PPFM Support as has the COPCU contingency budget of $2,559,875. In calculating Activity 4 (the Basic Financial Information System), the following activity numbers from the MOFED March 14, 2011, budget were included: 1.2, 1.4, 1.8, 1.9, 1.10, 2.3. In calculating Activity 9 (Distributed Basic Financial Information System), the following activity numbers from the MOFED March 14, 2011, budget were included: 1.1, 1.3, 1.5, 1.6, 1.7. In calculating Activity 10 (ERP financial information system), the $18 million for a pilot Oracle ERP is not funded under the C1, but I have included it here, since it is part of the PFM strategy and is now being funded by the World Bank.

and irregularities by both the government and the World Bank in procuring the two computer systems. The scale of underfunding of in-service training by the C1 project is staggering. At the specific request of the minister of finance, the Channel 1 assessment team reviewed the training needs for the next five years; it estimated that the demand for IST to sustain the PFA was about 182,000 staff, at a cost of $21.2 million over five years.[17] The DSA project introduced the new financial systems over twelve years and spent over 80 percent of its $34.4 million budget on developing the training materials and then delivering training to more than 72,000 officials.

There were several reasons that 82,000 staff needed IST after 2008: virtually no training had been done since 2007 in the large regions; BPR had removed most of the 72,000 trained officials trained under the DSA project (BPR had no funds for training); and the small regions that had been late to the reform needed their staff to be trained. The C1 project's IST budget was just $3 million, thus underfunding training by 86 percent. What little IST was conducted was of shocking quality. The twelve-year reform had developed a robust training program whose key features were class sizes of no larger than forty officials trained by two resource persons over ten days for the core courses. Under C1 funding, one zone in the Southern Region trained 575 staff over eight days in two separate classes. Only 5 of the 575 participants passed the course exam—a .09 percent pass rate.[18]

The IMF's program for public finance: shoot for the stars

If the World Bank's program was poorly designed and implemented, the IMF's was a bigger mess.[19] It focused on introducing the most sophisticated techniques in the PFM toolbox—it truly was shooting for the stars. This space travel is presented in an October 2011 IMF report, "Ethiopia Public Financial Management Reform Priorities: Next Steps."[20] Written by a team led by Pokar Khemani, the current head of the fiscal affairs department of the IMF, the report is a poster child for foreign aid at its worst:

1 It ignored recent reports on the status of financial systems. The IMF report cited only IMF documents, many of them outdated.[21]
2 It ignored decentralization, the government's priority. The report clearly stated that it "focuses on the federal government budget and does not extend to regional budget considerations."[22] It failed to address the serious constraints facing regions, zones, and weredas, which was where PFA deterioration was happening.
3 It emphasized inappropriate techniques such as program budgeting, accrual accounting, a high-end Oracle IFMIS, and medium-term planning.[23]
4 It proposed a new reform program to be driven by the IMF without any mention of the PBS II C1 program, funded by the World Bank and other donors.
5 It sought to restore the zero treasury balance system. This had been introduced in 2004, but had been suspended in 2008 because MOFED had found it to be unworkable.

6 It discussed the need to strengthen internal controls yet made no mention of the impact of BPR, which has seriously compromised internal controls.

7 It failed to mention the need to support external audit.

8 It recommended that the government introduce an Oracle IFMIS while failing to note its potential risks, given the weak and limited bandwidth of Ethiopia's ICT (information communication technology) infrastructure. Until the ICT is strengthened, an Oracle IFMIS cannot reach zones or weredas.

9 Its assessment of the existing financial system was for the most part disparaging and self-serving, thereby justifying the IMF's own reform program.[24]

10 It shows a lack of understanding of how such inappropriate reforms divert MOFED staff from providing support to the regions. The Channel 1 assessment had found this lack of support to be a chronic and serious problem in all regions surveyed.

In sum, the IMF in this report ignored all of the accomplishments of the government's Expenditure Management and Control Program (EMCP) reform. What the IMF proposed was in effect an employment program for IMF technical assistance staff and not a suitable strategy for Ethiopia. The IMF is obsessed with program budgeting. But what impact will such budgeting have on the delivery, in the short and even medium term, addressing the deterioration of the financial basics needed for effective implementation of the two largest donor projects in the country—PBS II and the PSNP funds which feed 9 million Ethiopians? But the fallacy of the IMF program is that cash is going missing—there is weak external control—and reforms of internal control such as program budgeting do not address this fundamental weakness. Internal control assumes external control is effective. It is not.

The government of Prime Minister Meles Zenawi made it clear in 1996 that it did not want Bretton Woods involvement in its financial reform. Yet the IMF pressed the government in 2005 to introduce program budgeting just as the DSA-designed budget reform was being rolled out in the large Oromia region (discussed in chapter 4). That action created chaos and was professionally irresponsible. The IMF's 2011 report also shows that after six years of IMF assistance, its program budget reform is in disarray.

Unfortunately, officials of the Bretton Woods agencies seem to have lost a sense of modesty and of their limited role, especially in matters of public expenditure management. This is made clear in the presentation by Robert Lacey to the Harvard Institute for International Development seminar on the "the link between planning and budgeting."

> Like most of my colleagues at the World Bank and the International Monetary Fund, I am an observer rather than an actor in the drama of public expenditure management. Anything that I say has therefore something in common with the backseat driver who always persists in making a nuisance of himself by telling the real driver what he is doing wrong and rarely what

he is doing right. The real driver's understandable annoyance at this practice is heightened by this certain knowledge that if the backseat driver were by some unfortunate sequence of events to be placed behind the wheel the results would be worse than disastrous.[25]

Since 2008 Ethiopia has embarked on a road of perpetual reform that can be summarized as a leap from administration to management, from PFA to PFM—as Lacey said, worse than disastrous, as measured by the World Bank's own metrics. The Channel 1 assessment found that frontline service delivery and a core, if not the core, government policy of decentralization has been neglected. Regions, zones, and especially weredas are struggling to establish good administration generally and PFA specifically. The road the Ministry of Finance and its foreign backers have adopted does not meet the needs of decentralization. This road is a perfect storm: BPR has degraded control, the World Bank PBS II C1 reform has further weakened control by slashing training and external audit, which has been underfunded for over a decade. Worst, the bank and the IMF are urging the government to shoot for the stars with inappropriate advanced PFM techniques. If there is one principle agreed on by most finance professionals it is that one must first have good control (PFA) before leaping to management (PFM).[26] The actions and advice of the World Bank and the IMF have violated this principle.

The road Ethiopia should have taken and still needs to take: sustaining the PFA reform

Since 2008, Ethiopia has taken the wrong road in public finance. Using our framework of the drivers of reform presented in chapters 1 and 2—context, ownership, purpose, and strategy—the right road would have been:

Ownership: Government, both federal and regional
Purpose: PFA that supports decentralization
Strategy: Sustain

The wrong road was:

Ownership: Bretton Woods agencies
Purpose: Experiment with PFM techniques in the federal government
Strategy: Change

The wrong road was taken for three reasons. First and foremost, MOFED did not understand the magnitude of the reform because it had not involved itself in the countrywide reform. Second, MOFED was weak and disorganized, lacked initiative, and had difficulty keeping its own house in order. Third, MOFED had become accustomed over twelve years to letting others (the regions and the DSA project) do the donkey work of reform and in 2008 outsourced the reform to the foreigner—the firm of Dulcian, headed by an inexperienced owner who had never worked outside the United States. MOFED's failure to weigh in on the serious weakening of finance control caused by the government's own BPR reform, discussed earlier, speaks volumes of its lack of due diligence and failure to assume responsibility for maintaining probity in public finances. In his work on systems development, Burton Swanson's core conclusion explains why the wrong road was taken: "We only really understand a ... system when we know about its implementation."[27] MOFED did not know how to implement the reform of the system.

In October 2005, more than a year prior to the end of the Phase 4 contract, which was to roll out the reform to the rest of the country, I submitted to MOFED a detailed report on what was needed to sustain the reform when the DSA was no longer providing technical assistance to the reform after twelve years of having done so.[28] The report stressed the government's role in maintaining the reform within a complex political and policy context and "development partners'" role in supporting the government in this.

This advice was never heeded.[29]

MOFED's four big mistakes

Sadly, the primary responsibility for taking the wrong road rests with government. It would be nice to be able to place the blame on the foreign aid agencies, which elbowed their way into the public finance reform terrain in 2008 after being specifically excluded for twelve years—as explicitly sanctioned by the prime minister and enshrined in the government's CSRP report. Despite the problems created by the Bretton Woods agencies, especially their push to introduce new reforms that the country wasn't ready for, it is MOFED which made four crucial mistakes that led to the wrong road.

1   The wrong strategy for the Phase 4 of the DSA Project.
2   Mismanagement of the Reform Support Unit 3. Failure to create a public finance steering committee.
3   Failure to make MOFED's takeover of the reform a priority.

MOFED mistake 1: the wrong strategy for Phase 4 of the DSA project

The origins of the wrong turn had its roots in the design of the final phase of the DSA project, Phase 4, which was to run for twenty months, from July 1, 2004, through November 30, 2006. The Phase 4 technical proposal outlined the three activities of the reform and estimated that these would take a total of six years: introduce, one year; support, two years; and institutionalize, three years (see table 8.3).[30] The introduction activity involved a number of tasks:

*   Simplification of budget structures
*   Simplification of financial management (single treasury system)
*   Development of procedures

Table 8.3 Six-year time frame to introduce, support, and institutionalize the Civil Service Reform Program's financial reforms to the regions, FY2001 to FY2007 (European calendar)

(1) Task number. Reform. Number of years required.	(2) FY2001 July 2001 to July 2002	(3) FY2002 July 2002 to July 2003	(4) FY2003 July 2003 to July 2004	(5) FY2004 July 2004 to July 2005	(6) FY2005 July 2005 to July 2006	(7) FY2006 July 2006 to July 2007	(8) FY2007 July 2007 to July 2008	(9) Date completed or projected completion date
				DSA Phase 4 starts July 1, 2004		DSA Phase 4 ends November 30, 2006 Phase 5 begins December 1, 2006	DSA Phase 5 ends January 31, 2008	
1 **Budget reform.**[a] Introduce. One year.	Federal	SR	Amhara Tigray Oromia	Oromia Bene Addis Dire	Harari Afar Gambela Somali Addis Dire			Completed in FY2005. Except for Somali, which did not do the reform.
2 Support. Two years.		Federal	Federal SR	Federal SR Amhara Tigray	SR Amhara Tigray Oromia Bene	Oromia Bene Harari Afar Gambela Somali Addis Dire	Harari Afar Gambela Somali Addis Dire	Completed in FY2007. Does not include Somali as it did not do the reform.
3 Institutionalize. More than three years.					SR Federal	SR Amhara Tigray Federal	Tigray Amhara	FY2010. Except for Somali, which did not do the reform.

Reform step							Notes
4 **Accounts reform.**[b] Introduce. One year.	Federal	SR, Tigray, Amhara	SR, Amhara, Addis, Dire	Oromia, Bene, Addis, Dire, Harari	Afar, Gambela, Somali		Completed in FY2006. Except for Somali, which did not do the reform.
5 Support. Two years.		Federal	Federal, SR, Tigray, Amhara	Federal, SR, Tigray, Amhara	Federal, SR, Oromia, Bene, Harari, Addis, Dire	Oromia, Bene, Harari, Afar, Gambela, Somali, Addis, Dire	Projected to be completed in FY2009. Except for Somali, which did not do the reform.
6 Institutionalize. More than three years.					SR, Tigray, Amhara, Federal	SR, Tigray, Amhara, Federal	Projected to be completed in FY2012. Excludes Somali which did not do the reform.
7 **Budget planning.**[c] Introduce. One year.	Federal	SR	SR	Amhara, Tigray, Oromia	Bene		Completed in FY2006
8 Support. Two years.		Federal	Federal, SR	Federal, SR	Amhara, Tigray, Oromia	Amhara, Tigray, Oromia	Projected to be completed in FY2009
9 Institutionalize. More than three years.					SR	SR	Projected to be completed in FY2012

Source: Peterson (2004: 10–11).

Notes

a Oromia was provided with limited support in budget reform during FY2002.

b In FY2004, the project introduced the single treasury system in the Southern and Amhara regions. Support was required at the federal level beyond the period of two years (in FY2005 and FY2006) to assist with consolidation of country-wide accounts and to support the additional rollout to federal public bodies.

c Support was required in the Southern Region beyond the period of two years (in FY2004 and FY2005) as the single treasury system was introduced in FY2004.

Key: Federal = federal government; Addis = Addis Ababa; Dire = Dire Dawa; Bene = Benishangul Gumuz; SR = Southern Region.

- Development of training materials
- Delivery of training
- Development and production of formats
- Development and installation of financial information systems

The support activity starts the year after a reform such as the reform of accounts is introduced and is scheduled to take two years. Introducing a financial reform does not mean it is fully and smoothly operating. Experience with these financial reforms has shown that considerable support is needed for several years after they are introduced. Support requires managerial, technical, and financial resources. Managerial support is needed because these reforms impose additional and significant management tasks. Technical support is needed for modification of procedures to regional requirements, follow-on training, assessment and fine-tuning of operations, supervising data processing, and document preparation. Financial support, too, is critical because financial reforms involve additional expenditures for commodities and services such as forms, training manuals, computer supplies, and travel for assessment and supervision. These financial reforms were welcomed by regions, but they did impose additional and in many cases significant burdens on local budgets.

The third activity, institutionalize, was planned to begin after the two-year support phase is completed. Successful institutionalization means that these financial systems can be fully managed, technically supported, and financially resourced by government.

If the design of the DSA project started in July 1996, and if each reform—budget; accounts; budget planning—took six years, that would mean that completion of all three activities would be 2012 (there is some overlap, which is why the completion date is 2012 and not 2014; see table 8.3, column 9). The Phase 4 estimate of sixteen years for a full rollout of the PFA reform in Ethiopia with its recent and ongoing deep devolution to weredas was not unrealistic in light of other international experience. For example, the Swedish International Development Agency (SIDA) states:

> A realistic time frame for PFM reforms that involve revised legislation, new systems and procedures would be not less than 10 years. A full rollout and change of culture and responsibilities down to service delivery levels may well take 15 years.[31]

Concerning the length of time needed to reform a financial system, SIDA is not explicit as to whether, in their time frame, government structures are centralized or decentralized, and if decentralized, what type of decentralization?[32] (SIDA's concept of a "full rollout" fits with the third activity, institutionalize.) In short, the end of the final Phase 4 of the DSA project in November 2006 meant that the reform would require another forty-three months to complete.

The challenge in April of 2004 as Phase 3 was coming to an end was to close the project down, even though the reform clearly was not finished. The rollout to all regions was nowhere near completion (see table 8.3, especially tasks 1, 2, 5, 6, 8, 9).

As the reform could not be completed by the end of Phase 4, what then should be the strategy for this phase? The project proposed a strategy to complete the reform in as much of the country as possible. Maintaining the reform sequence (introduction, one year; support, two years; institutionalize, three years) would mean that the introduction and support activities could be completed and institutionalization under way in the four big regions. With the reform embedded in the big four regions, 97 percent of total public expenditure in the country would be operating under reformed systems. Deepening and making sustainable the management of 97 percent of public expenditure should be a top priority and would significantly reduce the risk of retrenchment of the reforms. Speeding up the extension of the reform to the last 3 percent of public expenditure—the smaller regions—by not observing the six-year rollout sequence was risky because these regions still had their hands full implementing second-stage decentralization, to their weredas. Adding the additional burden of reforming their financial systems would in all likelihood exceed their capacity, especially since they were categorized as "low-capacity regions." The project argued that it was imprudent to introduce the reform to these regions and then depart without providing any follow-up support, which experience from the early reformers had shown to be so critical to the success of their reforms.

The explicit assumption of this proposed strategy was that if the reforms were well embedded in the federal government and four large regions, these governments could be twinned with the yet-to-be-reformed small regions and bring them along. In other words, five strong government entities would become the owners of the reform in their own jurisdictions and could also extend it.[33] The defining feature of the Phase 4 strategy was that government, not the DSA project, would complete the rollout of the reform, and, more important, sustain it.

The minister of finance disagreed with our strategy. He wanted a 100 percent rollout of the reform—he was not concerned with the support or institutionalization activities. I entered a meeting chaired by him and the three funders of the DSA project (the United States, the Netherlands, and Ireland) with an $8.1 million proposal for our two-track strategy and left with an unmanageable and inappropriate $14.6 million project with one track: finish the rollout to the whole country.

I argued. I stressed to the minister and the funders that their strategy would fail and ran the risk that the whole reform would not be successfully handed over to government, which would undermine the accomplishments of the twelve preceding years. I pointed out that the very ministry we were meeting in, the Ministry of Finance, was still dependent upon the project six years after the reforms had been introduced into the ministry for closing its and the nation's accounts and supporting the nation's financial information system, which ran budgeting and accounting. I pointed out that we were just starting the rollout of the reform to the huge Oromia region, which was akin to reforming the fifth-largest country in Africa, and the outcome of that reform was not certain. I also pointed out the precarious security conditions in some of the small regions, particularly Somali, where the Ethiopian military controlled less than half of the region and was combating an insurgency that moved in and out of the country from neighboring Somalia. The security issue alone, which made access for project staff difficult, meant that 100 percent rollout might not be achieved, regardless of the budget (the funders had offered an 80 percent increase in funding, which most project directors would be pleased about and delighted to surprise a home office with!). I did not mince my words with the minister and the funders: the minister's version of Phase 4 put the whole reform at risk.

I should have said no. Full stop. The principal impact of my failure to put a stop to this plan was that the project became very spread out; it could not focus on deepening the reform. The DSA project was forced to ramp up its staff, which pushed existing staff to the limit and also sacrificed quality. Depth was sacrificed for breadth. DSA project advisors were especially concerned about the nearly impossible task of reforming the last regions—Harari, Afar, Gambella, and Somali, especially Somali—in such a short time frame.

As Phase 4 neared its end in November 2006, MOFED became very nervous about how the rest of the project would be completed. USAID wanted to get out of the project, and MOFED pleaded with other donors for, first, an additional year and then for three additional eleventh-hour one-month extensions. We called this "extension phase" Phase 5 (see table 8.3, columns 7 and 8). Column 8 in table 8.3 shows the status of the reform in 2008, forty-three months from completion, and shows the lack of understanding on the part of MOFED of what was needed to implement and sustain this reform. For example, support and institutionalize, especially for the small regions, were not going to be completed by the time the DSA project ended.

MOFED mistake 2: mismanagement of the reform support unit

With a focus on rollout, not support, once the DSA project ended the reforms would need to be supported post-DSA. In November 2007, the minister of finance asked for a proposal on how to complete the reform and how to sustain it. The DSA project proposed the creation of the Reform Support Unit (RSU), to be located within MOFED.[34] It would retain the key Ethiopian staff of the DSA project and be supervised by the ministry. The RSU would be tasked with keeping the pressure on the government to take over sustaining the reform with its own staff. The RSU would operate for one year, and its scope was limited: finish the rollout of the reform to the small regions, support the existing financial information system, and do a modest upgrade of the financial information system.

The key to the RSU's success, I explained to the minister of finance, was the appointment of a credible director, who I believed should be an Ethiopian. The minister finally appointed an American, Paul Dorsey, the expatriate owner of the U.S. firm Dulcian, which had provided modest assistance for the DSA project. I was not at all comfortable with this decision: Dorsey was sort of a computer person with no relevant experience in public finance, nor had he ever worked in a developing country.

Dorsey and the RSU were due to start operations in February 2008, the month after the DSA project ended. Dorsey signed a $3 million-plus contract to direct the RSU and provide it with key technical assistance. The Ethiopian staff of the RSU did yeoman service in supporting the rollout of the reform and the existing financial information system, and did so without the leadership of Dorsey, who failed to honor his contractual obligation of being resident in-country and managing the RSU. When he finally arrived at the end of the year's contract he promptly fired the key Ethiopian staff who were making the RSU work because they kept MOFED informed as to his failure and that of his firm to meet their contractual obligations. In brief, Dorsey and Dulcian delivered virtually none of the technical assistance the company contracted to provide (Dulcian worked on but did not deliver the modest upgrade of the IBEX FIS). Worse, Dulcian used its RSU contract to develop a proprietary business tool for Dulcian applications outside Ethiopia.

Dorsey was the wrong person for the job. He and Dulcian proved to be the downfall of the RSU and virtually eliminated ministry support for the reformed systems in the federal government and the regional governments. The Dulcian saga demonstrated the inability of MOFED, particularly the head of the Expenditure Management and Control Program office, to manage relatively small-scale reform activities. Obviously it was not up to the challenge of managing large-scale programs—a major reason for the poor design and implementation of the $86 million financial component of the PBS II. The RSU was an innovative approach to sustaining the reform, but it ended up being stillborn.

MOFED mistake 3: failure to create a public finance steering committee

The DSA advised the creation of a public finance steering committee to oversee these systems throughout the country to be composed of the heads of the regional finance bureaus and chaired by the minister of finance. I viewed the establishment of such a steering committee as the most important resource in completing and sustaining the reform once the DSA project ended. Such an entity was needed to carefully monitor the introduction of new, broader management reforms such as BPR that would significantly impact PFA. Its members would understand the risks to the existing reforms inherent in adopting new financial reforms—especially sophisticated PFM systems that foreign donors championed—while the rollout of the existing reform was just ending and the crucial support and settling period was starting. Such a steering committee, if it worked as hoped, would have gone a long way toward ensuring that the senior finance officials of the country understood the lessons of the reform, the complexity of the reformed systems, and the resources needed to sustain these systems. A functioning steering committee may well have stopped the government from taking its wrong turn.

I lobbied the funders of Phase 4 to make such a committee a condition for their funding of Phase 4, and most of them lobbied MOFED to create it. But the ministry rejected the proposal.

MOFED mistake 4: failure to make takeover of the reform a priority

One of the most frustrating periods of this reform for the DSA project was the anemic response of MOFED to accept handover by the DSA project of support to the project. I am reminded of the adage about imperialism—easy in, hard out. Things were never easy in Ethiopia, but extricating the project after twelve years was the hardest task. Sustainability is an axiom of effective development and a hallmark of professionalism in this field. The DSA project was ending four years before the reform was finished, so our professional responsibility was to set in place as best we could resources such as the RSU that would sustain the reform and, it was hoped, involve MOFED in all facets of the reform. Unfortunately, MOFED was never serious about taking over support for the reform. It assembled a small group of officials who blithely said they could take over the reform with the proviso they receive an additional 1,000 Ethiopian birr—about $115—a month. They formed a committee whose official name was soon changed to the Committee on Delay and was soon disbanded for lack of attendance and action.

What needs to be done? Halting and reversing the deterioration of PFA in Ethiopia

The deterioration of public finances in Ethiopia since 2008 is the result of a failure of the federal Ministry of Finance and the regional finance bureaus to assume responsibility for a core government function, financial administration and management. These financial organizations' senior officials need to assume their professional responsibility to safeguard and provide stewardship of public money. They must ensure probity in response to any actions, foreign or domestic, that affect the finance function. This they have not done.

In September 2011 the Channel 1 assessment team gave the government and the foreign aid agencies a report that provides a comprehensive list of actions to be taken in the short and medium term to arrest the erosion of PFA. I also briefed the minister of finance in the presence of the mission director of the World Bank for Ethiopia about these recommendations.[35] We recommended that the government take five actions to halt and reverse the decline in the performance of its financial systems:

1   Reassert financial controls lost under BPR
2   Strengthen external audit, rapidly and thoroughly
3   Restart in-service training on the existing financial systems
4   Secure the IBEX 1.3 financial information system
5   Enforce the hard budget constraint

Complementing these five actions by the federal government, the ruling party must reinvigorate its discipline and ensure that cadres respect and promote the stewardship of public money.

But the fundamental issue is not a list of recommendations; it is who decides the future direction of Ethiopia's financial system. The Civil Service Reform Program was focused, its goal to support decentralization and to be owned by government. That focus has been lost. Of particular concern has been the failure of regional governments and finance officials to make their needs known and to be strong partners in policy decisions about financial administration throughout the country. I would argue that the "key sequence" of financial reform in Ethiopia is the evolution in the partnership of federal and regional finance officials, not the trivial obsession of foreign aid with sophisticated techniques and software.

Update: loss of government ownership

In June 2014 I spoke with an Ethiopian official who brought me up to date on recent developments. Ethiopia's financial system is going from bad to worse. The metric of this deterioration is the backlog of accounts, which was cleared under the reform. Now the Southern Region and Oromia both have backlogs, of three years and two years, respectively. Why is this happening?

One reason is poor stewardship. Senior officials are directing that funds be spent in the absence of a budget for that spending. To close the annual accounts you have to finalize the adjusted budget—ensure that all the changes, such as moving funds from buying stationery to buying fuel, are recorded so that the details of accounts can match with the detailed line items of the budget. Thus, lacking an adjusted budget, regions are having difficulty finalizing the budget, and this is creating a backlog of accounts.

A second reason for the backlog is that the accounting officials responsible for closing the accounts don't know how to do so, even when there is an adjusted budget. This downgrading of capacity has resulted from a lack of in-service training and from counterproductive staff rotations undertaken as part of the business process reengineering reform introduced by the government.

Third, as if the backlog and the shrunken staff capacity were not bad enough, these problems have been compounded, not solved, by the World Bank's "solution": to fund contractors to manage the accounts in regional finance bureaus (ten accountants and ten information systems specialists) and zone finance departments (two accountants and two information systems specialists). These contractors come from the ranks of government, so the World Bank is decimating the government's finance staff while deskilling the local administrations. This new development of contracting out government financial administration is not sustainable and creates enormous risk to government finances. If the funding of such contractors dries up or the World Bank halts funding because of disputes with the government—or because of a national emergency such as a war—public finances in effect could not be done. In fact, foreign aid did decamp from the country from 1998 to 2000, during the war with Eritrea.

Conclusion

As of 2010 the World Bank had judged Ethiopia to have one of the best reforms in Africa in recent decades and, consequently, one of the best financial systems on the continent (the bank's assessments were actually made from mid-2008 to March 2010).[36] In light of the deterioration found by the 2011 Channel 1 Assessment, can it still be said that Ethiopia has one of Africa's best systems? For the answer to that question we shall have to await the results of a new PEFA assessment, which will be conducted in 2014 by donors and should be available in 2015. Whatever the PEFA verdict, Ethiopia can take steps to recapture its strong 2010 position.

Government financial systems are persistently challenged. Politicians decry their performance and bureaucrats seek technical solutions that promise better performance. For governments that are aid-dependent, their foreign benefactors often weigh in with unreasonable demands and inappropriate initiatives. A newly reformed financial system is especially vulnerable, for in its last phase, operation, when technical assistance is withdrawn and government itself must run the reformed system, the system "live[s] on borrowed time" until adequate support is put in place.[37] Since the end of technical assistance from the DSA project in January 2008, Ethiopia's reformed financial systems have faced severe challenges: they have not been adequately supported, and other reform programs have introduced irrelevant complications and some have undermined prudent practices. Ethiopia's twelve-year reform worked because of its alignment of context, ownership, purpose, and strategy (the COPS elements). Together they delivered a financial system that was fit for purpose and worked in the varied contexts of a decentralized country. The decline in the performance of public finance since 2008 has been due to the loss of this COPS alignment. The fundamental responsibility for the deterioration rests with government, although ill-advised foreign aid activities have also contributed.

In April 2011 as I was working on the Channel 1 assessment, I met Tolosa Degafa, head of the BOFED in Oromia, Ethiopia's largest region—in effect, Africa's fifth-largest country (Degafa, had taken over from Retta Bedada). Oromia had introduced the budget reform in 2004 and the accounts reform in 2005. I asked his opinion of the financial reform and its status in his region. He candidly said that the procedures were good, but the reform needed to settle. Six to seven years on, the reform had not settled. Like fine wine, reforms must age.

Notes

1 The European Commission suspended assistance to the Productive Safety Nets Program in 2010 but was forced to restart its support after the serious crop failures in 2011.
2 The deterioration in financial reporting was documented by Parminder Brar, the task manager for the PBS II C1 component (the financial component) responsible for providing support to the public finance system (see Brar 2010, 2011). For a description of the PBS II project see World Bank (2009a); on the PSNP project, see World Bank (2006).

3 There are in effect seven channels, what I call lines of financial management, by which public funds flow in Ethiopia. Some are exclusively for domestic funds, some are both domestic and foreign, and some are exclusively for foreign aid funds. See Peterson et al. (2011: 15–18).
4 The five regions covered in the Channel 1 assessment included the big four regions (Amhara, Oromia, Southern, Tigray) and one small region (Benishangul Gumuz).
5 Peterson et al. (2011: 36).
6 Peterson et al. (2011: 38). None of the finance offices in the Southern Region where the reform was piloted had proper cash control.
7 Peterson et al. (2011: 36).
8 In the first two months of Ethiopian FY2003 (July and August 2010), the delays in transfers of PSNP funds meant these payments created the longest delays to clients in four years. See World Bank (2011a: 2).
9 See World Bank (2009a, 2009b, 2010b, 2011a).
10 World Bank (2009a, 2012c).
11 As initially conceived, reengineering was intended to harness the power of micro-computers to transform business processes (Hammer and Stanton 1995).
12 The modified accrual basis of accounting not only is complex but also allows laxity in the execution of the budget. Expenditures can be committed in fiscal year 1 but actually neither reach beneficiaries nor are settled until well into year 2. This creates reams of complications on the ground, including delayed payments to beneficiaries. With modified accrual accounting, prompt reporting cannot be separated from prompt execution of the budget.
13 Peterson et al. (2011: 27–8).
14 World Bank (2009a: 18–23).
15 Included in these figures is the $18 million for the Oracle IFMIS pilot.
16 The government was billed $3 million for the upgrade of the DSA-developed IBEX 1.3 system, called IBEX 2 by the follow-on contractor, Dulcian Inc., but the system was never delivered. Worse, although Dulcian's contract clearly specified that the IBEX 2 upgrade was to be developed in Ethiopia, they used these funds to build, off-shore, a proprietary software tool called BRIM for their business that they intended to license to the Ethiopian government. Dulcian planned to use it to generate software code for the IBEX 2. This violated the contractual arrangements that deliverables are the property of the government and not the contractor.
17 Peterson et al. (2011: 246–78).
18 Peterson et al. (2011: 2).
19 Despite years of failure of the PBS II C1 program to support financial systems—which threatens the completion of the bank's largest development aid project in Africa—the World Bank task manager for the C1 reform who designed this component, Parminder Brar, continues to be in charge of it. He has also been under investigation by the bank's own Office of Integrity for improper procurement of FIS services. This same task manager traveled to Harvard University in the summer of 2008 while I was teaching the university's Executive Program in PFM and lobbied me to support a sole-source contract for the IBEX 2 vaporware. I refused.
20 International Monetary Fund (2011).
21 The only reports referenced are IMF reports (Last and Robinson 2005; Last et al. 2009). No reference was made to the many World Bank assessments—JRIS reports, PEFAs, FRA—nor to the just-completed Channel 1 assessment. Though invited by the World Bank mission director to attend the debriefing of the Channel 1 assessment, the IMF was the only major donor that did not send a representative.
22 International Monetary Fund (2011: 14).
23 The IMF's 2011 program for PFM in Ethiopia runs contrary to its own findings. In a 2005 report it stated, "Computerization cannot be the solution if fundamental preconditions are lacking" (International Monetary Fund 2005: 52).

24 The 2010 PEFA assessment of regions found that the IBEX 1.3 fully met their requirements (World Bank 2010d: 69). Some statements in the IMF report about the existing systems are patently untrue, such as that the IBEX 1.3 does not operate in a WAN mode (International Monetary Fund 2011: 37).
25 Lacey (1989: 1).
26 As formulated by Schick (1966).
27 Swanson (1988: ix).
28 Peterson (2005).
29 After my October 2005 memo the DSA project continued to provide the minister of finance with briefs showing evidence of the government's failure to assume responsibility for the reform and to resource it adequately.
30 Peterson (2004: 5–7).
31 Swedish International Development Agency (2007: 93). This time frame is based on a study by Andersson and Isaksen (2003).
32 According to one view there are three types of decentralization: deconcentration—the center simply assigns responsibilities but retains control; delegation—the center assigns responsibilities often to para or non-state actors such as state corporations and NGOs; and devolution—autonomous local government (Cohen and Peterson 1999: 24–9).
33 Peterson (2005: 7).
34 The design of the RSU is presented in DSA M-107.
35 See Peterson et al. (2011: 76–82); the Channel 1 assessment is available on this book's website (http://stevepetersonpfm.com).
36 World Bank (2010a); Hedger and de Renzio (2010).
37 Swanson (1988: 40).

9 How to reform a public financial system

Public financial administration or public financial management?

I had two objectives in writing this book. The first was to document a successful financial reform in Africa from firsthand experience and with sufficient passage of time to see its impacts and how it fared. This has rarely been done. The second objective was to distill from this experience analytical frameworks that could guide other countries in financial reforms. The field of public financial management (PFM) does not have adequate frameworks—an issue I discuss here and in chapter 10. The PFM field has generated many lists of lessons, but absent analytical frameworks these lessons remain unconnected dots—findings relating only to a particular country's reform. Frameworks help practitioners connect the dots and provide a means of integrating different countries' experiences to guide future reforms.

Because public finance is an applied activity with elements of both theory and practice, it is difficult to develop frameworks that meet the rigor of theory and the relevance of practice. This challenge was well articulated by Hugh Dalton, who served as a minister of the Crown in the United Kingdom for eleven years and was chancellor of the exchequer for two turbulent years, 1945 to 1947, when his country was recovering from World War II:

> Every writer who aims at organizing a general discussion of public finance must be conscious of a conflict between two personalities, those of the practical and of the analytical man. And, in seeking to resolve this conflict, he is in danger of getting the worst of both worlds, missing both the perfection of theory, boldly guided by pure reason and the wisdom of statesmanship, cautiously guided by administrative officialdom.... Studies in public finance have ... a special fascination, but for the same reason, an excess of abstraction is apt, in this sphere, to seem especially unreal and an excess of conventional rule-of-thumb especially half-witted.[1]

To move the field of PFM forward so that governments can make better decisions and be better advised, frameworks are needed that bridge theory and practice. The foundation for such frameworks has been well established in the work of Frederick Brooks. He wrote one of the most significant and sensible books on the development and design of complex systems, *The Mythical Man-Month*, and argued persuasively about the need for coherence—which he called conceptual integrity.

> I will contend that conceptual integrity *is* [emphasis added] the most important consideration in system design. It is better to have a system omit certain anomalous features and improvements, but to reflect one set of design ideas, than to have one that contains many good but independent and uncoordinated ideas.... Conceptual integrity does require that a system reflect a single philosophy and that the specification as seen by the user flow from a few minds.[2]

Coherence does not come easy in the environment of a developing country, given the enormous need and the limited resources to meet that need. Indeed, one could argue that underdevelopment is the weakness of coherence (or its virtual absence in the case of failed states)—a fragmented state, poor infrastructure, and underperforming markets. The likelihood that the regime that emerged in Ethiopia in 1996 after seventeen years of civil war could establish a coherent reform program was slim. There were daunting obstacles to achieving coherence:

General sense of urgency—everything had to be done at once.
The government had to establish legitimacy and follow through, at least in principle, on its war slogan of self-determination, which in practice meant rapidly implementing ethnic decentralization.
Decentralization to regions was followed by a further massive second-stage decentralization to weredas, so the state was undergoing change.
Skilled manpower had been drained to the diaspora and those who remained were predominantly from the Amhara ethnic group, whose influence the regime sought to diminish.
Foreign aid poured in, bringing with it a confused reform agenda.
The leadership was young; though experienced in the art of revolution, it had no experience in the art of governing.

A coherent reform requires good management. The iron triangle of management of any project, and even of government itself, is scope, schedule (time frame), and budget. Scope is what is done, schedule is when it is done, and budget shapes how it is done. Defining scope should be the first-order task of a government, and any program it espouses. Once defined, scope determines the schedule and budget required. The key to good projects, programs, and governments is the management of scope. Unfortunately, although the *m* in PFM stands for "management," the iron triangle of management is typically ignored in discussions of PFM reform. One reason many financial reforms underperform or fail is because the iron triangle is not managed correctly. It is assumed that the magnitudes of the three sides of the triangle are irrelevant and do not need to be in balance—that, say, with a big budget, a comprehensive scope can be achieved on a short schedule. In fact, and unfortunately, big budgets and short schedules match the dominant priority of foreign aid agencies to disburse monies quickly. Many financial reforms, especially in Africa, have been driven by foreign aid—in fact, instigating them has often been a precondition for getting the aid. This view of the malleability of the three reform variables has led to reforms with absurd scope, gold-plated budgets, and unrealistic schedules that are not met. This pathological outcome can clearly be seen in the foreign aid–driven financial reforms in Ethiopia since 2008 (discussed in chapter 8).

The Ethiopian reform achieved coherence because the regime retained firm ownership of the reform and that ownership pursued a very clear policy: strengthening decentralization so to strengthen the regime. Scope was clear and was a matter of survival.

In this chapter I first present three frameworks, which when used together can guide governments in managing scope, schedule, and budget. Then I review the Ethiopian financial reform and the way the three management tasks (scope, schedule, budget) were done from the perspective of the three frameworks. Finally, I show why the financial reforms pursued since 2008 (presented in chapter 8) have not been coherent.

Three frameworks for guiding public financial reform

Achieving coherence in a reform requires managing scope, schedule, and budget and doing it right. My three frameworks can guide reformers in how to do the right things right. The devil is in the details and these frameworks show how to make the details cohere. Three frameworks shape the three management tasks of reform:

1   Drivers: Context, ownership, purpose, and strategy (COPS)
2   Platforms: Transaction, legal, policy
3   Phases: Translation, development, pilot, rollout, operation

The *drivers* framework provides a comprehensive view of a country's situation, which shapes public financial reform. The most general and nondiscretionary (not subject to change) driver of reform is context: a country's historical, cultural, economic, political, and bureaucratic legacy. Context frames the three discretionary drivers of a reform, about which governments have a choice: ownership, purpose, and strategy. The key to a successful public sector financial reform is the alignment—coherence—of the discretionary drivers with the nondiscretionary one.

The *platform* framework presents the three functions of a financial system— transaction, legal, and policy—from which the technical options of a reform are selected. Each platform is made up of systems and the attributes needed for their execution. For example, in the transaction platform, one of the systems is budgeting, and the attributes needed for its execution are institutions, organization, and staffing.[3]

The *phases* framework shows the steps of implementing a reform program: translation, design, pilot, rollout, and operation. This framework describes the distinctive roles of each step and the integration of government staff and technical assistance in delivering those roles and promoting the essential and little-discussed ingredient of a successful reform—learning.

The drivers of reform: context, ownership, purpose, and strategy

The four drivers of financial reform, nicknamed COPS, is a framework for understanding the legacies of a country that enable or disable a financial reform and the choices that need to be made, given that legacy, to introduce and achieve reform. (In chapter 2, I used this COPS framework to present an overview of the Ethiopian financial reform).

Context	Historical, cultural, economic, political, bureaucratic
Ownership	Government, foreign aid, contractor
Purpose	Financial administration or financial management
Strategy	Recognize, improve, change, sustain

Context

Context is a country's legacy that shapes reform and is historical, cultural, economic, political, and bureaucratic. Understanding context is a challenge, for it requires pinpointing features that a reform needs to overcome as well as build upon. This assessment needs to be incisive, not encyclopedic. It is hoped that understanding the context will make reformers stop, look, listen, and proceed appropriately.

Understanding the bureaucratic context is especially important for achieving coherence in a reform. A financial reform must fit with how the state operates. Financial reforms are not free-standing.[4] One can view the operation of the state as a continuum from weak administration to strong management. A coherent financial reform requires an alignment of the *purpose* of the financial reform, building financial administration or management, with the operation of the state, administration or management. A principal and possibly key reason that financial reforms have failed in developing countries, especially Africa, has been the attempt to insert financial management into states that have weak administration.

Understanding context is particularly important if the state is undergoing a transformation. The Ethiopian case provides insights into how a financial reform can be done while the state is being changed. The most dramatic change in Ethiopia was decentralization of government functions—first to regions and then to weredas. Within that broad and ambitious change, the government also sought to reform the state's operation as laid out by the Civil Service Reform Program (CSRP), which had five prongs: human resources, service delivery, top management systems, ethics, and expenditure management. Thus, the financial reform did not drive the broader reform of the state but was done simultaneously as the state changed.

The field of PFM has been virtually silent about the challenges that decentralization poses for reform. The Ethiopian case demonstrates that decentralization poses a challenge to keeping coherence in a reform because it involves managing multiple governments with varying capabilities, and this introduces leads and lags into the reform. Decentralization brings benefit to a reform for it allows piloting that can demonstrate success (e.g., the Southern Region) and failures (e.g., the Amhara budget and accounts reforms). Failures can be contained to one subnational government and provide powerful lessons.

Another area where the PFM field has been silent is the fact that it takes years for decentralization to settle—for the state to settle—which adds to the many years required to implement and embed financial reforms even when the state is not decentralizing. One of the few studies on this topic was done by SIDA in 2007. The study found that it takes twelve to fifteen years to implement a financial reform.[5] It should be noted that the SIDA study does not consider how much additional time is required for a financial reform in a country that is also decentralizing. The field has not adequately discussed the interplay of reforms—financial as well as broader bureaucratic and political—and their impact on the time frame of reform.

Ownership

That governments in developing countries must own their financial systems is a fundamental concept in public sector reform in general and financial reform specifically (even though in reality it is rare for them to do so). There are a number of reasons why this is important.

First, the management of public money goes to the heart of sovereignty, and no government should relinquish its control over the operation and reform of its finances.

Second, governments must have flexibility. No government has enough resources, so public finance is the "management of illusion." Financial management often requires moving funds about to meet needs. Some transactions may appear appropriate; others may seem, or be, inappropriate, but this is the political reality. This political reality of public finance means that no government, especially a poor and foreign aid–dependent one, wants outsiders looking at the books, and it certainly doesn't want foreigners doing the books. At times governments have to do things that foreigners don't like—like go to war with their neighbors (as occurred from 1998 to 2000 when Ethiopia and Eritrea were at war).

A third reason governments must retain ownership of their financial systems is that weakness in public finances is often the result of poor execution, not of inadequate systems or procedures.[6] Execution cannot be outsourced to foreigners or contractors; it must be done by the government, which ensures adequate resources and stewardship.

Fourth, governments must own a reform to ensure that it is sustained. The government must be fully involved and know the reform. As Burton Swanson stated, "We only really understand a ... system when we know about its implementation."[7] Ownership cannot be absentee.

The fifth reason why governments must own their reform is that foreign aid is fickle and fleeting and in all likelihood will not be around for the twelve to fifteen years it takes to reform public financial systems.[8]

Government ownership of this key function is often diminished in Africa because of the conditionalities required by foreign aid agencies before they will agree to provide loans or grants to a government.

It is not appropriate for foreign aid to demand, much less manage, the change of financial systems. It may be appropriate, within reason, to require and if need be help recipient governments strengthen the *execution* of their systems, but reforming the systems themselves is another matter. In Africa, as Ian Lienert pointed out, the systems are robust—they just are not executed.[9]

Purpose

The purpose of a financial reform can be viewed as two ends of a spectrum. The starting end is the basics—establishing external control, which is public financial administration (PFA). At the other extreme is sophistication—establishing internal control, which is public financial management (PFM). If PFA is not robust, then PFM is premature. Generally a financial reform is located between these two endpoints. The Ethiopian expenditure planning reform demonstrated that it is possible to evolve to more advanced techniques, such as performance budgeting, but to do so innovatively by building on and incorporating the features of basic systems.[10] In any event, history has shown and current achievements in Africa demonstrate that PFM is not a precondition for economic development.

The field of PFM is weak because it relies on a weak framework, the sequencing of sophisticated financial techniques (SFTs). The sequencing of SFTs does not address the core issue of financial *control*. I contend that the defining sequence in financial reform is not through a series of SFTs but from external to internal control—that is, the establishment of adequate external control, public financial *administration* (PFA), followed by the evolution to internal control, public financial *management* (PFM). The PFA-PFM distinction is crucial, highlighting not just the difference between internal and external control but also the salient features of the context: whether the state is one of weak administration or strong management. As stated previously, financial systems are not free-standing—they are embedded in how a state functions. The fundamental source of coherence in a financial reform is that purpose (PFA or PFM) is fit for context—how the state operates. The problems inherent in the PFM field's reliance on the SFT sequencing framework and the relevance of the PFA-PFM distinction to this issue are discussed in depth in chapter 10.

Strategy

The fourth driver of public sector financial reform is strategy. There are four possible strategies of reform: *recognize* what exists; *improve* what exists; *change* what exists; *sustain* the improvements and changes that have been introduced. Too often reform is viewed myopically as involving only change. Yet in most cases a specific reform should involve more than one of these strategies, such as a combination of recognize and improve, with some change. Furthermore, one of the most important aspects of reform is sustaining it, yet for many reformers how to sustain a reform is an afterthought, if they do not forget it altogether.

RECOGNIZE

Recognizing—understanding and respecting what exists—should always be part of a reform, yet it is often the most neglected. Governments in developing countries often do not understand the strengths of their systems and are too quick to change them, often on the advice of outsiders. The common practice in Africa of making at most a cursory review of existing systems before leaping to major financial reform is akin to the reengineering movement of the 1990s, which advocated looking only cursorily at existing business processes because they were going to be replaced anyhow.[11] If, as some specialists have argued, public financial systems in Africa are robust but not executed, one must thoroughly understand the existing systems in order to have confidence that they are indeed robust, and if they are, to decide what should be done with them.

Recognition is also needed to ensure that financial reform fits with the nature of the state—weak administration or strong management. The recognition strategy of reform is central, for it focuses on the definition of the problem, not, prematurely, on a solution. Many financial reform projects have started out pinpointing solutions—techniques and their sequence—without taking time to define the problem. First, the hard questions must be asked: Is change needed, and if so, how does that improve outcomes, the sustainability and quality of public expenditure? Focusing on finding solutions rather than on defining the problems makes financial reform an end, not a means.

Not only is recognition the right strategy at the start of a reform program, it should be revisited at the end to assess whether the sustaining reform is being done well and whether the reform is respected, not ignored.[12]

IMPROVE

Karl Weick has argued that successful public sector reforms are often the result of securing incremental improvements, or "small wins," an approach that "addresses social problems by working directly on their construction and indirectly on their resolution."[13] The most egregious source of error in financial reforms in Africa has been the failure to recognize the political and state arrangements that enable or disable PFA and PFM reforms. Improving what exists is the essence of a small win. Improving also fits with the reality found in most African governments, where systems are robust but not adequately executed.[14] The most persuasive argument for an improve strategy of reform is that it works within the political and bureaucratic arrangements for administration or management and promotes coherence. Toning up what exists and focusing on strengthening execution—for example, by means of in-service training, and reorganization of finance functions—can have significant payoffs at modest cost. Reforms that focus on improving rather than changing are faster, cheaper, less risky, and less disruptive of daily operations. Reform as improvement also ensures that government remains in the driver's seat of managing and operating its financial system.

CHANGE

Change should be undertaken judiciously and should be justified in terms of improving the quality of PFA and PFM outputs such as sectoral allocation and composition of expenditure (that is, the allocation of funds among ministries and tiers of government and between the recurrent and capital budgets). Changing rather than improving PFA and PFM entails significantly higher risk and thus requires clear rules to manage risk and avoid failure. Change can be within PFA and within PFM, and can also be the movement from PFA to PFM. As noted earlier, change to advanced techniques in Africa, from PFA to PFM, has often not been supported by change in administration, or the mode of execution. It is ironic that financial reforms demanded by foreign aid agencies and made part of conditionalities for rapidly disbursing aid to the recipient country are principally reforms of change rather than reforms of recognize-improve-sustain. Yet reforms of change are inherently more, not less, risky, and they take much longer, which is at odds with the short time frames of disbursing aid. This signals a major disconnect, a lack of coherence.

SUSTAIN

Governments the world over typically underfund operating and maintenance (o&m) expenses and give priority to new expenditure, often capital expenditure. Sustaining is the "o&m" of a financial reform, and like most o&m expenditures, it has few advocates. This means that sustaining a reform is the orphan of the reform process. Sustaining lacks constituents because many advocates of reform, including foreign aid agencies, are always eager for the glamour of effecting more and more change, not for the more mundane tasks involved in maintaining what has been achieved. Sustaining, unlike changing, does not lend itself to the types of discrete benchmarks that foreign aid agencies prefer to have as a condition for continuing aid. Further, it is axiomatic that sustaining must be led and resourced domestically. This is because the sustaining horizon is long term—indeed, perpetual—and must not be beholden to fickle foreigners. Sustaining a reform is the key to effective execution of systems, and the lack of sustaining has undermined many financial reforms in Africa.[15] The dearth of resources for sustaining existing financial systems is a reflection of the broader problem of public expenditure, namely, poor composition of expenditure.

The platforms of public financial administration/management

Platforms define the menu of reform. A good public finance system performs three functions:

1 It handles a myriad of *transactions*.
2 It ensures that transactions are *legal*.
3 It ensures that transactions implement *policy*.

These functions are delivered by the transaction, legal, and policy platforms of PFA and PFM (for short, PFA/M). The three functions overlap. For example, information about budgets from the transaction platform is needed to formulate budget strategies in the policy platform, while legislative oversight of the legal platform is needed to evaluate expenditure.

> *The Platforms of Public Financial Management and Some of Their Systems*
> **Transaction Platform**
> Budget
> Accounts
> Cash management
> Internal audit
> Revenue
>
> **Legal Platform**
> Legal framework
> External audit
> Legislative oversight
>
> **Policy Platform**
> Macroeconomic framework
> Medium-term expenditure frameworks
> Budget policy
> Program budgeting
> Revenue policy

   Much of PFA/M is about handling transactions, such as paying for goods and services (fuel, salaries, weapons)—hence the transaction platform. Within the transaction platform are several systems (budgeting, accounting, and so forth).
   In the legal platform the systems are the legal framework of public finance such as the constitution, budget law, financial regulations; external audit; and rules for legislative oversight such as public accounts committees.

The policy platform is the locus of fiscal management (for example, the macroeconomic framework) as well as performance systems such as performance budgeting.

The platform framework provides a reform menu of the three functions and the systems of those functions (for example, budgeting in the transaction platform) that the PFA/M of any country must carry out.

In 2002 I developed the platform framework and used it to organize the PFM Executive Program at Harvard University. In 2005 a very different platform concept that assumed foreign aid to be a relevant platform emerged from the literature on policy-based foreign aid and the conditionalities donors and lenders needed to reduce fiduciary risk. This idea was set forth in "A Platform Approach to Improving Public Financial Management," published by the UK's Department of International Development. The thesis was elaborated by Peter Brooke, who extolled the virtues of this foreign aid platform approach, arguing that it provides "greater clarity to both the governments and donors about the rules of engagement and disbursement and what each expects of the other in the partnership."[16] There are two problems with the foreign aid platform and the premises of its advocates. First, it focuses on the wrong thing: advanced PFM techniques and their sequence instead of on the COPS drivers in a particular country. Second, the advocates of this platform view financial reform as driven by the real or perceived needs of foreign aid agencies, not by the needs of governments. My platform approach is generic and locates reform within the three functions of PFA and PFM and is applicable to all governments: fragile, developing, transitional, developed.

In summary, the platform framework provides a comprehensive menu of the measures a government can select in designing its pathway to reform. One possible pathway could begin with focusing exclusively on a system of the legal platform (say, the law of appropriation), followed by strengthening a system of the transaction platform (say, improving the existing formats for budget bids). No government has the capacity to reform all of the systems of all of the platforms at once. A key factor determining the success of a PFA and PFM reform is the process of selection from the platform menu. Appropriate selection in the initial stages of reform of the right number and priority of components promotes coherence and generates crucial momentum. Inappropriate selection of too many components or the wrong priorities can derail or stymie reform.

The phases of a reform project: getting the right people on the bus at the right time

In his best-selling 2001 classic on management, *Good to Great: Why Some Companies Make the Leap ... and Others Don't*, Jim Collins offered a corrective to the obsession in the corporate world with strategy. He argued that what counts is people, not strategy; for firms to become great they must "*first* get the right people on the bus (and the wrong people off the bus) *before* [they] figure out where to drive it."[17] Put another way, the right people will *learn* what to do.

Getting the people right in a reform was a lesson I learned after eight years of reforming financial systems for the government of Kenya. Before I left Kenya in 1994 I wrote up the lessons from the various reforms I had worked on and found that indeed the critical success factor was people: the "saints," senior government officials who supported and protected the reforms, and the "wizards," the specialists. For a reform to succeed, the "demons," the detractors of reform, had to be managed—put off the bus.[18]

The field of PFM could take a page or two out of Collins's book, for the field is obsessed with systems and their sequence—with irrelevant strategies and not with the right people. Doing the right thing right in a reform requires aligning the people involved, government officials and technical assistance, who together deliver the three processes needed to realize a reform: design, implementation, utilization. The phases framework focuses on an issue that has largely been ignored in the PFM field—*learning*. Too much current PFM reform is about blueprints—techniques and the sequence of introducing them—an approach that has been anointed as "international best practice." But this means that it has been practiced somewhere else. Reform is contextual. It requires a learning, not a blueprint, cookie-cutter, approach.[19] Governments must not just own and authorize a reform—they need to understand it intimately for only then can they sustain it.

With the phases framework we get into the nuts and bolts of "how to do it," which is also rarely discussed in the PFM field, in part because most of the PFM pontificators have never done a reform.

The phases framework

The phases framework comprises five elements:

1 Processes of reform: design, implementation, utilization.
2 Roles that reformers perform: architect, builder, user.
3 Personnel who deliver the roles: government officials, technical assistance.
4 Resources personnel can provide: expertise, experience, management, funding.
5 Phases of reform: translation, development, pilot, rollout, operation.

Figure 9.1 shows how the three processes of reform—design, implementation, and utilization—are delivered throughout the life of a reform project. Each process spans several phases, and the processes overlap. The design process occurs over three phases (translation, development, pilot) and overlaps with the implementation process in Phases 2 and 3 and overlaps with the utilization process in Phase 3. (See box 9.1 for a description of the activities done in each of the five phases.)

The key challenge to doing reform right lies in establishing a working relationship between the people who share the burden of work, government officials and technical assistance staff, by an appropriate division of labor. This good

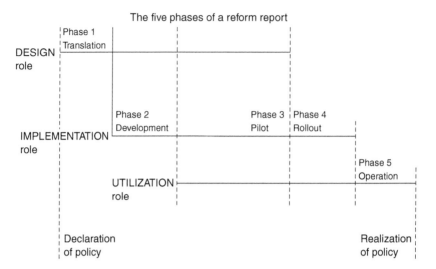

Figure 9.1 Delivery of reform processes throughout the five phases of a reform project (source: adapted from Swanson 1988: 39).

working relationship promotes the key objective of all five phases: learning. In his insightful work on how systems are reformed, E. Burton Swanson argues that "system realization takes place by means of the mutual informing of system participants over the system's life course."[20] Much lip service is paid in the PFM field to the need to understand context; Swanson clearly states that people are the fount of context: "Realism in system design requires an understanding of other people."[21] Learning is critical to getting a good design that is fit for context, to getting smooth implementation, and to embedding the reform in government so there is seamless utilization. The objective of learning is also to start the handover of the reform at the earliest possible time from technical assistance staff to government officials so that the reform is sustained. This process of takeover should not be begun in the waning hours of a project, when the experts are departing.

The phases framework is adapted from Burton Swanson's work on systems development.[22] What resonated with the experience in Ethiopia was Swanson's core conclusion: "We only really understand a … system when we know about its implementation."[23] I shall return to this theme, for it goes a long way toward explaining why the federal government in Ethiopia has not properly sustained the reform.

How Ethiopia achieved coherence in its financial reform

Successful reforms are coherent. Coherence is achieved by good management of the reform's scope, schedule, and budget. Of these the most important is scope. Our three frameworks shed light on how Ethiopia's reform was well managed.

Box 9.1 The five phases of reform

Phase 1. Translation (role: design)

A reform begins with the declaration of a policy. A design phase follows, which translates the policy into a strategy and specific activities of a program of work. This phase comes to a productive end only with the engagement of the prospect of implementation.

Phase 2. Development (roles: design, implementation)

Enter the implementer. Implementation begins in earnest with the commitment of significant resources to system realization, based typically on the approval of a design and its execution as embodied in a project document (technical and financial proposal). System development is marked by a design-implementation dialog.

Phase 3. Pilot (roles: design, implementation, utilization)

Implementation enters its second and core stage, the pilot stage, when operation and use of the system begins. The dialogue among designer, implementer, and user is now complete. Adaptation of implementation based on utilization feedback is undertaken, and adaptation of design also continues as before. This phase is the crucial one in the overall realization process. Only here is there mutual learning among all participants.

Phase 4. Rollout (roles: implementation, utilization)

Implementation begins its third and final stage with the near cessation of design activity. This phase includes only adaptation of implementation. Dialogue takes place principally between the implementer and the client.

Phase 5. Operation (role: utilization)

Reforms need to be sustained and even made continuously relevant by marginal updating as circumstances change. If they are neglected, they go into disuse. Realization of policy may eventually conclude some time after implementation itself has ceased. That is, benefits may continue to accrue to the client, although the designer or implementer no longer allocates resources to the reform. Absent an active implementer, however, the reform lives only on borrowed time.

Source: adapted from Swanson (1988: 34–40).

Scope

The three frameworks—drivers, platforms, phases—explain how the scope of the financial reform was determined: from the broad sweep of history, the political imperatives of decentralization, the weaknesses of the state, the need to work with and rapidly improve the financial system that existed, the need for external control, and the organization of the reform process.

Drivers

Context. The recent history of the emergence of revolutionary movement after seventeen years of civil war defined the scope not just of the financial reform but of the overhaul of state and society from the old order to the new. The regime that came to power had done so with a promise of ethnic self-determination, which meant that decentralization to ethnic regions was a priority. The bureaucratic context, then, was decentralization—first to regions and then a leap to weredas, most of whom had little or no capacity. Strengthening administration at all levels, including the federal government, was a priority of the regime. The Office of the Prime Minister undertook a thorough assessment of the civil service.[24] The findings of this assessment confirmed that the state was in serious need of reform and that reform should be about strengthening administration and not making a leap to management.

Ownership. The Civil Service Reform Program that emerged from the assessment by the Office of the Prime Minister was from the start firmly owned by the government—the prime minister had personally chaired the committee that produced the task report. The CSRP was done in secret by the government without any financial or policy input by foreign aid agencies. When the government presented the reform plan to the foreign aid community it made it clear that the government would direct the reform, the reform would be under its control, and no foreign aid agency would be allowed to influence the direction of reform. In particular, the IMF and the World Bank, which typically dominate financial reforms on the continent, were excluded from the reform.

Purpose. Strengthening weak administration at both the federal and regional levels (first-stage decentralization) meant that the purpose of the financial reform was public financial administration (PFA), not public financial management (PFM). The regime was very concerned that corruption was increasing and that decentralization would accelerate it. Putting strong external controls (PFA) in place was urgently needed; indeed, the first activity of the CSRP was the passage of a new financial law with specific criminal and financial penalties for misuse of funds.[25]

Strategy. Rapid strengthening of financial systems meant a strategy of recognizing what existed and improving where necessary. The regime could not wait for a decade-long process of changing procedures. The Civil Service Reform Task Force report found that the existing financial systems—it focused on budgets, accounts, and cash management—could be made to work if improved. The rapid expansion of the regions' responsibilities and the regime's desire to reduce the influence of the Amhara ethnic group, which had dominated the state for centuries, required that an in-service training program be rapidly put in place to train officials outside of the Amhara region. So the strategy of reform was one of recognize and improve what exists and sustain the existing and improved system by means of in-service training.

Platforms

The first step of the financial reform, the new financial law and supporting financial regulations, was on the legal platform. The second step was to reform the transaction platform, especially the systems of budgeting, accounting, and cash management. As for the policy platform, policy was made by party cadres, not the state, and the process was not open to public scrutiny. The CSRP made no recommendations for the development of economic policy and its linkage to financial systems.

Phases

The CSRP document made it very clear that the reform was to be done by government officials; technical assistance would support, not lead, this process. The financial reform began with the establishment of reform teams for budgets and accounts that were chaired by senior government officials and had technical assistance staff assigned to them. The first two phases of reform, translation and development, which used the CSRP document as a point of departure, specified a scope and a work program to achieve the reform and was done by these reform teams. The follow-on reform phases of piloting and rollout—also driven by government-led teams supported by technical assistance—promoted learning how to fit the agreed-to systems to regional and subregional contexts. In the next section, "Schedule," I explain how the schedule of the financial reform can be understood in terms of the phases framework.

Schedule

Once the scope of a reform is defined, the schedule and budget follow. The schedule of the financial reform would be determined by the pace of decentralization. The immediate need was to strengthen the federal government and the four largest regions, which handled approximately 97 percent of public expenditure. The small, "emerging" regions would receive the financial reform much later, once their basic administrative systems had been strengthened. The phases framework of financial reform explains how the reform was scheduled (see table 9.1, chapter 4, on the budget reform, and chapter 5, on the accounts reform, are organized around the phases of the reform and show in considerable detail how alignment of staff and roles was done in those two reforms. The phases framework points to the key quality of a successful reform—learning: why learning takes time, why it is essential with decentralization, and why reform "blueprints" are inappropriate.

1 Translation

The first phase of reform is the translation phase. In the Ethiopian case this involved taking the recommendations from the task force report, reviewing them

Table 9.1 The alignment of roles, processes, and phases in the Ethiopian reform

	Phase				
	Translation	Development	Pilot	Rollout	Operation
ROLES					
Typical	Architect	Architect, Builder	Architect, Builder, User	Builder, User	User
Ethiopia reform	Architect	Architect, Builder, User	Architect, Builder, User	Architect, Builder, User	User
PROCESSES					
Design					
Government officials	Applicable Driver's seat? Local experience	Applicable	Applicable	Applicable	Not applicable
Technical assistance	Driver's seat Expertise Experience (int'l) TA model: hands-on				
Implementation					
Government officials	Not applicable	Applicable Joint driver Expertise Experience (local)	Applicable Driver Management Expertise Experience (local)	Applicable Driver Management Expertise Experience (local)	Not applicable
Technical assistance		Joint driver Expertise Experience (int'l) Funding TA model: hands-on	Driver Management Expertise Experience (modified int'l) Funding TA model: elbows near	Passenger Management Expertise Experience (modified int'l) Funding TA model: elbows near	

Utilization				
Government officials	Not applicable	Not applicable	Applicable	Applicable	Applicable Driver Management Expertise Experience (local) Funding
Technical assistance					Not applicable

Source: author.

with government officials, and crafting a terms of reference for a project that would implement the agreed-to recommendations. In this phase, although technical assistance (TA) was in the driver's seat, TA and the governmental enjoyed remarkable access and frank discussion of the task force report's recommendations and what, in the given context, made sense.

2 Development

The second phase, development, was atypical in the Ethiopian reform, for it involved all three roles and not just the two that typify this phase, architect and builder. Especially different was the intensive involvement of officials who performed all three roles. This was achieved by the use of the budget reform team and the accounts reform team, which brought officials and technical assistance together to design the reform. The involvement of officials in the roles of architects, builders, and users brought an uncommon realism to the reform's design and made it fit for purpose. The officials tossed out irrelevant recommendations from the task force report, they confirmed a reform strategy of recognize-improve-sustain, and they rejected the change strategy. More fundamentally, they ensured government ownership where the rubber meets the road in reform—its development. Government ownership was not a slogan—it was real. Officials and TA took turns driving the bus, but at the end of the day it was a government official who parked the bus.

3 Pilot

The third phase is the most complicated, since it typically involves all three roles. I would argue that the pilot phase at both the federal level and in the first region where the reform was rolled out, the Southern Region, was greatly facilitated by the involvement of officials performing all three roles rather than, say, TA performing the roles of architect and builder. Pilots are proof of concept, so regardless of whether they succeed or fail, the outcome will result in learning. The reform experienced successes and failure in the pilots. The failure that occurred in one region (Amhara) was instructive and quite possibly necessary for follow-on regions to reform successfully. The reform of the largest region, Oromia, was a daunting challenge, given the scale of the task in this country-size region. I think it is likely that the failure of the second-largest region, Amhara, the year before was sobering to the regional officials and prompted them to craft an appropriate reform and allocate adequate resources. They learned from the early reformers.

   The pilot phase is also characterized by the complexity of the management task. The core task of implementation is management. Remember Swanson: "We only really understand a … system when we know about its implementation." How the management task is shared between officials and TA is crucial. If TA are the managers, which is often the case, especially since they usually provide the bulk of funding, officials fail to learn to manage. The need for a project to meet its contracted deliverables often means that TA is typically far more hands-on than it should be in this phase. Indeed, a true pilot is a test of a reform in design, implementation, and use. This means that TA should be starting to withdraw during the pilot phase. Throughout the reform, the DSA project pursued an "elbows near," not "hands on," approach to TA, the ideal model of technical assistance in this phase.[26]

4 Rollout

Rollout should be simpler than the pilot, for it typically involves only two roles: builder and user. Again, the case in Ethiopia differed because all three roles were needed—a result of the variations of decentralization, which required the continued presence of an architect. A good example of the role of the architect in the rollout phase was the development of a single pool for concentrating the finance staff in the finance organization in weredas rather than distributing the finance task to sector organizations. This innovation was needed with second-stage decentralization to weredas and had to be adapted for regions' varying requirements.

The scale of the rollout phase perforce means that TA has limited capacity to be widely engaged. At its height, the DSA project had a total of sixty-three staff members, more than half of whom were providing support for the rollout. This contingent could not possibly fully engage in a country as large and diverse as Ethiopia. The rollout was accomplished by the 72,000 officials who were trained in the course of the reform. Rollout demands by far the most funding—training those 72,000 officials requires a considerable investment—and a technical assistance project's key contribution in this phase is to assist in meeting those funding needs. But even in funding, the government should be increasing its presence during rollout. In the last phase of the DSA project—completing the rollout of the reform nationwide—the government did step up to the plate and provide more funding than the other three funders, the governments of the United States, the Netherlands, and Ireland.

5 Operation

The Ethiopian reform has not been adequately sustained since the end of the DSA project in 2008 and the departure of technical assistance. This has contributed to the deterioration of public finance since 2008.[27] Swanson's comments on what often happens in the operation phase are prescient for Ethiopia: "Benefits may continue to accrue to the client although allocation of resources to the reform no longer takes place.... In the absence of an active decision maker, however, the system lives on borrowed time."[28] (The operation phase of reform is discussed in detail in chapter 8, "The tests of time.")

Three years after the DSA project ended, I directed an assessment of the causes of poor financial performance at the request of the government and foreign aid agencies (the Channel 1 assessment is presented in chapter 8). At the conclusion of our team's review of the Amhara region we met with senior financial officials and briefed them on our findings. I asked them several questions, and the one that raised the most discomfort was my request to review the region's plan for in-service training and its proposal to the Ministry of Finance for funding that plan. With much handwringing the answer came: there was no proposal for in-service training; the region had not requested training funds from the Ministry of Finance. The region had failed to do the most obvious task needed to sustain reform. Most shocking was the question from the head of the regional Bureau of Finance and Economic Development: "When is the DSA project coming back?" It confirmed all too clearly Swanson's point about reforms living on "borrowed time" absent an active builder. The user wanted the previous architect and builder to come back.

The importance of getting good alignment of officials and TA is of the greatest consequence when it comes to sustaining a reform—ensuring that time is not "borrowed" but continues to be paid for. As the DSA project was closing down after twelve years, there was a huge crisis in the government's takeover of the reform. The end date of the project was extended by four emergency contracts over fifteen months in a desperate attempt to buy time so that the government, especially the federal government, could take over the reform. It never did. There were many reasons for this (discussed in chapter 8), but the best explanation is that government preferred a "let the project do it" approach rather than fully engaging in implementation itself. The federal government was especially negligent in understanding and participating in the reform process in the regions, which differed in many respects from the federal reform.

The first, broad, lesson from the phases of this reform is the need for governments not just to "own" a PFA/M reform but to "know it" through deep engagement in its implementation. Success in implanting and sustaining a reform rests on whether there is learning by the top leadership as well as the rank and file. A lesson specific to PFA/M reform in decentralized governments is that the center must pay particular attention so that it is able to understand the variations of subnational systems.

A lacuna of the PFM field has been the lack of understanding of "how long it takes" to do a reform. A financial reform, especially a public sector reform, with a realistic proposed schedule is as rare as hen's teeth. Peter Silkin, the technical assistance advisor to the Office of the Prime Minister and the principal architect of the Civil Service Reform Program volumes, thought that the financial reform could be done in two years—an optimistic forecast that reflected his lack of experience.

The Swedish International Development Agency's handbook on PFM is refreshing for its realism:

> A realistic time frame for PFM reforms that involve revised legislation, new systems and procedures would be not less than 10 years. A full rollout and change of culture and responsibilities down to service delivery levels may well take 15 years.[29]

The ten- and fifteen-year time frames of reform suggested are not definitive, but they are supported by the experience of the Ethiopian reform. Furthermore, the findings of and SIDA (Swedish International Development Agency) schedules did not take into consideration the challenges to achieving PFA/M reform in a deeply decentralized country such as Ethiopia. For Ethiopia, clearly a ten- to fifteen-year time frame is reasonable; indeed, it may well be quite optimistic.

Since many of the financial reforms in Africa are driven by the conditionalities attached to foreign aid, two questions need to be asked. Why aren't foreign aid agencies transparent with governments concerning the long time frames needed? Why don't they clarify the risk of starting reform with aid funds that in all likelihood will not be available over the many years that these reforms take?

The right budget

Next question: "How much should reform cost?" As with time frames, the PFM field has been virtually silent on budgets for reform. Furthermore, the components of cost—technical assistance, training, FIS software, FIS hardware, etc.—have not been broken down. The Ethiopian reform cost $34.4 million over twelve years, broken down as follows: training, $27.6 million (80.2 percent); technical assistance and administration, $4.8 million (14 percent); and FIS (software and hardware), $2 million (5.8 percent). There is a 26 percent USAID overhead for universities implementing USAID contracts, and the amount paid to Harvard University from all of the categories named was nearly $9 million.[30]

These figures highlight some relevant points. First, financial reforms are not that expensive, especially with a reform strategy of recognize-improve-sustain. Change was limited, and the changes that were put in place evolved from and were closely connected to the improved systems. Second, training is the key task not only to put the reform in place but also to sustain it. The DSA was fundamentally a training project that trained nearly 72,000 government officials. This reform was also unusual for the relatively small amount invested in financial information systems ($3.2 million). Training is core and needs to be well funded. Attempts to cut corners on training must be resisted.

The budget for the World Bank's C1 component of the PBS II program, whose purpose is to support PFA and introduce PFM reforms, has a very different composition: FIS gets 49.8 percent while training gets just a paltry 4.6 percent. The principal reason PFA has deteriorated since 2008 has been the anemic funding of training. Meanwhile, FIS systems are big-ticket items that serve as commodity dumps welcomed by foreign aid because they allow them to disburse large sums quickly. Consequently, FIS systems often are barely scrutinized in terms of their budgets. "Gold-plating," spending a lot of money on glitzy, big-ticket items, is common and difficult to resist, for these procurements offer potential rents to all parties: the government, the funder, and the contractor.

Foreign aid agencies like to move money, and aid-dependent countries like external resource flows, regardless of their origin. In general, the budgets for financial reforms are far too big (to be sure, neither the funders nor officials in aid-dependent countries will welcome this view). The fact is, you cannot buy reform. You cannot achieve reform by throwing money at an ill-chosen target. Too much money will actually hamper genuine reform. True reform in a developing country needs to be lean and mean. Lean and mean means that from the very start of a reform the focus is on using and leveraging the existing resources of government. Prime Minister Meles Zenawi, who chaired the Civil Service Reform Program, was very clear that it would not be gold-plated. He vetoed overseas degrees, experience-sharing junkets, and the importation of foreign organizations to deliver in-service training. Bootstrapping was the order of the day. The more financially slim and fit a reform is, the greater the likelihood that it can be sustained with local resources, which by definition is required. Fred Brooks again is insightful on this issue: "The worst buildings are those whose budget was too great for the purpose to be served."[31]

Why the financial reforms since 2008 are not working

The three frameworks—drivers, platforms, phases—demonstrate why the financial reforms pursued since 2008 have not worked and are causing the deterioration of financial performance. The first framework is the COPS drivers: context, ownership, purpose, strategy. In terms of context, the raison d'être—supporting decentralization—has gone by the board. The 2011 IMF blueprint for Ethiopia's financial systems focuses on the federal government.[32] Ownership has been handed over to the World Bank and the IMF. These agencies have brought big checkbooks to the table, and the government has not resisted. Purpose is now reaching for the stars of PFM rather than embedding PFA. The strategy is now one of change. The change stance fails to recognize not only what the CSRP did over twelve years but even what other foreign aid agencies are doing. For example, the 2011 IMF blueprint makes no mention of the World Bank's financial component under the PBS II program.

One can understand why the reforms since 2008 are not working in terms of the platforms framework. The DSA project focused on toning up the traditional budget, evolving the accounting system to double-entry bookkeeping and a modified cash basis, and developing a custom-designed financial information system, the IBEX 1.3. These measures improved and evolved the basics. Foreign aid agencies are leaping to the most sophisticated systems of a financial transaction platform: a commercial off-the-shelf Oracle integrated financial management information system and an accrual basis of accounting. In the policy platform, foreign aid has overlooked the Type 1 performance budget developed in the Southern Region and has pursued the summits of program budgeting.

In the phases framework, the emphasis has shifted from in-service training and learning over a realistic, extended schedule to the quickie imposition of blueprints imported from other locales.

Conclusion

Establishing coherence is the key to a successful financial reform. Coherence is achieved with a clearly defined and appropriate scope followed by a schedule that promotes learning and a budget that is spare but adequate. Achieving this understanding, by both foreign technical assistance and local officials, takes time, but it is time well spent. Gaining deep understanding should begin at the start of the reform. This promotes government ownership every step of the way and prepares governments to fully assume the design and management of a reformed financial system when technical assistance departs. Foreigners' tendency to propose and even impose blueprints from afar must be resisted.

I developed the three frameworks from my experiences over the course of twelve years managing the DSA project and teaching government officials in the Executive Program in PFM at Harvard University which I co-founded and directed for most of its twenty-four-year history. In 2000 I started to use these frameworks to organize both the PFM executive program and my graduate courses in PFM at the Harvard Kennedy School.[33] The frameworks resonated with many of the 1,600-plus senior government officials from over fifty-three countries and even foreign aid officials who attended the executive program. One of the common takeaways by these officials at the end of the program was their "Aha!" realization, "What we have is not so bad!" They learned that what they have should be improved before it is changed.

This brief overview of what has happened to public finances in Ethiopia since 2008 in terms of my three analytical frameworks provides a foundation for the subject of the final chapter: Why is the field of PFM so weak, and what can be done about it?

Notes

1 Dalton (1954: 3–4).
2 Brooks (1995: 42, 49).
3 By institutions I mean the rules that guide officials' behavior. Organization is the formal structure of government agencies.
4 Hepworth (2013: 3).
5 Swedish International Development Agency (2007: 89).
6 Lienert (2003: 63).
7 Swanson (1988: ix).
8 The estimate of twelve to fifteen years comes from Swedish International Development Agency (2007: 89).
9 Lienert (2003: 63). Deficiency in execution of financial systems may be caused not by the lack of resources or training but by the lack of stewardship.
10 An example of introducing management into budgeting is Type 1 performance budgeting (discussed in chapter 7).
11 Hammer and Stanton (1995: 19).
12 My eight years working on financial reforms in the government of Kenya convinced me that reformed systems should be "revered and feared" so that the temptation for continual reform is tempered. See Peterson (1998: 58).

13 Weick (1984: 40).
14 Lienert (2003: 63).
15 Stevens (2004); Lawson (2012).
16 Department for International Development (2005); see also Brooke (2003, 2).
17 Collins (2001: 44).
18 Peterson (1998: 37).
19 David Korten's pathbreaking work on the need for a learning rather than a blueprint approach in development was recognized as the best article in the *Journal of Public Administration* in 1980. His insights are still very relevant today. See Korten (1980).
20 Swanson (1988: 37).
21 Swanson (1988: 35).
22 I am grateful to Burton Swanson for his insights into the management challenges of reforming systems, which I absorbed as a graduate student at the Anderson School of Business at UCLA.
23 Swanson (1988: ix).
24 Office of the Prime Minister, Task Force for Civil Service Reform (1996b).
25 See Article 64 of the financial law (Federal Democratic Republic of Ethiopia 1996: 312–13).
26 The reform of financial management information systems often requires that TA take a hands-on approach. That was the case in this reform, but once the systems were in place, they were operated by government staff. The maintenance of the FIS, as opposed to its operation, is still in the hands of contract staff, not government officials, in Ethiopia and many other governments.
27 Peterson et al. (2011: 1–3).
28 Swanson (1988: 40).
29 Swedish International Development Agency (2007: 91). This assessment was based on a review of Swedish and Norwegian aid programs for PFM reforms. See also Andersson and Isaksen (2003).
30 The overhead for universities does not apply for goods costing over $500, so the computer hardware was exempt from this overhead. Most of the cost of the reform went to salaries, stationery, etc.
31 Brooks (1995: 47).
32 International Monetary Fund (2011).
33 The syllabi for the PFM Executive Program I directed at Harvard as well as the syllabi from my graduate courses at Harvard in PFM can be found on the website that supports this book: http://stevepetersonpfm.com. I am currently applying my approach to teaching officials and graduate students in PFM using these frameworks in my courses at the University of Melbourne.

10   Recreating the field of PFM for the twenty-first century

We live in financial times. The global financial crisis that began in 2007 and persists as this book goes to press is a wake-up call that the management of public money must be done better. The field of public financial management (PFM) is weak and has not served governments or global governance well. This indictment is not just about poor results in sub-Saharan Africa. A remarkably frank recent assessment by the World Bank found "virtually no correlation whatsoever" between foreign aid and improving PFM in North Africa and the Middle East.[1] Richard Allen, recently retired from the Fiscal Affairs Department of the IMF, concluded at the end of one of the frequent conferences on PFM:

> The uncomfortable truth to my mind is that the old consensus on budget reform ... based broadly on the idea that developing countries should follow the approach to reform followed in advanced countries, has proved largely unsuccessful. According to the World Bank's CPIA [Country Policy and Institutional Assessment] ratings, PFM systems in developing countries hardly increased during the last ten years.... African countries include many notable examples of this failure.[2]

In this concluding chapter I examine why the field is so weak and what can be done about it. The significance of Ethiopia and the widely acknowledged success of its financial reform makes it a credible source of insights for improving the whole PFM field.

Why the field is weak

The field of PFM is weak, first, because there is little or no learning and, second, because its guiding framework, the sequencing of techniques, is inadequate. The observations of three specialists—Allen Schick on PFM, David Korten on learning, and Jon Moris on technical assistance to sub-Saharan Africa—illustrate the lack of learning and the focus on technique that has weakened financial reforms not only in Africa but in other settings.

Any field, be it theoretical or applied, must have critical scrutiny to be legitimate and to advance. PFM lacks critical scrutiny. Allen Schick, a respected authority on budget theory and a governance fellow at the Brookings Institution, has eloquently stated the need for scrutiny and the value of questioning orthodoxy:

> I think that there is a powerful inhibition in the PFM community not to discuss certain things—how reforms truly work, how successful they are, or whether they make a difference.... We rarely have a frank discussion about when reforms do work [and] when they don't work. There is not enough attention in the PFM community to failure. Failure is a better teacher than success! If I could see one change in the PFM community, I'd like to see a more open and forthright conversation regarding success and failure in PFM innovation.[3]

The field of PFM consists too much of implanting techniques from other contexts that are often justified as best practice. Yet financial systems must be appropriate to context. This "blueprint" or turnkey approach, where a system is taken over lock, stock, and barrel from another country—has not promoted learning because local factors have been ignored in both the implementation and the postmortem. The prominent economist and former Harvard Business School professor David Korten drew on the findings from the fields of business policy and organizational design—which stress the need for "finding the fit" among task, context, and organization—to posit that finding the fit was also the key to successful rural development projects. In the unique, complex contexts of development projects, a blueprint approach—in which fit is predetermined—simply does not work. In the development environment a learning process approach is needed to achieve a custom-tailored fit among

> beneficiary needs, program outputs, and the competence of the assisting organization. The key was not preplanning [blueprints], but an organization with a capacity for embracing error, learning with the people, and building new knowledge and capacity and institutional capacity through action.[4]

The error of technique-driven development was critically assessed almost four decades ago, in 1977, by the East Africa–born anthropologist Jon Moris, who currently writes on anthropology as applied to international development. Moris drew on his long experience in the field in Africa when he wrote about the "transferability of western management concepts and programs" to that continent:

> After bitter trial and error, one can only conclude that it is the system itself that is the problem, capable of rendering almost any input ineffective— whether trained staff, new equipment, sensible policies, or fresh projects.... The literature on comparative administration abounds with warnings that the export of techniques alone is risky, more likely to complicate than to expedite management in non-Western contexts.[5]

What stymies learning in the field of PFM? How do these problems in turn reinforce the inappropriate sequencing framework that guides the field?

Why there is so little learning in the field of PFM

Learning requires critical scrutiny, dissemination of findings, and constructive dialogue.

In the PFM field, four types of entities should be involved in this learning: foreign aid agencies, recipient governments, consultants, and academia. Yet all four entities have provided virtually none of the critical scrutiny needed to advance the field.

Why foreign aid agencies do not promote critical scrutiny

Foreign aid agencies, specifically the Bretton Woods agencies, the International Monetary Fund, and the World Bank, dominate the field of PFM. The defining feature of the sequencing framework that I discuss in the next section is that it is driven by foreign aid. The Bretton Woods agencies view themselves as the gate-keepers of financial reform—"an honest broker of reform," as Richard Allen put it—and their practices become the orthodoxy of this field.[6] Even when an orthodox practice has proved to have serious deficiencies, these agencies maintain confidence in it because it is theirs.[7] This self-conviction precludes self-criticism and learning.

A second reason for the lack of critical scrutiny by foreign aid agencies is that a failure of a specific country's reform is often not openly reported by either funder or recipient. To do so would threaten the continuance of aid flows. Acknowledging failure runs against the short-term interest of both recipient and funder, so they collude in keeping mum about performance failures.

Third, foreign aid agencies must have models of success to justify their role in changing recipient government financial systems and disbursing money to do so. Even if the reforms have serious blemishes and are limited in impact, criticisms are glossed over and the reform is actually trotted out as a model. For several years the PFM reform in Tanzania was considered the shining success in Africa; its head, Peter Murphy, who weighs heavily in the field and now with the IMF, held it out as a model for the rest of Africa. The reality did not bear scrutiny. PR has taken the place of critical scrutiny.[8]

Fourth, the obverse of touting models that have little relevance is ignoring models that do have relevance but in which the Bretton Woods agencies have had no involvement.[9] Even though the Ethiopian reform was scored one of the best in Africa for the first decade of the millennium, it has received scant attention, so the lessons of this reform have remained undocumented and have not been taken on board by the PFM community. The field has not learned from this success. Why? I believe the answer is simple, and it is disconcerting. It has been ignored because the Ethiopian government intentionally excluded the Bretton Woods agencies from this reform, and Bretton Woods, the self-appointed opinion makers about all things PFM, would not extol a reform they were not a part of. The Ethiopian reform was especially galling to the Bretton Woods because, although not of their own making, it comes out on top when judged by their very own metrics.

Finally, what is striking is that even when foreign aid is candid and reflective of the failures in this field, the talk in reports does not translate into the walk in the field. The rethink by the Bretton Woods about their past advice on financial information systems and the near failure of these reforms in Africa has not led to change in practice—witness the IMF's 2011 roadmap of reform for Ethiopia, which recommends an Oracle IFMIS (integrated financial management information system), a type of system that is utterly inappropriate (as explained in detail in chapter 6).[10] There are many other examples. So even the critical scrutiny that does take place does not impact practice.

Why governments that receive foreign aid do not promote critical scrutiny

Recipient governments must meet conditions to receive aid, and PFM reforms are often part of the package of these conditions. So governments agree to undertake a PFM reform as a quid pro quo, but often are not really committed to it. If the reforms perform poorly or fail, the flow of aid is threatened. So government officials don't tell the agencies—or anyone else—of the failure, to keep the funds flowing.

Second, the contracting of PFM reforms provides significant scope for rents to government officials—abuses that have been most notable in big-ticket items such as IFMISs.

Third, many government finance officials view foreign aid agencies as potential employers and as a ticket from low government wages to high international pay. They are unlikely to criticize the potential hand they hope will feed them.

Why consultants are not a source of critical scrutiny

Consultants and practitioners rarely write up and disseminate frank findings about their work in the field. An esteemed colleague, Subramanian Ramakrishna, the senior budget advisor of the Harvard University team working with the Ministry of Finance in Kenya, turned the publish-or-perish adage on its head, advising me while I was serving as an advisor in the Kenya government not to write about this field—"In technical assistance, to publish is to perish." Like aid-recipient governments, consultants and their firms do not want to cast doubt on the appropriateness or success of a funder's aid program and the PFM conditionalities that often accompany these programs. Typically, consulting firms leverage their activities in one country to a new assignment in another country. They are not going to publicize the failure of projects that are popular with funders, even if the failure was not their fault and the failure therefore doesn't reflect on their firm or individual employees. Leveraging previous work also promotes the practice of imposing blueprints from other contexts. Leverage is all about change, not about recognize-improve-sustain.

Why academia is not a source of critical scrutiny

One would think that the academy would be a source of learning. Sadly, it falls far short of delivering this role because practical experience is the basis of the kind of learning that is needed, which few academicians have. Furthermore, like the aid-dependent countries and their officials themselves, too many are beholden to foreign aid for contracts for research and consultancies. Instead of extensive field-work, most pontificators from the ivory tower take the lazy research route of relying on secondhand and sanitized field reports and mining PEFA (Public Expenditure Financial Accountability) assessments—a limited metric at best (discussed in a later section of this chapter).

Illustrative of the poverty of academic thinking in PFM is a silly though colorful theory of PFM reform put forth by Matt Andrews, a former official of the World Bank.

As would be expected, Andrews views financial reform as a foreign aid, not a government, process; indeed, he states that government has to be literally guarded so that it doesn't ruin everything. In a colorful PowerPoint presentation he delivered in 2008 at Harvard's Kennedy School, Andrews argued that successful PFM reform requires three actions of foreign aid officials: "hippo minding," "camel seeking," and "oasis building." By "hippo minding" he means that foreign aid officials must "mind" senior government officials, the hippos. His presentation showed an official of the foreign aid agency guarding dozing hippos in a tent, under a crescent moon. Foreign aid officials are also called "camel seekers" meeting the challenge of finding the right consultants (the camels) to do the reform. And by "oasis building" he means the financial reform and its wonderful outcome, which foreign aid agencies specify and direct the consultants to build. Robert Lawrence, a highly respected trade economist from the Kennedy School who attended the event, was the first to comment, and his comment says it all: "What has this got to do with anything?"

Another weakness of the academy is that it ignores the achievements of past practitioners and theoreticians—as Allen Schick states, this field does not learn. Their claim to learnedness rests on jazzy-sounding new terms such as "problem-driven iterative adaptation."[11] This certainly sounds a lot like, well, learning and the virtue of an incremental approach, as put forth and elaborated on by Charles Lindblom in 1959. In 1980, David Korten drew on Lindblom's work when he recommended using notions of incremental learning as a basis for the design of development projects. In 1984 Karl Weick built on Lindblom and Korten when he argued for a "small wins" approach to achieving better public policy. In 1988, Aaron Wildavsky built on all of this work and argued that trial and error is a device for courting small dangers in order to avoid or lessen the damage from big ones.[12]

One would assume that a university setting is a space devoted to developing objective, critical views. In the PFM field that confidence is misplaced. Academics who have been formed by and are still beholden to the Bretton Woods agencies cannot be relied upon to be objective. They have no real critique, just marginal suggestions, because any serious critique would mean questioning the fundamental assumption: that foreign aid must drive PFM reforms. So they make it a bit silly—hippos and camels and "problem-driven iterative adaptation." And, of course, critical scrutiny would jeopardize their lucrative relationship with foreign aid (via contracts with the World Bank). Not all members of the academy are completely lightweight or lack independence from foreign aid, but one can ask why established figures in the field do not act more decisively to promote the critical scrutiny so needed. Given the importance of financial management and its egregious mismanagement in recent years by the public and private sector alike, improving our knowledge of how to reform PFM is a very important task.

A few academics have taken on the orthodoxy; here the work of Howard Mellett and his colleagues is exemplary. Mellett and his team debunked the orthodoxy now swirling around the field of PFM that both developed and developing governments should adopt accrual accounting. His study of the impact of accrual accounting in use for over twenty years in the UK's National Health Service found that this technique did not improve management of services.[13] Robin Gauld and Shaun Goldfinch's work on public sector information systems in New Zealand—considered to have one of the best public finance systems in the world—also questioned the virtue of large-scale off-the-shelf systems.[14]

Anthropology is a discipline in which contextual and cultural features are as critical as they are to PFM—a point Bronislaw Malinowski recognized and expressed forcefully from the beginning of his career.[15] The same goes for PFM in developing countries. To the pontificators of academe I say: "Get thee to the field!" Few have.

One can only conclude that there are powerful incentives for inaction. Yet the lack of critical scrutiny in this field has been very costly—indeed, the costs are incalculable. Governments have been poorly advised, scarce resources have been used improperly or completely wasted, and valuable time has been lost.

The lack of critical scrutiny has allowed the perpetuation of the dominant framework of the PFM field—the sequencing of techniques of PFM. I now critically examine this framework.

The wrong PFM framework: sequencing techniques

The dominant framework of PFM is sequencing of advanced financial techniques—"international best practice"—many of which are imported from the private sector. Accrual accounting is perhaps the most notable example of a sophisticated technique whose imposition on the financial activities of a developing nation can be ruinous if not well run—which few developing and even developed countries can do.

The conceptual origins of the sequence framework is Allen Schick's seminal 1966 article, "The Road to PPB: The Stages of Budget Reform," in which he postulated that control, management, and planning form the fundamental sequence of reforming public budgets.[16] Schick confined his argument to the evolution of budget formats—control achieved via line-item budgeting, management achieved via performance budgeting, and planning achieved via program budgeting. He did not apply his sequencing idea to PFM writ large. The nuances of Schick's framework were lost on the field, while the notion of sequencing stuck.

The virtues and limitations of Schick's framework have not been well understood by the field, which has, in my view, led to confusion on the part of both practitioners and academics.

The sequencing framework of PFM currently in vogue was most recently stated in January 2013 by Jack Diamond, of the Fiscal Affairs Department of the IMF, in a 156-page paper, "Background Paper 1: Sequencing PFM Reforms," which was widely circulated in the PFM field.[17] It highlights much of what is wrong with the field and—emanating as it does from the IMF—shows the font of confusion. Diamond defines financial reform as a sequence of sophisticated financial techniques (SFTs). In other words, effective reform is seen as occurring as ever more sophisticated financial systems are implemented. Financial reform should also be foreign aid–driven. In particular, the Bretton Woods agencies supposedly know best. Furthermore, the International Monetary Fund is, according to Diamond's former IMF colleague Richard Allen, "an honest broker of reform."[18] There are numerous problems with this sequencing framework, especially when it is applied to the reform of financial systems in developing countries. Understanding these problems serves as a point of departure in crafting a more appropriate framework for the field.

Problem 1. Sophisticated financial techniques are not needed for economic development

The field of PFM assumes that SFTs are needed for economic development and is silent on the actual validity of this premise. Yet the early industrializers in Europe and those that followed such as the United States did not have sophisticated financial systems. So what is the justification for governments of developing countries to adopt PFM reforms that introduce sophisticated techniques and, worse, put workable financial systems at risk? Ethiopia is considered by some observers of economic development in Africa to be one of the seventeen emerging countries on the continent—the "cheetahs." Its annual GDP growth from 1996 to 2008, the exact years of its financial reform, was 4.1 percent, second only to Mozambique's 5.3 percent.[19] The Ethiopian cheetah was certainly growing without SFTs.

Problem 2. Value of SFTs unproven

The value of sophisticated techniques on improving public sector management has not been proven, as shown in the study of accrual accounting on the management of the National Health Service in the United Kingdom.[20]

Problem 3. Faulty premises underlie the sequencing obsession

The focus in the PFM field on sequencing SFTs is based on two faulty assumptions. First is the cherished but misguided belief that technique can improve financial outcomes. V. O. Key long ago dismissed the idea that the allocation of public resources can be reduced to technique.[21] The second assumption is that techniques from the private sector are applicable to and needed by the public sector—that the public sector lacks efficiency and performance and such techniques can supply them. This "technique envy" toward the private sector extends beyond simply finance techniques to balanced score cards, process reengineering, and other such new things—many are management fads that come and go. The oft-intoned mantra that governments should adopt accrual accounting is illustrative of technique envy. To be sure, accrual is one of the four bases of accounting for the private sector, but why assume that it makes sense for the public sector? It may make sense for companies that can take advantage of the tax deductibility of depreciation, that need statements of financial position to access equity and debt markets, and that require valuation for purposes of sale— but these issues do not apply to governments.

Private sector and public sector finance are two different animals. The task of private sector finance is simple: determine marginal cost and thus profit. The task of the public sector is complex: achieve public purpose (assuming the political system can clearly define purpose). Sophisticated techniques can be used by the private sector because the task is so simple. The capital asset pricing model (CAPM), which is the core paradigm of corporate finance, is elegant and simple—there is a linear relationship between risk and return for a fully diversified portfolio of assets. The public sector has no equivalent to the CAPM. Public sector finance is very complicated, and, again as Key showed in 1940, the core task of allocation cannot be reduced to technique.

The consequences of the obsession with techniques are more than merely technical. There is a dark side to complex financial techniques. Sophisticated financial engineers in the private sector cooked up toxic instruments that led to the global financial crisis that persists today. Indeed, these techniques undermined the bottom (Y axis) of the CAPM—risk could not be determined.[22] Complexity allowed firms to deceive. In the public sector, too, the use of advanced techniques has led to diminished transparency and outright deception. Indeed, the virtue of the traditional budget, deemed a dinosaur by the proponents of SFTs, is that it makes very clear the link between appropriation and agency.[23] Aaron Wildavsky has argued that the wildly heralded innovation of program-based budgeting failed in the U.S. government because it lost the link between the budget appropriation and the agency charged with its implementation.[24] And some finance specialists have argued that SFTs such as performance budgeting actually promote deception.[25]

There is never enough money. Good public financial management is about equity—"making everyone equally unhappy"—not maximizing the shareholder value of equities.[26] It is about creating systems that deliver rough justice, and sometimes this requires managing illusion. Such systems may not deliver the best, but their goal of equity can be met if they can deliver the second and third best. But they have to deliver, and to do this they must be risk-free to the greatest extent possible. The traditional budget endures not because it is the best but because it is what is feasible. Viewed from the summits of corporate finance, this may look like a low common denominator, but it is the reality of public finance. There is a fundamental misconception in the PFM field about the need for the "best," a misconception enshrined in the oft-uttered mantra "international best practice."

Problem 4. Faulty definition of performance

The sequencing paradigm focuses on performance, defined as the level of sophistication of techniques rather than as the management of risk and the reliable delivery of financial services. As long ago as 1978 Aaron Wildavsky explained that the virtue and persistence of the line-item budget, the first stage of Schick's reform sequence, lay in its ability to deliver all the functions of budgeting, even if not all are done brilliantly. It is superior to more sophisticated formats because the latter fail to deliver some functions.[27] Reliability in the delivery of public money—not level of sophistication—should be the defining criterion of performance. Diamond devotes one third of his work on sequencing to risk, yet he makes no mention of either a metric of risk (such as foreign aid's own Fiduciary Risk Assessment tool) or of the more serious risk, when reforms are driven by the conditionality of foreign aid, of distorting the management of reform (scope, schedule, and budget) and introducing volatile short-term external funding of financial reforms, which in reality require long-term stable funding.

Problem 5. False reliance on nonexistent standards

The sequencing paradigm focuses on systems and relies on an assumption that standards exist for systems, especially sophisticated systems. Ergo, these standards can be used to assess the systems. This is a faulty assumption. There is still disagreement in the accounting profession over the applicable "guidelines" (not standards) to be followed for the simplest basis of accounting, the cash basis; no standards at all exist for the modified cash basis or the modified accrual basis of accounting (the types of accounting systems that most governments should probably aspire to). The paradigm has reified guidelines into standards derived from statistics and monitoring of financial systems rather than financial practice. The Bretton Woods agencies impose a rigid standard of what a country's budget structure should be that is based on the COFOG (Classification of the Functions of Government) framework, thus ignoring the first-order role of a budget structure, which is to facilitate budget administration, not to generate statistics.

Problem 6. Execution gets short shrift

The sequence paradigm focuses on systems and ignores their execution. Ian Lienert argued many years ago that in Africa the financial systems were for the most part robust—they just were not executed.[28] If simple systems are not executed properly, what hope is there that sophisticated systems will be executed? Execution of existing systems is a crucial step in public finance reform.

Problem 7. Faulty assumptions regarding government capacity

SFTs can only be used when a government has a well-established, smoothly functioning culture of management and related business processes. This is typically not the case in developing and even transition countries.[29] Indeed, one can argue that government operations should be reformed before either basic or sophisticated financial techniques are addressed.[30]

Problem 8. Inappropriateness of SFTs with decentralization

The PFM field is virtually silent on the appropriateness of SFTs to a decentralized structure of government, especially in developing countries. Diamond makes no mention in his report about the structure of government. While the development community is still pondering what the Millennium Development Goals should be after 2015, it is clear that delivery of social services will continue to be core and that decentralized service delivery will be high on the agenda. Decentralization complicates the functions of government and especially complicates the delivery of foreign aid, which works best when there is one checkbook, located in the central government. At a minimum, when a financial reform is being considered, the weakest link in the chain, not the strongest, should determine the starting point of reform, to ensure that systems are fit for context. In a decentralized government, generally the strongest link is the central government and the weakest is the lowest tier. Thus, reformers must pay attention to the capacities at the lowest tier. A negative example: the IMF's 2011 program for financial reform for Ethiopia focused on advanced techniques for the center and ignored the weakest link, the weredas, the lowest administrative unit (discussed in chapter 8).

Problem 9. Incorrect empirical basis (metric)

The empirical basis of the sequencing framework, which is focused on performance, is the PEFA (Public Expenditure Financial Accountability) Framework. This metric is limited to the throughput of a financial system at a point in time and ignores the inputs and outputs of a financial system. As a metric of throughput, the PEFA is not able to determine the sources of poor performance—the inputs—so it is not appropriate for a reform program to be designed around it.

The PEFA guidance documentation clearly warns against this: *"The [PEFA] report does not make recommendations* for the reform program of the government and does not include a judgment as to whether the government reform program addresses the right PFM weaknesses or whether the proposed reform measures are adequate [emphasis in original]."[31] The warning goes unheeded, and PEFAs are used to design reforms as opposed to monitoring them. For example, in his 2013 report Diamond specifically recommends "the use of PEFA indicators in deciding lower level sequencing," and in his colorful graphic "The Risk Based Approach to Sequencing Reforms," his penultimate stage 3 is "reform actions to reach PEFA targets."[32]

The PEFA also does not have the capability to assess PFM in a decentralized structure of government.[33] A further problem with the metric is that although there is documentation to guide PEFA evaluators on how to score the twenty-eight indicators of performance, grading is subjective, and errors, some egregious, do occur.[34]

The PEFA Framework has become like a hammer in a small child's hand. Its limits are ignored and it is pounded in areas for which it is not applicable. Illustrative of this is the use by some agencies of the mechanical translation of PEFA indicators into fiduciary risk assessment indicators.[35] Performance, at least as measured by the PEFA, does not equal risk.

Problem 10. Wrong people in charge

A serious problem of the sequencing framework is its underlying premise that PFM reform is and should be a foreign aid–driven process. Foreign aid should be in the driver's seat and the government should at best be a junior partner and at worst a passive bystander in these reforms. Implicit in this framework is the conviction that foreign aid is justified in driving the reform because, after all, these agencies and their staff have to look after "their" money. Dependency on foreign aid enormously complicates political state relationships; indeed, foreign aid agencies (first and foremost the Bretton Woods agencies) too often end up acting as a second government. It is astounding that much of the discussion in PFM is mum on this complication, although not all aid officials have remained mum. In his insightful 2004 study of financial reform in poor countries, Mike Stevens, formerly of the World Bank, argued persuasively that the institutions and incentives in these countries and those of foreign aid agencies were not supportive of the practices of good financial control. "The reasons are partly technical," writes Stevens,

> … but for the most part they are about stakeholder incentives. Many of these incentives favor maintaining the status quo. This, in turn, explains the surprising stability of poor country ways of managing personnel and financial resources. Other incentives derive from the aid process itself. These have long been ignored by the [World] Bank and bilateral donors, and while there has been some recognition in recent years and efforts made to remedy

negative effects, in broad terms much more needs to be done to understand the influence of the aid process on counterpart responses, and to confront and change donor policies and processes when they are shown to be negative.[36]

Stevens's advice over a decade continues to be ignored. Diamond's 2013 paper, "Background Paper 1: Sequencing PFM Reforms," is in effect a manifesto of how foreign aid should determine a country's PFM:[37]

The position taken in this paper is that *reform actions should be advanced to attain certain PFM outcomes. If the risk of not attaining a significant part of these outcomes is too great (or "intolerable"), the reform should not proceed.* When applying this guideline it should be recognized that the risk appetite of donors will vary [emphasis in the original].

Diamond's manifesto goes on to state that governments need to be carefully watched—not unlike Matt Andrews's hippo minding:

Letting the authorities lead reforms is not always desirable. Obviously, getting the authorities to own and lead reforms is essential, but in some contexts making this the prime driver of reform could prove risky and may involve unacceptable PFM trade-offs. . . . Donors should perhaps more explicitly re-examine how far technical PFM considerations should be compromised to fit a country's political economy context.

Diamond actually stated, "Donors conceded too much to local politicians. Choosing reform activities on the basis of local demand also has its downside."
  Perhaps the best illustration of the paradigm's focus on foreign aid as the driver of reform is Peter Brooke's "platform approach" to packaging reform to help international finance agencies and donors.[38] Diamond extends the foreign aid role by lamenting that focusing on the basics of PFM is a hard sell to donors and recipient governments. A hard sell? When millions of dollars in loans are dangled in front of the nose of a government official living on a shoestring salary in an African ministry of finance, the only thing that is "hard" about the sell is that it is hard for these officials to say no to SFTs and rents.

Problem 11. Distortion of the host country's governance

The management of public resources goes to the heart of sovereignty. Perhaps the single most important factor contributing to the success of the Ethiopian financial reform was its firm exclusion of the Bretton Woods agencies. The prime minister and deputy prime minister "got" that a Bretton Woods–driven PFM reform introduces distortions in a host country's governance. They wanted to avoid the serious problems of adopting an IMF program which set aggregate parameters on a country's finances (such as debt level) and then having IMF staff crawling all over the government to monitor the program. The concerns of Ethiopia's top leadership about Bretton Woods involvement were justified when the Fund just days before the commencement of war with Eritrea declared Ethiopia "off track" in its program. Ethiopia was not off track. The IMF baldly used political criteria to discipline the policy of a sovereign country—indeed, on a decision to protect its very sovereignty. Senior leadership of the government were furious with the IMF action.

Let the renowned and heterodox development economist Lord Peter Bauer have the last word on the problem of foreign aid–driven development:

> External doles ... tend to bias the development process in directions based on external prototypes, which are often inappropriate and therefore damaging. Such a sequence retards development rather than promotes it.... Adverse results are all the more likely when the expenditure within the country is undertaken by people who do not themselves bear the cost.[39]

The sequencing framework can be boiled down to inappropriate external prototypes—about foreign blueprints, not local learning. The principal lesson from the Ethiopian reform for other governments is that *you* must do it, and you *can* do it.

How to improve the PFM field

The field is weak because it lacks critical scrutiny, which has resulted in the use of a weak and inappropriate framework for guiding policy. In this section I first present a better framework for PFA and PFM, then discuss the challenges of promoting learning in the field of public finance reform, and conclude with some additional measures to improve the field.

The right sequence: first, public financial administration; then, public financial management

Ethiopia is judged by the field of PFM to have implemented from 2000 to 2008 one of the best reforms of the new century's first decade.[40] This assessment is not, strictly speaking, correct. Ethiopia implemented a public financial administration (PFA) reform, not a public financial management (PFM) reform. The distinction between public financial administration and public financial management goes to the heart of how governments allocate and monitor public money—how they control their finances.

Financial control is embedded in a country's political and state arrangements—it is not "free-standing."[41] PFA is defined by external control based on political and state arrangements that focus on *compliance*, which limits discretion. PFM is defined by internal control based on political state relationships that focus on *professionalism*—which promotes discretion. Thus, the crucial sequence of financial reform is to be seen on a spectrum of financial control—from external control (public finance administration) to internal control (public financial management). Management is fundamentally about discretion: about making choices with regard to objectives, about taking the risk of deploying resources to achieve those objectives, about being held accountable for decisions and having incentives to perform. The distinction between external and internal control was made clearly by Allen Schick in 1978 in a little-noticed article, "Contemporary Problems in Financial Control." Evolving from external to internal control is a sea change in how a government does business:

> Internal control is much more than a procedural matter. It represents a fundamental shift in attitude about government.... Internal control signifies that public agencies can police themselves, that it is much more important to get on with the job than to worry about preventing the misuse of funds.[42]

It was an important corrective to Schick's earlier and widely cited article on the stages of budget reform, which provided the conceptual basis of the current sequence framework, discussed earlier, and has been a source of confusion in the field.[43]

The financial trinity: control, management, and planning

Interpreting the work of Robert Anthony on operations research, Allen Schick in 1966 argued that public budgets perform three roles—control, management, and planning—and that budget reform is the sequence of introducing these roles, starting with control.[44] So the first stage of budget reform is control, delivered by the line-item budget format, followed by management, delivered by the performance budget format, and finally, planning, delivered by the program budget format. Even though Schick's article was very clear that the financial trinity applied only to budgets and not to all of the components of a financial system (accounts, audit), it has spawned much confusion. The principal confusion is that the trinity (control-management-planning) defines the sequence of how a financial system as a whole (budgets, accounts, audit, etc.) should evolve and therefore also defines how it is to be reformed. The second confusion is that each item of Schick's trinity is embedded in a budget format—for example, management is done by performance budgets, so if governments want to promote management of financial resources, they have to adopt performance budgets.

Arguably the most persuasive critique of Schick's financial trinity comes from Aaron Wildavsky, a pioneer and dean of the field of budgeting.[45] Wildavsky's 1978 work on why the traditional budget—the line-item budget—lasts refuted Schick's 1966 financial trinity model.[46] Wildavsky argued that not only is the line-item budget especially effective in promoting control, but also one of the principal virtues of this budget format is that it delivers *all three* roles, unlike more "advanced" budget types such as performance- or program-based, which fail to deliver some roles.[47] Wildavsky provided an important corrective to

Schick's trinity: namely, he clarified that the trinity was not rigidly rooted in budget formats. This point defines the second of the two attributes of the PFA-PFM distinction: the *focus of allocation*—inputs, outputs, outcomes. The first and defining attribute of PFA versus PFM is the *type of control*—external versus internal.

Unpacking Schick's financial trinity, the first stage of budget reform was control, accomplished by use of a line-item budget format, which focused on the allocation of inputs. The second stage of budget reform was management, which was to be done by a performance budget format, which focused on the allocation of outputs. The third stage of budget reform was planning, which was to be done by a program budget format, which focused on the allocation of outcomes. Wildavsky's corrective to Schick's trinity unbundles budget formats (line-item, performance, program) from their respective roles (control, management, planning) and their respective focus on resources (inputs, outputs, outcomes). That is, Schick erected a rigid structure whereby a line-item budget format provided the role of control and focused on outputs; a performance budget format provided the role of management and focused on outputs; a program budget format provided the role of planning and focused on outcomes. For Wildavsky, budgeting and financial administration or management are not as rigid as Schick's trinity suggests. A traditional budget does not preclude management or planning or a focus on outputs and outcomes.

Tweaking the paradigm, or, an organic sequencing framework

Building on these points, PFA and PFM each have two attributes: the type of control and the focus of resource allocation. PFA is defined by external control, and, à la Wildavsky—despite the resource focus especially on inputs—it does not preclude a focus on outputs and even outcomes.[48] PFM is defined by internal control with a resource focus on outputs and especially outcomes, although it does not totally overlook inputs. Ergo, PFM should not be attempted unless a robust PFA is in place, with good external control and well-monitored inputs.

What are the implications of the PFA and PFM distinction as here defined? The first implication is that this distinction shows the deficiencies of the current PFM sequencing framework. The sequencing framework makes no mention of the evolution of control. Further, sequencing in the form of introducing new budget formats is not needed because PFA has a resource focus that includes inputs and outputs and even outcomes. PFA is most focused on inputs, but it can and does focus on outputs. Outcomes are its weakest suit and thus *may* become an argument for adopting PFM.

The second implication of the PFA-PFM distinction is that PFA may be all that is needed by developing and transitional countries. PFM is not needed to support a country's economic development—but good PFA is needed. Indeed, it raises the question: Is PFM needed at all?[49] The two attributes of PFA—external control and a focus on inputs and outputs—are what developing countries must have. PFA, like the traditional line-item budget, is especially effective in establishing control, which is arguably the first-order task of a financial system. External control is particularly needed for aid-dependent countries, because—despite much lip service paid by foreign aid agencies to the need for performance indicators—the first task is to count the money from all sources, domestic and foreign. The field of PFM has said nothing about the financial performance of donor darlings in Africa, countries that receive much attention and much money from the foreign aid community. From Ghana in the 1960s to Kenya in the 1970s to Tanzania and Uganda in the 1980s, much money went missing with these donor darlings. Ethiopia is the latest darling—hopefully it will have a better ending. Strengthening external control prior to the ramping up of foreign aid is a crucial and continuous task, if only to ensure that domestic public money is accounted for and the financial system is not perverted.

In my critique of the sequence framework of PFM, I noted that it failed to take into account the structure of government, particularly decentralization. Decentralization clearly raises concerns about financial control, because responsibility for resources is moved to lower levels of government, which typically are less capable (some also speculate that decentralization creates a hospitable climate for increased corruption, but this has not been empirically proven).[50] Until decentralization is well established, there is need for good external control, if only to confirm to the central authorities the wisdom and the efficacy of this policy. Many developing nations attach great significance to meeting the Millennium Development Goals, which are about the provision of social services. Since decentralization facilitates frontline provision of social services, many of these nations will consequently be pursuing decentralization. If public money—domestic as well as foreign—is to be counted, external control will have to be in place.

The oft-heard critique of the traditional line-item budget is the focus on inputs to the exclusion of outputs and even outcomes. This is seen as a shortcoming that indicates the need for performance budgeting and preferably program budgeting. This critique is simplistic and false: PFA can deliver the first- and second-order tasks in resource allocation, inputs and outputs. It is too simplistic to assert that administrators cannot manage, that they cannot focus on the outputs which the inputs will produce. One finds extraordinary management talent in the administrative cadres of poor countries, who make a lot happen with very little. Do developing countries really need an elaborate performance budget format to achieve performance in outputs?

As to the focus on outcomes with program budgeting, even the most developed governments struggle with program budgeting. A focus on outcomes assumes a broader capacity of the state to allocate and coordinate across sectors and take on board complex tradeoffs—what is called "whole of government planning." An example of such planning would be thinking through what would be the best targets for public investment to improve health. The agencies responsible for water and sanitation or education may well be more effective targets than the agency that has official responsibility for handling health. The desirability of this type of planning for outcomes notwithstanding, first things must come first. Governments in developing countries must first get their inputs and outputs in order, and of course control the cash.

The sequencing framework that dominates the field of PFM is rigid and fails to show the all-important nuances. It specifies a lockstep sequence of techniques to move from the "primitive" basics of control (inputs) to the lofty heights of performance (outputs) and planning (outcomes) of international best practice. One such rigid rule is that to have performance one must have a performance budget. Not so. Financial systems and their reform are more organic than these simplistic rules would suggest. Reform should build on systems and tailor them to context, and it can. A good example of organic reform was the development of what we called in the DSA project a Type 1 performance budget. Complementing but lying outside the traditional line-item budget was a four-page performance agreement with key performance indicators and key performance targets.[51] This budgeting system thus built upon a well-functioning line-item budget that focused on control (inputs), yet introduced performance management (outputs). What is most striking is that this system was implemented at the lowest level of decentralization, the wereda, which has the weakest financial capacity. It worked because it evolved from the existing budgeting system and preserved the control established by this system. It worked because the performance metrics of the agreement were simple (though not simplistic) and were relevant to context. Financial reform is best when it is organic—fit for context. The conventional PFM sequencing framework is not organic—it is about inserting new, rigid, ever more complex techniques that do not build on what exists, using blueprints and "standards" from afar.

In thinking about the "right sequence" one must always bear in mind that PFA and PFM are ideal types. Ideal types never exist in pure form in reality. The utility of an ideal type should be judged by whether it is a useful way of looking at the world because it simplifies and aids comprehension. Does it facilitate the analysis of real situations?

In reality, elements of internal control are mixed with external control in PFA, and there are elements of both types of control in PFM. In practice, "pure" PFA and "pure" PFM are at either end of a continuum from more "basic" to less "basic" financial operations. Some more sophisticated accounting and bookkeeping techniques, such as modified cash-based accounting and double-entry bookkeeping, can be used with a line-item budget without taking the leap into "pure" PFM or getting on a sequencing treadmill. With the proper guidance and training, these "stepping stones" along the PFA–PFM continuum (see table 10.1) can be used to extend the reach of the traditional budget without incurring the costs and risks of a precipitous leap into risky international "best practice" of the outcome-based program budget. Owing no doubt to the lack of international standards for any but pure cash-based and pure accrual accounting, many advocates of "best practice" PFM are unfamiliar with or even wholly ignorant of the stepping-stone approach to incremental improvements in an accounting system (see next section).

In Ethiopia what was needed was a toned-up traditional budget with a sensible budget classification and chart of accounts that ties the financial systems together, and a clear link between the budget appropriation and the agency that

Table 10.1 PFA–PFM continuum for budgeting and accounting

	1 > "Pure" PFA	2 > Stepping stone	3 > Stepping stone	4 > Stepping stone	5 "Pure" PFM
Budgeting format	Line-item			Performance/ Program	Accrual
Accounting, basis	Cash	Modified cash	Modified accrual		Accrual
Accounting, bookkeeping	Single-entry	Double-entry			

Source: author.

is to implement the budget. What type of accounting is basic? Clearly the accounting system needs to be current, but—as shown in table 10.1—"the basics" can move beyond single-entry bookkeeping to perform functions toward the PFM end of the continuum.

The Ethiopian case shows that with a well-prepared in-service training program, officials with a twelfth-grade education are able to manage double-entry book-keeping and a modified cash basis of accounting. Complementing the procedural basics are clear budget and accounts forms with instructions that link seamlessly to an automated system. There is a range of options for a financial information system to link the financial systems (budget, treasury, accounts), as discussed in chapter 6. Another basic is good internal control, which is established by a legal framework, robust procedures, and trained staff. Officials of a state that principally operates by administration are not devoid of management abilities—indeed, the champions of successful financial reform to strengthen PFA are often deft managers who take the risk of reform, what I call the saints of reform.[52] The bottom line for introducing and sustaining any meaningful reform, whether the basics or sophisticated techniques—is a first-class in-service training program.

The lack of standards and need for contextual learning

Implicit in the PFM sequencing framework is the assumption that there are standards for the techniques that are advocated. Yet what is striking is how few standards exist. Take accounting. There are four bases of accounting—cash, modified cash, modified accrual, and accrual. There are IPSAS (International Public Sector Accounting Standards) guidelines for cash and accrual, yet even these are continually debated.[53] The ongoing discussion about the guidelines for the simplest basis, cash accounting, speaks volumes about the lack of firm footing of PFM techniques. One can argue that the intermediate stages of accounting, modified cash and modified accrual, are the most appropriate bases of accounting for developing countries, yet there are no guidelines. COFOG as originally presented was to be a guide, not a standard, in recognition of the fact that the organization of governments varied and that coding should first address the administration of the budget and not be a rigid standard for statistics.

The lack of clear standards in the field of PFM means that learning is imperative—systems must be designed not to meet a set of standards but to fit the context, which means that these context-sensitive systems become the basis of learning. Government staff and DSA advisors defined and modified Ethiopia's cash basis of accounting over time. They could not follow a blueprint—there wasn't one.

Promoting learning in the PFM field

The ongoing carnage of the recent financial crisis is a clear wake-up call that the responsible handling of public money is the most pressing need for the public sector. The PFM field must learn, and this learning must assert itself in face of the lack of learning on the part of foreign aid agencies, governments, consultants, and academics. But will it?

Clearly the major actor that needs to change is foreign aid, especially the Bretton Woods agencies, which have the contractual and financial wherewithal to "persuade" aid-dependent governments to do what they say. They also view themselves as having the competence and neutrality to weigh in on all things PFM.[54] That the Bretton Woods can change—become a "self-correcting" organization, in the words of the late Martin Landau, one of the deepest thinkers on organizations—is doubtful:

> We see the LSFO [large-scale formal organization] as much less the ideal problem-solving instrument than we thought it was: that it is not all that rational, all that scientific, as it claimed to be. On the contrary, bureaucratic systems appear to act as ends in themselves and their functionaries seem more protective of status and power than concerned with the search for rules of adequate solution. Where agencies committed to the canons of science must be open to correction, the modern bureaucracy devotes inordinate amounts of energy to the construction of barriers to review and account. And we can often observe that it masks itself with symbols of knowledge when no such knowledge in fact exists. Bureaucracies are chastised today as sluggish, unresponsive, rigid, closed, and thus resistant to change—which means they do not learn. Crozier has suggested that a bureaucratic organization is one that cannot correct its behavior by learning from its errors.[55]

In foreign aid agencies there is much talk—papers are written—about the sins committed and the need to change, but there is no walk. The Canterbury tales of endless conferences where hippos, "problem-driven iterative adaptation," and metaphors abound accord with Landau's point about the use of symbols of knowledge where no knowledge exists. There is no learning if the talk is not tested by the walk.

Ironically, the influence of the Bretton Woods on PFM may soon be on the wane because their business model is in trouble. The public finance types in these agencies are funded by fees from the loans taken out by developing countries. But countries are growing and so they need less financial and technical assistance, so the source of fees is drying up because the disbursements of these agencies are precipitously declining.[56] Also, with the global economy improving, it is quite possible that the IMF and the World Bank will be shrinking their PFM staff, as they were doing prior to the 2007 financial crisis. One could say that the Bretton Woods agencies are on the wrong side of history.

Additional measures needed to improve PFA/M

Beyond adopting a better framework and promoting learning by the Bretton Woods and other foreign aid agencies, some additional measures are needed.

Aid-dependent governments must better recognize and understand the systems they have and ensure that they are executed. Regardless of whether procedures should be retained, improved, or changed, governments' first duty is to sustain and execute them.

As to improving the quality of technical assistance in finance to developing governments, there is no simple solution to upping the professionalism of the consulting industry. One avenue, though, is to make available to governments undertaking a reform a panel of experts that would provide oversight and much-needed quality assurance. Such a panel could be assembled by active or recently retired civil servants from countries that are not providing bilateral aid to the host country. Such a panel could help governments monitor the performance of the reform and also that of foreign funders, consultants, and their own efforts.

Academics who profess on PFM matters must, first and foremost, be intellectually honest about what they do and do not know. Second, PFM consultants and academics should, like professional investment advisors, be transparent and disclose whom they are beholden to—their contractual obligations—for example, to a Bretton Woods or other government or private agency. Third, they should clearly state in detail their actual experience in the field and its relevance to the topic they are writing about or expounding upon.

Maps for unmarked roads

The PFM prescribers have been obsessed for some time with the need to move to an accrual basis of accounting, a very advanced technique, but the field has failed to develop guidelines for the interim bases of accounting—modified cash and modified accrual—which are easier for developing countries to operate and provide adequate functionality. Another area where an unmarked road needs some signage in the form of sensible guidelines is in the area of financial information systems that can run PFA, not PFM, systems. FISs with flexible functionality, meaning that they can manage multiple schemes of budget classification and charts of accounts that occur as a country's reform unfolds, are essential. The flexibility to evolve to new bases of accounting is also required.

A metric that matters

Returning to Wildavsky, the most important attribute of a financial technique is that it be reliable and not fail. Thus, the most important metric of all in public finance is one that assesses risks of a financial system. In order to guide the design of a reform program that mitigates risk, a risk assessment metric must assess the inputs of the financial system. In other words, garbage in, garbage out. Conversely, good inputs, greater likelihood of good outputs.

So far no such metric exists. The fiduciary risk assessment metric of foreign aid agencies focuses on the risk to their own funds from using the aid recipients' financial systems, not on risks to the financial systems themselves.[57] What is needed is a systems risk assessment metric that evaluates the overall risk of a government's financial system, regardless of the sources of funds, and that covers centralized as well as decentralized structures of government.

Advocates of the framework of sequencing SFTs have virtually ignored this lacuna. Instead of developing adequate metrics for risk, PFM professionals misuse the PEFA to measure performance, then assume that the performance deficits they have uncovered can also be expressed as risk, so that the performance metric in practice is used, falsely, as a measure of risk.[58] In truth, PEFA focuses on throughputs, not inputs. Throughputs are the wrong point in the process to evaluate risk. Risk must be assessed at the beginning of the causal chain. Risk metrics would examine the inputs of a system—the systems of budgeting, accounting, etc.—with the aim of pinpointing deficiencies. These deficiencies are risks, an awareness of which should inform the priorities of a reform program. Risk mitigation, not scoring an A on a performance indicator, should be the first order of business of a reform.

Why are risk metrics for PFM ignored? I believe the answer lies in the unwillingness of both the providers and receivers of foreign aid to scrutinize the recipient country systems too closely, for such assessments might well raise uncomfortable questions and even lead to the cessation of aid.

Professional development

There is a striking lacuna in academia when it comes to advanced training in the field of public financial administration/management. There are no degree programs specific to the field of public financial administration and management. For over twenty years I worked as a project manager for financial reform in Kenya and then Ethiopia, and government officials continually asked me for recommendations as to where they could go for training in this field. I could not advise them because such a program does not exist. Aside from short executive programs—I developed a three-week program at Harvard, which ran for twenty-four years—the only option was to send officials for a two-year MBA. Unfortunately, all too often this training had little to do with improving government finance and much to do with giving these officials a ticket to private sector employment to improve their personal finances. Allen Schick has weighed in on why this lacuna in academia exists:

I wouldn't say there is no interest in PFM in universities, but it is certainly not well defined in academia. I think academia does not pay much attention to it because the students and faculty interested in it gravitate toward business schools, rather than schools of public policy. Business schools offer courses in financial management, financial accounting, and cost accounting. One doesn't see these courses in public policy schools. So PFM gets overlooked in academia simply through natural selection of interests. Furthermore, the economics profession as a whole is not interested in PFM. It uses the data from accounting systems and audits, but is not interested in those systems per se. It is interested in policy analysis—which is the stock and trade of public policy schools and economics departments. The processes by which policies are formulated and implemented are less of interest to the economics profession.[59]

A one-year master's degree that covers PFA and PFM is needed. It would not only provide rigorous and relevant training but also make the very important distinction between public sector and private sector finance, between the disposition of public and private monies. The importation into the public sector of techniques from the private sector—which I have described as "technique envy"— has been a major contributor to the weakness of public sector finances.

Such a master's program would build both the capacity and, more important, the confidence of officials of governments to direct their country's reform. Ideally the presence of officials with this thorough training would allow governments to fully own their reforms and undertake them themselves. A master's program located in a well-established university would also promote an objective research agenda that could review the good, the bad, and the ugly cases of public sector financial reform. To bolster both the applied and theoretical sides of PFA/M, the program would need to twin government officials who bring current experience and practice into the classroom with academics who possess deep field experience and who can bring relevant frameworks and literature to bear on the discussions. Such a program could best be located in a country whose government has a respected public finance system.[60] This can serve as a model both for students and visiting government officials to study and also as an inspiration and model for governments that want to control their own reforms, without foreign aid and their conditionalities, and for forward-thinking foreign aid agencies that are committed to government ownership of reforms.

What the field can learn from Ethiopia's financial reform

The field of PFA/M can learn a great deal from Ethiopia's financial reform:

- About the impact of the reform within Ethiopia
- About the importance of PFA versus PFM for a developing country
- About broad lessons that are of value to other countries

The reform's impact within Ethiopia

Allen Schick recently opined that financial reform has not meant much.[61] Perhaps he meant that PFM reforms done in countries where the political and state arrangements did not support the techniques inserted have not worked and the reform has led to delayed development, the continuation of corruption, and public funds going missing. He cannot, however, have been speaking of Ethiopia!

The PFA reform implemented by the Ethiopian government between 1996 and 2008 led to major improvements in the financial function, from the central ministries down to the lowest tier of government, the weredas. Indeed, it could be argued that without an effective PFA reform at the wereda level, the government policy of relying on weredas to be the frontline deliverers and financers of social services could have failed in some locales, and decentralization might indeed have led to corruption.[62]

Budgeting was put in order with a streamlined budget classification system and chart of accounts, which in turn streamlined the accounts, audit, and financial information systems. Performance was introduced through a simple yet powerful performance agreement at the weredas, many of whom struggle to maintain a performing electricity supply. An output-conditional, needs-based unit-cost intra-regional fiscal transfer system was introduced that programmed the fiscal transfer to weredas. In accounting, a four-year backlog was removed so that accounting became current, not historical. Furthermore, the move from single- to double-entry bookkeeping and from a cash to a modified basis of cash accounting was a sea change. A treasury single account was introduced in weredas, which strengthened cash management and control. Budgeting, accounting, and cash management were tied together by an innovative low-cost financial information system that was so fit for context that it can, and does, run on the dangling telephone wires to the remotest weredas. A planning reform that includes a macroeconomic financial framework and a three-year rolling expenditure plan was introduced, and more than 72,000 officials were trained.

There is a relationship between public financial administration and aid flows and economic growth, and both aid flows and economic growth flourished as a result of this reform.[63] As stated earlier, from 1996 to 2008, the exact years of its financial reform, Ethiopia's annual GDP growth rate was 4.1 percent, second only to Mozambique's 5.3 percent.[64]

But the intangible impact of this reform was even greater and more significant than the tangible statistics. It built the professionalism and confidence of a civil service that had been neglected and demoralized from years of domestic strife. The bulk of the reform's $34.4 million cost went for training, representing an opportunity that changed many officials' lives decidedly for the better. They gained recognition, and for many who labored in remote areas and challenging circumstances, the reform provided an enormous morale boost and gave them hope. Genuine reform is not about sequencing techniques; it is about reaching the trenches of the bureaucracies and giving staff the knowledge and motivation to make their work more effective and their communities' lives better. Ethiopia's

PFA reform refutes Schick's assertion that financial reform has not meant much. In Ethiopia the reform meant a great deal.

Why a PFA, not a PFM, reform?

Recall that PFA is primarily external control and PFM is primarily internal control. Even though the Civil Service Reform Program Task Force report, the founding document of the reform, referred to the need for management, the Ethiopian government did not pursue PFM. There were several reasons for this (explained in detail in chapter 2, "The drivers of public sector reform").

The principal contextual factor that shaped the reform was the party-state relationship. In 1991, a revolution brought to power an ethnic-minority party, the Tigrayan People's Liberation Front (TPLF), which was based on the Leninist model, according to which the party is an organizational weapon for the penetration of society.[65] The party would brook no opposition nor would it be held accountable to the state, much less the citizenry, through parliamentary democracy. The party distrusted the state because the state was dominated by the Amhara ethnic group, which the party believed was a source of oppression and undermined a key tenet of the revolution, ethnic self-determination. The source of "external control"—not just of finances but also of the state itself—was to be the party.

A second reason why PFA, not PFM, was the party's desire to maintain external control: its agenda of reform was shaped by its policy of ethnic-based decentralization and the rapid evolution of decentralization to regions and then—in what is called the second-stage decentralization—to weredas. This decentralization to weredas, some of them in locations that are among the world's most remote areas, required that the rudiments of administration be established. The party was very concerned that decentralization would unleash corruption, which was already increasing and confirmed the party's distrust of the state.[66] Rapid and deep decentralization required that for the foreseeable future the party would exercise firm control over the state—external control.

A third reason for a PFA, not a PFM, reform was the diminished skill set of the available officials, for many of the best had fled during the previous regime. The rapid decentralization also required legions of new staff to be recruited, trained, and posted to remote regions and weredas, where there was a likelihood of high turnover.

Finally, Ethiopia relies on foreign aid for approximately one third of its public funding and, in addition to this support, crucially, has a blank check for food aid to cope with its frequent and devastating famines.[67] The party wanted to be sure that aid flows would not be disrupted by weak financial control.

Lessons for other countries

Chapters 4 to 7, on the budgeting, accounting, financial information systems, and planning reforms, present specific lessons. In addition, eight broader lessons can be drawn from Ethiopia's twelve-year reform:

1 PFA is adequate to support economic development; PFM is not essential.
2 There are four strategies of reform: recognize, improve, sustain, and change.
3 PFA, with its external control, is essential to supporting decentralization, especially in developing countries.
4 Managing the scope of a reform is key. Scheduling and budget follow.
5 Reform is about learning, not about following blueprints—about people, not about techniques.
6 Financial reforms take time and have to settle.
7 Don't forget execution.
8 Limit the influence of foreign aid.

1 PFA is adequate to support economic development. PFM is not essential

The economic development of a country requires effective public finance. Well-functioning PFA is good enough—PFM is neither a necessary nor a sufficient condition for economic development. Ethiopia has experienced robust economic growth with its PFA.[68] PFM did not exist when the early industrializers developed. PFM reforms are riskier than PFA reforms and may well delay and possibly retard economic development if these systems are not effective.

Thus, governments should focus first on PFA reforms to promote economic development—and so should foreign aid donors, by the way. The primary role of foreign aid is to support economic development, and that is where its focus should remain. Since PFM is not needed for economic development, there are no situations that justify the imposition of PFM by foreign aid. (See also, later in this chapter, "8. Limit the influence of foreign aid.")

2 There are four strategies of reform: recognize, improve, sustain, and change

Governments are ongoing entities whose financial systems have been operating for years, indeed generations. One positive legacy of colonialism in Africa is that adequate financial systems were put in place generations ago. Although some government financial systems are failing, the vast majority work. The PFM field's emphasis on change, the new, instead of on making what exists work better flies in the face of these on-the-ground facts. The literature makes virtually no mention of the importance and utility of recognizing and validating what exists.

Yet recognizing what exists is often a revelation. One of the most consistent takeaways of government officials who attended the Executive Program in PFM that I directed at Harvard was their recognition that "what we have is not bad." It would be refreshing to read a Bretton Woods report written after an assessment of the financial systems of a developing country that contained a statement such as "The existing systems are good. Here are some suggestions for improvements that government might implement on its own with modest financial assistance if needed."

A strategy of recognize-improve-sustain is far superior to a strategy of change. The former is premised on retaining government ownership and operation, is less risky, is less disruptive, is faster, and is cheaper. This strategy sweeps government officials into the reform process in a meaningful way.

Sustain is something of a reform "orphan"—rarely seen as an indispensable component of a reform. This was one of the mistakes made by the IMF and the World Bank, when they attempted to move the country rapidly to sophisticated public financial management and failed to sustain the existing system of public financial administration. Worse, in early 2014 the government itself failed to sustain the accounting component of its reform when it allowed the World Bank to introduce contract staff to operate the accounting systems in regions and zones, thus sidelining local staff who had been operating the "fit-for-purpose" system introduced by the DSA reform. The government now can no longer independently operate its own accounting system (see also chapter 8).

3 PFA and its external control is essential to supporting decentralization, especially in developing countries

Decentralization as devolution means assigning responsibilities to government tiers that typically have less capability than the central government. Decentralization, especially when it is rapid, creates enormous risks. A financial reform conducted at the same time as decentralization needs to limit its risk and limit the burden the reform places on changing government structures. PFA systems and reforms are far less risky than PFM reforms; therefore they are the preferred approach to financial reform that is part of a reform sequence that buttresses decentralization.

The literature on the conventional sequencing paradigm says virtually nothing on how the structure of government affects the sequencing of financial reforms. Instead, the sequencing paradigm promotes increasing sophistication at the center and ignores the problems of the periphery, or integration of the center with the other tiers. For countries that are decentralized, the weakest, not the strongest, tier should be the first focus of reform. The IMF's 2011 blueprint for next steps in Ethiopia's financial reform violates this recommendation for it has proceeded to insert sophisticated techniques such as program budgeting at the center and has ignored regions and weredas.[69]

4 First determine the scope of a reform. Schedule and budget follow

Governments and their advisors can only do so much. The challenge in a developing country environment is that everything seems to need doing immediately. But this is not possible. Priorities must be set. Effective reforms require effective management, and the first-order task is to limit the scope. A problem with many foreign aid–driven reforms is that they are driven by budget and schedule—yet their budgets are too large and the schedule is too short. Budget- and schedule-driven reforms have not had positive outcomes. The need to determine scope first is why governments, not foreign aid, should manage their reforms: determine the scope, provide the budget, and set the schedule.

5 Reform is about learning, not about following blueprints; about people, not techniques

Effective financial systems fit with the political and state arrangements of a country and the culture and the capacity of the state. To be effective they must be fit for context. Sustainable reform requires that government officials understand the assets they already have as well as the options for improving and if need be changing their systems. Changing systems is best done through building on and complementing what exists. Inserting techniques from other contexts has never worked well in Africa or in any other contexts. Learning can also produce remarkable results such as the powerful yet simple Type 1 performance budget developed for weredas. Learning makes reform organic: fit for context, and comprehended and owned by government officials. Jim Collins's thoughts on how to get corporate strategy right applies to financial reform in developing countries: get the right people in the right seats and the wrong people off the bus and the bus will drive itself to an appropriate destination.[70]

6 Financial reforms take time and have to settle

Learning takes time. There are no "quick fixes" in this field, despite the fervent wishes of some government and foreign aid officials. Research by the Swedish International Development Agency has established that financial reforms take ten to fifteen years to be fully implemented.[71] Even after this, they take time to settle, especially when a new government structure such as decentralization is also settling. The PFM sequencing framework ignores these time constraints. Reforms need to build a stable financial plateau and not charge forth to conquer new summits.[72] A financial plateau means embedding new practices in government: they are funded and operated by government and they are coherent. Systems and their execution fit with the broader administrative and management processes of government.

7 Don't forget execution

I have cited Ian Lienert, a senior IMF economist, numerous times in this book concerning his finding that financial systems in Africa are for the most part robust—they simply are not executed. The field of PFM has been overly focused on installing new systems—techniques—and has not adequately addressed the need for more effective execution of existing systems. Execution requires adequate staff who are well trained, well managed, and insulated from political pressures so that they can carry out their fiduciary responsibilities.

8   Limit the influence of foreign aid

There are three principal reasons to limit the influence of foreign aid. The Bretton Woods agencies, especially the IMF, have the financial clout to impose a program on an aid-dependent country that may be antithetical to that country's actual requirements or simply does not work, as the comment by Richard Allen, formerly of the IMF, with which we began this chapter confirms. For this reason alone the IMF should be excluded from coordinating, directing, and staffing financial reforms and providing a pool of substantial funds that it controls. When one funder funds the whole reform program, that funder has too much influence.

An even more crucial reason why the IMF should not be involved in a country's reform is that it holds the sword of Damocles over these governments in its role as the keeper of the economic program agreement. If the IMF feels that the country has gone off track from the program, it causes other aid providers to stop assistance. The IMF initiated this domino effect intentionally when it falsely declared Ethiopia off track with its program with the fund—coincidently days before Ethiopia went to war with Eritrea in 1998.

Funding in the form of loans is a third source of major risk to aid recipients. The best way to limit the influence of foreign aid is to negotiate individual grants from multiple donors, each of whom funds small, discrete slices of the reform program, not the whole cake. In other words, emulate the Ethiopian government: exclude the Bretton Woods agencies and manage bilateral assistance so that its contribution leverages genuine reform goals.

Achieving *Uhuru*

Good news is coming out of Africa as African "cheetahs" join the Asian "tigers."[73] Ethiopia is one of these fast-growing cheetahs. Its economic success is the result of the discipline that also made its financial reform a success. Fifty-eight years ago, when decolonization began in Africa, the cry was "*Uhuru!*"— Swahili for "freedom." In the twenty-first century, "*Yichalal!*" will bring about genuine *uhuru*. African governments can effectively manage public resources. They should fully own and operate their financial systems. By doing so they will fully secure their sovereignty.

Notes

1   Beschel and Ahern (2012: 74). In his work on transitional countries seeking accession to the European Union, Noel Hepworth points out the disconnect between the demands of financial management required of accession and the capabilities of these countries. See Hepworth (2013).
2   Allen (2013: 1).
3   Schick quoted in Sarteriale (2011: 1).
4   Korten (1980: 480).
5   Moris (1977: 75, 77).
6   Allen (2010).
7   One such orthodoxy is the long-held dictum that a commercial off-the-shelf (COTS)

integrated financial management information system is superior to a custom-designed one. Years of COTS failures are starting to crack the orthodoxy (Dener, Watkins, and Dorotinsky 2011: xvii–xviii).

8 Despite much PR by Peter Murphy about the achievements of his PFM project, Wynne (2005) and the World Bank's (2001) own early assessments raised concerns and showed the very limited features of this reform.

9 The World Bank's recent review (2013b: 3–4) of Ethiopia's civil service reform seeks to take credit for the PFA reform. This is factually incorrect. As I discussed in chapter 8, the World Bank failed to support the reform after the DSA left at the end of January 2008. The bank's 2013 report also discounts what the government did and extols the virtues of its own Public Sector Capacity Building Program. A book could be written on the failures of the PSCAP, but the most telling feature of the program was its attempt to hijack the expenditure management component of the civil service reform and move its direction from the Ministry of Finance to the Ministry of Capacity Building, which existed because of World Bank funds. As one could expect, the minister of finance was furious at this action and forbade it. One of the most egregious oversights of this capacity building program was its failure to strengthen the regional management institutes designed to build local capacity. On the design of PSCAP see World Bank (2004).

10 International Monetary Fund (2011).

11 MacDonald (2011).

12 Lindblom (1959); Korten (1980); Weick (1984); Wildavsky (1988).

13 Mellett, Macniven, and Marriott (2007).

14 Gauld and Goldfinch (2006: 10–11).

15 Malinowski (1922: Introduction).

16 Schick (1966).

17 Diamond (2013). A cottage industry has developed in papers on sequencing. Recent examples include Bietenhader and Bergmann (2010) and Tommasi (2009, 2010).

18 Allen (2010).

19 Radelet (2010: xvi).

20 Mellett, Macniven, and Marriott (2007).

21 Key (1940).

22 Bookstaber (2007: 35–50) clearly presents the financial engineering that meant that risk could not be modeled. This inability to model risk was in good part responsible for the financial crisis that started in 2007. I present the consequences of the financial crisis to the achievement of the Millennium Development Goals (MDGs) as developed countries turn their attention and finances to the Millennium Unwinding Goals, MUGs—the unwinding of public and corporate debt. See Peterson (2010: 29–35).

23 Wildavsky (1978).

24 Wildavsky (1969: 190).

25 Smith (1999).

26 Alan G. Morris, personal communication, November 2006. Morris, the chairman of the Commonwealth Grants Commission of Australia, provided short-term advice to the DSA project and the government of Ethiopia regarding lessons from other countries' experiences with fiscal decentralization.

27 See Wildavsky (1978); see also Smith (1999) on the dangers of performance budgeting and Kraan's recent blog post on the technique (Kraan 2012).

28 Lienert (2003).

29 On viewing the business processes of public bureaucracies in Africa as hierarchies and networks see Peterson (1997); and on business processes in transitional countries in Europe see Hepworth (2013).

30 This theme underpins the wise counsel Noel Hepworth has given to transitional countries preparing for accession into the European Community. See Hepworth (2013).

31 See PEFA Secretariat (2011: 5).
32 Diamond (2013: 144–5, figure 10.5).
33 Efforts are under way to develop the capability of the PEFA to assess PFM in decentralized systems. See PEFA Secretariat (2008a, 2008b).
34 A review of the scoring of the 2010 PEFA of regions in Ethiopia found serious deficiencies in how the PEFA evaluators did their scoring. See Peterson (2011a: 16–31).
35 Department for International Development (2011).
36 Stevens (2004: 26).
37 All quotes by Jack Diamond are from Diamond (2013: 111, 110, 98, 9, 8).
38 The foreign platform approach is presented in Brooke (2003).
39 Bauer (1971: 103).
40 Hedger and De Renzio (2010).
41 I am indebted to Noel Hepworth for the term "free-standing."
42 Schick (1978: 514).
43 Schick (1966).
44 Anthony (1965); Schick (1966).
45 In a December 2011 interview Schick said that Wildavsky was the one person living or dead he would want to have a conversation with (Sarteriale 2011).
46 Wildavsky (1978); Schick (1966).
47 Wildavsky (1978).
48 Wildavsky (1978).
49 If he were alive, I believe that Wildavsky would take exception to Schick's recent distinction that the traditional budget is the "basics" and not the "best" in budgeting. See Schick (2012: 4). For Wildavsky it was not at all clear that governments needed to—or even could—move beyond the logic of incrementalism and annularity, which are the hallmarks of the traditional budget ("budget annularity" means the budget is for a twelve-month period). See Wildavsky (1964: 128–45).
50 For an argument that decentralization promotes corruption see Prud'homme (1995).
51 The wereda performance agreement is presented in DSA P-63 and DSA P-66.
52 Peterson (1998).
53 The International Public Sector Accounting Standards Board periodically releases the IPSAS guidelines for various accounting issues such as for the cash basis of accounting.
54 In 2009, Richard Allen, the director of the IMF Fiscal Affairs Department, in an interview with the IMF's *Public Financial Management Blog*, stated:

> Emphasis should be given to (i) conducting more critical evaluations of TA [technical assistance] work in this field … and (iii) making use of an "honest broker" such as the IMF to provide genuinely impartial advice on PFM reform strategy and its implementation that is disengaged from donors' lending strategies.

Allen doesn't clarify who should be assessing the donors and their TA staff but implies that it is the IMF itself that should be providing oversight of TA providers by means of its own "impartial advice." See Allen (2009: 3 [accessed November 12, 2010]; this post has since been taken down).
55 Landau (1973: 533–4).
56 World Bank (2013a: 14; 2013f).
57 In 2011 I reviewed the current status of the fiduciary risk assessment (FRA) metric used by foreign aid in my Country Integrated Fiduciary Risk Assessment of Ethiopia (Peterson 2011a: 4–8). Examples of the work in progress on the FRA are Department for International Development (2011), and the World Bank (2008, 2013c) and World Bank, Financial Management Sector Board (2009).
58 The UK's Department for International Development (2011) has used PEFA scores and translated them into indicators of risk.
59 Sarteriale (2011: 2).

60 Locating PFM training in countries where the government has exemplary financial systems is the approach I am taking in developing programs for executive education in PFM. I have developed a program with the University of Melbourne for PFM executive education for the Pacific region, specifically the People's Republic of China. For more details see http://stevepetersonpfm.com.
61 Schick (2002: 9).
62 As argued by Prud'homme (1995).
63 Over the period of 1993–94 to 2010–11, aid flows have accounted for approximately 37 percent of public expenditure in Ethiopia (World Bank 2012a: 113).
64 Radelet (2010: xvi).
65 Jowitt (1978).
66 The government study that guided the design of the civil service reform, which included public finance, discovered significant instances of corruption and found that corruption was increasing. See Office of the Prime Minister, Task Force on Civil Service Reform (1996b: 2).
67 Food aid to Ethiopia is not monetized, so it is off budget and off accounts.
68 Annual GDP growth for Ethiopia from 1996 to 2008 was 4.1 percent, the second best on the continent (Radelet 2010: xvi).
69 International Monetary Fund (2011: 14). The IMF reform program not only has nothing to say about the lowest and weakest tier of government, weredas—it doesn't even consider the regions or zones, in the middle tier.
70 Collins (2001: 44).
71 Swedish International Development Agency (2007: 93).
72 Peterson (2011b, 2011c).
73 Radelet (2010).

References

Works cited—general

Note: DSA publications cited are listed in "Works cited—DSA project documents," pp. 314–17.

Adem, Getachew. 2001. "Decentralization and Economic Development in Ethiopia." Paper presented to the Symposium on Decentralization and Development: Issues of Empowerment and Civil Society in Ethiopia. Addis Ababa: October 26.

Allen, Richard. 2009. "The Challenge of Reforming Budgetary Institutions in Developing Countries." PowerPoint Presentation, *Public Financial Management Blog*, June 29 (accessed November 10, 2012).

——. 2010. "Two Very Modest Proposals for Making Technical Assistance More Effective." *Public Financial Management Blog*, September 17.

——. 2013. "Is There a 'New Consensus' on PFM Reform?" *Public Financial Management Blog*, December 2.

Andersson, Goran, and Jan Isaksen. 2003. *Best Practice in Building African Capacity for Public Management—the Experience of NORAD and SIDA.* Stockholm: SIDA.

Anthony, Robert. 1965. *Planning and Control Systems: A Framework for Analysis.* Boston: Harvard University, Graduate School of Business Administration, Division of Research.

Associates for Rural Development. 2006. "Ethiopia: Evaluation of the In-Service Training Program in Financial Management." Report to the USAID Mission to Ethiopia. Addis Ababa: July 21.

Ayenew, Meheret. 1998. "Some Preliminary Observations of Institutional and Administrative Gaps in Ethiopia's Decentralization Processes." Working Paper No. 1, Regional and Local Development Studies. Addis Ababa: Addis Ababa University, September.

Bauer, Peter. 1971. *Dissent on Development: Studies and Debates in Development Economics.* London: Weidenfeld & Nicolson.

Beschel, Robert P., Jr., and Mark Ahern. 2012. *Public Financial Management Reform in the Middle East and North Africa: An Overview of Regional Experience.* Washington, D.C.: World Bank.

Bietenhader, Daniel, and Andreas Bergmann. 2010. "Principles for Sequencing Public Financial Reforms in Developing Countries." *International Public Management Review* 11, no. 1: 52–65.

Bookstaber, Richard. 2007. *A Demon of Our Own Design: Markets, Hedge Funds and the Perils of Financial Innovation.* Hoboken, N.J.: Wiley.

Brar, Parminder. 2010. "Ethiopia: Strengthening Public Financial Management." Addis Ababa: World Bank, November 11.

——. 2011. "Comment on 'The Performance of Financial Reporting of the PSNP and PBS II Program.'" Addis Ababa: World Bank, October 17.

Brietzke, Paul H. 1995. "Ethiopia's 'Leap in the Dark': Federalism and Self-Determination in the New Constitution." *Journal of African Law* 39 (July): 19–38.

Brooke, Peter. 2003. "Study of Measures Used to Address Weaknesses in Public Financial Management Systems in the Context of Policy Based Support." Report prepared for the PEFA Secretariat. Washington, D.C.: World Bank.

Brooks, Frederick P., Jr. 1995. *The Mythical Man-Month: Essays on Software Engineering.* 2nd edition. Reading, Mass.: Addison-Wesley.

Brumby, Jim. 2008. "MTEFs: Does the Walk Match the Talk?" PowerPoint presentation, From Diagnosis to Action Workshop, Washington, D.C.: March 21 (www.powershow.com/view1/bcf87-NmE2M/MTEFs_Does_the_walk_match_the_talk_powerpoint_ppt_presentation).

Caiden, Naomi, and Aaron Wildavsky. 1980. *Planning and Budgeting in Poor Countries.* New Brunswick, N.J.: Transaction Publishers.

Canadian International Development Agency. 1998. "Regional States of the Federal Democratic Republic of Ethiopia: Summary Report." Addis Ababa.

Chole, Eshetu. 1994a. "Opening Pandora's Box: Preliminary Notes on Fiscal Decentralization in Contemporary Ethiopia." *Northeast African Studies* 1, no. 1: 7–30.

——. 1994b. "Issues of Vertical Imbalance in Ethiopia's Emerging System of Fiscal Decentralization." In *Fiscal Decentralization in Ethiopia.* Addis Ababa: Addis Ababa University Press.

Clapham, Christopher. 1995. "Nationalism, Nationality and Regionalism in Ethiopia." John Hack Memorial Lecture, Anglo-Ethiopian Society. Addis Ababa. November.

Cohen, John M. 1974. "Local Government Reform in Ethiopia: An Analysis of the Problems and Prospects of the Awraja Self Government Proposal, with Particular Emphasis on Rural Change, Local Participation and Potential Areas of External Assistance." Report to USAID. Washington, D.C.

——. 1987. "Villagization in the Arsi Region of Ethiopia: Assessment of the Ethio-Swedish Mission (December 1–14, 1986)." Report prepared for the Swedish International Development Agency. Addis Ababa.

——. 1994. "Transition Toward Democracy and Governance in Post Mengistu Ethiopia." HIID Development Discussion Paper No. 493. Cambridge, Mass.: Harvard University, Harvard Institute for International Development.

——. 1995. "Ethnic Federalism in Ethiopia." *Northeast African Studies* 2, no. 2: 157–88.

Cohen, John, William Hammink, and Emmy Simmons. 1994. "Evaluation Report: Ethiopia Democracy/Governance Support Project 633-0007). Draft Report Prepared for the Ethiopia Mission." Addis Ababa: USAID, May 10.

Cohen, John M., and Peter H. Koehn. 1977. "Rural and Urban Land Reform in Ethiopia." *African Law Studies* 14, no. 1: 3–61.

Cohen, John M., and Stephen B. Peterson. 1996. "Interim Field Report: Phase II Decentralization Support Activity (DSA)." Report prepared for the USAID Mission to Ethiopia. Addis Ababa: May.

——. 1999. *Administrative Decentralization: Strategies for Developing Countries.* West Hartford, Conn.: Kumarian Press.

Cohen, John M., Stephen B. Peterson, and Paul J. Smoke. 1996. "Field Report: Phase I Decentralization Support Activity (DSA)." Report prepared for the USAID Mission to Ethiopia. Addis Ababa: February.

Cohen, John M., and Stevens P. Tucker. 1994. "Democratic Transition in Ethiopia." Unpublished paper. Author's collection.

Cohen, John M., and Dov Weintraub. 1975. *Land and Peasants in Imperial Ethiopia: Social Background to a Revolution.* Assen, Netherlands: Van Gorcum.

Collins, Jim. 2001. *Good to Great: Why Some Companies Make the Leap … and Others Don't.* New York: HarperCollins.

Coopers & Lybrand. 1997. "Ethiopia and National Accountancy and Audit Programme." Report to the Ministry of Finance. Addis Ababa. April.

Dalton, Hugh. 1954. *Principles of Public Finance.* London: Routledge & Kegan Paul.

Dener, Cem, Joanna Alexandra Watkins, and William Leslie Dorotinsky. 2011. "Financial Management Information Systems: 25 Years of World Bank Experience on What Works and What Doesn't." World Bank Study. Washington, D.C.: World Bank.

Department for International Development (UK). 2005. "A Platform Approach to Improving Public Financial Management." Briefing note. London (www.learn4dev.net/fileadmin/Resources/General_Documents/DfID_A%20Platform%20Approach%20to%20PFM.pdf).

———. 2011. "Managing Fiduciary Risk When Providing Foreign Aid." How-to Note. London. June (www.gov.uk/.../system/.../how-to-fiduciary-fin-aid.pdf).

Diamond, Jack. 2013. "Background Paper 1: Sequencing PFM Reform." Washington, D.C.: PEFA Secretariat, January.

Diamond, Jack, and Pokar Khemani. 2005. "Introducing Financial Management Information Systems in Developing Countries." IMF Working Paper No. 05/196. Washington, D.C.: International Monetary Fund.

Dom, Catherine, Stephen Lister, and Manos Antoninis. 2010. "An Analysis of Decentralisation in Ethiopia." Oxford, UK: Mokoro Ltd., April 3.

Dorotinsky, Bill. 2003. "Technology and Corruption: The Case of FMIS." Washington, D.C.: World Bank (download: http://powershow.com/view1/1d70ec-MmQxO/Technology_and_Corruption_The_Case_of_FMIS_powerpoint_ppt_presentation).

Excellence Management & Accounting Consultants. 1998. "Financial Reporting System for the Use of Donor Funds, Final Report, Volumes 1 and 2." Report to the Ministry of Finance. Addis Ababa: September.

Fairly, Richard, and Mary Wilshire. 2003. "Why the Vasa Sank: 10 Problems and Some Antidotes for Software Projects." *IEEE Software*, March–April, 18–25.

Federal Democratic Republic of Ethiopia. 1995. *Proclamation of the Constitution of the Federal Democratic Republic of Ethiopia (No. 1/1995).* Addis Ababa: August 21.

———. 1996. *Proclamation No. 57/1996 Federal Government of Ethiopia Financial Administration Proclamation.* Addis Ababa. December 19.

Federal Democratic Republic of Ethiopia, Ministry of Finance and Economic Development. 2010a. "Public Expenditure Administration and Control Reform Program: 2003 Fiscal Year Plan and Implementation Schedule." Addis Ababa: August.

———. 2010b. "Ethiopia Integrated Regional Government PEFA Assessment." Report to the World Bank Mission to Ethiopia. Addis Ababa: October.

———. 2011. "Protection of Basic Services: Program II Sub-Program C1 (revised)." Addis Ababa: March 14.

Flyvbjerg, Bent, and Alexander Budzier. 2011. "Why Your IT Project May Be Riskier Than You Think." *Harvard Business Review* 89, no. 9 (September 2011): 2–4.

Gauld, Robin, and Shaun Goldfinch. 2006. *Dangerous Enthusiasms: E-government, Computer Failure and Information System Development.* Dunedin: Otago University Press.

Gladwell, Malcolm. 2000. *The Tipping Point: How Little Things Can Make a Big Difference*. Boston: Little Brown.

Hammer, Michael, and James Champy. 1993. *Reengineering the Corporation: A Manifesto for Business Revolution*. New York: Harper Business Books.

Hammer, Michael, and Steven A. Stanton. 1995. *The Reengineering Revolution: A Handbook*. New York: HarperCollins.

Hedger, Edward, and Paolo de Renzio. 2010. "What Do Public Financial Management Assessments Tell Us about PFM Reform?" ODI Background Notes. London: Overseas Development Institute, July.

Heeks, Richard. 2002. "Information Systems and Developing Countries: Failure, Success and Local Improvisations." *Information Society* 18: 101–12.

Hepworth, Noel. 2013. "Stages in the Development of Financial Management and Control." Unpublished paper. Author's collection.

Hirschman, Albert. 1967. *Development Projects Observed*. Washington, D.C.: Brookings Institution.

Hough, Jerry. 1969. *The Soviet Prefect*. Cambridge, Mass.: Harvard University Press.

Hyden, Goran. 1983. *No Shortcuts to Progress: African Development Management in Perspective*. Berkeley: University of California Press.

———. 2006. *African Politics in Comparative Perspective*. Cambridge, UK: Cambridge University Press.

International Monetary Fund. 1986. *A Manual on Government Finance Statistics*. Washington, D.C.: IMF.

———. 1994. "Ethiopia—Recent Economic Developments." IMF Staff Country Report No. 94/15. Washington, D.C.: IMF.

———. 2001. *Government Finance Statistics Manual*. Washington, D.C.: IMF.

———. 2005. "IMF Technical Assistance Evaluation: Public Expenditure Management Reform in Selected African Countries." Washington, D.C.: IMF, August 10.

———. 2006. "Selected African Countries: IMF Technical Assistance Evaluation—Public Expenditure Management Reform." Washington, D.C.: IMF.

———. 2011. "Ethiopia: Public Financial Management Reform Priorities: Next Steps." Washington, D.C.: IMF, Fiscal Affairs Department, October.

James, Clive. 2007. *Cultural Amnesia: Necessary Memories from History and the Arts*. New York: Norton.

Jowitt, Kenneth. 1978. "Leninist Response to National Dependency." IIS Research Series No. 37. Berkeley: University of California, Institute of International Studies.

Keen, Peter. 1991. *Shaping the Future: Business Design Through Information Technology*. Boston: Harvard Business School Press.

Key, V. O. 1940. "The Lack of Budgetary Theory." *American Political Science Review* 34, no. 6: 1137–44.

Korten, David. 1980. "Community Organization and Rural Development: A Learning Process Approach." *Public Administration Review* (September–October): 480–511.

Kraan, Dirk. 2012. "Performance Budgeting: Facing Up to the Hard Questions." *Public Financial Management Blog*, September 4. No longer available at website; in author's collection.

Lacey, Robert M. 1989. "Managing Public Expenditure: An Evolving World Bank Perspective." *World Bank Discussion Papers* 56.

Landau, Martin. 1973. "On the Concept of a Self-Correcting Organization." *Public Administration Review* 33, no. 6 (November–December): 533–42.

Landau, Martin, and Eva Eagle. 1981. "On the Concept of Decentralization." Project on Managing Decentralization. Report prepared for USAID. Berkeley: University of California, Institute of International Studies (http://pdf.usaid.gov/pdf_docs/PNAAL320.pdf).

Last, Duncan. 2003. "Options for Medium Term Expenditure Planning." Visit memorandum: Ethiopia, November 17–19. Daar es Salaam, Tanzania: East AFRICTAC, November 17–19.

Last, Duncan, Davina Jacobs, Marc Robinson, and Mark Schaeffer. 2009. "Next Phase in Program Budgeting." Washington, D.C.: International Monetary Fund, November.

Last, Duncan, and Marc Robinson. 2005. "Improving Management of the Federal Government of Ethiopia's Budget." Dar es Salaam, Tanzania: East AFRITAC.

Lawson, Andrew. 2012. "Evaluation of Public Financial Management Reform in Burkina Faso, Ghana and Malawi 2001–2010." Final Synthesis Report, prepared for the Swedish International Development Agency, the Danish International Development Agency, and the African Development Bank. Stockholm: SIDA, April (www.oecd.org/derec/afdb/publicmanagementregorm.pdf).

Lehmann, Glenn. 1986. "Kenya's Experience with a Forward Budget." EDI Training Materials. Washington, D.C.: World Bank, Economic Development Institute, July.

Leonard, David K. 1987. "The Political Realities of African Management." *World Development* 15, no. 7: 899–910.

Levine, Donald. 1965. *Wax and Gold: Tradition and Innovation in Ethiopian Culture.* Chicago: University of Chicago Press.

Lienert, Ian. 2003. "Comparison Between Two Public Expenditure Management Systems in Africa." *OECD Journal on Budgeting* 3, no. 3: 35–66.

Lindauer, David L., and Michael Roemer, eds. 1994. *Africa and Asia: Legacies and Opportunities in Development.* Oakland, Calif.: ICS Press.

Lindblom, Charles. 1959. "The Science of 'Muddling Through.'" *Public Administration Review* 19, no. 2: 79–88.

MacDonald, Lawrence. 2011. "One Size Doesn't Fit All: Lant Pritchett on Mimicry in Development." *Global Prosperity Wonkcast* (blog), Center for Global Development (website), March 14.

Malinowski, Bronislaw. 1922. *Argonauts of the Western Pacific: An Account of Native Enterprise and Adventure in the Archipelagoes of Melanesian New Guinea.* Oxford: Routledge.

Marcus, Harold. 1995. "A Breakfast Meeting with Prime Minister Meles." Unpublished paper. Author's collection.

Mellett, Howard, Louise Macniven, and Neil Marriott. 2007. "NHS Resource Accounting in Wales: Problems of Implementation—Executive Summary." Institute of Chartered Accountants Scotland (links to executive summary and full report at http://icas.org.uk/marriott).

Mishra, Satish. 1993a. "Public Expenditure Implications of Regional Economic Devolution." Internal memo to USAID Mission to Ethiopia. Addis Ababa: June.

———. 1993b. "USAID's Possible Contribution to Regional Devolution." Internal memo. Addis Ababa: USAID, August 17.

———. 1995. "The Economic Dimensions of Regionalization in Ethiopia." Report prepared for USAID Mission to Ethiopia. Addis Ababa: February.

Moris, Jon. 1977. "The Transferability of Western Management Concepts and Programs: An East African Perspective." In *Education and Training for Public Sector Management in Developing Countries*, edited by William Stifel, James Black, and James Coleman. New York: Rockefeller Foundation.

Office of the Prime Minister, Civil Service Reform Management Unit. 1997. "Ethiopian Civil Service Reform: Four-Year Plan (1997 to 2000)." Addis Ababa: January.

Office of the Prime Minister, Task Force for Civil Service Reform. 1996a. *Task Force Comprehensive Report.* 5 volumes. Addis Ababa: February 3. Volume 1: chapter 1, "Executive Summary." Volume 2: chapter 2, "Introduction to the Task Force"; chapter 3, "Organization of Central Institutions"; chapter 4, "Expenditure Management and Control." Volume 3: chapter 5, "Human Resource Management"; chapter 6, "Top Management Systems." Volume 4: chapter 7, "Aspects of Institutional Management"; chapter 8, "Service Delivery and Quality of Service"; chapter 9, "Ethics." Volume 5: Appendices.

——. 1996b. "Civil Service Reform in Ethiopia." Report. Addis Ababa: April.

——. 1996c. "Management of the Reform of the Civil Service and External Resource Requirements as of May 2, 1996." Addis Ababa, May 2.

Organisation for Economic Co-operation and Development. 2001. "The Hidden Threat to E-Government: Avoiding Large Government IT Failures." PUMA Policy Brief No. 8. Paris: OECD, March.

Oxford Policy Management. 2000. "Medium Term Expenditure Frameworks—Panacea or Dangerous Distraction." Paper 2. *OPM Review*, May (www.opml.co.uk/sites/opml/files/OPM%20Review%202_0.pdf).

Parry, Michael. 2005. "Why Government IFMIS Procurements So Often Get It Wrong." *ACCA International Public Sector Bulletin*, Issue 4.

Pattanayak, Sailendra, and Israel Fainboim. 2010. "Treasury Single Account: Concept, Design, and Implementation Issues." IMF Working Paper 10143. Washington, D.C.: International Monetary Fund, May.

PEFA Secretariat. 2008a. "Guidelines for Application of the PEFA Performance Measurement Framework at Sub-National Government Level, Volume 1—Main Guidelines." Washington, D.C.: March.

——. 2008b. Guidelines for Application of the PEFA Performance Measurement Framework at Sub-National Government Level, Volume 2—Annex. Washington, D.C.: March.

——. 2011. "Public Financial Management Performance Measurement Framework." Washington, D.C.: January.

Perkins, Dwight, Steven C. Radelet, Donald Snodgrass, Malcolm Gillis, and Michael Roemer. 1996. *Economics of Development.* 4th edition. New York: Norton.

Peterson, Stephen. 1990. "Recurrent Cost Issues in the Ministry of Agriculture and the Ministry of Livestock Development." Report prepared for the Republic of Kenya Ministries of Agriculture and Livestock Development and the World Bank. Nairobi: May.

——. 1991. "From Processing to Analyzing: Intensifying the Use of Microcomputers in Development Bureaucracies." *Public Administration and Development* 5: 491–510.

——. 1992a. "Financial Reform in Kenya: The Allocational Bias." Unpublished paper. Author's collection.

——. 1992b. "Project Design: Agricultural Sector Management Project II." Report prepared for the World Bank and the Republic of Kenya Ministries of Agriculture and Livestock Development. Nairobi: June.

——. 1992c. "Technical Proposal for the ASAO II Budget Management Project." Proposal submitted to the Republic of Kenya Ministries of Agriculture and Livestock Development. Nairobi: August.

——. 1996a. "Decentralization Support Activity Project Proposal." Technical proposal prepared for the President and Fellows of Harvard College, submitted to the USAID Mission to Ethiopia. Addis Ababa: November 27.

———. 1996b. "Financial Management Issues of the Government of Ethiopia." Report prepared for the Ministry of Finance, Government of Ethiopia, and the USAID Mission to Ethiopia. Addis Ababa: June.

———. 1996c. "Financial Reform in Kenya: Implementing the Public Investment Program in a Line Ministry." In *Public Financial Administration in Developing Countries*, edited by Naomi Caiden. Greenwich, Conn.: JAI Press.

———. 1996d. "Generic Issues in Financial Management for the Central Government." Report prepared for the public expenditure review for the Ministry of Finance. In Oxford University, Centre for the Study of African Economies, Social Sector Review/ PER II. Addis Ababa.

———. 1996e. "Making IT Work: Implementing Effective Financial Information Systems in Bureaucracies in Developing Countries." In Glenn Jenkins, ed., *Information Technology and Innovation in Tax Administration*. The Hague: Kluwer Law International.

———. 1996f. "The Strategy of Civil Service Reform." Memorandum to Peter Silkin, Civil Service Reform Program advisor in the Office of the Prime Minister. Addis Ababa.

———. 1997. "Hierarchy versus Networks: Alternative Strategies for Building Organizational Capacity in Public Bureaucracies in Developing Countries." In *Getting Good Government: Capacity Building in the Public Sectors of Developing Countries*, edited by Merilee Grindle. Cambridge, Mass.: Harvard University, Kennedy School of Government.

———. 1998. "Saints, Demons, Wizards and Systems: Why Information Technology Reforms Fail or Underperform in African Bureaucracies." *Public Administration and Development* 18, no. 1: 27–60.

———. 1999. "In-Service Financial Training Proposal." Technical proposal submitted to the USAID Mission to Ethiopia by the President and Fellows of Harvard College. Addis Ababa: August.

———. 2004. "Technical Proposal: In-Service Training Program in Financial Management." Proposal prepared for the President and Fellows of Harvard College, submitted to the USAID Mission to Ethiopia. Addis Ababa: May 14.

———. 2005. "Sustaining the Accounts, Budget and Expenditure Planning Reforms under the Civil Service Reform Program." Report to the Ministry of Finance and Economic Development. Addis Ababa: October 17.

———. 2006. "Technical Proposal: In-Service Training Program in Financial Management." Proposal prepared for the President and Fellows of Harvard College, submitted to the USAID Mission to Ethiopia. Addis Ababa: September.

———. 2007a. "Automating Public Financial Management in Developing Countries." In *Budgeting and Budgetary Institutions, and Budget Reforms for a More Responsible and Accountable Public Governance*, edited by Anwar Shah. Public Sector Governance and Accountability Series. Washington, D.C.: World Bank.

———. 2007b. "Imperfect Systems: IFMISs in Africa." Paper prepared for the World Bank and presented at the CABRI Conference on Budget Management and Public Financial Accountability, Ministry of Finance, Pretoria, South Africa, June 18–21 (http://siteresources.worldbank.org/PSGLP/Resources/225Peterson.pdf).

———. 2010. "Rethinking the Millennium Development Goals for Africa." Faculty Research Working Paper Series RWP10–046. Cambridge, Mass.: Harvard Kennedy School of Government, November.

———. 2011a. "Ethiopia: Country Integrated Fiduciary Assessment: Draft Interim Report." Report prepared for the World Bank Support Mission in Ethiopia. Addis Ababa: March.

——. 2011b. "Plateaus not Summits: Reforming Public Financial Management in Africa." *Public Administration and Development* 31, no. 3: 205–13.

——. 2011c. "Why IT Worked: Critical Success Factors of a Financial Reform Project in Africa." Faculty Research Working Paper Series, No. RWP 11-019. Cambridge, Mass.: Harvard University, Harvard Kennedy School of Government, March.

Peterson, Stephen, Mebrahtu Araya, Tesfaye Gashaw, Chekol Kidane, Abera Mengistu, Mearuf Nurhusien, and Dula Tessema. 2011. "The Performance of Financial Reporting of the Productive Safety Nets Programme and Protecting Basic Services II Programme (Draft)." Unpublished draft report prepared for the World Bank Support Mission in Ethiopia. Author's collection.

Pinckney, Thomas, John Cohen, and David Leonard. 1983. "Microcomputers and Financial Management in Development Ministries: Experience from Kenya." *Agricultural Administration* 14: 151–67.

Prud'homme, Remy. 1995. "On the Dangers of Decentralization." Policy Working Paper No. 1252. Washington, D.C.: World Bank, Transportation, Water, and Urban Development Department.

Radelet, Steven. 2010. *Emerging Africa: How 17 Countries Are Leading the Way.* Washington, D.C.: Center for Global Development.

Reinert, Erik. 2006. "Development and Social Goals: Balancing Aid and Development to Prevent 'Welfare Colonialism.'" DESA Working Paper No. 14. New York: United Nations, Department of Economic and Social Affairs (www.un.org/esa/desa/papers/2006/wp14_2006.pdf).

Republic of Kenya. 1986a. "Budget Rationalization Program." Nairobi: Ministry of Finance and Ministry of Planning and National Development, April.

——. 1986b. "Economic Management for Renewed Growth: Sessional Paper no. 1 of 1986." Nairobi: Ministry of Finance and Ministry of Planning and National Development. Nairobi.

Rickey, Branch, and John L. Monteleone. 1995. *Branch Rickey's Little Blue Book: Wit and Strategy from Baseball's Last Wise Man.* New York: Macmillan.

Robinson, Marc, and Duncan Last. 2009. "A Basic Model of Performance-Based Budgeting." Washington, D.C.: International Monetary Fund, September.

Roemer, Michael, and Christine Winton Jones. 1991. *Markets in Developing Countries: Parallel, Fragmented and Black.* Oakland, Calif.: ICS Press.

Royal Academy of Engineering and British Computer Society. 2004. "The Challenges of Complex IT Projects." Report of working group. London: Royal Academy of Engineering.

Sarteriale, Carla. 2011. "Are PFM Reforms Always Worth It?" Interview of Allen Schick. *Public Financial Management Blog*, December 7.

Schiavo-Campo, Salvatore. 2008. "Of Mountains and Molehills: The Medium-Term Expenditure Framework." Paper presented at the Conference on Sustainability and Efficiency in Managing Public Expenditures. Organized by the East-West Center and Korea Development Institute. Honolulu, July 24–25.

Schiavo-Campo, Salvatore, and Daniel Tommasi. 1999. *Managing Government Expenditure.* Manila: Asian Development Bank.

Schick, Allen. 1966. "The Road to PPB: The Stages of Budget Reform." *Public Administration Review* 26, no. 4: 243–58.

——. 1978. "Contemporary Problems in Financial Control." *Public Administration Review* 38 (November–December): 513–19.

——. 2002. "Does Budgeting Have a Future?" *OECD Journal of Budgeting* 2, no. 2: 7–48.

——. 2012. "Basics First Is Best Practice." *IMF Public Financial Management Blog*, July 27.

Schiller, Christian, Matt Davies, and Duncan Last. 2002. "Aide Memoire Ethiopia: Improving Fiscal Reporting under Decentralization." Washington, D.C.: International Monetary Fund, July.

Smith, James. 1999. "The Benefits and Threats of PBB: An Assessment of a Modern Reform." *Public Budgeting and Finance* 19, no. 3: 3–15.

Stevens, Michael. 2004. "Institutional and Incentive Issues in Public Financial Management Reform in Poor Countries." Paper prepared for the World Bank. Washington, D.C.: World Bank (www1.worldbank.org/publicsector/pe/StrengthenedApproach/7Institutionallssues.pdf).

Swanson, E. Burton. 1988. *Information System Implementation: Bridging the Gap Between Design and Utilization.* Homewood, IL: Irwin.

Swedish International Development Agency. 2007. *Public Financial Management in Development Co-Operation: A Handbook for SIDA Staff.* Stockholm: SIDA.

Tadesse, Tsega. 2010. "Ethiopian Commodity Exchange (ECX)—Connecting Farmers to the Market." Master's thesis, Orebro University, Swedish Business School, August.

Thompson, Dennis, Jorge Dominguez, Dale Jorgenson, and Dwight Perkins. 2000. "The Harvard Institute for International Development and Its Relationship to Harvard University: Report to the Provost." Cambridge, Mass.: Harvard University.

Tommasi, Daniel. 2009. "Strengthening Public Expenditure Management in Developing Countries—Sequencing Issues." Unpublished paper, available for download at Capacity4dev.eu.

Tommasi, Daniel. 2010. "The Basic PFM Functions and PEFA Performance Indicators." OECD Working Paper. OECD: Paris: May 9.

Transitional Government of Ethiopia. 1992. "A Proclamation to Define the Sharing of Revenue Between the Central Government and the National/Regional Self-Governments." Proclamation 33/1992. Addis Ababa.

Transitional Government of Ethiopia, Ministry of Planning and Economic Development. 1993. "Management of Economic and Technical Change (METC), Participatory Regional Development (Sub-Programme 5A.2)." Proposal to the UNDP Fifth Country Programme. Internal government document. Addis Ababa: April.

Tucker, Stevens. 1998. *Ethiopia in Transition, 1991–1998.* Brighton, UK: Writenet.

——. 1999. "Ethiopia Governance Assessment." Report prepared for the UK Department for International Development. Addis Ababa. November.

United Nations. 1980. *Statistical Papers, Series M, No 70.* New York: UN.

United Nations Development Program. 1996. *Human Development Report 1996.* New York: UN.

——. 2011. *Human Development Report 2011.* New York: UN.

Weick, Karl. 1984. "Small Wins: Redefining the Scale of Social Problems." *American Psychologist* 39, no. 1: 40–9.

Wildavsky, Aaron. 1964. *The Politics of the Budgetary Process.* 4th edition. Boston: Little Brown.

——. 1969. "Rescuing Policy Analysis from PPBS." *Public Administration Review* 29 no. 2 (March–April): 189–202.

——. 1973. "If Planning Is Everything, Maybe It Is Nothing." *Policy Sciences* 4, no. 2: 127–53.

——. 1978. "A Budget for All Seasons? Why the Traditional Budget Lasts?" *Public Administration Review* (November–December): 501–9.

——. 1988. *Searching for Safety.* Piscataway, N.J.: Transaction Publishers.

Wills, Eric. 2005. "Harvard, Justice Dept. to Settle Lawsuit," *Chronicle of Higher Education*, July 1.

World Bank. 1998. *Public Expenditure Management Handbook.* Washington, D.C.

——. 2001. "Country Financial Accountability Assessment—Tanzania." Report No. 25804-TZ. Washington, D.C.: World Bank, May (https://openknowledge.worldbank.org/bitstream/handle/10986/14524/multi0page.txt?sequence=2).

——. 2002. "Design and Implementation of Financial Management Systems: An African Perspective." Africa Region Working Paper Series No. 25. Washington, D.C.: World Bank.

——. 2004. "Ethiopia: Project Appraisal Document on a Proposed Credit in the Amount of SDR 66.9 Million (US$100 Million Equivalent) to the Federal Democratic Republic of Ethiopia for a Public Sector Capacity Building Program Support Project." Report no. 28191-ET. Washington, D.C.: March 25 (link to document at http://documents.worldbank.org/curated/en/2004/03/3066146/ethiopia-public-sector-capacity-building-program-support-project).

——. 2006. "Project Appraisal Document: Productive Safety Net APL II Project in Support of the Second Phase of the Productive Safety Net Program." Addis Ababa: March 12.

——. 2008. "Country Financial Accountability Assessments and Country Procurement Assessment Reports: How Effective Are World Bank Fiduciary Diagnostics?" Report No. 43395. Washington, D.C.: April 24.

——. 2009a. "Project Appraisal Document: Protection of Basic Services Program Phase II Project." Addis Ababa: April 22.

——. 2009b. "Protection of Basic Services (PBS) Program, Phase II: Joint Review and Implementation Support Mission (JRIS), 2009—Aide-mémoire." Addis Ababa: May 20–22.

——. 2009c. "Protection of Basic Services (PBS) Program, Phase II: Joint Review and Implementation Support Mission (JRIS), November 12–20, 2009—Aide-mémoire." Addis Ababa.

——. 2010a. "Joint Review and Implementation Strategy of the Protecting Basic Services Project II." Report. Addis Ababa.

——. 2010b. "Protection of Basic Services (PBS) Program, Phase II: Joint Review and Implementation Support Mission (JRIS), April 12–23, 2010—Aide-mémoire." Addis Ababa.

——. 2010c. "Protection of Basic Services (PBS) Program, Phase II: Joint Review and Implementation Support Mission (JRIS), December 14–15, 2010—Aide-mémoire." Addis Ababa.

——. 2010d. "Public Finance Management Assessment: Integrated Regional Government (Based on the Public Expenditure Financial Accountability Framework (PEFA)." Addis Ababa.

——. 2011a. "Protection of Basic Services (PBS) Program, Phase II: Joint Review and Implementation Support Mission (JRIS), May 9–19, 2011—Draft Aide-mémoire." Addis Ababa.

——. 2011b. "Protection of Basic Services (PBS) Program, Phase II: Joint Review and Implementation Support Mission (JRIS), October 31–November 14, 2011–Aide-mémoire." Addis Ababa.

——. 2012a. "Project Appraisal Document: Protection of Basic Services Program Phase III Project." Addis Ababa: August 29.

——. 2012b. "Protection of Basic Services (PBS) Program, Phase II: Joint Review and Implementation Support Mission (JRIS), May 7–18, 2012—Aide-mémoire." Addis Ababa.

——. 2012c. "Protection of Basic Services (PBS) Program, Phase II: Joint Review and Implementation Support Mission (JRIS), November 5–16, 2012—Aide-mémoire." Addis Ababa.

——. 2012d. "Public Financial Management Reforms in Post-Conflict Countries: Synthesis Report." Washington, D.C.

——. 2013a. "The Challenge of Accelerating Africa's Poverty Reduction." *Africa's Pulse*, volume 8 (October): 19, box 2.

——. 2013b. "Federal Democratic Republic of Ethiopia: Ethiopia Public Sector Reform Approach: Building the Developmental State—A Review and Assessment of the Ethiopian Approach to Public Sector Reform." Washington, D.C.: April 26.

——. 2013c. "Investment Project Financing Operational Risk Assessment Framework Guidance Note." Washington, D.C.: April 10.

——. 2013d. "Protection of Basic Services (PBS) Program, Phase III: Joint Review and Implementation Support Mission (JRIS), May 8–10, 2013—Aide-mémoire." Addis Ababa.

——. 2013e. "Protection of Basic Services (PBS) Program, Phase III: Joint Review and Implementation Support Mission (JRIS), November 11–14, 2013—Aide-mémoire." Addis Ababa.

——. 2013f. "World Bank Group Strategy." Washington, D.C.: October 12.

World Bank, Financial Management Sector Board. 2009. "Assessment of Fiduciary Risks in the Use of Country FM Systems in Bank-Financed Investment Projects: Interim Guidance Note for FM Staff." Washington, D.C.: World Bank.

Wynne, Andy. 2005. "Public Financial Management Reforms in Developing Countries: Lessons of Experience from Ghana, Tanzania, Uganda." Working Paper No. 7. Harare: African Capacity Building Foundation, December.

Young, John. 1996. "Ethnicity and Power in Ethiopia." *Review of African Political Economy* 23, no. 70 (December): 531–42.

——. 1998. "Regionalism and Democracy in Tigray." *Third World Quarterly* 19, no. 2 (June): 101–204.

Works cited—DSA project documents

A complete list of DSA documents and the documents themselves are available at http://stevepetersonpfm.com.

1 Accounts reform

A-1 "Report of Visits to Regions: Assessment of Training Needs in Accounting." James Yardley. August 1, 1997.

A-2 "Assessment of Training Needs in Accounting and Accounting Practices." James Yardley. August 1, 1997.

A-3 "Accounts Reform Project Training Strategy." James Yardley. August 12, 1997.

A-5 "Accounting Specialist Training: Training for Accountants in a Self-Accounting Unit." James Yardley. August 19, 1997.

A-11 "Report of Consultancy." James Yardley. August 22, 1998.

A-12 "Donor Accounting: A Need for Harmonization, Coordination and Integration." James Yardley, August 21, 1998.

A-13   "Description of the Ethiopian Government Accounting System: Accounting Cycles and Processes." September 28, 1998.

A-14   "Description of the Ethiopian Government Accounting System: Government Accounting Form." September 28, 1998. Updated June 13, 2000, Version 1.1 Draft. Revised on September 30, 2000.

A-20   "Report of Consultancy." James Yardley and Kelly Richmond. January 20, 1999.

A-27   "Accounts Reform Design Manual (Manual 3): Overview of Operations and Financial Reports, Details by Transaction." Accounts Design Team. August 1, 2001.

A-33   "Report on Accounting Backlog." October 2001.

A-34   "Report on the Accounts Reform Workshop, September 20 and 21, Addis Ababa Ghion Hotel." October 2001.

A-35   "Manual 3: FGE Accounting System—Volume I: Accounting for Modified Cash Basis Transaction." January 2002.

A-61   "The Strategy for Implementing the Accounts Reform in Amhara Region in FY 1995." February 18, 2003.

A-66   "Assessment of Accounts Reform Implementation in Amhara Region." August 25, 2003.

A-67   "Assessment Report for Oromia Region." August 5, 2003.

A-90   "Civil Service Reform Program—Expenditure Management and Control Sub-Program: Assessment of the Accounts Reform in Tigray Region." David Lynch. August 24 2004.

A-166 "Manual 3: FGE Accounting System." Volume 1, version 1.3 (final draft). May 24, 2007.

A-167 "Manual 3: FGE Accounting System—Chart of Accounts." Volume 2, version 1.3. May 24, 2007.

2 Budget reform

B-11   "The Process of Parliamentary Approval and Appropriation for the Budget." Revised. December 12, 1998.

B-16   "Budget Reform Design Manual Version 2.1." January 24, 2000. Updated, February 17, 2000.

B-17   "Budget Information System—Results of Initial System Study, Proposed Future Activities, and Work Completed to Date." Version 1.0. Shaun McGrath. February 2000.

B-19   "Unit Costs and Their Role in the New Budget System." Perran Penrose. May 2000.

B-27   "Strategic Plan for Implementing the Budget Reform at the Federal Level for EFY1994." October 2, 2000.

B-31   "Data Management Plan for Implementing the Budget Reform by Federal Public Bodies using the Budget Information System (BIS)." January 11, 2001.

B-37   "FY1994 Approved Budget for the FDRE, Volume 1, Budget Summary." Amharic version.

B-38   "FY1994 Approved Budget for the FDRE, Volume 2, Budget Details." Amharic version.

B-39   "FY1994 Approved Budget for the FDRE, Volume 1, Budget Summary." English version.

B-40   "FY1994 Approved Budget for the FDRE, Volume 2, Budget Details." English version.

316 *References*

B-46   "Civil Service Reform Program: Assessment of the Implementation of the Budget Reform for the Preparation of the FY 1994 Federal Budget." December 3, 2001.

B-213   "Ministry of Finance and Economic Development; Revised Federal Budget Manual." Version 1.0, draft version 1.15. February 27, 2007.

3 Cash management [no documents cited]

4 Debt management [no documents cited]

5 Public investment and expenditure reform

P-15   "PIP FY's 1991–1993, volume 1, English."

P-16   "PIP FY's 1991–1993, volume 2, English."

P-49   "Civil Service Reform Program: SNNPR Budget Reform—Developing a Formula for Block Grant Allocations to Woredas." Perran Penrose. February 2002.

P-54   "Presentation by Perran Penrose—Seminar on Budget Planning at the Global Hotel from December 11 to 12, 2003." December 11, 2003.

P-63   "Impacts (Outcomes), Objectives, Outputs, Targets and Indicators—the SNNPRG Bloc Grant Performance Structure." Perran Penrose. May 2004.

P-64   "Regional Economic Policy Review—Policy for Growth and Competitiveness in the Southern Region—Background Paper for the 1998 Budget Planning Cycle." December 2004.

P-65   "Presentation of the Regional Economic Policy Review (REPR) in the Southern Nations Nationalities and Peoples' Region." Perran Penrose. December 2004.

P-66   "Planning Reform in the Southern Nations, Nationalities and Peoples' Region—Update, Issues and Actions." Perran Penrose. December 2004.

P-74   "Civil Service Reform Program: Revised Structure of the SNNPR Regional Fiscal Transfer and Allocation System." Perran Penrose. September 2006.

6 Policy advice to the prime minister's office

PA-1   "The Potential for Cereal Exports from Ethiopia." Richard Goldman. October 16, 1997.

PA-2   "The Results of the Visit to Ethiopia." Dwight Perkins. December 19, 1997.

PA-3   "Trip Report: My Visit to Ethiopia." Malcolm McPherson. February 14, 1998.

PA-4   "A Macroeconomic Model for Ethiopia." Malcolm McPherson and Tzvetana Rakovski. February 7, 1998. Updated July 7, 1999.

PA-5   "A Note on Macroeconomic Management in Ethiopia." Malcolm McPherson. March 3, 1998.

PA-6   "Strategy for Development of the Coffee Sector." Mike Westlake. October 24, 1998.

PA-7   "Low Wages Are Not Enough: An Analysis of Industrial Growth in Ethiopia." David Lindauer. June 1999.

PA-11   "Terms of Reference for a Study for the Development of a System for the Trading of Grain Warehouse Receipts at a Commodity Exchange." Mike Westlake. September 15, 2000.

PA-12   "Regional Economic Policy Review: Briefs on Agricultural Policy and Budgetary Options." Draft (not for circulation). Mike Westlake. March 2005.

7 Training strategy for accounts, budget, public investment/expenditure planning

T-1   "The Training Strategy for Accounts, Budget and Financial Planning Under Civil Service Reform." September 10, 1997.

T-2   "Trip Report: Assessment of the Region 1 Management Institute." November 14, 1997.

T-6   "Meeting on In-Service Training in Financial Management at the Ethiopian Civil Service College." June 16, 1996.

T-28   Accounts Training Module 1 v1.1: "FGE System of Accounting—Trainer Manual." April 2000.

T-29   Accounts Training Module 1 v1.1: "FGE System of Accounting—Trainee Manual." April 2000.

T-30   Accounts Training Module 1 v1.1: "FGE System of Accounting—Guide to Trainers." April 2000.

T-31   Accounts Training Module 1 v1.1: "FGE System of Accounting—Workbook for Trainees." April 2000.

T-32   Accounts Training Module 1 v1.1: "FGE System of Accounting—Overheads for Trainers." April 2000.

T-33   Accounts Training Module 1 v1.1 "FGE System of Accounting—Forms [Overheads] for Trainers." April 2000.

T-34   Accounts Training Module 1 v1.1 "FGE System of Accounting—Test Questions and Answers." April 2000.

T-35   Training Manual for Training Module A v. 1.0: "Introduction to FGE Accounting System." December 2000.

T-103   Budget Training Manual: "Budget Classification and the Chart of Accounts, Public Expenditure Programming: Concepts and Methods, Budget Preparation and Presentation, Budget Execution." Draft. November 19, 2002.

8 Miscellaneous reports

M-10   "Comments on the Draft Final Report on Financial Reporting System on the Use of Donor Funds by the Excellence Management and Accounting Consultants." October 2, 1998.

M-18   "Wereda Level Financial Management: Discussion Paper Prepared by the DSA Project." March 13, 2003.

M-23   "Minutes of the Regional Workshop on Financial Management: The Awassa Meeting of April 8–9, 2003." April 25, 2003.

M-24   "Strategy for Implementation of the Accounts Reform—Amhara Region." March 6, 2003.

M-34   "Trip Report—Amhara Region: Budget and Accounts Reform Status." January 13, 2004.

M-39   "Assessment Report on the Accounts Reform in SNNP Region." March 8, 2004.

M-42   "Operation of a Wereda Support Unit (WSU) in the SNNPR." Draft report. May 27, 2004.

M-56   "Civil Service Reform Program—Estimating the Current Revenue Potential for the SNNPR. Draft document." James M. Warner. July 2005.

M-70   "Overview of the DSA Project: Reform Strategy and Components of Reform

(Budget Planning, Budgeting, Accounting and Financial Information Systems)." June 8, 2006.

M-107 "Civil Service Reform Program—Proposal to Establish a Reform Support Unit (RSU) in the Ministry of Finance and Economic Development." November 25, 2006.

9 DSA project quarterly reports

Q-23　"Report of Project Activities: October 1st to December 31st, 2002." April 18, 2003.

10 Information technology

IT-IBEX-1　"Integrated Budget and Accounts Computer System: IBEX Functional Specifications." November 5, 2003.

IT-IBEX-2　"Integrated Budget and Accounts Computer System: IBEX Technical Design Document." February 11, 2004.

IT-IBEX-3　"Integrated Budget and Expenditure System (IBEX): Functional Requirements Document." March, 2004.

IT-002　"Phase IV Strategic IT Plan." February 3, 2004.

IT-010　"Procuring a New Financial Information System: Issues to Consider." March 11, 2005.

IT-BIS/BDA　"An Assessment of the DSA Project Information Systems." September 20, 2003.

11 Computer media [no documents cited]

12 Minutes of the meetings of the project steering committee [no documents cited]

13 Outside reports involving the DSA project [no documents cited]

14 In-service financial training project quarterly reports, prepared by the DSA project [no documents cited]

Index

Page numbers in *italics* denote tables and boxes, those in **bold** denote figures, n refers to a note.

324 *Index*

International Federation of Accountants 130
International Monetary Fund (IMF) 9, 13, *14*, 35,
41, 53, 58n5, 81, 83–4, 118n19–20, 162–3, 175,
194n4, 203, 212, 221, 225, 232, 235–6, 247n21,
247n23, 248n24, 262, 273, 275, 279, 285, 292,
300, 303n69; advice on budgeting 86, 119n26;
head 218; mistakes 298; program for public
finance 234, 247n23, 270; *Public Financial
Management Blog* 41, 302n54; reform *123*, 235,
303n69; reform program for Ethiopia 276, 282,
284, 298, 303n69; report 234, 247n21, 248n24;
resident representative 204, 219; staff 83,
196n40, 285; senior economist 299; statistical
manual 118n17; team 83, 218; technical guide
85; technical assistance staff 235
International Public Sector Accounting Standards
Board (IPSASB) 130
IPFs *see* indicative planning figures
Ireland xxvii, 58n4, 149, 241, 267; Irish Aid 149,
167, 206
iron triangle of management *see* project
management

JBAR (Joint Budget and Aid Review) *see* World
Bank, JBAR
Johannes, Haile *see* Haile Johannes
Jowitt, Kenneth 18

kebele 19, 38n27
Kedru Abza 109, 197
Kelly, Kevin 197
Keen, Peter 170
Kenya 9, 73, 93, 96, 200, 205, 221n5, 222n14, 288;
blueprint for development 222n14; budget 75,
117, 199, 212, 221n6; budget reform 221n5;
development 222n14; Egerton Agricultural
College 118n2; financial issues 50; financial
reform 39, 50, 59n21, 198, 259, 271n12; SP in
293; foreign aid 221n6, 288; government 44, 64,
199, 259, 271n12, 276; HIID 45; Harvard team
in 276; Ministry of Agriculture, Livestock
Development and Marketing 199; Ministry of
Finance 64, 78, 117, 118n2, 276; Ministry of
Planning 9, 198; Ministry of Planning and
National Development 198; multiyear
incremental budgets 212; PFM executive
training program 118n2; PIP 205; planning
reforms 198, 200; policy advisory team 222n14;
see also Peterson, Stephen B.
Key, V.O. 68, 280
Kifle, Melaku *see* Melaku Kifle
Korten, David: learning 272n19, 277; successful
rural development 273–4

Lacey, Robert M. 221n5, 235–6
Landau, Martin 37n17, 291
Last, Duncan 83–6, 118n20, 218–19, 222n29,
247n21
Layne, Tamirat *see* Tamirat Layne
learning 87, 96, 103, 139, 148, 272n17; and
alignment 3, 10–11; contextual 290; in PFM
275, 291
least-developed countries 14, *15*
Leonard, David K. 58n2, 113
lessons of Ethiopia's financial reform 223–71,

294–300; accounts reform 163–4; budget reform
101–3, 115; FIS reform 187–9; planning reform
for other countries 296–300
Levine, Donald 7–8, 30; *see also Wax and Gold:
Tradition and Innovation in Ethiopian Culture*
(Levine)
Lienert, Ian 254, 271n9, 282, 299
Lindblom, Charles 277
line-item budget 165n11, 212, 279, 281, 286;
traditional 68, 70, 147, 211, 216, 287–9
Lomanism 188

McGrath, Shaun 87–8, 184, 186
macroeconomic fiscal framework (MEFF) *52*; *see
also* planning reform, MEFF
Malinowski, Bronislaw 278
Manual 3, 136, 150, 158; *see also* accounts reform,
new accounting system
mashashaya 8, 34, 157, 229
medium-term expenditure frameworks (MTEFs)
76, 257; definition 76; regional 213; *see also*
planning reform, MTEFs
Mekonnen, Derege *see* Derege Mekonnen
Mekonnen, Samson 170
Mekonnen Abraha 114, 156
Melaku Kifle 92, 161, 205, 217
Meles Zenawi xxvii, 17, 34, 37n6, 58n5, 136, 202,
204, 235, 237; leadership of reform 40, 46, 262,
270
Mellett, Howard 278
Mengistu 120n47
metrics 53; performance 289; risk 293; World
Bank's 227, 232, 236, 276
Microsoft: Excel 169; SQL Server 172, 193
Ministry of Economic Development and
Cooperation (MEDAC) 25, 31, 91–2, 94, 98–9,
101, 137, 210
Ministry of Finance (MOF) 29, 63, 82–3, 86,
88–9, 94, 98, 122, 137, 140, 156, 169, 195n30,
207, *233*, 236, 241, 284, 301n9; accounts
department 78, 140; advisor 188, 276; backlog
of accounts 147–8, 165n15; budget information
system 101; building 67; cap on revenues 56;
data influx 125, 131; directives 25, 124;
disbursing for food relief 74; failures 26, 158,
244; federal 24–5, 244; finance function
166n38; finance specialists 226; funding
in-service training 268; head of accounts 140;
head of information technology 167; key sector
officials 99; management weakness 132, 180;
meeting in 28, 241; personnel 109; merged with
MEDAC 94; responsibilities 124; review of
compliance 57; senior accounts 141; staff 141;
strategy 66; support withdrawn 229; technical
assistance 188; Track 2 pilot design 99–101;
Treasury Department 97, 101; World Bank loan
194n2
Ministry of Finance and Economic Development
(MOFED) 26, 74, 91–2, 94, 99, 167, 174,
195n30, 207, 229, *233*, 242; accounts
department 96, 176; consultant 188; failed
160–1, 180–1, 237; federal finance 166n38, 175,
217; created from merger 94, 229; minister
briefed 158; mistakes 237, 242–4; officials 207;
organizational constraints 216; reform 236;

For Product Safety Concerns and Information please contact our EU
representative GPSR@taylorandfrancis.com
Taylor & Francis Verlag GmbH, Kaufingerstraße 24, 80331 München, Germany

www.ingramcontent.com/pod-product-compliance
Ingram Content Group UK Ltd.
Pitfield, Milton Keynes, MK11 3LW, UK
UKHW021020180425
457613UK00020B/1005

* 9 7 8 0 3 6 7 8 7 2 3 1 1 *